China's Local Public Finance in Transition

CHINA'S LOCAL PUBLIC FINANCE IN TRANSITION

Edited by
Joyce Yanyun Man
and
Yu-Hung Hong

LINCOLN INSTITUTE OF LAND POLICY
CAMBRIDGE, MASSACHUSETTS

© 2011 by the Lincoln Institute of Land Policy

All rights reserved.

Library of Congress Cataloging-in-Publication Data

China's local public finance in transition / edited by Joyce Yanyun Man and Yu-Hung Hong.
    p. cm.
    ISBN 978-1-55844-201-6
  1. Local finance—China.   2. Finance, Public—China.   3. Intergovernmental fiscal relations—China.   I. Man, Joyce Y.   II. Hong, Yu-hung.
    HJ9590.C44 2011
    336'.01451—dc22

                                                                                                      2010036711

Designed by Westchester Book Services.

Composed in Minion Pro by Westchester Book Services in Danbury, Connecticut. Printed and bound by Puritan Press, Inc., in Hollis, New Hampshire.

♲ The paper is Rolland Enviro 100, an acid-free, 100 percent recycled sheet.

MANUFACTURED IN THE UNITED STATES OF AMERICA

Contents

List of Illustrations   *vii*

Foreword   *xi*
GREGORY K. INGRAM

Introduction

1   Local Public Finance in China: An Overview   3
JOYCE YANYUN MAN

Local Expenditures

2   Assessing the Assignment of Expenditure Responsibilities   21
JORGE MARTINEZ-VAZQUEZ and BAOYUN QIAO

3   Fiscal Decentralization, Infrastructure Financing, and Regional Disparity   41
WEIPING WU

4   Financing Local Public Infrastructure: Guangdong Province   57
JOHN L. MIKESELL, JUN MA, ALFRED TAT-KEI HO, and MEILI NIU

Local Revenue Sources

5   Provincial Tax Revenue   91
DONALD J. S. BREAN

6   Tax Structure and Economic Growth   113
JOYCE YANYUN MAN and XINYE ZHENG

7   Fiscal Reform and Land Public Finance: Zouping County in National Context   125
SUSAN H. WHITING

8   The Path to Property Taxation   145
JOHN E. ANDERSON

9   Integrating the Proposed Property Tax with the Public Leasehold System   165
YU-HUNG HONG and DIANA BRUBAKER

Intergovernmental Transfers

10 The Determinants of Intergovernmental Transfer   191
    LI ZHANG and XINYE ZHENG

11 Central Government Transfers: For Equity or for Growth?   203
    SHUANGLIN LIN

12 Fiscal Reform and Rural Public Finance   227
    RICHARD BIRD, LOREN BRANDT, SCOTT ROZELLE, and LINXIU ZHANG

Future Reform

13 Intergovernmental Fiscal Relations and Local Public
    Finance: What Is Next on the Reform Agenda?   247
    ROY W. BAHL

Contributors   273

Index   275

About the Lincoln Institute of Land Policy   285

Illustrations

TABLES

1.1	National Government Revenue of Central and Local Governments, 2008	7
1.2	Per Capita Tax Revenue and Ratio of Subnational Tax Revenue to GDP by Province, 2007	9
1.3	Taxes on Land and Property, 2008	10
1.4	Importance of Land Revenue by Province, 2007	13
2.1	Relative Shares of Expenditure at Different Government Levels, 2003	28
2.2	Composition of Budget Expenditure at Different Government Levels, 2003	30
2.3	Aggregate Expenditure Composition at the Subnational Level, 2005	31
2.4	Most Important Extrabudgetary Expenditures, 2004	32
2.5	Per Capita Expenditure Disparities Across Provinces, 1990–2005	34
2.6	Subnational Expenditures per Capita, 2005	35
3.1	Urban Maintenance and Construction Revenues, 1990–2004	45
3.2	Level of Urban Infrastructure Services by Region, 1996–2005	49
3.3	Per Capita Urban Maintenance and Construction Revenues by Province, 1996–2004	51
3.4	Descriptive Statistics for Prefecture-Level Cities	52
3.5	OLS Regression on GDP Growth Rate	53
4.1	Capital Construction Investment in Selected Sectors in Guangdong Province, 1996–2006	68
4.2	Capital Construction Investment in Selected Provincial Sectors	69
4.3	Guangdong's Budgetary Spending on Infrastructure-Related Items, 1996–2006	70
4.4	Revenue Sources for the Guangdong Department of Construction, 2004	72
4.5	Accomplishments of Public Infrastructure Investment	73
4.6	Expanding Infrastructure in Urban Districts of Guangzhou City, 1990–2005	75
4.7	Growth Rates of the GDP, Population, and Infrastructure Investment in Guangdong, 1996–2006	76
5.1	Total Tax (Central + Local) to GDP, 1978–2006	93
5.2	Central Share of Total Tax Revenue, 1978–2006	93
5.3	Total Provincial Tax to National GDP, 1978–2006	93

5.4	Provincial GDP per Capita, 1999–2005	97
5.5	Provincial Tax Revenue per Capita, 1999–2005	99
5.6	Provincial Tax Revenue as Percent of Provincial GDP	100
5.7	Per Capita Taxes by Category and Province, 2005	102
5.8	Tax per Capita, 2005: Average Annual Percentage Change by Category and Province, 1999–2005	104
5.9	Revenue Elasticity, Based on 1999–2005 Changes	106
5.10	Total Provincial GDP per Capita and Gini Coefficient, 2005 and 2015	109
5.11	Total Provincial Taxes per Capita, 2005 Actual and 2015 Projected	110
5.12	Provincial Tax Gini Coefficients, 2005 Actual and 2015 Projected	111
6.1	Descriptive Statistics of Selected Variables	116
6.2	Estimation Results Under Alternative Specifications of Tax Variables for per Capita GDP	118
6.3	Estimation Results Under Alternative Specifications of Tax Variables as Ratio to GDP	119
6.4	Estimation Results Under Alternative Specifications of Tax Variables for Annual Growth Rate of per Capita GDP	121
6.5	2SLS Estimation Results Under Alternative Specifications of Tax Variables for per Capita GDP in Logarithm	122
7.1	The "Two Ratios," 1984–2005	127
7.2	Revenue Assignments: Central, Local, and Shared as of 2002	129
7.3	Distribution of Revenues across Subnational Governments as of 1999	131
7.4	Sources of Budgetary Revenue (percent share)	137
7.5	Sources of Budgetary Revenue (level)	137
7.6	Sources of Budgetary Revenue (percent increase)	138
7.7	Land Requisitioned at Zouping and Gaoxin, 2004–2006	139
8.1	Comparative Static Effects of Taxation on Structural Density and Development Timing	156
8.2	Comparative Static Effects of Development Fees on Structural Density and Development Timing	159
9.1	Revenues and Expenditures of Prefecture-Level Cities	177
9.2	Summary of Results of Three Hedonic Regression Studies	179
9.3	Descriptive Statistics of Variables	180
9.4	Capitalization Estimates of Property Tax and Public Goods	182
9.5	Land-Related Taxes, 2006	183
10.1	Transfer Results for All Counties	196
10.2	Regression Results for NDPCs and Non-NDPCs	197
10.3	Results for Rural Counties and Urban Counties	198
10.4	Impact of Tax-for-Fee Reform on Different Components of Transfers	199
10.5a	Different Impacts of Rural Tax-for-Fee Reform on Urban and Rural Counties	200
10.5b	Different Impacts of Rural Tax-for-Fee Reform on Urban and Rural Counties (Without Considering Impact of Reform)	201
11.1	Budgetary Revenues and Expenditures of Central and Local Governments	206

11.2	Shares of Central Government Revenue and Expenditure for Selected Countries, 2004	208
11.3	Per Capita Regional Government Expenditures	210
11.4	Provincial per Capita Transfers from the Central Government, 1995–2005	217
11.5a	Summary of Statistics of Variables	218
11.5b	Correlation Coefficients of Variables	219
11.6a	Regressions of Real per Capita Transfers from the Central Government, 1995–2004	221
11.6b	Regressions of Real per Capita Transfers from the Central Government, 1995–2000	223
11.6c	Regressions of Real per Capita Transfers from the Central Government, 2000–2004	223
12.1	Summary Table of Village Fiscal Balance, 2000 and 2004	229
12.2	Per Capita Fiscal Revenue: Sources of Funding	231
12.3	Inequality Measures for Fiscal Revenues and Expenditures	232
12.4	Per Capita Total Fiscal Expenditure: Composition of Expenditures	233
12.5	Funding of Public Investment by Project Type	235
12.6	Summary of Township Fiscal Health, Including Summary of Operating Budget, Capital Budget, and Debts, 2000 and 2004	238
12.7	Correlations Between Measures of Township Fiscal Reform and Village Fiscal Health, 2000 and 2004	240
12.8	Regression Results Explaining Villager Satisfaction, 2004	241
13.1	Distribution of Government Expenditure and Taxes by Level of Government, 2003	251
13.2	China's System of Intergovernmental Transfers	260
13.3	Central-Provincial Intergovernmental Transfers: Vertical and Horizontal Shares	261
13.4	Property Tax as Share of GDP	263

FIGURES

1.1	Subnational Government Share of Budgetary Revenue and Expenditure in China, 1978–2008	6
1.2	Subnational Government Share of Total Government Revenue and Expenditure in a Comparative Perspective	6
1.3	Share of Property Tax in Local Tax Revenue or Local Revenue in Selected Countries	12
1.4	Importance of Land Transfer Fees by Province, 2007	13
2.1	Assignment of Expenditure Responsibilities Between Central and Subnational Governments	27
3.1	Urban Maintenance and Construction Revenues by Region, 2002 and 2003	50
4.1	Infrastructure Decision-Making Process by Municipal Governments	61
7.1	China's Government Structure	128

8.1	Effect of an Increase in the Marginal Cost of Waiting on Development Timing and Density When Density Demanded Is Rising Over Time	154
8.2	Effect of an Increase in the Marginal Cost of Waiting on Development Timing and Density When Density Demanded Is Falling Over Time	155
8.3	Land and Improvements Tax Rate Options	161
9.1	Components of Land Value and Corresponding Beneficiaries Under Public Leasehold Systems	168
9.2	Relationship Between Land Value and Property Tax Under Scenario 1	171
9.3	Relationship Between Land Value and Property Tax Under Scenario 2	172
9.4	Relationship Between Land Value and Property Tax Under Scenario 3	174
9.5	Relationship Between Land Value and Property Tax Under Scenario 4	175
10.1	Division of Expenditure Responsibilities for Central and Local Governments	193
10.2	Division of Revenue Between Central and Local Governments	194
10.3	Transfer Categories over Years	194
11.1	Per Capita Government Expenditure by Region, 2000 and 2005	209
11.2	Per Capita Government Expenditure on Education, Health Care, and Welfare, by Region, 2005	211

Foreword

For the past 30 years, China's economy has developed rapidly following the implementation of economic reforms that have facilitated investment, expanded trade, and introduced market mechanisms and practices. At the same time, reforms of China's public finances have also proceeded, albeit at a somewhat slower pace and with less publicity. The major reform of public finances implemented in 1994 shifted a large share of fiscal revenues from local governments to the central government. This reform set the stage for the issues addressed in this volume because, while successfully moving revenues from local governments, the reform did not substantially transfer expenditure responsibilities from local governments. Following the 1994 reform, local governments were left with 46 percent of revenues and responsibility for 77 percent of public expenditures.

This overall revenue shortfall at the local government level motivated local governments to exploit new revenue sources, many of which were outside of the general budget. Revenue from the conversion of land from rural use to urban use has been one of the most important extrabudgetary revenue sources for many local governments. Conversion involves compensating farmers for their land based on its value in agricultural use, and then converting the land to urban use and selling it for development at its adjusted and much higher urban value. The difference in land values accrues to the local government.

The revenue from land sales has been a major source of funding for investment in infrastructure capital, often required to provide services to the newly converted urban land. In areas where urban land is in short supply, the revenue realized has been large, and the incentive to produce revenue has led to excessive conversion of land to urban use. Symptoms of such excess conversion have been the low density of development in the periphery of some metropolitan areas and the large areas of urban land that remain undeveloped. This is a surprising, and potentially unique, unanticipated land use consequence of a fiscal reform motivated by a need to increase central government revenues.

However, opportunities to convert land to urban use vary greatly across municipalities, and many local governments have received little revenue from this source. Cross-provincial disparities in revenues and expenditures, which have long been significant, have been exacerbated by cross-provincial differences in urban land values.

Three major policy options explored in this volume can address the underlying imbalance between revenues and expenditures at the local level in China. The first is to institute new sources of local revenue, such as a property tax, and much attention has been devoted to this approach in recent years. The second is to reform and enhance transfers of revenue from the central government to local governments, a promising approach that could also address cross-provincial disparities in revenues and expenditures. The third is to revisit the assignment of expenditure responsibilities and to shift some of these from local governments to the central government so that expenditure assignment aligns better with revenue assignment.

The end result is likely to be a mix of all three policy options as part of an incremental reform that will strengthen fiscal decentralization while attempting to reduce cross-provincial fiscal disparities. Current intergovernmental transfers do little to address these disparities. The policy challenge is to reduce these disparities while preserving incentives for local fiscal efforts to raise revenue.

Gregory K. Ingram
President and CEO
Lincoln Institute of Land Policy

Introduction

Local Public Finance in China: An Overview

JOYCE YANYUN MAN

Since 1978, China has undertaken a range of changes and reforms that have fundamentally transformed the country from social, economic, and government finance perspectives. As a result, China has moved from a command-based to a market-oriented economy; from a closed, self-sufficient, and rural society to a powerhouse nation of international commerce and rapid urbanization; from a country with a high reliance on the agricultural sector to an increasingly industrialized economy with a large proportion of manufacturing and service sectors; from a low-income country with a poverty rate of nearly 60 percent to a nation with a growing and increasingly affluent middle class and a poverty rate of less than 10 percent. The rapid growth in the past 30 years has propelled China into the position of the third-largest economy in the world, eager to exert its due influence in every aspect of world affairs.

However, China has lagged in its public finance reform and political reform. The fiscal policy instruments of taxation and spending have been limited in their utilization and influence. The country's tax structure is far from the optimal level of efficiency and equity. In particular, fiscal reforms in the past 30 years have not addressed the assignment of expenditure responsibilities among China's central and subnational governments to be compatible with their revenue capacity and intergovernmental transfer system. China's local governments (provincial, prefecture, county, and township) have not been granted any legal authority for taxing or borrowing and are overloaded with unfunded central mandates. As a result, many local governments turn to extrabudgetary revenue sources such as land leasing fees and numerous other fees and surcharges, as well as indirect borrowing from banks, to finance infrastructure investment and local economic development. At a time when fiscal and administrative reforms have been moved to the top of the Chinese central government's agenda, the efforts and studies in this book are certainly timely and important.

Evolution of China's Fiscal System and the Development of Local Public Finance

The past 30 years have witnessed a structural change in the Chinese public finance system, albeit far from an adequate one. China has been going through a process of fiscal decentralization to promote local governments' fiscal responsibilities and administrative autonomy while maintaining an adequate degree of fiscal control in the central government (Shen, Jin, and Zou 2006). This trend is in striking contrast to the central control and planning system that existed for 30 years before the current economic reforms. In general, China's fiscal system has experienced three significant stages of change since 1949.

Fiscal Centralization Between 1949 and 1978

Before the economic reforms started, in 1978, China had a control system under which the consolidated budget system was initiated, approved, and administered by the central government. The subnational governments served as agents of the central government with little discretionary spending power. Local governments received appropriation and operating budgets from the central government to deliver public services, including education, public safety, health care, social security, and housing. At the same time, local government authorities were commanded to run local enterprises according to the central planning system. Revenues were collected largely from the taxes and fees and the profit sharing from state-owned enterprises (SOEs). An intergovernmental transfer system was set up to balance the fiscal gap between the revenues collected by local governments and the local spending needs approved by the central government. Any fiscal surplus was transferred to the central government, and shortfalls were covered automatically by the central government through budget appropriations. It was a highly redistribution-oriented system. However, it lacked fiscal incentives for subnational governments to promote local economic development and the effective and efficient provision of public goods and services.

Fiscal Contract System Between 1979 and 1993

Since the beginning of economic reform in 1978, the central government has initiated a number of fiscal reforms to provide incentives to local governments to promote local economic development and mobilize revenue collection. In 1980 a revenue-sharing system was put in place as an alternative to the highly centralized fiscal structure. Under this system, the central government established the revenue-sharing rules for the central and provincial governments, and each province set the rules for the provincial government and municipalities. The higher-level government determined the revenue-sharing rules for its lower levels of government. Local finance bureaus were largely responsible for revenue collections, which consisted of three types of revenues: central-fixed revenue, local-fixed revenue, and shared revenue (which was split 80–20 between the central and subnational governments). As a consequence of this uniform revenue-sharing structure, fiscal disparity in revenue collection among subnational governments, due to the differences in economic bases and tax efforts, prompted the central government to rearrange this tax-sharing system in 1985. The new revenue-sharing formula took account of the subnational governments' budget balances in previous years and allowed less affluent provinces to retain more revenues; less was allowed for those with high tax capacity. In 1988, the Chinese government implemented a "fiscal contracting system" under which one of six types of revenue-sharing contracting methods would be applied to the provinces (Agarwala 1992; Ma 1997; Shen, Jin, and Zou 2006). However, this tax-and-profit contract system resulted in a drastic decline in revenue collection as a share of GDP and the central government's portion of total revenue. For example, the ratio of total government revenue to GDP dropped from 22.2 percent in 1985 to 12.3 percent in 1993, and the ratio of the central government to the total government revenue decreased from 38.4 percent in 1985 to 22 percent in 1993 (National Bureau of Statistics, various years). The fiscal constraints experienced by the central government and its dependence on local remittances to finance its outlays led to a major fiscal restructuring in 1994.

Tax Sharing System Since 1994

In an effort to mobilize revenue collections and increase revenue shares of the central government, a significant fiscal reform was launched in 1994 that introduced a value-added tax (VAT) to replace the turnover-based product tax; implemented an excise tax on tobacco, liquor, and some luxuries; unified and simplified the corporative income tax; and improved the central-local revenue-sharing arrangements. The tax administration was separated into national tax services (NTS), which were responsible for the revenue collection of central fixed and shared taxes, and local tax services (LTS), which were in charge of local taxes (Bahl 1999; Ma 1997; Shen, Jin, and Zou 2006; Wong 1997). Since the introduction of the tax-for-fee and valued-added tax, central government revenue has experienced rapid growth. By 2008, the central government share of total revenue had increased to 53 percent from 22 percent in 1993. The portion of the tax revenues for the central government reached 64 percent of total tax revenue in China. The ratio of total government revenue to GDP was up by 8.1 percentage points, from 12.3 percent to 20.4 percent between 1993 and 2008.

However, the fiscal reforms implemented in 1994 dealt only with revenue assignments, leaving expenditure assignments intact. On the expenditure side, local governments are responsible for the provision of a wide range of public goods and services, including education, health, social services, and economic services. As figure 1.1 indicates, the tax assignment system has resulted in an even bigger fiscal imbalance between revenue and expenditure for local governments in China. For example, subnational governments in China account for 79 percent of total government expenditure but only 47 percent of total government revenues. The mismatch of revenue and expenditure assignments at the subnational level of government in China has led to an increasing reliance on indirect borrowing and on extrabudgetary fees and charges such as land leasing fees to meet the demand for basic public goods and service provision. As figure 1.2 reveals, such a fiscal imbalance far exceeds that of other developing countries, transitional countries, and even OECD countries (Dollar and Hofman 2008).

FIGURE 1.1

Subnational Government Share of Budgetary Revenue and Expenditure in China, 1978–2008

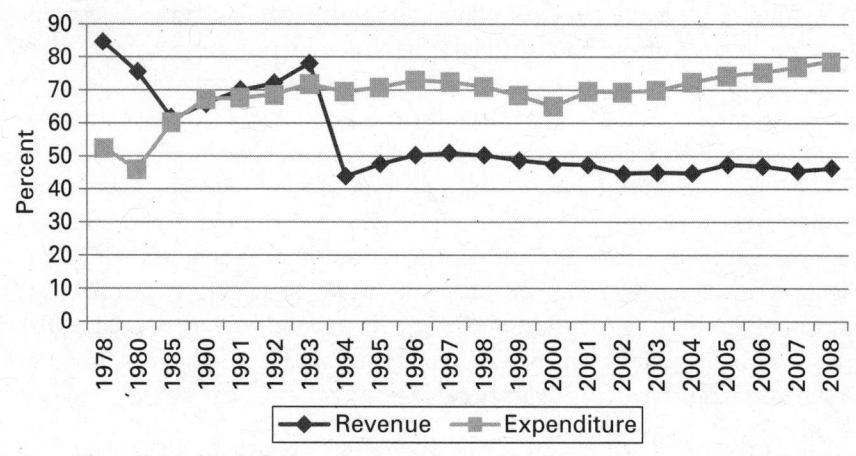

SOURCE: *Chinese Statistical Yearbook*, various years.

FIGURE 1.2

Subnational Government Share of Total Government Revenue and Expenditure in a Comparative Perspective

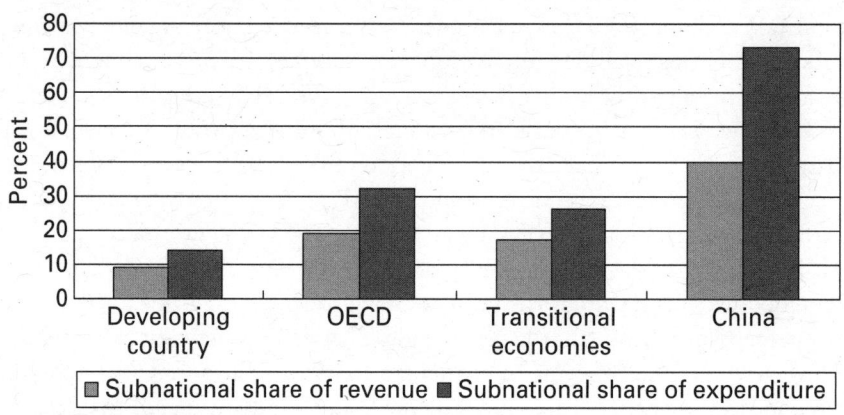

SOURCE: Dollar and Hofman, 2008.

Local Tax Structure and Fiscal Disparity

The fiscal reforms in 1994 established a tax-sharing system between the central and subnational governments and assigned a number of tax revenues to subnational governments as local taxes. Local government revenues include local tax revenues and shared tax revenues. As table 1.1 indicates, a number of taxes were assigned to local governments as local taxes, including the urban land use tax, land value-added tax, real estate tax, deed tax, vehicle and vessel tax, tobacco tax, farmland occupation tax, and others. In addition, provincial and local governments can share with the central government the revenues from the VAT, business tax, individual and

TABLE 1.1
National Government Revenue of Central and Local Governments, 2008

Item	National Government Revenue (100 million yuan)	Central Government (%)	Local Governments (%)
National government revenue	61330.35	53	47
Total tax revenue	54223.79	57	43
Domestic value-added tax	17996.94	75	25
Domestic consumption tax	2568.27	100	0
VAT and consumption tax from imports	7391.13	100	0
VAT and consumption tax rebate for exports	−5865.93	100	0
Business tax	7626.39	3	97
Corporate income tax	11175.63	64	36
Individual income tax	3722.31	60	40
Resource tax	301.76	0	100
City maintenance and construction tax	1344.09	1	99
Real estate tax	680.34	0	100
Stamp tax	1311.29	72	28
Stamp tax on security exchange	979.16	97	3
Urban land use tax	816.90	0	100
Land appreciation tax	537.43	0	100
Tax on vehicles and boat operation	144.21	0	100
Tax on ship tonnage	20.12	100	0
Vehicle purchase tax	989.89	100	0
Tariffs	1769.95	100	0
Farm land occupation tax	314.41	0	100
Deed tax	1307.53	0	100
Tobacco leaf tax	67.45	0	100
Other tax revenue	3.68	4	96
Total nontax revenue	7106.56	24	76
Special program receipts	1554.10	13	87
Charge of administrative and institutional units	2134.86	17	83
Penalty receipts	898.40	4	96
Other nontax receipts	2519.20	44	56

SOURCE: *China Statistical Yearbook*, 2009.

corporate income tax, resource tax, and urban maintenance and construction tax. As a result, local governments' revenue accounted for 43 percent of total tax revenue in 2008.

Local taxes are administered by subnational governments, and the resulting revenues are used to finance local government activities and expenditure programs. Provincial governments have been granted certain legislative rights for some local taxes. For example, provincial governments have a right to design the implementation details for the real estate tax, urban maintenance and construction tax, vehicle use tax, and urban land use tax and to set the tax rate within the range approved by the central government. In 2007, local taxes generated 287.13 billion yuan and accounted for 14.9 percent of total subnational government tax revenues. Local taxes cover only 12.2 percent of local expenditures, demonstrating that they are not an adequate revenue source for provincial and subprovincial governments to finance public goods and services and economic activities carried out by Chinese local governments.

The current fiscal structure in China has also resulted in enormous fiscal disparities among subnational governments. As table 1.2 shows, the per capita tax revenue ranges from 709 yuan and 730 yuan in Tibet and Gansu, respectively, to 11,165 yuan in Shanghai and 9,140 yuan in Beijing in 2007.

When the share of tax revenue is compared to GDP, table 1.2 also reveals that Guizhou, Gansu, and Tibet were among the lowest in tax revenue per capita, while Shanghai, Beijing, and Tianjin were at the top of the list. This indicates that the tax-sharing reforms in 1994 have achieved the goal of reversing the downward trend in government revenue collection and the central government's share of government revenues, but have failed in achieving fiscal balance among the central, provincial, and local governments. The fiscal inequality poses big challenges to policy makers and public finance scholars in designing a balanced fiscal structure that supports sustained growth and social justice and harmony.

Land and Property Taxation

The Chinese property market is based on a land-use rights system. The ownership of urban land resides with the government. The government leases the land to developers and other users for specified periods of time, and those leases can be bought and sold on the land and housing market. Due to the separation of land ownership and property ownership, property owners are liable for taxes on the property they own and the land they lease from the government in the form of the urban land use tax and the real estate tax. When the transaction occurs, the Chinese government levies a deed or contract tax and a land value-added tax.

Urban Land Use Tax

China has separate taxes on land and housing. The dual land system divides land into state ownership in urban areas and collective ownership in rural areas. The urban land use tax was launched in 1988 and is based on the amount of urban land used by domestic companies, individuals, and some nonprofit organizations. When the land located in an urban area is used, users are required to pay a tax based on the size of the land area acquired, at a rate between 0.6 yuan and 30 yuan per square meter. Before 2007 the rate was 0.2–10 yuan per square meter. Until 1 July 2007, the tax was collected only from domestic taxpayers and foreign companies; individuals were exempted. Since then, individuals have been required to pay this tax, as well, and the entire tax revenue belongs to the local government. As indicated in table 1.3, the revenue generated from the urban land use tax accounts for only 3.5 percent of the total tax revenues of local governments in China.

TABLE 1.2
Per Capita Tax Revenue and Ratio of Subnational Tax Revenue to GDP by Province, 2007

Rank	Province	Tax Revenue per Capita (yuan)	Rank	Province	Tax Revenue / GDP (%)
1	Shanghai	11,165	1	Shanghai	17.02
2	Beijing	9,140	2	Beijing	15.96
3	Tianjin	4,847	3	Chongqing	10.74
4	Zhejiang	3,260	4	Tianjin	10.70
5	Guangdong	2,948	5	Shanxi	10.43
6	Jiangsu	2,935	6	Guizhou	10.40
7	Liaoning	2,519	7	Yunnan	10.27
8	Inner Mongolia	2,047	8	Liaoning	9.82
9	Fujian	1,953	9	Ningxia	9.00
10	Shandong	1,789	10	Guangdong	8.96
11	Shanxi	1,762	11	Hainan	8.85
12	Chongqing	1,572	12	Zhejiang	8.78
13	Xinjiang	1,364	13	Shaanxi	8.69
14	Ningxia	1,312	14	Jiangsu	8.69
15	Hainan	1,282	15	Xinjiang	8.11
16	Shaanxi	1,268	16	Sichuan	8.10
17	Jilin	1,175	17	Inner Mongolia	8.08
18	Heilongjiang	1,152	18	Fujian	7.56
19	Hebei	1,137	19	Anhui	7.38
20	Yunnan	1,078	20	Qinghai	7.24
21	Sichuan	1,047	21	Jiangxi	7.09
22	Hubei	1,036	22	Ganxu	7.06
23	Qinghai	1,027	23	Guangxi	7.03
24	Hunan	954	24	Hunan	6.59
25	Henan	921	25	Shandong	6.45
26	Jiangxi	893	26	Hubei	6.40
27	Anhui	889	27	Heilongjiang	6.23
28	Guangxi	878	28	Jilin	6.07
29	Guizhou	758	29	Tibet	5.89
30	Gansu	730	30	Hebei	5.76
31	Tibet	709	31	Henan	5.74
Average		2,114	Average		8.55%
Median		1,268	Median		8.10%

SOURCE: National Bureau of Statistics, 2008.

Real Estate Tax

The real estate tax established in 1986 is levied on the original value or rental income collected from businesses; individuals have to pay the tax only when their property is rented for commercial use. There is no tax on owner-occupied houses. Real estate tax is calculated and paid on the basis of the original value of the property minus a deduction of 10–30 percent. The specific deduction is determined by the people's government of the provinces, autonomous regions, and municipalities

TABLE 1.3
Taxes on Land and Property, 2008

Tax	Implemented Date	Tax Base	Tax Rate	Collection Stage	Share of Local Tax Revenue (%)
Urban land use tax	1/11/1988	Taxable land size (only on domestic taxpayers before 2007)	30 yuan/m² to 0.6 yuan/m²	Possession (recurrent)	3.51
Real estate tax	1/10/1986	Real estate for business use	1.2% of original value or 12% of rental income	Possession (recurrent)	2.93
Land value-added tax	1/1/1994	Land appreciation value	Progressive tax rate (30–60% on the LAV)	Transaction (nonrecurrent)	2.31
Farmland occupation tax	1/4/1987	Farmland size	yuan 1–10/m² (yuan 5–50/m² after 2008)	Land development (nonrecurrent)	1.35
Deed tax	1/10/1997	Self-reported value of land and house transfer	3–5%	Transaction (nonrecurrent)	5.62

SOURCE: National Bureau of Statistics, 2009.

directly under the central government. The tax rate is 2.9 percent when based on property value and 12 percent when based on rental income.

Before 1 January 2009, foreign companies and individuals were required to pay a separate tax with a tax base and rates similar to those of the real estate tax. The urban real property tax, implemented on 8 August 1951, was based on the market value or rental income of property unless the property was for nonbusiness uses. Local governments were granted the authority to give tax exemptions and tax rate deductions at their discretion. In 2009 property tax reform consolidated the real estate house tax and urban real property tax into a single "real estate tax" to achieve equity and administrative simplicity. Since 1 January 2009, the real estate tax has been levied on real property owned by foreign individuals and enterprises according to the provisional regulations of the People's Republic of China with respect to the use of the tax, basis of tax assessment, tax rate, preferential treatment, exemptions, and management of tax collection.

Land Value-Added Tax

China also collects taxes on land value appreciation, defined as the difference between the original purchase value and the sale price. All businesses and individuals receiving income from the transfer of state-owned land use rights or buildings and their attached facilities are liable for the LVAT. This tax is collected when the transfer of real estate occurs and is levied at the transaction stage with a rate between 30 percent and 60 percent of value appreciation. It is levied upon the land appreciation value, defined as the balance of proceeds received by the taxpayer on the transfer of real estate after deducting the sum paid for the acquisition of the land use rights, the costs and expenses for development of the land, and the costs and expenses for the construction of new buildings and facilities or the assessed value for used properties and buildings. The tax is computed and collected when the transfer of real estate takes place. A progressive tax rate of 30–60 percent on the land appreciation value (LAV) is applied with four brackets as follows:

For LAV <50% of deductible items	30%
For LAV >50% but <100% of deductible items	40%
For LAV >100% but <200% of deductible items	50%
For LAV Over 200% of deductible items	60%

Other Land and Real Estate Taxes

Users of farmland have to pay a farmland occupation tax that has been levied at a rate of 5–50 yuan per square meter since 2008 but at the lower rate of 1–10 yuan per square meter prior to 2008. The deed tax is a tax levied on the contractual value of land use rights and housing during the transaction stage of real property for sales on the market. If the self-reported transaction value of the transferred property is too low, the taxing authority may use an estimated value or the published land base value as the tax base.

Unlike many other countries, China does not tax residential property that is not used for business. But several taxes play the role of property tax. The four main types of taxes relating to real property in China are the urban land use tax, the land value-added tax, the real estate tax, and the farmland occupation tax. These four taxes generated about 2,347 billion yuan in 2008, accounting for only 10.1 percent of local government tax revenue and 8.2 percent of total local government revenue in China. Compared with that of the developed and developing countries in the world shown in figure 1.3, China's land and property tax share of local tax revenue is among the lowest, in the league of Argentina (5.0 percent) and Nicaragua (6.4 percent). It is lower than that of Russia (13.4 percent), Poland (14.01 percent), South Africa (20.3 percent), Indonesia (67.1 percent), and many developed countries.

Land and property tax revenue varies greatly among provinces due to inconsistent enforcement practices, different tax bases, and pressures from interjurisdictional tax competition and other factors. Not surprisingly, Beijing and Shanghai have the highest property tax per capita. The degree of reliance on property tax revenue varies among provinces, as well. It ranged from 1.95 percent of total revenue in Tibet and 7.51 percent in Qinghai Province to 21.26 percent in Jiangxi and 22.55 percent in Shandong Province in 2008. On average, it accounts for 14.64 percent (National Bureau of Statistics, 2009). Such disparity, however, is likely to result in differential effects of the property tax on economic activities in China.

FIGURE 1.3

Share of Property Tax in Local Tax Revenue or Local Revenue in Selected Countries

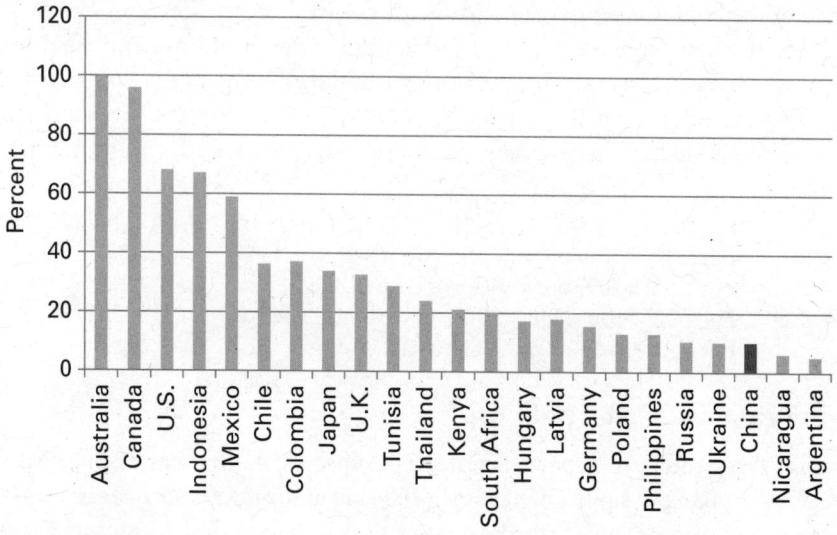

SOURCES: Richard M. Bird and Enid Slack, *International Handbook of Land and Property Taxation*; Joan M. Youngman and Jane H. Malme, *An International Survey of Taxes on Land and Buildings*; Government website of each country; China's data are compiled by the author.

Extrabudgetary Activities and Land Transfer Fees

The Chinese government also relies heavily on extrabudget revenue that is excluded from the revenue accounts compiled by the Ministry of Finance. Extrabudget revenue usually includes user charges for public utilities; fees for public services; surcharges on taxes; earmarked levies for specific purposes or funds, such as education; and revenues from commercial or business undertakings by government enterprises or agencies. Extrabudget revenues amounted to 661.7 billion yuan, or 2.2 percent of GDP, in 2008 (National Bureau of Statistics, 2008).

The imbalance of expenditure and revenue assignments facing provincial and local governments and consequent pressure of fiscal stress and interjurisdictional competition have made local governments turn toward extrabudgetary revenues for government financing, as well (Song, Chu, and Cao 1999). In recent years, most local governments have relied on the sales of land rights for much needed revenue to finance basic public services demanded by their residents and comply with mandates from the central government. As a result, land transfer fees increased from 9.3 percent of total local budgetary revenue in 1999 to 43.5 percent in 2008, as shown in figure 1.4. The revenue from land transfer fees was about 21 percent of total local expenditures in 2008, up from 5.7 percent in 1999, indicating an increasingly heavy reliance on land transfer fees as a revenue source and possible evidence of the existence of so-called land public finance at the local level.

In 2007, per capita land transfer fees revealed large variations among provinces, as indicated in table 1.4. When they are ranked according to the ratio of land trans-

FIGURE 1.4
Importance of Land Transfer Fees by Province, 2007

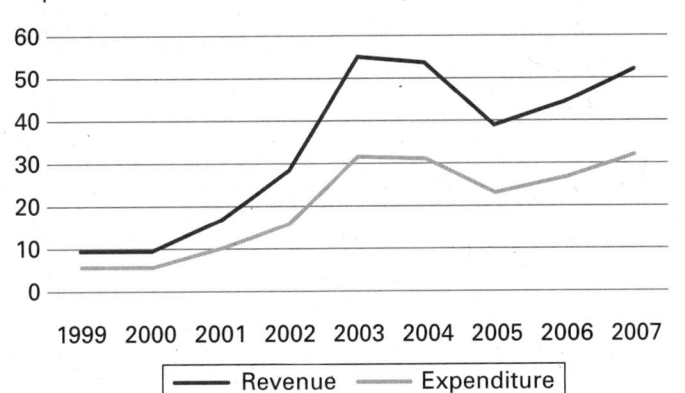

SOURCE: *Chinese Statistical Yearbook of Land Resources*, 2008.

TABLE 1.4
Importance of Land Revenue by Province, 2007

Rank	Province	Land Revenue / GDP (%)	Province	Land Revenue / Fiscal Revenue (%)	Province	Land Transfer Fees per Capita
1	Sichuan	5.40	Sichuan	66.66	Tianjin	1794.6
2	Chongqing	4.31	Chongqing	40.18	Beijing	1107.9
3	Tianjin	3.96	Anhui	38.40	Liaoning	764.7
4	Hainan	3.24	Tianjin	37.02	Fujian	713.2
5	Liaoning	3.00	Fujian	36.65	Sichuan	697.3

Rank	Province	Land Revenue / GDP (%)	Province	Land Revenue / Fiscal Revenue (%)	Province	Land Transfer Fees per Capita
27	Yunnan	0.45	Shanghai	5.50	Jiangxi	67.1
28	Tibet	0.38	Yunnan	4.43	Yunnan	47.3
29	Gansu	0.31	Gansu	4.40	Tibet	45.6
30	Beijing	0.19	Qinghai	2.39	Gansu	30.9
31	Qinghai	0.17	Beijing	1.21	Qinghai	24.5

SOURCE: National Bureau of Statistics, 2008.

fer fees to total revenues, we can see that the ratio varies from 1.21 percent in Beijing to 66.6 percent in Sichuan Province in 2007. The five provinces that have the highest ratio of land transfer fees to local revenue are Sichuan Province, Chongqing (40.18 percent), Anhui (38.4 percent), Tianjin (37.02 percent), and Fujian (36.65 percent). The fees from land leasing account for about 5.4 percent of GDP in Sichuan Province and 3.24 percent in Hainan. Not surprisingly, Shanghai and Beijing were among the provinces with the lowest portion of land leasing fees in their local revenue.

Such large variations among subnational governments indicate the need for further analysis of the impacts of land-related taxes and fees on the housing market, the net rate of return on capital, and the economic growth in China.

This Volume

In 2007, a joint initiative created The Peking University–Lincoln Institute Center for Urban Development and Land Policy to give Lincoln Institute of Land Policy's China program a presence in China's political capital. Annual conferences on various land-related topics were convened, and this volume collects the proceedings and papers from the 2008 conference entitled "Local Public Finance and Property Tax in China."

An overview of subnational government finance and the tax structure in China reveals that the reforms of the past 30 years have significantly improved the country's fiscal system but have left many tasks unfinished and the mission incomplete. The most noticeable are the much needed fiscal reforms at the subnational level of government—county and township governments, in particular—and the assignment of expenditure responsibilities among central, provincial, and local governments. The fiscal imbalance between expenditure and revenue assignments among subnational governments may lead to a large disparity in revenue sources and expenditure and, consequently, income inequality. Without a timely correction of this problem, it may result in the underprovision of basic public goods and services, unfounded mandates on local governments, lack of accountability, overreliance on land-related extrabudgetary revenue sources, and a hotbed for corruption. It may also lead to the inefficient use of land and natural resources, unsustainable economic growth, and social instability.

To help understand and solve the current problems in China, this book includes chapters written by scholars in the fields of economics, public finance, urban studies, and business administration from universities, academies, and research institutes in the United States, Canada, and China. The book is organized in five parts, including this overview as part 1. Part 2 describes the local expenditure situation in China, with the focus on such aspects as fiscal decentralization, expenditure assignment, and infrastructure-financing practices; part 3 presents the issues of local revenue sources, land finance, and property taxation; part 4 focuses on local intergovernmental transfers; and part 5 elaborates the fiscal reforms of the past and shows the direction for future reform.

In chapter 2 Jorge Martinez-Vazquez and Baoyun Qiao present an assessment of the assignment of expenditure responsibilities in China, as well as the common problems encountered in the international experience. The chapter provides a road map and practical recommendations for the reform of expenditure assignments in China. It argues that a stable, efficient, and fair decentralized system of public finance in China will require an unambiguous and well-defined institutional framework in the assignment of expenditure responsibilities among the different levels of government.

Chapters 3 and 4 focus on public infrastructure financing. In chapter 3 Weiping Wu explores the patterns of financing infrastructure development across different cities and discusses the relationship between infrastructure investment and regional economic performance. While outlining how successive waves of fiscal decentralization in China during the reform era have affected local financing and autonomy, the chapter also examines the increasing disparity in the ability of cities to finance infrastructure development. The conclusion is drawn that infrastructure investment is a statistically significant predictor of regional economic performance, though further research is needed to ascertain the positive contribution of public infrastructure to economic performance.

In chapter 4 John L. Mikesell, Jun Ma, Alfred Tat-Kei Ho, and Meili Niu use Guangdong Province to examine the institutional arrangements and politics of the infrastructure-financing mechanism, to analyze the issues related to "extrabudgetary" revenues and control, and to provide recommendations regarding the current system of capital budgeting and financing. The chapter reveals that the Chinese government still lacks a systematic approach for handling long-term capital improvement plans and developing a regular, comprehensive capital budget. It is important to increase the transparency of capital budgeting decisions and the oversight power of the People's Congress, so that the government can be held more accountable for infrastructure policies and spending decisions.

Donald Brean, in chapter 5, presents an empirical overview of provincial taxation in China, focusing on the recent performance of seven specific provincial taxes in 31 provinces over the years 1999 to 2005. The seven taxes include the value-added tax, operations tax, company tax, individual income tax, resource tax, city construction tax, and contract tax. The chapter also projects the fiscal conditions to 2015. The author's analysis indicates that the disparity of GDP per capita combined with the provincial cross-section disparity in GDP growth rates will eventually give rise to greater disparity in each tax category on a per capita basis.

In chapter 6 Joyce Man and Xinye Zheng empirically test the effects of taxation on economic growth using provincial data from China. Specifically, taxes on business capital income and on land and real property have a negative correlation with economic growth after controlling for fixed effects and simultaneity bias. Results support the hypothesis that distortional taxation lowers economic performance. The results of the study may indicate that sustained growth in China may be achieved by lowering the overall tax burden; reducing taxes on capital income, physical capital, and land; and mobilizing tax resources with efficient administration and enforcement.

Susan H. Whiting, in chapter 7, describes the evolution of the fiscal system since the economic reform and examines the nature of revenue and expenditure assignments, intergovernmental fiscal transfers, and the implications of these factors for coping with revenue inadequacy at the local level and fiscal equalization across local jurisdictions. The chapter introduces some political issues that exacerbate the problems in central-local fiscal relations and develops a case study of one of China's "top 100" counties to examine how it has exploited land to promote revenue generation. The survey of official revenue sources and expenditure responsibilities highlights the fiscal gap that exists for many local governments.

In chapter 8 John Anderson summarizes the major economic impacts of development fees and ad valorem property taxes with applications to the contemporary policy setting of China. Dynamic models of the development process indicate that the policy switch from a lump-sum fee to a property tax would have uncertain effects on both development timing and structural density. Policy insights based on the analytic results for both fees and taxes, with special emphasis placed on transition issues, are provided for the current Chinese situation. More work is necessary to develop appropriate models of a transition from a land-leasing regime to a quasi-ownership regime with taxes or fees used to fund local government provision of public goods.

Using China as a case, Yu-Hung Hong and Diana Brubaker in chapter 9 examine a topic related to real property taxation in transitional countries: taxing public leasehold land. Four scenarios are composed to project property tax impacts on leasehold revenue and land value. By applying the scenarios to China based on ideas of tax and public spending capitalization into property prices, the authors estimate capitalization of property tax liabilities and public goods provision using a random effects regression model and panel data from 1999–2006. Finally, they suggest potential policy implications for the implementation of the proposed property tax reform in China. More research is needed to estimate the capitalization rates of tax and spending.

In chapter 10 Li Zhang and Xinye Zheng discuss the determinants of intergovernmental transfer in China. An empirical analysis based on county-level data sets examines how transfers are allocated to each county. This study analyzes total transfers, as well as different types of transfers. By differentiating between the two broad categories of transfers and two subgroups—NDPCs and non-NDPCs—and then urban and rural counties, the authors found that, due to the effects of the tax rebate, the total government transfer is prorich, although the equalization transfer does play its designated role to equalize fiscal capacity, especially in poor and rural areas.

In chapter 11 Shuanglin Lin examines the determinants of central government transfers, consisting of tax rebates and grants, to provinces. The author found that, even though grants are equity promoting, tax rebates are virtually growth stimulating. The data from 1995 to 2004 for 31 provinces shows that tax rebates dominated the equity-promoting grants in central government transfers; provinces with a higher level of income received more per capita transfers than provinces with a lower level of income; and provinces with a higher growth rate received more per capita transfers than provinces with a lower rate of growth. Thus, the current transfer system is ineffective in reducing the regional fiscal inequality and reforming the transfer system is imperative.

Drawing on a survey carried out by Richard Bird, Loren Brandt, Scott Rozelle, and Linxiu Zhang, chapter 12 provides an analysis of the changes in township and village finance between 2000 and 2004. The survey extends to one hundred villages in fifty townships in twenty-five counties in the five provinces of Jilin, Hebei, Shaanxi, Sichuan, and Jiangsu. This chapter suggests that the development of more responsive and sustainable local fiscal management in China will inevitably require both the devolution of more decision-making power over public finance to local governments and the development of local governments that are more directly responsible to the local people whom they are supposed to serve.

In the last chapter of the book, Roy Bahl reviews the theory and practices of fiscal decentralization and examines whether international practice holds any useful lessons for China. The chapter presents the three key instruments used to decentralize fiscal structures: expenditure assignment, revenue assignment, and intergovernmental transfers. The author compares the international experience with the Chinese practice and examines the special role of the property tax in fiscal decentralization—in OECD countries, low-income countries, and China. The author argues that if China were to develop a local government finance system, international practice could provide good lessons to guide China with intergovernmental fiscal policy.

Given the breadth of the chapter discussions, this book will be a resource for government officials, public finance practitioners, academic researchers, college students, and members of the general public who are concerned with government tax and expenditure policies and practices in China. University instructors will also find this book useful as a supplemental textbook for public finance and economic development courses.

REFERENCES

Agarwala, Ramgopal. 1992. China: Reforming intergovernmental fiscal relations. Discussion Paper No. 178. Washington, DC: World Bank.

Bahl, Roy. 1999. *Fiscal policy in China: Taxation and intergovernmental fiscal relations.* San Francisco: 1990 Institute.

Bird, Richard Miller, and Naomi Enid Slack. 2004. *International handbook of land and property taxation.* Northampton, MA: Edward Elgar.

Dollar, David, and Bert Hofman. 2008. Intergovernmental fiscal reforms, expenditure assignment, and governance. In *Public finance in China: Reform and growth for a harmonious society,* eds. Jiwei Lou and Shuilin Wang. Cambridge, MA: World Bank Publications.

Ma, Jun. 1997. China's fiscal reform: An overview. *Asian Economic Journal* 11(4):443–458.

National Bureau of Statistics. Various years. *China statistical yearbook.* Beijing: China Statistics Press.

———. Various years. *China statistical yearbook of land resources.* Beijing: China Statistics Press.

Qiu, Dong. 2005. *China fiscal federalism.* Beijing: Central University of Finance and Economics.

Shen, Chunli, Jing Jin, and Heng-fu Zou. 2006. *Fiscal decentralization in China revisited.* Beijing: Central University of Finance and Economics.

Song, Shunfeng, George S. F. Chu, and Rongqing Cao. 1999. Real estate tax in urban China. *Contemporary Economic Policy* 17(4):540–551.

Wong, Christine P. W. 1997. *Financing local government in the People's Republic of China.* Hong Kong: Oxford University Press.

Youngman, Joan M., and Jane H. Malme. 1994. *An international survey of taxes on land and buildings.* Derventer, Netherlands: Kluwer.

Local Expenditures

Assessing the Assignment of Expenditure Responsibilities

JORGE MARTINEZ-VAZQUEZ AND BAOYUN QIAO

China has been carrying out a significant fiscal decentralization policy for over three decades. However, reforms have largely concentrated on the revenue side of budgets, and generally they have not been coordinated with an explicit strategy for the decentralization of expenditure assignments. Although significant strides have been made in the areas of tax assignments and tax administration, other areas—in particular, the assignment of government functions—have advanced much less. Yet a stable, efficient, and fair decentralized system of public finance in China will require an unambiguous and well-defined institutional framework in the assignment of expenditure responsibilities among the different levels of government. The assignment of responsibilities is by no means the only condition, but it is the most important, and it should also be the first in a well-sequenced decentralization reform effort.[1]

This chapter reviews the most important current issues surrounding the assignment of expenditure responsibilities in China.[2] In order to put those issues in the proper perspective, an overview is provided of the general principles of expenditure assignments and the common problems encountered in the international experience. The chapter also provides a road map and practical recommendations for the reform of expenditure assignments in China.

Principles of Expenditure Assignments in Theory and Practice

The Role of the Public Sector in the Economy

Before the question of expenditure assignment is addressed, it is necessary to define clearly the roles of the private and public sectors in the economy. Many countries,

---

[1] See Bahl and Martinez-Vazquez (2006b) for a discussion of the sequencing of decentralization reforms.
[2] See Bahl and Martinez-Vazquez (2006a) for a wider perspective of decentralization reform in China.

especially transitional countries, have undergone massive privatization of state and local enterprises involved in what can basically be considered private-sector economic activities. While there has been privatization in China in some cases, it has yet to begin in earnest in other areas of the economy. Thus, a first step to expenditure assignment reform in China is to define the responsibilities of the public sector and ascertain what activities can be privatized. In theory, the role of the public sector should be limited to those services and activities that private markets will not supply efficiently—either because of the difficulty of charging a price or because of joint-consumption benefits—and those with desirable redistributional value.

The Primacy of Expenditure Assignment in Intergovernmental Fiscal Relations Design

Most experts in decentralization policy agree that the first fundamental step in the design of a system of intergovernmental fiscal relations should be a clear assignment of functional responsibilities among different levels of government. The international experience shows that instability, controversy, and, ultimately, inefficiency in public service delivery can follow when the decentralization laws are silent or unclear about the competencies and expenditure obligations of different levels of government.

Designing the other important pieces of a system of decentralized finances, including revenue assignments and transfers, in the absence of a clear expenditure assignment is to put the cart before the horse. Decentralization initiatives in Latin American countries (e.g., Colombia, Ecuador, Bolivia, and Nicaragua) over the past several decades have made this type of mistake. Revenues were assigned to subnational governments and transfers put in place before it was decided what functional competencies would be transferred from the central government to subnational governments. This led to weak decentralized systems and fiscally overburdened central governments in those countries for years to come.

General Principles of Expenditure Assignments

The theory of public finance suggests some fundamental rules for the assignment of expenditure responsibilities in a decentralized system. However, these rules do not provide an absolute best way for deciding which level of government should be responsible for particular public services. Together with the rules or best principles, the adequacy of any functional assignment has to be judged in terms of how well it achieves the goals or objectives set up by the government in its decentralization strategy.

The critical role of the efficiency criterion. The efficient provision of government services requires that government satisfy the needs and preferences of taxpayers as well as possible. In plainer words, government expenditure that does not address the needs and preferences of citizens is partially or absolutely wasted. The approximation of needs and preferences is best achieved via the "subsidiarity" principle.[3]

---

[3] The principle is widely accepted by fiscal decentralization experts and has also been adopted as a practical guide. For example, the European Charter of Local Self-Government formally adopts the subsidiarity principle as the most prominent guide for expenditure assignments.

What this principle says is that the responsibility for the provision of services should be at the lowest level of government compatible with the size of the "benefit area" associated with those services. The benefit area for sanitation services is clearly the local community, but for air traffic control the benefit area may be the entire national territory. The provision of services with smaller benefit areas by smaller governments makes it more likely that there will be a good match between the services provided and the local residents' preferences. However, leaving the supply of public services with wider benefit areas to smaller units of government is likely to result in the inefficient underprovision of services in the case of economies of scale in the production of services or in the presence of jurisdictional externalities (e.g., a tertiary hospital solely financed by a single municipality but providing regional services). Further efficiency in the provision of public services can be achieved when service provision is linked to the costs of service provision via fees, service charges, or local taxes; these "pricing" mechanisms also can help reveal taxpayers' place of residences to local officials.

The objectives of redistribution and stability in public service provision. It is generally agreed that expenditures undertaken by government for equity or income equalization reasons, such as social welfare programs, should be the domain of the central government or at least should be financed by the central government. It is thought that local or regional governments would have difficulties sustaining independent programs of this nature because they risk attracting the needy from other areas and would thus have to tax their (potentially mobile) residents more heavily to sustain the level of expenditures. But, while funding for such programs should be a central government responsibility, implementation can, in many cases, be left to local governments, which may have informational and other comparative advantages in delivering the service. Expenditures undertaken for the stabilization of the economy, such as massive investment or unemployment compensation, are generally ascribed to the central government because of their scale; subnational governments may be too small to be effective, and their efforts may be quickly diluted within the rest of the national economy (Martinez-Vazquez and McNab 2003).

But no matter how the general principles above are implemented, the conclusion needs to be that there is no single best assignment. What is considered the best assignment is likely to change over time with changes in costs and technological constraints, as well as in citizens' preferences. However, decentralized systems of finance work much more smoothly when at any given moment there is a concrete, clear, and stable assignment of expenditure responsibilities.

Expenditure Assignments in the International Experience

Not surprisingly, the assignment of expenditure responsibilities among different levels of government varies widely in the international experience. This variety reflects different approaches to decentralization, as in the case of federal and more decentralized countries, and unitary and more centralized countries, and differences in policy objectives. It may also reflect problematic choices of assignments in some cases.

Often, expenditure assignments broadly agree with generally accepted principles. For example, there is a general correspondence between the geographical dimension of benefits from a particular service and the level of government responsible for provision of that service. By and large, the functions allocated to the central government have a national dimension. These include defense and internal security, the justice system, foreign relations, and research. Some expenditures with macroeconomic and redistributional implications, such as pensions and unemployment compensation, are often the responsibility of the central government, as well, and those expenditures are financed by extrabudgetary funds (Bahl 1999; Bahl and Martinez-Vazquez 2006a; Wong 1997). Correspondingly, most of the expenditure responsibilities of subnational governments involve services with regional or local benefit areas, such as tertiary hospitals, primary education, fire protection, and sanitation. Appearances can be misleading, however, and a number of countries have several important problems in their expenditure assignments.

Common Problems with Expenditure Assignments

The international experience with expenditure assignments also provides some valuable lessons in what to avoid, including the following:

- *Lack of formal assignment.* A common problem found in the international experience, especially in the case of transitional countries during the 1990s, is the lack of a formal assignment of responsibilities. Although it is true that highly decentralized countries, such as the United States, lack a formal assignment of expenditure responsibilities in the law, such countries have a de facto assignment that has been achieved through many trials and tribulations over a long period of time—in some cases, centuries. Countries that are newly decentralizing are better served by adopting explicit assignments of responsibilities. The preferred vehicle for the assignment of expenditure responsibilities is the decentralization law or budget code. Some countries list expenditure responsibilities in their constitutions. Although it may be wise to put into the constitution some general principles for expenditure assignments (for example, a general respect for the subsidiarity principle), detailed expenditure assignments enshrined in a constitution prove difficult to change.
- *Inefficient assignments.* A second common problem in the assignment of expenditure responsibilities is wrong or inefficient assignments. This is the case, for example, in the assignment of expenditure responsibilities for social protection and welfare exclusively to local governments. Other examples include the assignment of responsibilities for national defense locally or of local fire protection services or water and sewerage services nationally. A more common mistake is the assignment of all capital expenditure responsibilities to the central level, regardless of the level of government responsible for provision of the services associated with the capital infrastructure. Such a decision is typically guided either by assumptions about the central government's capacity to finance large projects or by the belief that only central government officials are qualified to make capital investment decisions. Dichotomizing the responsibilities for building (by the

central government) and maintenance and operations (at the subnational level) can introduce "moral hazard" problems leading to a lack of proper maintenance of capital infrastructure.

- *Wide cosharing of responsibilities.* The cosharing of responsibilities within a particular public service is likely to cause confusion leading to inefficiencies. In an ideal world, all inputs for the delivery of a particular service would be simultaneously decided by a single authority. Fragmentation of duties within a service is more likely to cause, for example, a relative disproportion of funds to be spent on salaries and much less on operations; similarly, maintenance may be reduced to a minimum. On the other hand, the cosharing of responsibilities for a single service may be necessary given national political objectives. For example, subnational governments may be responsible for primary and secondary education, but curricula and textbook production may be carried out by the national government. The cosharing of responsibilities becomes less of a problem when particular attributes and tasks (e.g., for financing, regulation, and implementation) in a common service are clearly assigned to different levels of government. Problems arise when the assignment of these attributes is unclear—for example, when two different levels of government are responsible for financing and regulation for the same basic service.

Challenges with Expenditure Assignments in China

China is a large and diverse country with no single decentralization law and seemingly without an explicit decentralization strategy.[4] The current model of expenditure assignments is roughly based on the role of designing catchment areas for services. China's current decentralization system provides subnational governments with considerable expenditure autonomy (World Bank 2002), but the system may not necessarily be providing the most desirable mix of public goods and services at the local level.

The elements of the current system of expenditure assignment in China that present problems include (1) the mismatch between expenditure responsibilities and revenue sources at the lowest levels of government (counties and townships), where many important social services are concentrated; (2) a general lack of clarity of expenditure assignments aggravated by the lack of formal assignments; (3) several wrongly assigned responsibilities, such as pensions and unemployment insurance, at the lowest level; and (4) the lack of horizontal accountability mechanisms, with possibly important undesirable consequences, including the underprovision of basic public services.

How the System Got Here

The current system of intergovernmental fiscal relations in China is the result of successive fiscal reforms starting at the beginning of the 1980s. Before that time, China had been under a central planning system since 1949, when the People's Republic of China was created. The recent reforms—of the fiscal responsibility system, starting at the beginning of the 1980s; the fiscal contracting system, starting

---

[4] This section draws on Martinez-Vazquez (2006).

in 1988 (Bahl and Wallich 1992); and the tax sharing system, starting in 1994—have the striking feature of putting almost exclusive emphasis on improving revenue assignments and transfers and practically ignoring the question of expenditure assignments.[5]

This means that the assignment of expenditure responsibilities remained virtually unchanged until some of the more recent reforms described below. To a large extent, expenditure assignments in many areas are still a legacy of the Maoist economy, in which the division of responsibilities was unimportant, as every unit strove to be self-reliant. For example, to a large extent the current responsibility for providing social services at the lowest government levels is a legacy of the system of collective agriculture, under which the communes and brigades of the People's Republic financed education, health, and social welfare.

Current Expenditure Assignments

As we have mentioned, expenditure responsibilities in China are highly decentralized. The budget law confers substantial autonomy and quite broad expenditure responsibilities on each level of subnational government. However, expenditure assignments are far from being transparent and clear, mostly because of the lack of formal assignments and the extensive concurrent expenditure responsibilities among different levels of government. This conspicuous presence of concurrent responsibilities can be traced back to the planned economy era. At that time, it was not considered necessary to separate the responsibilities of different spheres of government as providers of public services (local governments acted as agents of the central government, carrying out assigned tasks only), nor was it considered necessary to separate the expenditure responsibilities of governments from those of state-owned enterprises (SOEs). The latter fact was due to the cohesive functions of the government in both the public and private sectors; in fact, government before the mid-1980s jointly determined fiscal expenditures and the expenses of the SOEs.

As defined by the current legislation, the division of the main expenditure responsibilities among the central and provincial governments is summarized in figure 2.1.

In practice the main characteristics of the current assignment of expenditure responsibilities can be summarized as follows:

- *A blurred distinction between the public and private sectors.* During the process of transition from the planned economy to the market economy, government gradually relied more heavily on market mechanisms and gave up direct intervention in the private sector. However, government's expenditure responsibilities are still very wide. Currently, a significant number of enterprises are still owned by (or belong to) governments at different levels, and there is still a variety of channels through which governments can directly or indirectly encroach into private-sector activities through their SOEs (Qiao and Shah 2006). The low level of development of the legal framework that regulates the behavior of governments and government officials has led to high levels of administrative discretion.

---

[5] See Martinez-Vazquez (2006) for a discussion of the reform stages.

FIGURE 2.1
Assignment of Expenditure Responsibilities Between Central and Subnational Governments

Main expenditure responsibilities of the central government
Defense
Foreign affairs
Operation of the central government
Operational expenses for cultural, educational, scientific, and public health undertakings at the central level
Key capital construction
Technical renovation and new product development in centrally owned enterprises
Agriculture
Subsidies
Macroeconomic control and regional coordination of economic development
Social security
Debt

Main expenditure responsibilities of subnational governments
Operation of subnational governments
Operational expenses on cultural, educational, scientific, and public health undertakings at the subnational level
Subnational capital construction
Technical renovation and new product development in locally owned enterprises
Agriculture
Urban maintenance and construction
Social security
Subsidies

SOURCE: Zhang and Martinez-Vazquez, 2003.

Thus, China is still in the process of clearly differentiating between private- and public-sector activities and aligning the responsibilities of the government sector to fit the development of the market economy.

- *Extensive use of concurrent responsibilities and highly decentralized responsibilities for basic public services.* There has been no apparent change in policy or practice in expenditure assignment between the central government and local governments and among subprovincial governments since the initiation of the market-oriented reforms. Most recently, the 1994 tax-sharing system reform restated the pre-reform expenditure assignments. It is particularly important that the expenditure assignment for subprovincial governments is still entirely left to the discretion of the provincial government. To improve the expenditure assignments at the subprovincial government level, the central government's Ministry of Finance (MOF) issued "Suggestions on Improving Subprovincial Fiscal Relations" in December 2002, with the objective of providing further guidelines on subprovincial expenditure assignment, but these fall short of an explicit expenditure assignment.

Concurrent responsibilities between the central and subnational levels of government are still the norm, and usually these are ad hoc. Exclusive responsibilities at the central and subnational levels are few. The central government tends to be exclusively responsible for national defense issues, and local governments exclusively

TABLE 2.1

Relative Shares of Expenditure at Different Government Levels, 2003 (percent)

Expenditures	Central	Provincial	Prefecture	County and Under
Total	30	18	22	30
Capital investment	44	23	22	11
Agriculture expenditure	12	46	11	31
Education	8	15	18	59
Scientific research	63	23	9	5
Health care	3	22	32	43
Social security	11	39	32	18
Government administration	19	11	22	48
Public security & procuratorial agencies, court of justice	5	25	34	36
National defense	99	1	0	0
Foreign affairs	87	13	0	0
Foreign aid	100	0	0	0
Other	29	16	25	30

SOURCES: National Bureau of Statistics of China; Ministry of Finance.

provide services on urban maintenance and construction. Other public services show concurrent or coshared responsibilities. The relative shares of expenditures for different levels of government in 2003 are listed in table 2.1.

Although there has been a slight trend toward centralization in recent years, the provision of basic public services is still mainly the responsibility of subprovincial governments, particularly county-level governments. The three most important categories of social services are basic education, health, and social welfare.

Education services are divided into basic education, higher education, and vocational training.[6] Most vocational education is now left to private market institutions. County-level governments, which include cities and urban districts, are mostly responsible for basic education services. The role of the central government is that of policy maker and overall planner. In addition, the central government has responsibility for teachers' training and for setting up special education funds for subsidizing basic education in poor and minority areas. Provincial governments have the overall responsibility for formulating the development plan for basic education in their territories and providing assistance to counties to help them meet recurrent expenditures in education. The responsibility for actually implementing compulsory education programs, including the financing of basic education, lies with the cities, or districts of large cities, in urban areas and with counties in rural areas.

The provision of basic education services in rural areas is one of the major current concerns for the central government because of the generally worse service conditions there. Some new initiatives, especially "The Decision on Further Strengthening Rural Education," issued by the State Council in September 2003, have expanded the expenditure responsibilities of the central government for basic educa-

---

[6] See "Implementation Suggestions of the State Council on the Guidelines for the Reform and Development of Education in China," issued in July 1994.

tion. With that initiative, the implementation of compulsory education became a central government shared responsibility. The central government's goal was to support students from poor families by waiving their textbook, tuition, and miscellaneous fees and by subsidizing housing expenditures for elementary and secondary education students. The central government, as well as provincial governments, started setting up special funds for the support of this program in 2003. All students who meet the requirements of the poverty standard are supposed to have been enjoying the listed benefits since 2006.

The assignment of expenditure responsibilities for higher education differs from that for basic education. In general, private institutions of higher education in China are few, and they account for a very small portion of these services; private institutions tend to concentrate on vocational training. Public higher education institutions are divided into two groups: one belongs to the central government, and the other belongs to subnational governments. Thus, expenditure responsibilities for higher education are shared between the central government and the provincial governments. The central government has responsibility for the national development of higher education and provides direct support to the higher education organizations that belong to the central government. The provincial governments have responsibility for the provincial development of higher education and support the higher education institutions that belong to the provincial governments.

Health care services are mostly the responsibility of the county level of government and below. The central government has continued to announce its commitment to public health care,[7] but in practice its responsibility for health care has been minimal for years. The huge rural-urban divide that exists in many aspects of daily life in China—in particular, in access to public services—takes on special meaning in the area of health services. For this reason, coverage of rural health care has recently become one of the stated major concerns of the central government. "The Decision of the Central Committee of the Communist Party of China and the State Council to Further Strengthen Rural Health Care," issued by the central government in October 2002, provided detailed responsibilities for the provision of rural health care services among different levels of government. The central government now has the responsibility for designing the overall plan for rural public health care, the provincial governments have responsibility for its implementation, and the county governments have overall responsibility for rural public health care delivery. In addition, the central government is responsible for subsidizing programs for the prevention and control of highly infectious diseases, endemic diseases, occupational diseases, and so on in poorer areas; provincial governments are responsible for subsidizing health programs of county (city) governments and for paying the costs of planned vaccinations; and county governments are responsible for the delivery of all rural public health services.

One of the newest initiatives in health services is the rebuilding of the rural collaborative health care system, which began in January 2003. This program expanded the responsibilities of both the central government and provincial governments

---

[7] For example, "The Decision on Public Health Reform and Development by the Central Government," issued in January 1997, requires that public spending on health care at both the central government and subnational government levels increase at a higher rate of growth than general budgetary expenditures.

regarding health care. It established, among other measures, that from 2003 on, in addition to the contribution of 10 yuan per resident every year, the central government should pay 20 yuan and provincial governments no less than 20 yuan a year for each rural resident who joins the rural collaborative health care system. The provincial governments were given discretion to arrange the sharing of their contribution among the different subnational government levels in their jurisdictions.

Social security remains mainly the responsibility of subnational governments. The main component of current social security expenditure is the minimum living standard paid to urban dwellers. Thus, the expenditure responsibilities in this area are more concentrated at the provincial and prefecture levels, and less responsibility is placed at the county level of government and below, the vast majority of whose population are rural residents, who have much less coverage under the social security system.

Operation-oriented local expenditure structure. Subprovincial governments have always given priority to current administrative needs over other spending needs. Currently, the expenditure pattern in some areas, particularly in poorer areas, is still regarded as "feeding finance" (*chi fan cai zhen*) or just meeting government administration costs. The structure of the components in total government expenditures at different levels is shown in table 2.2. Typically, subnational governments give priority to administration spending, local public security agencies, and courts of justice in their expenditure decisions. By design, most government personnel are concentrated at lower levels of government; in many cases these local governments have been acting as employers of last resort. This has led to the growth of local expenditures on employees.

TABLE 2.2

Composition of Budget Expenditure at Different Government Levels, 2003 (percent)

Expenditures	Central	Provincial	Prefecture	County and Under
Total	100.0	100.0	100.0	100.0
Capital investment	20.5	17.4	14.1	5.0
Agriculture expenditure	1.8	11.6	2.4	4.7
Education	3.2	9.4	9.7	23.8
Scientific research	2.6	1.5	0.5	0.2
Health care	0.3	3.8	4.7	4.5
Social security	1.9	10.9	7.5	3.0
Government administration	5.4	4.7	8.5	13.4
Public security & procuratorial agencies, court of justice	1.0	7.3	8.4	6.1
National defense	25.4	0.5	0.0	0.0
Foreign affairs	0.9	0.2	0.0	0.0
Foreign aid	0.7	0.0	0.0	0.0
Other	36.2	32.6	44.1	39.3

SOURCES: National Bureau of Statistics of China; Ministry of Finance.

Basic public services do not represent a significant share of local expenditures. In particular, in the total expenditures of county-level governments, which are the main providers of basic public services, the sum of education, health care, and social security counts for approximately 30 percent, as shown in table 2.2. In subnational government aggregate expenditures, the same services count for around 25 percent on average, while in some provinces it counts for less than 17 percent (table 2.3).

On the other hand, it appears that in provinces where the services are more decentralized, service delivery outcomes are improved. For example, in provinces where the provincial government remains the main spending authority, infant mortality rates are higher than in provinces where counties have the main spending authority (Uchimura and Jütting 2007).

Hierarchical expenditure managing model. Nowadays each subnational government has its own budget, but practically speaking, the budget of each government includes both its own budget and the consolidated budget of all the governments under it; of course, for the lowest government, the township government, its own budget is equivalent to a consolidated budget. The government budget at each level is approved by the People's Congress at that level, which also checks the consolidated budget. The approved budget of each subnational government is submitted to the next level of government, and so on up to the MOF, for the record and for the compilation of the upper-level government's consolidated budget and eventually the national consolidated budget. The national budgets are the last to be approved. The main issue with this approach is that local residents' input into the shape and content of local expenditure budgets is limited. Instead, local expenditure management is conducted mostly through the bureaucratic hierarchy.

Significant administrative autonomy for local expenditure decisions. Currently, subnational government officials still practice "administrative autonomy" to increase their effective autonomy and go beyond the confines and constraints imposed by the local budget and related regulations. In general, the management of

TABLE 2.3
Aggregate Expenditure Composition at the Subnational Level, 2005 (percent)

Expenditures	Max.	Min.	Avg.	C.V.
Capital construction	30.41	4.81	11.60	0.49
Agriculture	4.76	1.49	3.57	0.22
Education	18.80	10.99	14.72	0.15
Public health	6.20	2.80	4.08	0.21
Subsidies for social security programs	16.62	1.72	6.86	0.55
Government administration	15.07	4.19	9.75	0.22
Public security & procuratorial agencies, court of justice	10.11	4.42	6.58	0.20
City maintenance	11.77	0.23	4.50	0.52
Underdeveloped areas	2.57	0.00	1.05	0.75

SOURCES: National Bureau of Statistics of China; Ministry of Finance.
NOTE: C.V. is the coefficient of variation.

funds is through a "distributive model," whereby various government agencies and divisions of the finance department make their own expenditure decisions, and some expenditures may not be included in the budget. One manifestation of the administrative autonomy at the subnational level is the prevalence of extrabudgetary funds. It is important to note that a significant portion of subnational government expenditures do not go through the regular budget channels. Fundamentally, extrabudgetary expenditures do not differ that much from ordinary budgetary expenditures. As shown in table 2.4, the largest share of the officially recorded extrabudgetary funds is spent on government administration (72 percent for 2004). Other uses of extrabudgetary funds overlap considerably with those of ordinary budget items.

As the central government has taken various measures to transform its extrabudgetary expenditures into budgetary expenditures (Wong 1998; 2000), extrabudgetary funds at the central government level have decreased dramatically (Qiao and Shah 2006). In contrast, extrabudgetary expenditures still play a very important role at the subnational level, despite the central government's long effort to reduce their use and importance and transform extrabudgetary funds into ordinary budgetary funds. As a matter of fact, the ratio of extrabudgetary to budgetary expenditures for subnational governments was still around 20 percent in 2004.

The use of revenues from the sale of land in off-budget funds is another manifestation of administrative autonomy. In addition, soft-budget constraints are still a problem in China's system. One manifestation of a soft-budget constraint is in the dealings between SOEs and government. Some SOEs are generally not very competitive and rely heavily on government to survive; however, they also help the interests of local governments.[8]

In recent years the central government has taken steps to improve expenditure management processes, including the creation of budgeting departments, according to which each government agency and public service unit has a single budget that combines all budgetary and extrabudgetary funds; the introduction of a treasury system and the centralization of payment administration, by which all expenditure

TABLE 2.4
Most Important Extrabudgetary Expenditures, 2004

Item	Percent of Total
Capital construction	6.6
Public administration	72.0
City maintenance	4.5
Township expense	4.7
Other	12.2

SOURCE: National Bureau of Statistics of China, 2006.

---

[8] According to China's 1994 budget law, subnational governments are forbidden from borrowing on the capital market except with special approval from the central government; however, they can effectively borrow through SOEs.

funds for each government are controlled in a single account of the central bank; and the standardization of governmental procurement practices.

Main Issues with Expenditure Assignments

Little has been done to reform policy and clarify expenditure assignments over the past several decades. This is especially true at the subprovincial level. The main challenges facing the current system in expenditure assignments include the following:

- *A mismatch of expenditure responsibilities and revenue sources at the lowest levels of administration.* Local governments (especially county and township levels) have very heavy expenditure responsibilities in education, health, and social insurance that are out of line with international practice. While the tax-sharing system reform has recentralized revenue assignments, there has been considerable devolution of expenditure responsibilities to local governments. More important, the vertical imbalances caused by revenue centralization and expenditure decentralization have not been adequately offset by intergovernmental transfers (Jia 2004).
- *Significant regional disparities in fiscal performance.* The current system of decentralized finance in China yields significant horizontal fiscal disparities (Qiao, Martinez-Vazquez, and Xu 2008). These disparities occur across provinces but also within provinces, especially between urban and rural areas, and there is evidence that they are expanding. The expanding disparities in expenditure per capita and in service delivery are likely to be harmful for cohesion of the country. The increasing trend in expenditure disparities, which was temporarily stopped for several years starting in 1998 as several intergovernmental transfer programs were newly introduced by the central government, has continued since 2000. Since 2003, reforms in intergovernmental transfers to improve rural basic public services have slightly decreased the disparity. (See table 2.5.) In 2005, public expenditures per capita in the best-off province were 7.9 times larger than those for the worst-off province, and the coefficient of variation across provinces was 0.73. These disparities are very large by international standards.
- *Serious underprovision of basic public services in poor jurisdictions.* For county governments that have only limited revenues, the ability to spend on local public goods depends heavily on intergovernmental transfers (Uchimura and Jütting 2007). But without adequate resources at the lower levels of government, the current levels of intergovernmental transfers and the budget priority decisions taken by the local governments have led in many cases to the underprovision of basic public services (Martinez-Vazquez, Qiao, and Zhang 2008). China's system of intergovernmental finance is far from achieving the goal of providing all citizens with similar access to basic public services. While the average per capita educational expenditure is 352 yuan, the poorest jurisdiction spends only 171 yuan, less than half of the national average and less than one-sixth of what the richest jurisdiction spends. The underprovision in some areas of public health services and social security is even more significant. The poorest jurisdiction spends 39 yuan per capita on health care, which represents 37 percent of the

TABLE 2.5
Per Capita Expenditure Disparities Across Provinces, 1990–2005 (yuan)

Year	Max.	Min.	Avg.	C.V.
1990	613	99	251	0.57
1991	664	102	280	0.56
1992	729	112	296	0.56
1993	958	122	372	0.57
1994	1,452	157	444	0.69
1995	1,837	226	538	0.71
1996	2,348	278	632	0.72
1997	2,806	308	698	0.77
1998	3,211	347	811	0.76
1999	3,620	409	943	0.76
2000	3,635	225	1,075	0.70
2001	4,387	532	1,383	0.73
2002	5,307	655	1,620	0.75
2003	6,361	741	1,792	0.77
2004	7,936	905	2,082	0.75
2005	9,259	1,165	2,538	0.73

SOURCE: National Bureau of Statistics of China for the years cited.
NOTE: C.V. is the coefficient of variation.

average and only 9 percent of what is spent by the richest jurisdiction. In the case of social security programs, the lowest jurisdiction spends 29 yuan per capita on subsidies for social security programs, which represents 19 percent of the average and 7 percent of what is spent by the richest jurisdiction (table 2.6).

- *Lack of horizontal accountability mechanisms.* An important question is whether local governments are prioritizing local budget expenditures according to the needs and preferences of their residents (Oates 1972; 2005). The generally low horizontal accountability of local government officials to their residents has likely exacerbated problems with the delivery of services. Accountability of government officials to residents has been further reduced because an increasing number of people have migrated internally without the official documents and are "illegally" residing in urban areas, especially in the eastern provinces, without a right to access basic services. But even in the poorer areas, the limited fiscal resources have not prevented local governments from expanding into areas with heavy overhead expenditures that in many other countries are left to the private sector. In China there continues to be no clear delineation for government responsibilities between the public and private sectors.
- *The undesired consequences of lacking a clear assignment of responsibilities.* The lack of explicit expenditure assignments at the subprovincial level has led to considerable overlapping of responsibilities and eventually lower accountability because of the difficulty of identifying what level of government should be accountable for the delivery of particular services. Inefficient underprovision of services is more likely in the presence of extensive concurrent responsibilities. The lack of explicit assignments has also meant considerable murkiness as to which level is responsible for financing expenditures and how the financing responsibilities

TABLE 2.6
Subnational Expenditures per Capita, 2005 (yuan)

Expenditures	Max.	Min.	Avg.	C.V.
Total	9,259	1,165	2,538	0.73
Capital construction	2,077	76	358	1.35
Agriculture	216	38	82	0.49
Education	1,029	171	352	0.59
Public health	427	39	105	0.80
Social security programs	405	29	156	0.69
Government administration	1,009	118	231	0.71
Public security & procuratorial agencies, court of justice	549	70	162	0.70
City maintenance	499	16	117	1.03
Underdeveloped areas	152	0	24	1.26

SOURCES: National Bureau of Statistics of China; Ministry of Finance.
NOTE: C.V. is the coefficient of variation.

are divided. This has facilitated the convenient offloading of responsibilities down the hierarchical structure of government. In education, for example, despite the fact that in many cases resources are inadequate, counties have been called on in recent years to finance basic education reform. Some of these upper-level government measures can be considered as unfunded government mandates. The lack of explicit assignments has also led to significant differences in the distribution of responsibilities among local governments across provinces. Although in theory there is nothing wrong with variety in approaches to expenditure assignments, the absence of a holistic approach to expenditure (and revenue) assignments means that matching revenue sources with expenditure functions at each local level is made more difficult, as is targeting pass-through transfers from the central government to lower-level local governments. The absence of a unified approach to expenditure assignments also makes the tasks of setting standards for the provision of public services and monitoring performance harder, and it can be expected to contribute to wide variation in the standards of services.

- *Several inefficient expenditure assignments.* Several of the current expenditure assignments are problematic. The most conspicuous example is the responsibility assigned to city- or county-level governments for pensions, unemployment, and income support schemes. Such assignments are hardly replicated anywhere else in the world; general pension schemes, unemployment insurance, and other social security measures tend to be central government responsibilities. Either provincial or national pooling would seem to be the correct approach to the assignment of these services. These types of social security schemes require a level of risk pooling and redistribution that cannot be matched at the level of county governments.[9] Whereas welfare benefits are almost nonexistent in rural areas, in urban areas there is often a lack of redistribution because poorer communities with the highest needs are least financially able to fund these expenditures. The

---

[9] See, for example, Ahmad (1995) and the references therein.

inability of many local governments to finance the social safety net has led in recent years to widespread pension arrears and defaults that have forced the central government to intervene with subsidies.

A Road Map for Reform

Setting up formal and stable expenditure assignments to clarify the responsibilities of all government levels must become a priority for reform. A clear and explicit assignment of expenditure responsibilities at all levels could (1) facilitate a more efficient organization and provision of basic public services; (2) significantly improve the accountability of public officials to residents; (3) help eliminate government encroachment in the private sector; and (4) help address the issues of vertical and horizontal fiscal disparities.

In the past two decades, China has made considerable progress in separating government from SOEs and redefining the functions and responsibilities of government in the economy. But there are still significant problems from an expenditure assignment perspective (Martinez-Vazquez 1998). In particular, a stable and transparent expenditure assignment at all levels of government, emphasizing exclusive over concurrent responsibilities, is desirable.[10]

The other option is to continue with the current system and muddle through until an acceptable system presents itself through piecemeal reforms. Practice can substitute for explicit assignments in the law, but relatively younger decentralized countries like China may avoid costly transactions through more explicit and clear assignments. When concurrent responsibilities are desirable, assignments should be clarified by explicitly assigning the multidimensional array of attributes that go with each function, including (1) actually producing a good or delivering a service; (2) providing or administering the service; (3) financing the service; and (4) setting standards, regulations, and policies for the provision of services. In addition to clarifying assignments, it will be important to improve coordinating institutions across levels of government to address different interpretations and conflicts arising from concurrent assignments.[11]

But the question is how to proceed with comprehensive reform in expenditure assignments. The rest of this chapter provides practical guidelines that can be followed in this reform process. Among the most important steps to accomplish reform is the appointment of a high-level intergovernmental reform commission charged first with mapping out the current de facto expenditure assignments and providing a blueprint for reform options. Further below, we list the steps for comprehensive reform. However, first, because comprehensive reform can be politically difficult, some worthwhile reforms that can be made piecemeal follow:

- *Reassign selected expenditure responsibilities.* The financing and provision of social security services (pensions, disability and survivor benefits, and unemployment)

---

[10] For example, in many decentralized large countries, including Australia, Brazil, Canada, the Russian Federation, and the United States, a number of responsibilities are exclusively assigned to local governments.

[11] For example, Australia, Canada, and New Zealand use periodic formal meetings of elected officials and bureaucrats at different levels to discuss mutually important expenditure assignments and other fiscal issues.

should be recentralized, at the provincial or central government level. The recent policy measures assigning more responsibility for social security at the central level are steps in the right direction.

- *Address the existing large fiscal disparities and align the decentralized fiscal system more properly to ensure that all citizens have access to basic public services regardless of where they happen to live.* Addressing the existing fiscal disparities will require, at a minimum, significantly enhancing the role of equalization grants in the current intergovernmental system. This will require at the center an increase in the pool of funds dedicated to equalization, the consolidation of many existing small transfers with equalization objectives, and a distribution formula that takes into account fiscal capacities and expenditure needs. At the subcentral level, clear guidelines for the provinces, prefectures, and counties (if applicable) would need to be legislated to introduce (1) sufficient funding for equalization grants for the governments immediately below; and (2) distribution formulas that capture, to the extent the data allow, the differences in fiscal opportunity and expenditure needs of subordinate local governments. A small set of conditional sectoral grants could also be considered in order to guarantee some minimum standards of service throughout the national territory. In this regard it may be worth considering the use of national minimum standards for basic public services and the use of conditional grants to ensure that all subnational governments have the means to finance them.

- *Improve the accountability and quality of local expenditure management.* A significant feature of China's decentralization system bearing on the issue of efficiency is that the accountability of subnational government officials to local residents is weak; the direct appointment of officials tends to make them mostly accountable to the upper and central government authorities. The system needs to introduce adequate accountability mechanisms to provide incentives to subnational governments to properly weigh spending on economic development and construction and other public services, especially those in the social areas. Besides local elections, different approaches are used internationally to better empower communities. For example, local governance in some countries is reinforced by institutions that facilitate the involvement of civil society in the delivery of public services.[12] For example, in the education sector, there is now evidence that community-managed schools can lower teacher absenteeism and improve schooling outcomes.

Important Preliminary Questions

There are several important questions that need to be considered by the authorities before moving on to reform the current system of expenditure assignments:

- *What should be the scope of the reform in expenditure assignments and privatization?* A benefit of extending the scope of the reform to all activities within the

---

[12] For example, in Canada, Local Boards are not-for-profit, community-based organizations composed of volunteers from business, labor, education, and community groups that support local governments in a variety of ways. Similar institutions exist in the United States.

fiscal system is that we can identify activities at the central and subnational levels that do not serve a public function and that by their nature can be better provided in the private sector. The reform of expenditure assignments provides an excellent opportunity for the privatization of activities that do not belong in the public sector.

- *Should assignments be distinguished as "delegated" or "own" responsibilities?* In determining expenditure assignments we may want to make a distinction between voluntary (or "own") responsibilities and mandatory (or "delegated") functions of subnational governments. A decision needs to be made as to whether it is desirable to differentiate between what subnational governments *can* do and what they *must* do. However, doing this is not a requirement for a clear assignment of expenditure responsibilities. Delegated responsibilities are typically paid via conditional or tied grants.
- *How far should "exclusive" (as opposed to "concurrent") assignments be taken?* Exclusive responsibility is more conducive to accountability and generally a more efficient provision of services; however, in practice, exclusive responsibilities are not always possible, and they may not be desirable in some cases.
- *Which general approach—"general competence" or "closed list"—should be used for expenditure responsibilities?* Here the choice is between a "general competence" approach followed by some exclusions or exceptions and a "closed list" of competences. A closed-list approach is more cumbersome, but it can offer more protection to subnational governments from encroachment by central or upper-level governments. Typically, the question boils down to what level of government may have "residual powers," in case a particular (new) function does not appear in the law in the closed list of any one level of government.
- *What legal instrument should be employed to specify expenditure assignments?* Because an assignment should be stable over time, especially given the time needed for strategic planning and capacity building, it should be in the law—for example, in the decentralization law or the budget code. It is less preferable to introduce expenditure assignments in the constitution.
- *How much needs to be specified in the law, and how much can be left to coordination or even interpretation by the courts?* No expenditure assignment can ever be detailed enough to preempt the need for dialogue and coordination among different levels of government, but there is the matter of the level of specificity in the law. That is, how much should we rely on the legal text and implementation rules vis-à-vis a more general text that will be subject to interpretation as we go, by practice and coordinating institutions, and ultimately be left for interpretation and rulings by the courts of law?
- *Should expenditure assignments be determined at all levels or just between the central and the "aggregated" subnational level?* When there is a single tier of government below the central government, the assignment of functions must cover all government levels. However, when there are two or more tiers of government at the subnational level, there are several choices of approach. An explicit assignment at all levels is more transparent and efficient but, of course, less flexible in adapting to specific characteristics of subnational units.

- *Should the assignment of asymmetric responsibilities be considered?* Some local jurisdictions may be too small to realize economies of scale in the delivery of public services; they may lack adequate fiscal capacity and tax base and also lack administrative and managerial capacity. Although there are some ways to get around the small scale, such as privatization of services, the creation of special districts, or associations of local governments, the most preferable solution to the problem is the amalgamation of smaller local governments into larger units with adequate size and capacity. If amalgamation is not politically feasible, the solution could be an asymmetric assignment of expenditure responsibilities, in which more or less responsibilities are assigned according to the capacity of local governments.

Identifying Who Should Be Involved

It may be assumed that in the case of China, the determination of expenditure assignments is the prerogative of the national or central authorities. As mentioned earlier, leadership of the reform should be assigned to an intergovernmental reform commission with wide representation of the most important stakeholders at the central and subnational levels. The commission, with support of a technical secretariat or working group, would need to establish the general strategy and scope of the reform, as well as an implementation plan with an explicit time schedule. If there is no commission, perhaps the Ministry of Finance could take the lead in the reform effort. However, that is likely to be less than ideal.

Determining What Information Is Needed

Setting up to conduct comprehensive reform of expenditure assignments will require significant amounts of data on actual and potential expenditures and expenditure needs associated with the reassignment. Getting all of this information on a timely basis may be one of the most significant hurdles to expenditure assignment reform. But it will be important that adequate resources are dedicated to this task.

Enforcement

One of the big difficulties with expenditure assignments, and in other policy areas, as well, is that there may be significant differences between what the assignments are in practice and what is specified in the law and regulations. These problems will tend to be minimized if the process of reform is highly participatory, involving all stakeholders, and the reforms are well publicized. The added clarity to the assignment of expenditure responsibilities by the reform should also contribute to reducing differences between practice and law. Intergovernmental institutions for cooperation and dialogue among the different levels of government can also work well in this context.

Acknowledgments

We are thankful to Andrey Timofeev, Bert Hofman, and Dana Weist for helpful comments to previous drafts and to J. Vernon Henderson for his comments.

REFERENCES

Ahmad, Ehtisham. 1995. A comparative perspective on expenditure assignments. In *Reforming China's public finances*, eds. Ehtisham Ahmad, Gao Qiang, and Vito Tanzi, 77–94. Washington, DC: International Monetary Fund.

Bahl, Roy. 1999. *Fiscal policy in China: Taxation on intergovernmental fiscal relations*. San Francisco: 1990 Institute.

Bahl, Roy, and Jorge Martinez-Vazquez. 2006a. Fiscal federalism and economic reform in China. In *Federalism and economic reform*, eds. T. S. Srinivasan and Jessica. S. Wallach, 249–300. New York: Cambridge University Press.

———. 2006b. Sequencing decentralization. Policy Research Working Paper No. 3914. Washington, DC: World Bank.

Bahl, Roy, and Christine Wallich. 1992. Intergovernmental fiscal relations in China. Policy Research Working Paper No. 863. Washington, DC: World Bank.

Jia, Kang. 2004. *Local fiscal issues*. Beijing: Economic Science Publishing House.

Martinez-Vazquez, Jorge. 1998. The assignment of expenditure responsibilities. Mimeo. Atlanta: Georgia State University, Andrew Young School of Policy Studies.

———. 2006. Expenditure assignments in China. Background Paper for presentation at the Roundtable Conference on Public Finance for a Harmonious Society, Beijing (June 28–27).

Martinez-Vazquez, Jorge, and Robert M. McNab. 2003. Fiscal decentralization and economic growth. *World Development* 31(9):1597–1616.

Martinez-Vazquez, Jorge, Baoyun Qiao, and Li Zhang. 2008. The role of provincial policies in fiscal equalization outcomes in China. *China Review* 8(2):135–167.

Ministry of Finance of China. 2004, 2006. *China fiscal statistical yearbook*. Beijing: China Financial and Economic Publishing House.

National Bureau of Statistics of China. 1991–2006. *China statistical yearbook*. Beijing: China Statistics Press.

Oates, Wallace E. 1972. *Fiscal federalism*. New York: Harcourt Brace Jovanovich.

———. 2005. Toward a second-generation theory of fiscal federalism. *International Tax and Public Finance* 12(4): 349–373.

Qiao, Baoyun, Jorge Martinez-Vazquez, and Yongsheng Xu. 2008. The tradeoff between growth and equity in decentralization policy: China's experience. *Journal of Development Economics* 86(1):112–128.

Qiao, Baoyun, and Anwar Shah. 2006. Local government organization and finance: China. In *Local government in developing countries*, ed. Anwar Shah, 137–166. Washington, DC: World Bank.

State Council. 1994. "Implementation Suggestions of the State Council on the Guidelines for the Reform and Development of Education in China," Beijing (July).

Uchimura, Hiroko, and Johannes Jütting. 2007. Fiscal decentralization, Chinese style: Good for health outcomes? Working Paper No. 264. Paris: OECD Development Centre.

Wong, Christine P. W., ed. 1997. *Financing local government in the People's Republic of China*. Hong Kong: Oxford University Press.

———. 1998. Fiscal dualism in China: Gradualist reform and the growth of off-budget finance. In *Taxation in modern China*, ed. Donald J. S. Brean, 187–207. New York: Routledge.

———. 2000. Central-local relations revisited: The 1994 tax-sharing reform and public expenditure management in China. *China Perspectives* 31 (September–October): 52–63.

World Bank. 2002. *China national development and subnational finance: A review of provincial expenditures*. Washington, DC: World Bank.

Zhang, Zhihua, and Jorge Martinez-Vazquez. 2003. The system of equalization transfers in China. International Studies Program Working Paper No. 0312. Atlanta: Georgia State University, Andrew Young School of Policy Studies.

Fiscal Decentralization, Infrastructure Financing, and Regional Disparity

3

WEIPING WU

Rapid urbanization in China's reform period has resulted in a very high demand for basic urban infrastructure and the need for sustained mechanisms of financing. How China accommodates its increasingly urban population is critical not only directly for the well-being of an increasing number of its people but also more indirectly for its sustained economic development (Wong and Bird 2004). Public ownership has been the predominant form through which urban infrastructure is provided. As the Chinese economy moves more and more toward a market-oriented economy, the role of state enterprises in infrastructure development has diminished (Lin 2001). Consequently, municipal authorities have become the key providers.

Infrastructure financing in urban China is fundamentally different from infrastructure financing in most other countries. In industrialized countries, borrowing is widely used as a key method because of the capital-intensive nature of much urban infrastructure, especially in upfront costs (Bird 2004; Chan 1998). Most such borrowing is directly from a functioning capital market and relies on a system of municipal bond rating. Large cities tend to have better access to bond markets than small cities. Excluding borrowing, local taxes are the most important source of infrastructure financing, counting on average a 40 percent share (Chan 1998). Taxes are followed by grants and subsidies, and then other sources, including user charges. Although the situation in developing countries various substantially, local property taxes dominate the revenue structure and loan financing tends to be a small source.

Municipal governments in China, on the other hand, have neither sufficient tax resources to finance infrastructure nor the authority to borrow externally (Wong and Bird 2004). Under reform, the decentralized fiscal system has mostly worked to the advantage of municipal governments, allowing them better incentives to mobilize local resources. At the municipal level, new mechanisms of financing arising from such fiscal freedom have contributed to significant expansion of infrastructure investment. However, the central government assigns heavy responsibilities for the provision of nearly all public services to local governments without adequately supporting them through either revenue assignments or an intergovernmental transfer system. Continuing fiscal decentralization, in addition, has affected regional patterns of infrastructure financing. As economic growth becomes more concentrated in the coastal region, there has been a sharp rise in interregional disparities in fiscal spending, accompanied by gradual deterioration in public services provided in inland regions. Some attempt to reverse the trend of growing regional inequality began around 1998, when the government started redirecting fiscal resources toward equalization, including the "Go West" development strategy launched in 1999. A major driver of this transfer policy appears to be concern for the growing regional disparities that many consider to have marred the country's impressive growth performance (Wong and Bird 2004).

The main purpose of this chapter is to explore patterns of financing infrastructure development across cities of different regional location and the relationship between infrastructure investment and regional economic performance. First, the chapter outlines how successive waves of fiscal decentralization in China during the reform era have affected local financing and autonomy. Second, it analyzes the expanding range of mechanisms in financing urban infrastructure, paying particular attention to the use of funds outside of the budgetary process. Third, it examines the increasing disparity among cities of different geographic locations in their ability to finance infrastructure development and their performance in doing so. Last, using statistical data on large, prefecture-level cities in China, the chapter presents preliminary results from a regression analysis on the relationship between urban infrastructure investment and economic performance. This chapter uses the limited definition of urban infrastructure often called "urban maintenance and construction" in China. It includes public utilities (water supply and drainage, residential gas and heating supply, and public transportation), municipal works (roads, bridges, tunnels, and sewerage), parks, sanitation and waste management, and flood control. Housing, power, telecommunications, and other transportation sectors (ports, airports, and railway) are not counted as a part of urban maintenance and construction (Wu 1999).

Central-Local Fiscal Relations

Public finance matters for the provision of urban infrastructure. China's record of investment in infrastructure such as highways, ports, power plants, and a variety of urban services has been nothing short of astonishing (Wong and Bird 2004). But its fiscal system remains in transition, the product of decentralization. Much like the macroeconomic reforms, fiscal decentralization has been gradual and incremental, responding to immediate problems with short-term fixes. There continues to be a mismatch of expenditures and revenues between levels of government. As a result, the operation of local governments in public financing is often chaotic, as they cope with fund shortfalls through a variety of off-budget mechanisms.

Prior to the economic reform, China's fiscal system was characterized by centralized revenue collection and fiscal transfers. All taxes and profits were collected by local governments, remitted to the central government, and then transferred back to the provinces and municipalities according to their expenditure needs as approved by Beijing. Under that fiscal system, municipal revenues were shared with the central or the provincial government for redistribution. For many years revenue retention rates for municipal authorities were very low and insufficient to allow significant expansion of infrastructure and adequate maintenance. Capital expenditure funding, in the form of either grants or credit, was largely unavailable to the service sector and directed mainly to the production sectors (World Bank 1993). The paramount importance of the central government derived from its control of the fiscal revenue and expenditures of local governments—and, therefore, financing and investment for urban construction. In the three general levels of governments (central, provincial, and municipal), the lower levels were entirely subordinate to governments of higher rank in fiscal matters (Wong 1997).

The central government controlled urban maintenance and construction revenues mainly through central budgetary allocation, supplementary project funding, and the public utility surcharge levied on enterprises and commercial users. There were no earmarked taxes or funds for urban construction, and user charges were minimal. As a result, there was no guaranteed steady flow of funds to urban construction from year to year. Indeed, central funding for the urban sector dried up between the 1950s and the 1970s as Beijing focused on building inland defense facilities. As a result of the rigid central-local fiscal relations, municipalities also did not have the local finance systems necessary to support infrastructure projects (Chan 1998; Dowall 1993). At the local level, the infrastructure sector was a low priority when funds were allocated through municipal budgets. Because of the bias toward industrial production, capital outlays for urban construction were determined by a population count, according to household registration, and tended to be very limited, often not exceeding one-tenth of total municipal expenditures (Wu 1999).

Central-local fiscal relations have been altered significantly by decentralization efforts since 1980. First, the central government introduced a new decentralizing fiscal regime that visualized each provincial entity as a "separate kitchen" for fiscal purposes. This, together with subsequent fiscal reform by provinces, allowed many municipalities to retain higher rates of revenue and to allocate funding more freely. In 1980 a new system of fiscal contract was introduced, which designated separate types of taxes or revenue. Under this arrangement participating provinces and municipalities were allowed a share of revenue. They retained all income collected in excess of this share. In exchange for being given a bigger slice of revenue, they were required to accept responsibility for most items of expenditure.

Yet another new set of reform measures were introduced at the beginning of 1994 to further streamline central-local fiscal relations. Three areas of concern were addressed: providing adequate revenues for governments, particularly the central government; building a more transparent tax structure; and improving central-local revenue sharing arrangements (Wong 1997). Taxes were reassigned between the central and local governments, and a shift was made from a negotiated system of general revenue sharing to a mix of tax assignments and tax sharing (Wong and Bird 2004). For the first time, local governments were assigned some taxes as local with significant revenue-generation capacity. Related to urban construction, an urban land use tax, a real estate tax, and an urban maintenance and construction tax are now among the local taxes. Another positive element in the new system is a mandate to reduce government involvement in microeconomic management.

There are, however, substantial distortions associated with the new tax-sharing system created through the 1994 reform. First of all, by sharing value-added tax revenues with local governments at a flat rate by origin, the system introduced a highly disequalizing feature to revenue sharing, ensuring that revenue-rich regions would keep more. Specifically, coastal provinces gained revenue shares relative to inland provinces. From 1993 to 1998, for instance, the ratio of provincial per capita fiscal expenditures grew in Shanghai from 2.8 to 4.5 and in Beijing from 2.0 to 3.0 times the national average. In contrast, the ratio fell in Gansu, from 0.76 to 0.61, and in Hunan, from 0.60 to 0.52 (Wong and Bird 2004). Second, the reform recentralized revenues but left expenditure assignments unchanged. This created a huge fiscal gap for local governments.

Urban Infrastructure Financing

As the public finance system continues to be reformed, mechanisms for infrastructure financing are broadening, particularly through nonstate channels (see table 3.1). There are four general sources of funds available for urban infrastructure development. The first is budgetary allocation from central and local governments, consistently making up about 15 percent. The second is local fiscal revenues: the urban maintenance and construction tax (collected by local governments as a surcharge on the combined value of the value-added tax, product tax, and business tax—7 percent in cities, 5 percent in towns, and 1 percent elsewhere) and the public utility surcharge (collected by local governments at a rate of 5–8 percent from the turnover of water, electricity, natural gas supplies, public transportation, and local telephone service) (Chan 1998; World Bank 2000). The third is nonfiscal sources, including primarily fees and user charges, although most such revenues were recorded in the "Other Sources" category in the 1990s. The fourth is borrowing, from both domestic and foreign sources, including foreign investment. An additional significant source is self-raised funds, providing 10–20 percent of revenues.

There are problems in the collection of the so-called two-item funds—the urban maintenance and construction tax and the public utility surcharge—although as earmarked funds they could have become the backbone of urban infrastructure financing. The rate is set by the central government and is low relative to the financing need of many cities. The former is collected as a surcharge on three taxes levied on the output of industrial and commercial enterprises and incomes of enterprises in transportation, hotel, catering, and other service sectors. Therefore, it fluctuates with output levels of these enterprises and does not apply to public institutions (*shiye danwei*). As a result, the two-item funds have accounted for a declining share of urban maintenance and construction revenues (see table 3.1).

TABLE 3.1

Urban Maintenance and Construction Revenues, 1990–2004 (billion yuan)

	1990	1993	1996	2002	2003	2004	2004 (%)
Budgetary allocation							
Central budgetary allocation	1.09	2.70	1.04	7.60	7.71	5.26	1.00
Local budgetary allocation	1.98	5.95	8.63	39.27	53.29	66.58	12.66
Local taxes							
Maintenance and construction tax	6.51	9.8	15.78	31.60	37.17	44.63	8.49
Public utility surcharge	2.26	3.3	5.56	4.99	5.57	5.90	1.12
Fees and user charges							
Water resource fee	0.28	0.48	0.61	1.24	1.60	2.07	0.39
Infrastructure connection fee				8.66	9.44	10.68	2.03
User charges[a]				8.94	10.61	12.27	2.33
Land transfer fee				28.30	50.68	109.96	20.92
Borrowing							
Domestic loans	0.88	4.46	9.57	87.39	133.18	144.55	27.49
Foreign capital[b]	0.25	1.38	5.59	6.11	6.81	7.42	1.41
Bonds				0.29	1.60	0.06	0.01
Stock financing				0.68	0.03	0.29	0.06
Self-raised funds	2.58	4.59	11.95	60.08	76.97	90.02	17.12
Other sources[c]	5.21	25.47	26.05	30.47	32.96	26.06	4.96
Total	21.04	58.13	84.78	315.62	427.62	525.76	100.00

SOURCES: Wu, 1999; Ministry of Construction, 2002–2004.

NOTES: [a]User charges primarily include tolls on roads and bridges, wastewater treatment fees, and garbage treatment fees. [b]Foreign capital includes both direct investment and loans. [c]A major component of other sources prior to 2002 was infrastructure connection fees.

An increasingly important mechanism of financing is the collection of fees and user charges, including the infrastructure connection fee (similar to the impact fee in the United States). Such income now counts for between 15 and 25 percent of urban maintenance and construction revenues. But the increasing fee and user charge income in China may be misleading, as revenue from leasing land use rights has become an important component (a share of 21 percent in 2004; see table 3.1). A more serious problem lies in the wide range of fee scale and fee items across cities. Some municipal authorities have included a multitude of infrastructure services in the fee collection and often have asked for exorbitant amounts of money (Wu 1999). This is shown in the case of some 28 different fees imposed on various aspects of real estate development in Shanghai (Bird 2004).

Revenue from borrowing is rising, from only about 5 percent in 1990 to about 30 percent in 2004. Such borrowing includes not only cash and deposits but also treasury and other financial bonds and equities. Bank credit also is emerging as an important source of borrowing. China increasingly resembles market economies in which surpluses generated in the household sector are loaned to the enterprise sector to finance a portion of public investment. But banks sometimes are reluctant because infrastructure investment is large, with long terms and lower return rates, and regional (Zhang and Wu 2005). In addition, foreign capital (including government and commercial loans, direct investment, and international bonds) has begun to play some role in financing urban infrastructure. When China started to open infrastructure to overseas investment in the late 1980s, foreign companies responded enthusiastically. China has since attracted money for truly commercial projects, such as joint ventures to build and operate roads and bridges, where costs are expected to be recovered through toll collection. The central government offers a series of incentives to prospective investors, including tax advantages, customs duty exemptions, a wider variety of permitted activities, and relative operational autonomy (Wu 1999). Public-private partnerships (or joint ventures) tend to be a common form of foreign participation in which both sides contribute funds or services (frequently by providing property or land on the Chinese side), and the public sector often is represented by a company directly or indirectly owned by the government (Bellier and Zhou 2003; Bird 2004). Since 1995, more concessional projects have emerged, particularly in the form of BOT (build-operate-transfer) projects.

Fiscal reforms have selectively allowed certain provincial-level entities the right to issue construction bonds domestically. Aimed at capturing the high level of household savings, this practice has been growing but remains a small source of infrastructure financing. Borrowing from international sources is in principle not permitted at the local level, with exceptions approved only by the central government. The dilemma of external borrowing is illustrated by Shanghai's experience—debt services for such borrowing must be underwritten by profit-making activities often unrelated to infrastructure development. In 1986, the city was authorized to borrow US$3.2 billion from international financial institutions (Qiu 2005), and, given its lack of local fiscal resources, it was allowed to create an independent economic entity (Shanghai Jiushi Company) for debt services to bundle together profit-making projects with public works, financing the works through borrowed funds to be repaid by the profits. Its investments in hotels, factories, and so on were considered successful, and many similar quasi-public companies were subsequently set up not only in Shanghai but in many other cities, as well (Wong and Bird 2004). Shanghai eventually established 10 large government investment companies as the main financing entities, covering industry and urban construction. The establishment of those companies for loan services facilitated several key infrastructure projects, such as the new railway station, Nanpu and Yangpu Bridges, Inner Ring Road, and the No. 1 Metro Line (Qiu 2005).

The emergence of new mechanisms has resulted in the increasing importance of extrabudgetary funds, which are still in the public sector but are not subject to central or provincial budgetary control. This is an indication of a higher degree of municipal fiscal independence. The formal budget is only a part of the fiscal story and not necessarily the most important part. A broad definition of extrabudgetary funds is that they constitute all resources managed directly or indirectly by administrative branches of the government outside the normal budgetary process. Extrabudgetary funds generally include fees and funds that are not taxes, such as the water resource fee, infrastructure connection fee, and user charges (see table 3.1). While budgeted funds are under strict supervision, extrabudgetary funds are easier to manipulate and soften the budgetary constraint for municipal governments. The primary motivation for the development of extrabudgetary funds at the local level is revenue enhancement rather than earmarking (Wong and Bird 2004). For instance, authorities in some cities have created "revolving funds" for small-scale investments. These funds have transformed ordinary fiscal grants into repayable loans. Repayment of the principal as well as interest is channeled back to the revolving fund, gradually building available resources. Such funds are operated in a legal gray area and often opposed by officials of the banking system (Yusuf and Wu 1997).

Self-raised funds are an even grayer area in local financing. Though not collected as taxes or budgetary items, extrabudgetary funds nonetheless are specifically authorized by some government body. Sometimes called extra-extrabudgetary funds, off-budgetary funds, or extra-system revenues, self-raised funds are not specifically authorized as a fee or a fund (Wong and Bird 2004). Such revenue is irregular and often nonrecurring, raised by central ministries, local governments, or public institutions. It is an example of how fiscal burdens can be passed on to the enterprise sector, which is then forced to finance public services. For instance, in Dongguan, Guangdong Province, local authorities have experimented with a new method to raise funds. It involves the creation of an energy and communications company that raises money from state, collective, and private sources for the construction of roads and power plants. The company pays interest on these funds and will repay the capital by collecting user fees and tolls (Harral 1992). An example of privately funded infrastructure services is the rise of premium water networks in some cities. Beginning in the mid-1990s, select residential communities began to bypass municipal tap water supply systems through the construction of small-scale secondary pipe networks for purified drinking water (Boland 2007).

The difficulty in sorting out local public finance in China is further demonstrated by the practice of land leasing and transfer. For many localities, land transfer fees are considered self-raised funds because they are not specifically authorized as fees and the revenue varies from year to year. But for others, revenues from land transfer are treated as extrabudgetary. In current practice, land leasing and transfer are driven by short-term interests of local governments. Since land is the most valuable commodity under the control of a municipal government, generating revenues from leasing land use rights and charging land use fees has become a popular local practice. Many local governments have been dependent on the sale of leases for a considerable fraction of their revenues and have at the same time been increasingly involved in land and real estate development. Local government's role is critical to the acquisition of land for development, especially when the conversion of farmland is involved (Wong and Bird 2004). The use of state assets by the government and its agencies to raise off-budget revenues, however, is a major source of inefficiency, distorted incentives, and loss of state assets (Wong and Bird 2004). In addition, sold land use rights represent relinquished sources of income. It is unlikely that cities can count on revenue from asset sales as a major, lasting source of funding to expand infrastructure construction and maintenance.

Regional Disparity in Infrastructure Provision and Financing

Regional disparity in economic performance and income has been long-standing in China. Before 1949, more than 70 percent of China's industries were concentrated within a narrow coastal belt on the eastern side of the country. This was largely due to the development of precapitalist (nationalist) modes of production in the early twentieth century—mainly in port cities under partial colonization by advanced capitalist countries. Since the establishment of a socialist state, central planning of development has become more economically self-reliant. It was the inland area or "periphery" of China that was emphasized. Later, in the 1960s, due to concerns for national security, a belt of mountainous, dispersed, and tunneled locations within the inland region were targeted for development. This was known as the Third Line and was no doubt aimed at reducing the disparity between the coastal and inland regions. After 1979, the tune of socialist planning in China changed to one of economic efficiency and spatial deployment. Policies introduced since then favor a reorientation to coastal or "core" development, indicating China's new effort toward further technological and economic expansion. As a result, the eastern region has experienced the most rapid economic growth.

There are now noticeable differences in nearly all available indicators of urban infrastructure services across regions, even though China has made significant progress on an aggregate level (table 3.2). Cities in the eastern region uniformly enjoy higher levels of service in all sectors; a markedly higher percentage of the population has access to piped water and wastewater treatment. In many inland provinces, local infrastructures, such as public transportation systems, roads, streets, water supplies, and waste treatment systems, are in poor condition. The major reasons for the slower infrastructure growth there include low government spending on infrastructures caused by low government revenues (Lin 2001). The growth of local government revenues, in general, is low. In 1978, local government revenues were 95.65 billion yuan, while in 1998 they were 134.37 billion yuan when adjusted for inflation. The annual growth rate of local government revenues was only 1.7 percent. Local governments have become increasingly dependent on the central government for transfers. Before 1985, local government revenues were larger than expenditures, and local government remitted revenues to the central government. In 1998, 35 percent of local government expenditures were financed by subsidies from the central government (Lin 2001). Lower local government revenues resulted in lower expenditures on local infrastructure construction and maintenance.

Continuing fiscal decentralization also has affected regional patterns of infrastructure financing. In particular, there are substantial distortions associated with the new tax-sharing system created through the 1994 reform. Specifically, coastal provinces gained revenue shares relative to inland provinces. On the other hand, there is yet to be a supporting system in place to ensure minimum standards of service provision across regions. As wealth has become more concentrated in the coastal region since the 1990s, there has been a sharp rise in interregional disparities in fiscal spending, accompanied by a gradual deterioration in public services provided in the inland provinces (Wong and Bird 2004). The western region, for instance, relies much more on budgetary allocation and borrowing to finance urban

TABLE 3.2
Level of Urban Infrastructure Services by Region, 1996–2005

	1996	2002	2003	2004	2005
Water coverage rate (percent)					
Eastern region	97.67	86.23	90.02	93.39	94.36
Central region	91.39	75.84	81.66	84.61	86.75
Western region	96.07	60.59	83.71	85.21	85.32
National average	94.89	77.85	86.15	88.85	91.09
Gas coverage rate (percent)					
Eastern region	83.88	82.25	87.60	90.41	90.63
Central region	59.97	58.57	64.93	68.90	72.21
Western region	60.07	43.98	66.42	65.70	67.79
National average	73.21	67.17	76.74	81.53	82.08
Public transportation vehicles (per 10,000 persons)					
Eastern region	8.88	8.06	8.57	10.06	9.80
Central region	5.73	5.62	6.52	6.85	7.16
Western region	7.92	5.25	7.05	8.75	9.01
National average	7.29	6.73	7.66	8.41	8.62
Per capita road area (square meters)					
Eastern region	8.90	9.56	10.53	11.67	12.21
Central region	6.55	7.06	8.10	8.66	9.35
Western region	7.44	5.04	7.91	8.93	9.57
National average	7.56	7.87	9.34	10.34	10.92
Wastewater treatment rate (percent)					
Eastern region	27.93	46.07	48.43	51.94	—
Central region	17.76	32.85	37.18	39.29	—
Western region	20.39	30.07	31.48	34.66	—
National average	23.62	39.97	42.39	45.67	—

SOURCES: Hou, 1998; National Bureau of Statistics of China, 2006; Ministry of Construction, 2002–2004.
NOTE: — = data not available.

infrastructure and has much less ability to raise funds from extrabudgetary sources (see figure 3.1). In general, very large cities tend to rely less on budgetary allocation and more on self-raised funds.

There is a general regional disparity in the level of urban infrastructure financing, although the patterns are not uniform within region. Overall, provinces in the eastern region have fared better. From 1996 to 2004, for instance, Beijing, Shanghai, and Zhejiang enjoyed per capita urban maintenance and construction revenues at more than twice the national averages. But there is substantial variation within the coastal region. Provinces on the southeast coast, such as Guangdong, Fujian, and Hainan, saw their revenue levels decline relative to national averages. Some provinces in the western region, particularly Chongqing and Sichuan, experienced more rapid growth in the level of urban infrastructure financing (see table 3.3). The central region in general, on the other hand, lagged behind.

The regional patterns in urban infrastructure financing appear to have shifted in tandem with the progress of economic reforms across China. In 1996, provinces

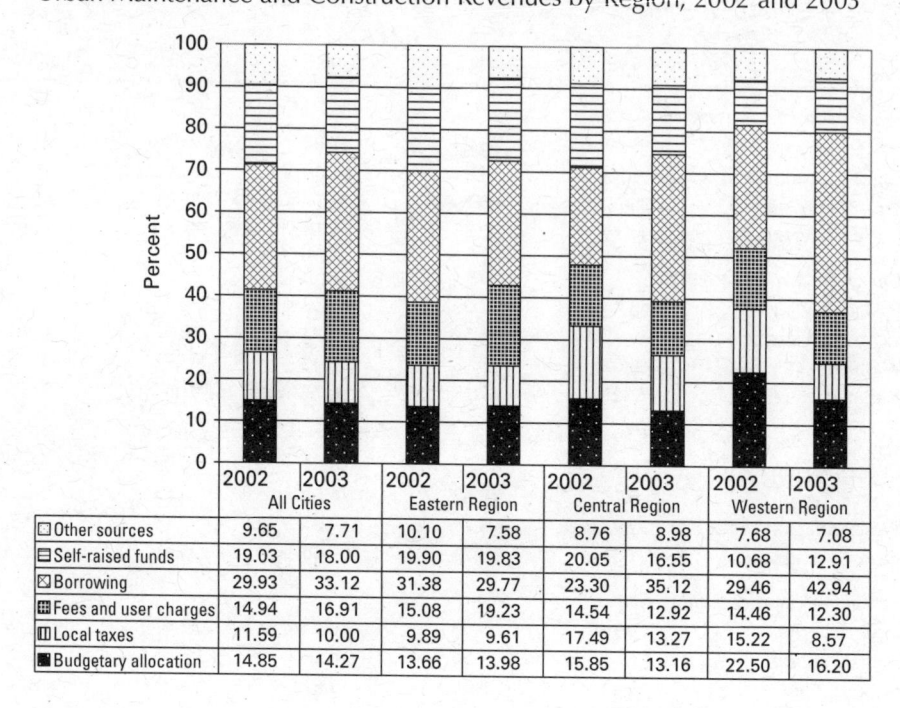

FIGURE 3.1
Urban Maintenance and Construction Revenues by Region, 2002 and 2003

	All Cities 2002	All Cities 2003	Eastern Region 2002	Eastern Region 2003	Central Region 2002	Central Region 2003	Western Region 2002	Western Region 2003
Other sources	9.65	7.71	10.10	7.58	8.76	8.98	7.68	7.08
Self-raised funds	19.03	18.00	19.90	19.83	20.05	16.55	10.68	12.91
Borrowing	29.93	33.12	31.38	29.77	23.30	35.12	29.46	42.94
Fees and user charges	14.94	16.91	15.08	19.23	14.54	12.92	14.46	12.30
Local taxes	11.59	10.00	9.89	9.61	17.49	13.27	15.22	8.57
Budgetary allocation	14.85	14.27	13.66	13.98	15.85	13.16	22.50	16.20

with the highest levels of per capita urban maintenance and construction revenues, including Guangdong, Fujian, and Shanghai, tended to be on the southeast coast. That is where market reforms took hold earlier. As reforms spread north and west, the growth of the Yangtze Delta area has become more prominent, and the Bohai area also is rising. Provinces in these areas, such as Zhejiang, Shanghai, Jiangsu, Tianjin, and Beijing, clearly stand out as heavy investors in urban infrastructure. Some of the poorest provinces continue losing ground in their capacity to finance urban infrastructure.

Does Infrastructure Financing Matter for Regional Economic Performance?

The regional unevenness in infrastructure development will have long-term effects on economic development. World Bank studies correlate a 1 percent increase in gross domestic product (GDP) with a 1 percent increase in infrastructure stock across all countries (Ingram and Kessides 1994; World Bank 1994). Munnell (1990) shows that, in the United States, those states that have invested in infrastructure tend to have greater output, more private investment, and higher employment growth (cited in Lin 2001). To explore whether infrastructure investment contributes significantly to urban economic performance, a database of prefecture-level Chinese cities (including large cities and provincial capital cities excluding Lhasa) has been

TABLE 3.3
Per Capita Urban Maintenance and Construction Revenues by Province, 1996–2004

	\multicolumn{4}{c	}{Investment (yuan)}	\multicolumn{4}{c}{Index (national average = 1)}
	1996	2002	2003	2004	1996	2002	2003	2004
Eastern region								
Beijing	613	2,905	2,429	4,884	1.37	3.24	1.92	3.17
Tianjin	436	1,305	2,219	2,744	0.97	1.46	1.75	1.78
Hebei	304	1,097	1,306	1,440	0.68	1.22	1.03	0.94
Liaoning	361	722	835	1,103	0.80	0.81	0.66	0.72
Shanghai	1,325	4,059	2,951	3,824	2.95	4.53	2.33	2.48
Jiangsu	706	1,436	2,307	2,367	1.57	1.60	1.82	1.54
Zhejiang	1,038	2,567	3,645	3,142	2.31	2.86	2.88	2.04
Fujian	614	615	1,063	1,304	1.37	0.69	0.84	0.85
Shandong	350	634	1,013	1,280	0.78	0.71	0.80	0.83
Guangdong	711	907	835	1,071	1.58	1.01	0.66	0.70
Guangxi	466	766	1,213	1,828	1.04	0.85	0.96	1.19
Hainan	496	451	442	1,391	1.10	0.50	0.35	0.90
Central region								
Shanxi	259	370	427	551	0.58	0.41	0.34	0.36
Inner Mongolia	219	716	1,057	1,141	0.49	0.80	0.84	0.74
Jilin	327	441	615	714	0.73	0.49	0.49	0.46
Heilongjiang	170	375	690	789	0.38	0.42	0.55	0.51
Anhui	362	444	668	806	0.81	0.50	0.53	0.52
Jiangxi	227	671	1,238	1,165	0.51	0.75	0.98	0.76
Henan	299	397	601	621	0.67	0.44	0.47	0.40
Hubei	163	287	507	664	0.36	0.32	0.40	0.43
Hunan	480	771	1,199	1,347	1.07	0.86	0.95	0.87
Western region								
Chongqing	—	395	1,645	2,296	—	0.44	1.30	1.49
Sichuan	385	328	1,796	1,784	0.86	0.37	1.42	1.16
Guizhou	301	415	558	487	0.67	0.46	0.44	0.32
Yunnan	494	612	931	1,220	1.10	0.68	0.74	0.79
Tibet	84	386	110	110	0.19	0.43	0.09	0.07
Shaanxi	347	484	992	1,315	0.77	0.54	0.78	0.85
Gansu	202	310	384	428	0.45	0.35	0.30	0.28
Qinghai	242	869	761	866	0.54	0.97	0.60	0.56
Ningxia	221	605	891	869	0.49	0.67	0.70	0.56
Xinjiang	310	936	1,446	1,330	0.69	1.04	1.14	0.86
National average	449	896	1,265	1,540	1.00	1.00	1.00	1.00

SOURCES: Hou, 1998; Ministry of Construction, 2002–2004.
NOTE: — = data not available.

constructed. In the strictest sense of the term, a *prefecture-level city* is not the equivalent of a city or municipality. Instead, it is an administrative unit comprising both an urban core (a city in the strict sense) and surrounding rural or less urbanized areas. Prefecture-level cities nearly always contain multiple counties, county-level cities, and other similar units. As a result, they can be considered the Chinese version of the term *metropolitan area*, used in many other countries. Official statistics collected on these cities includes data on both the entire jurisdiction of a prefecture-level city (*quan shi*) and the urban core (*shi qu*). This study used the former as the level of analysis and, hence, shows patterns at the level of metropolitan area.

An OLS (ordinary least squares) model used the GDP growth rate as the dependent variable. Because of the limited data availability, estimating a Cobb-Douglas production function at the level of metropolitan area was not feasible. As a result, GDP growth rate was analyzed as a function of public investments (in infrastructure and education) and other variables. Predictor variables included per capita urban maintenance and construction revenues, per capita investment in education, and per capita foreign direct investment. Unemployment rate was used to control for both cyclical and long-term trends in productivity (Andrews and Swanson 1995). Per capita foreign direct investment was used to approximate the level of private investment, since there was no adequate information on other types of private investment. Data were drawn from the *China Statistical Yearbook for Cities* and the *China Urban Construction Statistical Report* for 1999 and 2000, when information on all related variables was available. There were 236 prefecture-level cities in 1999 and 262 in 2000. After observations with missing data on key variables were excluded, 458 records were used in the analysis.

Descriptive statistics on the variables show that GDP growth rate varied substantially, with the standard deviation of 6.81 percent similar to the mean value of 7.20 percent (see table 3.4). Per capita urban maintenance and construction revenues follow a pattern of even greater dispersion, in which the standard deviation of 702.56 yuan exceeds the mean value of 686.62 yuan. The maximum level of 6,335.80 yuan for Ningbo (Zhejiang Province) is more than 380 times the minimum level of

TABLE 3.4
Descriptive Statistics for Prefecture-Level Cities

	Mean	SD	Minimum	Maximum
GDP growth rate (percent)	7.20	6.81	−39.80	30.93
Unemployment rate (percent)	3.56	2.47	0.00	22.32
Per capita foreign direct investment (US$)	139.86	340.43	0.00	3762.77
Per capita investment in education (yuan)	148.60	129.06	2.00	1673.00
Per capita urban maintenance and construction revenues (yuan)	686.62	702.56	16.48	6335.80

SOURCES: *China Statistical Yearbook for Cities*, 2000, 2001; *China Urban Construction Statistical Report*, 1999, 2000.

NOTE: Data are from the National Bureau of Statistics *(China Statistical Yearbook for Cities)*, except those on per capita urban maintenance and construction revenues, which are from the Ministry of Construction *(China Urban Construction Statistical Report)*. SD = standard deviation.

16.48 yuan for Yulin (Shaanxi Province). The distribution of per capita investment in education is about equally dispersed. Perhaps the most substantial variations occur for per capita foreign direct investment, with the standard deviation of US$340.43 more than twice the mean value of US$139.86. The maximum level was recorded for Dongguan (Guangdong Province), China's foremost center for export processing, while a number of cities received no foreign direct investment. It is clear that there are significant disparities across cities in economic performance and public investment, as well as private investment.

The purpose of the OLS model is to estimate and compare the effects of the predictors. It is not meant to fully account for the variations in GDP growth rate, as some important variables are not present in the model. The model is run with simultaneous entry, not stepwise, procedures, because the latter tends to capitalize on random variations in the data. There is no problem of multicollinearity in the OLS model, since no variables display tolerance levels lower than 0.2. As regression coefficients are unit dependent, discussion focuses on standardized coefficients in assessing the extent to which each predictor is influential.

The OLS results indicate that per capita infrastructure revenues are a statistically significant predictor for GDP growth (see table 3.5). Controlling for the effects of other factors, this predictor can explain close to 3 percent of the variance in the growth rate of GDP (partial coefficient $r = 0.167$). Granted this represents a small influence, but it is one that should not be overlooked. Per capita investment in education is not a significant contributor, nor is per capita foreign direct investment. These results are similar to those reported by studies on U.S. states (Munnell 1990) and 73 countries worldwide (Kelly 1997)—public capital in infrastructure has a far more significant effect on economic performance than social expenditures. However, per capita investment in education may not be the best indicator of the quality of educational services, since such investment tends to be channeled to physical facilities. Despite China's record of success as the largest recipient of foreign direct investment among developing countries, there is a general consensus that its growth has been driven predominantly by domestic investment. Extremely high domestic saving and investment rates have led gross domestic capital formation

TABLE 3.5
OLS Regression on GDP Growth Rate

	Standardized Coefficient	t-value	Significance	Tolerance
Constant		7.413	0.000	
Unemployment rate	−0.049	−1.061	0.289	0.963
Per capita foreign direct investment	0.096	1.606	0.109	0.571
Per capita investment in education	0.075	1.291	0.197	0.602
Per capita urban maintenance and construction revenues	0.178	3.612	0.000	0.833
Adjusted R^2	0.076			

SOURCES: National Bureau of Statistics of China, 2000, 2001; Ministry of Construction, 1999, 2000.
NOTE: OLS = ordinary least squares.

to surpass 40 percent of GDP. The share of foreign direct investment in GDP has been gradually drifting downward since the mid-1990s (Naughton 2007).

Findings from this analysis are preliminary, given that data constraints affect the number of variables included, as well as the choice of variables. In addition to the need for a better measure of education quality, per capita infrastructure revenues may not be the best indicator of the quality or quantity of physical infrastructure. For one, a city may have a very low baseline of infrastructure stock, and a higher level of investment in one year may not affect economic growth immediately. It may take several years for the effect of public investment in infrastructure to materialize in terms of better economic performance. Consequently, capital stock of infrastructure, which is used in most of the studies mentioned earlier, is likely a better indicator. This indicator should take all of the different categories, such as highways, airports, railways, communications, water and energy supplies, and public utilities, into consideration.

Summary

Research at the national and regional levels has pointed to the positive contribution of public infrastructure to economic performance. Differences in public capital facilities also appear to have a significant effect in accounting for regional income disparities. While still facing the daunting task of equipping its cities with modern infrastructure, China has made great strides in providing basic services and perhaps has performed better than most of its counterparts with similar income levels. However, there is an increasing disparity among cities of different geographic locations in their ability and performance to finance urban infrastructure. Since the regional unevenness in infrastructure development has long-term effects on economic development, this chapter represents an attempt to show how infrastructure investment may be connected with regional economic performance in China.

China's experience in infrastructure financing is a significant departure from the international norm—the capacity of municipalities to borrow externally is lacking, local property and land taxes are nearly absent, and extrabudgetary funds allow for softer budgetary constraints. The local problems, to a large extent, stem from the changing central-local fiscal relations. Though decentralization has allowed more incentives for local governments to mobilize resources, the 1994 tax reform has left significant distortions. These distortions have spatial implications, leaving poorer provinces in inland areas further behind in their capacity for revenue retention.

It is clear that levels of infrastructure service differ substantially across cities in the three large regions, as do their methods and abilities to finance public facilities. The western region, in particular, has much less ability to raise funds from extrabudgetary sources. Cities there rely much more on budgetary allocation and borrowing to finance urban infrastructure. Overall, provinces in the eastern region also have experienced higher levels of financing. Specifically, Zhejiang, Shanghai, Jiangsu, Tianjin, and Beijing stand out as heavy investors in urban infrastructure. The central region in general has lagged behind in this respect. Some of the poorest provinces continue losing ground in their capacity to finance urban infrastructure.

An analysis using data on prefecture-level cities shows that infrastructure investment is a statistically significant predictor for regional economic performance. GDP growth rate is regressed as a function of per capita urban maintenance and construction revenues, per capita investment in education, and per capita foreign direct investment. On their own, per capita urban maintenance and construction revenues can explain close to 3 percent of the variance in the growth rate of GDP. The two other predictor variables do not seem to have significant effects. To better ascertain the contribution of public investment in infrastructure to regional economic performance in China, future research needs to construct better measures and data on the quality and quantity of infrastructure capital stock.

REFERENCES

Andrews, Kim, and James Swanson. 1995. Does public infrastructure affect regional performance? *Growth and Change* 26(2):204–216.

Bellier, Michel, and Yue Maggie Zhou. 2003. Private participation in infrastructure in China: Issues and recommendations for the road, water, and power sectors. Working Paper No. 2. Washington, DC: World Bank.

Bird, Richard M. 2004. Getting it right: Financing urban development in China. International Tax Program Paper 0413. Toronto: University of Toronto, Institute for International Business (November).

Boland, Alana. 2007. The trickle-down effect: Ideology and the development of premium water networks in China's cities. *International Journal of Urban and Regional Research* 31(1):21–40.

Chan, Kam Wing. 1998. Infrastructure services and financing in Chinese cities. *Pacific Rim Law & Policy Journal* 7(3):503–528.

Dowall, David E. 1993. Establishing urban land markets in the People's Republic of China. *Journal of the American Planning Association* 59(2):182–192.

Harral, Clell G., ed. 1992. *Transport development in southern China.* Discussion Paper No. 151. Washington, DC: World Bank.

Hou, Jie, ed. 1998. *China urban and rural construction development report, 1997.* Beijing: China Urban Press (*Zhongguo Chengshi Chubanshe*).

Ingram, Gregory, and Christine Kessides. 1994. Infrastructure for development. *Finance and Development* 31(3):18–21.

Kelly, Trish. 1997. Public expenditures and growth. *Journal of Development Studies* 34(1):60–84.

Lin, Shuanglin. 2001. Public infrastructure development in China. *Comparative Economic Studies* 43(2):83.

Ministry of Construction. Various years. *China Urban Construction Statistical Report.* Beijing.

Munnell, Alicia H., with the assistance of Leah M. Cook. 1990. How does public infrastructure affect regional economic performance? *New England Economic Review* (September–October): 11–33.

National Bureau of Statistics of China. 1999. *Cities in China 1949–1998* [Xin Zhongguo Chengshi Wushinian]. Beijing: Xinhua Publishing House.

———. 2000–2001. *China statistical yearbook for cities.* Beijing: China Statistics Press.

———. 2006. *China statistical yearbook.* Beijing: China Statistics Press.

Naughton, Barry. 2007. *The Chinese economy: Transitions and growth.* Cambridge, MA: MIT Press.

Qiu, Wenjin. 2005. Exploration and practice of reform on urban infrastructure financing: Mechanism in Shanghai. Paper presented at the Practitioners' Conference on Mobilizing Urban Infrastructure Finance in a Responsible Fiscal Framework: Brazil, China, India, Poland and South Africa. Organized by the World Bank, Jaipur, India (January 6–8).

Wong, Christine P. W. 1997. Overview of issues in local public finance in the PRC. In *Financing local government in the People's Republic of China*, ed. Christine P. W. Wong, 27–60. Hong Kong: Oxford University Press for the Asian Development Bank.

Wong, Christine P. W., and Richard Bird. 2004. China's fiscal system: A work in progress. Paper presented to the Conference on China's Economic Transition, Pittsburgh (November).

World Bank. 1993. *China: Second Shanghai Metropolitan Transport Project*. Washington, DC.

———. 1994. *World development report 1994: Infrastructure for development*. New York: Oxford University Press for the World Bank.

———. 2000. Workshop on China's urbanization strategy: Opportunities, issues, and policy options. Sponsored by the State Development Planning Commission, the Ministry of Construction, and the World Bank Group.

Wu, Weiping. 1999. Reforming China's institutional environment for urban infrastructure provision. *Urban Studies* 36(13):2263–2282.

Yusuf, Shahid, and Weiping Wu. 1997. *The dynamics of urban growth in three Chinese cities*. New York: Oxford University Press for the World Bank.

Zhang, Yaoqing, and Qingling Wu. 2005. *Urban infrastructure provision and management*. Beijing: Economic Science Press.

Financing Local Public Infrastructure: Guangdong Province

4

JOHN L. MIKESELL, JUN MA, ALFRED TAT-KEI HO, AND MEILI NIU

The People's Republic of China is in the process of substantial economic, social, and demographic change. A great population shift from rural to urban areas has accompanied increased industrialization and greater prosperity in the country. New prosperity brings new demands, and the centralization of finances that occurred in the mid-1990s brought transfers of fiscal responsibilities from the central government to local governments. These changes have put new pressure on local governments for delivery of services, particularly in urban areas. During the period of 1978 to 2006, the percentage of urban population in China increased from 17.9 percent to 44.9 percent (National Bureau of Statistics of China 2007). Local governments must respond to their citizenry with expanded and enhanced services and must, accordingly, find ways to finance those services. Using local fiscal resources has many advantages, such as allowing greater responsiveness, flexibility, and incentives for efficiency in the delivery of services that are of greatest interest to the local population.

This chapter examines the institutional arrangement and politics of the infrastructure financing mechanism, analyzes the issues related to "extrabudgetary" revenues and control, and provides recommendations regarding the current system of capital budgeting and financing by the Chinese government. By developing an in-depth understanding of these finances in Guangdong Province, it will be easier to analyze the conditions elsewhere and devise responsive strategies to deal with the process of urban development.

Decision-Making Mechanisms of Infrastructure Development in Guangdong

In Guangdong Province, there are three major steps in the formal decision-making process for infrastructure development: (1) preparation and evaluation of an initial project proposal to the Development and Reform Commission (DRC); (2) preparation and approval of a feasibility report if the initial proposal is approved; and (3) preparation of a project blueprint and budgetary estimate.

The initial project proposal is mainly a planning document that demonstrates the necessity of the project. The feasibility report provides information on how to get the project done. The blueprint gives the detailed design of the project, and the budgetary estimate focuses on its financial viability. Responsible entities must approve all three major documents before the project breaks ground.

Preparation and Evaluation of the Initial Project Proposal

The decision to finance an infrastructure project starts with a request by a functional department, which sees the need for the project based on assessment of the socioeconomic conditions of the community. The functional department is responsible for putting together an initial project proposal and submitting it to the DRC for review.

The Guangdong DRC is the regulatory agency responsible for monitoring the implementation and performance of macroeconomic policies and approving major infrastructure projects. Its jurisdiction includes education, health, water and sewage, solid waste, environmental protection, office building construction, public transportation, and streets and public highways. However, infrastructure investment made by nongovernmental entities, such as toll roads and utility projects constructed and managed by private companies, does not require the direct oversight and approval of the DRC. The 2004 China reform relinquished the DRC's traditional authority over approval of all investment projects (including private investment) and confined its authority solely to the review and approval of infrastructure projects using public money.

An initial proposal by a functional department typically includes the following information:

- The size of the project, such as the number of miles of a local road to be constructed or the size of an office building.
- The total manpower required.
- An estimate of the total financial investment.
- A financing plan.

The DRC evaluates an initial proposal by analyzing the needs suggested by the functional department and whether the proposed scope of the project matches the need. It also consults with the finance department, which is responsible for evaluating the financial feasibility of the project. For example, the proposal may require the use of resources from various sources, such as general fiscal revenue, specific funds designated for the functional departments, and other financing schemes (described below). The finance department must know which accounts will be drawn upon to finance the proposed project, whether those accounts have sufficient funds to support the project, whether there are legal concerns about the project, and whether the project conflicts with the financing priorities of the provincial government. If the project needs funding from the central government or if the project scope reaches a certain threshold, the functional department must also work with the Guangdong DRC to seek approval from the national DRC and coordinate with its counterpart ministry at the central government.

Once the finance department replies positively with regard to the feasibility of the proposal, the Guangdong DRC forwards the initial proposal to the General Office of the Governor (GOG) for consideration. According to a study by Ma and Zhou (2006), provincial leadership often plays a critical role in providing support for the infrastructure initiatives of functional departments under their jurisdictions, picking "high-profile" projects, and exerting informal influence over the decisions made by the finance department and the DRC to approve or reject the initial proposals. The involvement of provincial leadership undoubtedly broadens the scope of consideration in the decision-making process, reflecting that the process is driven by political factors as well as scientific analysis. Once the GOG and the central government, if involved, also respond positively, the DRC approves the initial proposal and sends a formal notice to the functional department to proceed to the next step.

Preparation and Evaluation of the Feasibility Report

Once the functional department receives approval of the initial project proposal from the DRC, it can start working on the feasibility report. This report provides more technical details, including physical asset planning, construction planning, estimates of various spending needs, and the financing strategy. If part of the financing is to be raised from nongovernmental sources, such as bank loans, domestic private investment, foreign investment, and donations (see the following section for more details), the department must provide the specifics about how and when the money will be raised. The feasibility report may also provide an estimate of the social and economic benefits of the project.

Compared to the initial project proposal, the feasibility report provides more detailed and specific information that explains how the department plans to realize the project. Because of its technical nature, many functional departments subcontract the writing of the feasibility report to a consulting company or research organization. Once the feasibility report is complete, the DRC reviews it and makes the approval decision.

Preparation and Approval of the Blueprint and Budget Estimate

If the DRC approves the feasibility report, the department may proceed to the final stage, which is to prepare the construction blueprint and the detailed capital budget. The provincial construction department is responsible for reviewing and approving the blueprint submitted by the functional department, while the DRC is responsible for reviewing and approving the budget estimates. If the estimate is over 50 million yuan, the DRC entrusts a professional agency to evaluate the estimates before it approves the budget.

Once a functional agency gets all necessary documents approved, the construction department starts an open bidding process to find a construction company to implement the project. It also uses a bidding process to find an oversight agent to monitor the project's progress and ensure that the construction work follows the plan. After construction is complete, the monitoring agent evaluates the results of the project. If the work is satisfactory, the functional department asks the finance department to pay for the work. During this process, an evaluation unit of the finance department also conducts a financial audit before making a final payment.

Exceptions and Variations

In general, all infrastructure projects funded by fiscal revenues must go through these three approval steps. However, there are exceptions to and variations in the decision-making process because of the following factors: (1) there is no formal capital budget power to group together all decisions on capital expenditures; and (2) spending authority continues to be fragmented, even though reforms have been made over the past decade to consolidate power in the finance department. Therefore, the financing schemes for capital projects can be diverse, and the organization with the strongest voice in decision making is usually the one that provides the primary source of funds for the project. For instance, if the project money comes primarily from the DRC, the DRC usually has the final say on the approval decision of the project. If a project is funded by money controlled by the finance department, the finance department is likely to have the strongest influence in the process. Likewise, if a project is supported by money directly raised by or earmarked for a specific functional department, both the DRC and the finance department tend to grant de facto authority to that department. If funding comes from many sources, negotiation and coordination among multiple parties may be needed to determine the spending authority of the project.

The Infrastructure Policy-Making Process at the Municipal Level

The process at the municipal level is similar to the process at the provincial level described above, except that the entity responsible for approving major public capital projects is the Development and Reform Department (DRD) instead of the DRC. Also, all large-scale local projects exceeding a certain investment scale must seek the approval of the provincial government. Figure 4.1 provides a brief outline of the local process using a municipal government in Guangdong Province as an example. In the first step, the DRD evaluates and approves the initial project proposals based on the policy priorities of the government and the financial feasibility of the project. The process is similar to the provincial process, except that in Guangdong Province, local DRDs usually have greater policy and budgetary power than their provincial counterpart (the DRC). As a result, local DRDs play a more important gate-keeping function in approving local infrastructure projects.

Once a project is approved, the DRD discusses with other related departments, such as the Department of Land and Resources, the Department of Construction, and the Department of Transportation, to select the appropriate site for the project. The Department of Environmental Protection may also be asked to assess the environmental impacts of the project. The Department of Land and Resources will also begin to draft a land use plan based on the needs of the project, the results of

FIGURE 4.1
Infrastructure Decision-Making Process by Municipal Governments

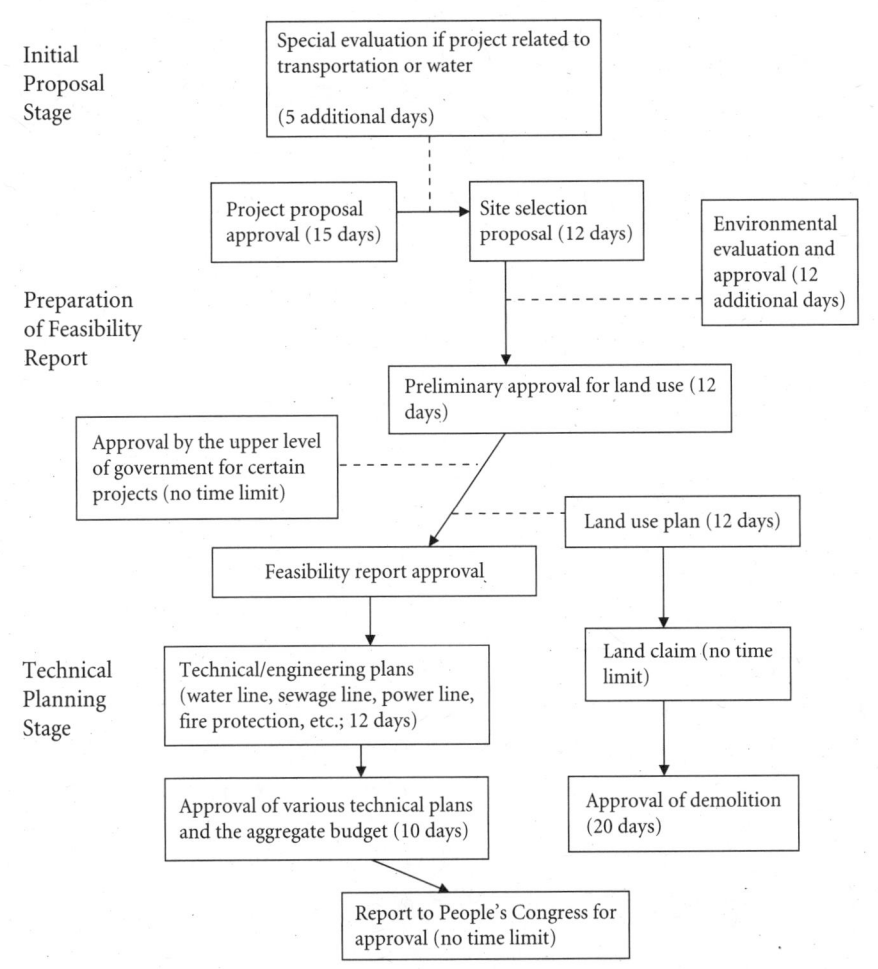

Initial Proposal Stage
- Special evaluation if project related to transportation or water (5 additional days)
- Project proposal approval (15 days)
- Site selection proposal (12 days)

Preparation of Feasibility Report
- Environmental evaluation and approval (12 additional days)
- Preliminary approval for land use (12 days)
- Approval by the upper level of government for certain projects (no time limit)
- Land use plan (12 days)
- Feasibility report approval

Technical Planning Stage
- Technical/engineering plans (water line, sewage line, power line, fire protection, etc.; 12 days)
- Land claim (no time limit)
- Approval of various technical plans and the aggregate budget (10 days)
- Approval of demolition (20 days)
- Report to People's Congress for approval (no time limit)

coordination with other related departments, and the aggregate land use policy established by the local People's Congress. Compared with the provincial process, local departments of land and resources have more control over land use because most land is owned by the municipality rather than the province. As a result, municipalities play a more active role in infrastructure planning and site selection. Once there is no major concern about the site, the Department of Land and Resources finalizes the land use plan. For large-scale projects that have significant policy and fiscal implications, the draft land use plan should be submitted to the upper level of government for approval.

When the land use plan is finalized, the government can make plans for reclaiming the land use rights from the existing tenants of the land. Compensation plans and reallocation plans are prepared and communicated to the tenants affected by the land use changes. How long it takes to relocate the residents and prepare the land for an infrastructure project depends on the size of the project and whether there is any resistance to move from existing tenants, any legal challenges to the government's land use plan, or any technical concerns with changing the land use. If there is no major problem and existing residents are successfully relocated, the government will issue approval for demolition.

While the local government is busy with land use planning and resident relocation, technical departments, such as the departments of construction, transportation, water, sewage, and other utilities, will begin to make technical plans to ensure that the site will have road access and utility services. Based on the technical plans drafted by various departments, the local finance department will estimate the total costs of the project and develop an aggregate budget. Every year, the finance department compiles all the budgets for infrastructure projects and submits them to the local People's Congress for approval. Once the People's Congress approves the project list and the budgets, demolition and project construction work can begin. The finance department may also implement the financing plans to pay for the projects.

The Financing Mechanism of Infrastructure Development in Guangdong

Provincial and local finance departments face tremendous pressure in financing many large-scale infrastructure projects as a result of rapid economic development in Guangdong Province and elsewhere in southern China and the policy mandates and directives from different entities of the Chinese political system. Because relying solely on current tax revenues to finance long-term capital projects is neither sufficient nor efficient, many provincial and local governments have developed other financing mechanisms to meet their spending needs. These can be categorized into five major financing sources.

Financing Through the General Budget

The first source of funding is through the general governmental budget. The primary revenue sources for general budgetary spending are (1) general taxation; (2) operating profit from state-owned assets; (3) administrative fees; (4) miscellaneous revenues such as fines; (5) transfers from higher levels of government; and (6) fund balance transfers from the prior year. Among these sources, intergovernmental transfers are relatively more important for poorer provinces and projects that have significant effects outside the province.

Capital projects that generate significant public impacts and projects that cannot be self-financed easily through tolls or private investment are often financed through the general budget. In the 1980s, when Chinese economic reforms were still in their initial phase, the general budget played a critical role and occupied a significant share of total infrastructure spending (Zhu 2005). However, as economic reforms have continued to expand and the Chinese banking and enterprise system become more developed, the relative share of the general budget in supporting infrastructure spending has declined, especially in richer provinces that can rely on nonbudgetary revenue.

Financing from Extrabudgetary Funds

The financial management reforms introduced in the 1990s and early 2000s have significantly constrained the discretionary power of individual departments to create, collect, and disperse extrabudgetary funds, which are obtained primarily from user fees and charges. Departments today can still collect many user fees and charges, but they must put these extrabudgetary revenues into a special account managed and overseen by the finance department. The annual departmental budget regulates how departments can use these funds in the special account, and all transactions are overseen by the finance department.

Many departments, especially those that manage highways, various transportation facilities, sewage, water, and other utilities, can easily collect tolls on the services provided. Also, many activities conducted by businesses and individuals are regulated by the government, allowing the government to collect user fees. These revenues, often extrabudgetary, are important financing sources for infrastructure projects in some cases.

Loans from the National Government

Loans from the national government are also important for large-scale projects. According to the Chinese budget law, local governments are not allowed to borrow on their own. The central government issues debt for provincial and local governments, which are then responsible for paying the principal and interest costs. Provincial and local governments do not have full autonomy in deciding how much debt they want to take on from the national government. Macroeconomic control and central policy priorities significantly influence how much the Chinese government wants to borrow in a particular time period. After the amount has been determined and is issued, different national ministries receive their shares based on the policy priorities and decisions of central government leaders. The money is then allocated by these central ministries to support provincial and local projects that require such financing. In the process of allocation, many factors are considered, such as the fiscal capacity of an area and the financing needs of different projects. Usually, rich provinces such as Guangdong do not get a significant share. For example, in 2001 Guangdong received national loans of 1.97 trillion yuan, which was about 1 percent of total provincial budgetary spending. In 2005, the amount of national loans dropped even further, to 292 million yuan, which was about 0.1 percent of total budgetary spending (Ministry of Finance 2002; 2006).

Self-Fundraising through Governmental and Proprietary Funds

A provincial or local department may "self-raise" funds for capital projects through

- revenues of its service units and enterprises;
- retained earnings or transfers from its service units and enterprises; and
- revenues from the leasing of land use rights.

Besides functional departments, Chinese provincial and local governments have many quasi-public service units that generate business income. For example, public universities collect tuition and fees, and within a university, cafeterias and dormitories have regular business income. The tourism department of a local government may operate souvenir shops at public parks and scenic places to generate extra revenues. These businesslike activities can bring in additional revenues for the departments, which can be used to finance capital projects. The revenues constitute a part of so-called self-generated funds.

A government can also raise funds through the leasing of land use rights. Because land cannot be privately owned in China, the land is "leased" through long-term contracts to developers and users who pay the government for the right to use the land, not for the ownership of the land. Since the 1994 fiscal reform, which centralized a large amount of revenues from the local to the central government, land-leasing revenues have been an important source of funding for local governments in financing infrastructure development. If the land is public land in an urban area, local governments have the full legal authority to reclaim the land from existing residents and lease the use rights to private developers or developers of mixed ownership for new development projects. Existing residents are entitled to some compensation according to legal requirements; such compensation, including moving costs, is subject to negotiation. If the land is agricultural, ownership belongs to a rural collective. The collective may lease the use rights of the land to private developers or developers of mixed ownership for residential and commercial purposes, or, more likely, the collective may form its own development and investment company to redevelop the land. If the government wants to use agricultural land (rural land), it must first transfer the land's ownership from the collective to a governmental or state-owned entity in order to gain the use rights.

Self-Fundraising through Domestic Private Bank Loans

A department may go outside the government to finance a public capital project. However, because the official policies of the Chinese government do not allow provincial and local governments to borrow on their own, money must be borrowed indirectly in one of two ways:

- Through service units or enterprises operated by the government.
- Through partnerships with private investors and businesses.

Service units and government-run enterprises can use their sales revenue as security for private bank loans. They can also sell the operating rights of some of their business activities, such as a sewage plant, to a private business for a number of years and use the revenue to pay off the loans.

If the government does not want to borrow through its own service units, it can arrange domestic bank loans by partnering with private businesses in infrastructure development and let its business partners borrow for the projects. The loans can be paid off by the future revenue streams of the infrastructure project, such as real estate development.

Land leasing and indirect borrowing may be related. For example, the government may first reclaim some land for development purposes. Then the land use rights can be leased to a private developer, which usually must borrow money to pay for it. Hence, land leasing is another way for a local government to access bank loans.

However, the government can also access bank loans that go beyond the direct proceeds from land-leasing sales. This is done primarily through government-owned investment and development companies and the China Development Bank (CDB). First, a local government designates certain urban infrastructure projects to a government-owned investment company. Then the company applies for a long-term loan from the CDB, which will cover a land parcel with several infrastructure projects in the area. The land leasing right is required as security for the loan, and the guarantee of the local government is needed.

The CDB has played a leading and active role in this kind of indirect borrowing for infrastructure investment since 1994. As a state-owned policy bank, CDB finances many key state and local infrastructure projects. It created and promoted the research and practice of development financing and the "parcel loan" (*da kun dai kuan*). As of the end of 2003, CDB's outstanding balance on loans for urban infrastructure construction projects in China stood at 226.9 billion yuan (US$27.4 billion).[1]

Guangdong local governments are major CDB clients. Long-term loans for Guangdong (excluding the Shenzhen Special Economy Zone) exceeded 101.4 billion yuan at the end of 2006. These loans support key infrastructure projects for energy, transportation, and urban services, such as the Guangdong highway system, city infrastructure in Guangzhou, and electricity network repair. On 5 August 2005, the Guangdong provincial government signed a Development Financing Cooperation Agreement with the CDB that granted 100 billion yuan for infrastructure construction in Guangdong for 10 years.

Besides the CDB, other commercial banks are also deeply involved in infrastructure loans with local governments. For example, Hubei Province received 80 billion yuan from the China Transportation Bank, 30 billion yuan from the China Agriculture Bank, 100 billion yuan from the China Commercial Bank, 70 billion yuan from the China Construction Bank, and 100 billion yuan from the Bank of China to complete the strategic development of China's central region. In 2006, the China Construction Bank granted 180 billion yuan to the Guangdong government, of which 130 billion yuan was used for infrastructure spending on transportation, urban construction, and manufacturing industries.

Hence, even though local governments are not allowed to borrow officially, they can access bank loans indirectly through their quasi-public investment and development companies. Such indirect borrowing is potentially less transparent than if local governments had the autonomy to borrow on their own. Whether controlled local borrowing would be more or less transparent than this indirect borrowing is not clear.

---

[1] See further discussion in Guangdong Provincial Government (2006), Shi (2007), and Sun (2006).

Self-Fundraising Through Foreign Investment

In addition to domestic bank borrowing, many local infrastructure projects that can generate business income are open to foreign investment. In Guangdong Province, for example, some highway projects are financed and managed by companies from Hong Kong, Taiwan, and other Asian countries. Usually, foreign companies are given the right to operate and earn revenues from the infrastructure for a fixed time period. At the end of the contract term, the operating right returns to the government.

Private Donations and Funding from International Organizations

Finally, the government may receive private donations to support infrastructure development. This is especially common in areas of social services, such as education and health care. Also, certain projects, especially those related to rural infrastructure, environmental protection, and the restoration of historical and cultural heritage sites, may receive grants from international organizations, including the World Bank, the Asian Development Bank, and the International Monetary Fund. However, the amounts are relatively small compared to total infrastructure investment.

Analyzing Infrastructure in Guangdong Province

The preceding discussion provides a framework for examining infrastructure projects and their financing in Guangdong Province. A more definitive analysis, however, is prevented by several limitations to the data:

- Because departmental budgets are still classified as secret information under Chinese law, the analysis in this chapter must rely on official statistics published by various agencies, such as the *Guangdong Statistical Yearbook*, the *Guangdong Finance Yearbook*, and the *Guangdong Land and Resources Yearbook*.
- The Chinese government classifies "capital-related spending" as (1) capital construction spending; (2) enterprise restructuring and related funds; (3) geological research expenses; (4) agricultural development and subsidies for agricultural and rural production; (5) urban maintenance expenses; (6) subsidies for underdeveloped areas; or (7) miscellaneous construction expenses incurred by commerce and business development agencies.[2] Because the focus of this chapter is investment in public infrastructure, such as highways, roads, public facilities, sewage, water, and other utility facilities, and not capital spending by enterprises, such as spending on factories or warehouses, only data for capital construction spending (category 1) and urban maintenance expenses (category 5) are analyzed here. Capital construction spending is approved by the provincial DRC (or local DRDs) and finance departments. Projects for urban maintenance, on the other hand, are supervised by the provincial and local finance departments. This analysis does not include government investment in state owned enterprise (SOE) technology upgrades and real estate development because those spending items are mostly for enterprises and private purposes.

---

[2] Refer to the statistical tables in the 1995 *Finance Yearbook*.

- Within the capital construction category of investment, only sectors that have a considerable public character and externality effects are analyzed. These include transportation, utilities, telecommunication, water conservation and environmental protection, education, health and welfare, public services, facilities and services to households, culture, sports and entertainment, and government/public and social organizations. Sectors excluded from the analysis are agriculture and forestry, mining, manufacturing, construction, computer and software services, wholesale and retail, hotels and catering, finance, real estate, leasing and business services, and geological and scientific research.
- The budgetary analysis relies on the data published in the *Guangdong Finance Yearbooks*. However, the yearbooks do not contain any data on fund budgets and other extrabudgetary revenues or borrowing by service units and government-owned investment enterprises. While they provide some data about the sources of funding for capital construction projects, they do not differentiate the data by industrial sectors (e.g., agriculture, manufacturing, energy, and utilities). As a result, there is no way to determine how much public infrastructure spending is supported by various self-fundraising sources, such as fees and charges that are extrabudgetary, domestic bank loans, foreign investment, and other sources of financing.
- For revenues from the leasing of land use rights, the analysis uses the data reported in the *Guangdong Yearbook on Land and Resources* and the *China Yearbook on Land and Resources*. These reports are likely to have underestimated the true amount of land-related revenues to local governments, but there are no other official published sources that can give a better estimate of land leasing revenues.

In 2006, Guangdong Province invested about 212 billion yuan (about US$30 billion) in various public capital construction projects. This amount was more than 3.5 times the amount invested in 1996 (see table 4.1). However, the percentage of the provincial GDP has remained relatively stable at about 8 percent to 9 percent. Comparing the spending changes between 1996 and 2006, sectors that had the fastest increase were culture, sports, and entertainment; public services and facilities; and utilities. The pattern reflects the rapid economic growth of the province during the past decade and the changing demands and public expectations for public facilities and services. Capital construction projects for government and public organizations, on the other hand, had the slowest relative growth—only about 38 percent over the past 10 years. These are the sectors least likely to be able to generate revenue through charges and similar sources.

To provide a comparative perspective of Guangdong's capital construction investment, we have analyzed similar data from four other provinces: Zhejiang, Jiangsu, Shandong, and Guangxi. The first three of the four are coastal provinces and relatively rich. Zhejiang and Jiangsu Provinces are located south of Shanghai, and Shandong Province is located south of Beijing. The three provinces together with Guangdong have been the major economic engine of China for the past two decades and have had the largest provincial GDP in China. Guangxi, on the other hand, is a relatively poorer province. Located west of Guangdong in the southern inland part of China, it is primarily an agricultural province with some tourism hot spots, such as Guilin.

TABLE 4.1

Capital Construction Investment in Selected Sectors in Guangdong Province, 1996–2006 (billion yuan)

Selected Industries	1996	2000	2004	2005	2006	Percentage Change
Transportation	17.946	22.032	43.74	53.634	62.13	246.21
Utilities	13.041	15.301	38.583	55.807	59.696	357.76
Telecom	7.406	6.924	7.227	5.454	4.867	−34.28
Water conservancy and environment	2.148	3.416	4.614	6.678	7.291	239.43
Education	4.215	4.946	17.013	18.356	13.893	229.61
Health and welfare	1.135	1.494	2.393	4.852	4.563	302.03
Public services/facilities and services to households	7.424	21.379	31.53	42.374	46.391	524.88
Culture, sports & entertainment	0.94	2.875	4.173	6.07	5.905	528.19
Government/public & social organizations	5.335	8.79	13.023	8.932	7.354	37.84
Total of selected industries	59.59	87.157	162.296	202.157	212.09	255.92
Gross domestic products	651.91	1,074.13	1,886.46	2,236.65	2,620.45	301.96
Ratio of capital construction investment to GDP	9.14%	8.11%	8.60%	9.04%	8.09%	

SOURCE: Guangdong Statistical Department, 1997, 2001, 2005, 2006, 2007.

Table 4.2 compares the capital construction investment by these provinces in the early 2000s.[3] Among the four relatively richer provinces, capital construction generally occupied about 7 percent to 8 percent of the provincial GDP. Compared with Guangdong, Jiangsu and Zhejiang occasionally invested a larger share of their GDP in capital construction in the early 2000s. In terms of per capita investment, Guangdong tended to spend more than the other three provinces. Compared with Guangxi, the relatively poorer province, Guangdong's per capita spending on public capital construction was clearly higher. However, Guangxi, like many other poorer provinces in China, has tried to catch up in the economic development process and has been devoting a relatively larger share of its GDP to infrastructure than the richer provinces have in recent years.

What also makes Guangdong unique is the level of its general budgetary investment in infrastructure projects. In the early 2000s, general budgetary appropriations for capital construction and urban maintenance by the Guangdong provincial and local governments reached almost 2 percent of GDP. The percentage of budgetary spending in those areas in other coastal provinces was usually no greater than 1 percent. If one compares the per capita amount of budgetary appropriations in those areas, the provincial and local governments of Guangdong have clearly invested more governmental resources than other rich provinces have.

---

[3] We compared data only up to 2004 because after that, many provinces no longer reported detailed data for capital construction.

TABLE 4.2
Capital Construction Investment in Selected Provincial Sectors

Province	Year	Public Capital Construction Investment, Society-Wide (billion yuan)	Percentage of GDP	Capital Construction and City Maintenance Spending in the General Budget (billion yuan)	Percentage of GDP	Population (10,000)	Public Capital Construction Investment per Capita, Deflated Year 2000 (yuan)	Capital Construction and City Maintenance Spending per Capita, Deflated Year 2000 (yuan)
Guangdong	2000	87.2	8.1	20.7	1.9	7,707	1,130.9	268.4
	2004	162.3	8.6	34.0	1.8	8,304	1,799.2	377.2
Jiangsu	2000	61.7	7.2	9.3	1.1	7,327	841.5	126.7
	2002	89.2	8.4	14.1	1.3	7,381	1,206.9	190.5
	2004	167.9	10.8	22.1	1.4	7,433	1,941.7	256.1
Shandong	2000	57.8	6.8	6.8	0.8	8,997	642.7	76.0
	2002	67.0	6.6	9.9	0.9	9,082	751.8	106.2
	2004	106.6	6.9	14.9	1.0	9,180	1,024.9	142.9
Zhejiang	2000	69.6	11.3	6.1	1.0	4,501	1,547.2	136.7
	2002	n/a		10.7	1.4	4,552	n/a	234.1
	2004	n/a		13.5	1.2	4,577	n/a	267.9
Guangxi	2000	22.9	11.1	3.3	1.6	4,751	481.0	70.3
	2002	21.5	8.8	7.7	3.1	4,822	436.5	156.1
	2004	47.7	14.4	6.8	2.1	4,889	895.7	128.1

SOURCES: Guangdong Statistical Department, 2001, 2003, 2005; Guangxi Zhuang Autonomous Region Statistical Department, 2001, 2003, 2005; Jiangxu Statistical Department, 2001, 2003, 2005; Shandong Statistical Department, 2001, 2003, 2005; Zhejiang Statistical Department, 2001, 2003, 2005.

NOTE: Only sectors listed in table 4.1 are included in the calculation of public capital construction investment. Sectors excluded from the analysis are agriculture and forestry, mining, manufacturing, construction, computer and software services, wholesale and retail, hotels and catering, finance, real estate, leasing and business services, and geological and scientific research. No analysis has been done for the capital construction investment in Zhejiang Province in 2002 and 2004, because after 2000, the *Zhejiang Statistical Yearbook* no longer reported the detailed breakdown of investment by industries.

Table 4.3 provides more details of Guangdong's budgetary spending on infrastructure projects. Although the amount of capital construction spending has increased almost threefold and urban maintenance spending almost fourfold, their share of the total general budget actually declined from 15.4 percent and 5.4 percent, respectively, to 10.7 percent and 4.7 percent, respectively, between 1996 and 2006. This primarily reflects the rapid growth of general government spending, which was even faster than these infrastructure-related items.

Within general budgetary spending on capital construction, only about 16 percent came from intrabudgetary accounts in 1996. The share gradually increased to about 30 percent in 2006. This change reflects the general trend of power reallocation from functional departments to the finance department, as well as success in reducing departments' reliance on extrabudgetary revenues. In other words, some of the reforms appear to be having their intended impact.

Occasionally, Guangdong Province also borrows through the central government to raise capital for infrastructure development needs. However, as shown in table 4.3, the total amount of national loans issued for Guangdong Province has been relatively small. The province and its local governments also receive central government transfers to support certain infrastructure development projects. For example, in 2005, transfers from the central government were about 488 billion yuan, about 21 percent of total budgetary spending. However, because no public data are available to show the detailed breakdown of central government grants, it

TABLE 4.3

Guangdong's Budgetary Spending on Infrastructure-Related Items, 1996–2006 (billion yuan)

Item	1996	2000	2004	2005	2006	Percentage Change
1. Total general budgetary expenditures	60.123	106.986	185.295	228.907	255.334	324.69
1a. Expenditure for capital construction by the general budget	9.283	15.335	25.413	26.443	27.269	193.75
—from intrabudget accounts	1.519	3.887	4.964	5.015	8.245	442.79
1b. Expenditure for city maintenance	3.223	5.348	8.611	10.62	12.079	274.78
Total of 1a and 1b	12.506	20.683	34.024	37.063	39.348	214.63
2. Expenditure by using loans of national debt	0	3.256	0.5	0.492		
Total of 1a and 1b as percentage of total general budgetary expenditures	20.80	19.33	18.36	16.19	15.41	
Total of 1a, 1b, and 2 as percentage of "Public Capital Construction" investment shown in table 4.1	20.99%	23.73%	20.96%	18.33%	18.55%	

SOURCE: Guangdong Statistical Department and Guangdong Finance Department, 1997, 2001, 2005, 2006, 2007.

is impossible to determine how much of the transfer has been used to support capital construction spending.

It is worth noting that general budgetary spending on infrastructure projects by Guangdong Province occupies only about 20 percent of the society-wide investment in public infrastructure. The remaining 80 percent comes from extrabudgetary revenues and various kinds of self-fundraising mechanisms, as discussed previously.

Because there are no public data available to provide a detailed breakdown of these funding sources, this part of infrastructure financing has remained obscure. However, land sale revenues are understood to have been a major source of funding for local infrastructure development (at the city and district levels). For example, according to the 2005 *China Land and Resources Yearbook* (Ministry of Land and Resources of China 2006), the revenue from leasing land use rights was 23.9 billion yuan in 2004. Adding this source of revenues to the budgetary appropriations and the expenditures financed by national loans, we estimate that about 40–50 percent of the total investment in public capital construction in 2004 was financed by budgetary and extrabudgetary resources, and the remaining half was funded by private investors, government-owned investment companies, and various forms of public-private partnerships.

While no public data are available to account for the major revenues of the whole pool of public infrastructure investment, the Chinese Ministry of Construction releases some provincial and local data on how it and its subordinate provincial and local departments finance various urban and rural infrastructure and maintenance projects. The Department of Construction (DOC) at the local level is responsible for urban planning, government building projects, and urban infrastructure construction and maintenance, including water supply, central heating, local roads and bridges, sewage, flood control, landscaping, and environmental sanitation. It also regulates the construction sector, develops standards for construction and utility companies, and works with other departments to monitor the work quality and progress of public infrastructure projects. Because of these official responsibilities, the department also participates actively in setting and implementing policies related to land use, long-term economic planning, and energy and utilities.

Table 4.4 provides a detailed breakdown of the revenue sources for urban construction and maintenance projects handled by the Guangdong DOC in 2004. Of the aggregate revenue total of about 38 billion yuan, less than 20 percent came from in-budgetary sources such as the urban maintenance and construction tax, supplemental fees from utilities, and budgetary allocation from the central and local government. About 18 percent came from extrabudgetary fees and charges such as water treatment fees, tolls on bridges and roads, and waste management fees, which are now monitored and managed by the Department of Finance rather than the DOC itself. Another 50 percent came from various kinds of self-generated funds, such as foreign investment and domestic bank loans and earnings of the department's service units and enterprises. Land lease revenue did not have a major role in the department's finances because land-related revenues are often earmarked to support large-scale infrastructure handled by other departments.

Because many departments in the Chinese bureaucracy, such as transportation, education, and irrigation, can have their own extrabudgetary revenue sources and

TABLE 4.4
Revenue Sources for the Guangdong Department of Construction, 2004 (million yuan)

Revenue Sources	Amount	Percent
In-budget revenues:		
urban maintenance and construction tax	2,269.9	5.9
supplemental fees from utilities	607.9	1.6
central financial allocation	79.6	0.2
local financial allocation	3,882.5	10.1
National loans financed with local budget	3.6	0.01
Extrabudgetary revenues from fees & charges	7,073.3	18.4
Self-fundraising through domestic loans	8,310.5	21.7
Self-fundraising through foreign investment	201.6	0.5
Self-fundraising through enterprises, service units, and institutions	10,454.9	27.3
Land-leasing revenues	1,500.4	3.9
Other revenues	3,970.9	10.4
Aggregate total	38,354.9	100.0

SOURCE: Ministry of Construction, 2005.

enterprise units, and because each of those departments' policy responsibilities can be borne by different government leaders (e.g., deputy governors or mayors), the DOC oversees only part of the infrastructure investment. This phenomenon is reflected in the finances of the DOC. In 2004, the Guangdong provincial and local governments collected a total of 5.5 billion yuan from urban maintenance and construction taxes. Those governments also spent a total of 8.6 billion yuan on urban maintenance in their general budget (Ministry of Finance of China 2005). These figures are significantly larger than the DOC's in-budget revenues. Also, the total of land-leasing revenues of Guangdong reached 23.9 billion yuan in 2004, most of which was spent on infrastructure development. Comparing this amount with the DOC's share of the total land-leasing revenues shows that the management and financing of infrastructure projects by the Chinese government is complex. It involves many departments and many financing mechanisms.

Evaluation of Current Decision-Making and Financing Mechanisms

Accomplishments During the Past Decades

Tremendous growth in public infrastructure. The accomplishments of infrastructure spending in Guangdong Province and its cities over the past decade and a half are very concrete and clear. The province is now well connected by various railway and highway systems. Within many cities, the basic infrastructure that is essential to the daily life of residents, including local roads, water, sewage, and other utility services, is well developed and maintained to keep pace with the demand of rapid economic growth (see table 4.5). For example, the length of highways

TABLE 4.5
Accomplishments of Public Infrastructure Investment

	1990	1995	2000	2005	Percentage Change, 1990–1995	Percentage Change, 1995–2000	Percentage Change, 2000–2005
Length of highways (km)	54,671	84,563	102,606	115,337	54.68	21.34	12.41
Length of city road extended (km)	34.93	89.08	187.47	178.33	155.02	110.45	-4.88
Number of civil motor vehicles	402,086	1,147,348	1,729,054	3,772,891	185.35	50.70	118.21
Length of civil aviation routes (km)	107,979	296,226	500,322	1,080,706	174.34	68.90	116.00
Total freight traffic volume (10,000 tons)	85,809	111,063	119,216	133,992	29.43	7.34	12.39
Volume of freight handled by waterways (10,000 tons)	16,198	32,952	31,649	70,926	103.43	-3.95	124.10
Volume of freight handled by railways (10,000 tons)	85,809	111,063	119,216	158,470	29.43	7.34	32.93
Volume of freight handled by civil aviation (10,000 tons)	8	21	31	73	162.50	47.62	135.48
Length of city sewage pipelines (km)	15.98	70.12	64.37	309.06	338.80	-8.20	380.13
Disposal capacity of city sewage (10,000 tons/day)	6	74	250	969.5	1133.33	237.84	287.80
Capacity of city tap water supply (10,000 tons/day)	270.8	1,600	865	2,668.2	490.84	-45.94	208.46

SOURCE: Guangdong Statistical Department, 1991, 1996, 2001, 2006.

in the province doubled between 1990 and 2000 and grew another 12 percent between 2000 and 2005. The length of city road also grew multiple times in the 1990s. Similarly, the capacity of water supply and the capacity to handle sewage have expanded exponentially in the same period to meet the demands of population growth and industrial development.

The dramatic expansion of infrastructure has been particularly clear in Guangdong's urban centers, such as Guangzhou. Table 4.6 shows the phenomenal growth in many areas between 1990 and 2005, particularly in local road construction and public green space.

Success in Diversifying Financing Sources. Table 4.7 compares the growth rate of infrastructure investment with that of the GDP and the provincial population for the past decade. In general, the growth rate of society-wide investment in public capital construction in selected sectors has been able to keep pace with the double-digit growth in the provincial GDP and has outpaced the growth of the population. The general budgetary spending on capital construction and urban maintenance also grew at a pace similar to that of the provincial GDP between 1996 and 2004 and has slowed only in recent years. Even with a slower pace of growth, the general budgetary spending in capital construction and urban maintenance increased at an average annual rate of 7.5 percent.

One of the key reasons for Guangdong's ability to maintain a high and steady growth rate in infrastructure investment is its willingness to partner with the private sector and diversify its funding sources for infrastructure investment. As discussed previously, general budgetary spending of the government only accounts for 20–25 percent of the society-wide investment in various public infrastructure sectors. Even if one includes the use of land sales revenues, we estimate that only about half of the investment comes from the public sector. The rest of the financing comes from the private sector, including public-private partnerships and foreign investment.

This financing strategy is critically important for sustaining the province's economic growth since provincial and local governments are not allowed to issue their own loans. Even if they could take a share of the national borrowing, the amount is often out of the province's or local government's discretionary control. For rich areas such as Guangdong, the amount of national loans allowed is also not very significant. Therefore, finding other creative ways to support long-term, large-scale infrastructure investment is a critical task for the finance department of a province or city. One of the key solutions is to find different ways to partner with the private sector. Guangdong has been very successful in using private capital to support various infrastructure projects, such as toll highways, the subway system, the sewage system, and the water supply.

Significant Progress in Institutionalizing a Capital Investment Process. Another major accomplishment of Guangdong's infrastructure development policies is its progress in regularizing the decision-making process of infrastructure investment. As all major capital projects must go through a three-stage process to get the approval of the DRC (or the DRD at the local level), the finance department, the land

TABLE 4.6
Expanding Infrastructure in Urban Districts of Guangzhou City, 1990–2005

Item	1990	1995	Percent Change, 1990–1995	2000	Percent Change, 1995–2000	2005	Percent Change, 2000–2005	Percent Change, 1990–2005
Registered population (10,000 persons)	357.9	385.4	7.7	566.7	47.0	617.3	8.9	72.5
Length of roads (1,000 m)	945	1,809	91.4	2,053	13.5	5,076	147.2	437.1
Area of roads (10,000 sq mi)	1,085	1,983	82.8	2,805	41.5	8,325	196.8	667.3
Number of bridges	265	524	97.7	685	30.7	1,142	66.7	330.9
Number of street lights	39,138	59,643	52.4	92,279	54.7	230,409	149.7	488.7
Length of sewer pipelines (1,000 m)	1,217	1,535	26.1	1,952	27.2	4,827	147.3	296.6
Percentage of population with access to tap water	100	98.2	−1.8	99.01	0.8	98.24	−0.8	−1.8
Per capita living space (sq mi)	7.99	9.61	20.3	13.13	36.6	18.87	43.7	136.2
Public green areas (ha)	1,132	1,485	31.2	2,705	82.2	6,988	158.3	517.3
Volume of garbage disposal (10,000 tons)	105	155	47.6	166	7.1	280	68.7	166.7

SOURCE: Guangzhou Statistical Department, 1991, 1996, 2001, 2006.

NOTE: In 2000 Guangzhou City expanded from eight districts to ten districts. The table shows the population of ten districts; it was 413.9 for eight districts.

TABLE 4.7
Growth Rates of the GDP, Population, and Infrastructure Investment in Guangdong, 1996–2006

	1996	2000	Average Annual Percentage Change, 1996–2000	2004	Average Annual Percentage Change, 2000–2004	2006	Average Annual Percentage Change, 2004–2006
GDP (billion yuan)	651.91	1,074.13	13.30	1,886.46	15.12	2,620.45	17.86
Year-end population (in 10,000)	6,896.77	7,706.80	2.82	8,303.70	1.88	9,304.00	5.85
Society-wide investment in capital construction in selected sectors related to public infrastructure (billion yuan)	59.59	87.16	9.97	162.30	16.82	212.09	14.32
General budgetary spending on capital construction and urban maintenance (billion yuan)	12.51	20.68	13.40	34.02	13.25	39.35	7.54

SOURCE: Guangdong Statistical Department, 1997, 2001, 2005, 2007.

and resource department (if transfer of land use rights or change of land use is involved), the construction department, the environmental protection agency (if environmental impact assessment is needed), and the key leaders of the government. Once an initial proposal has been approved by the government, the development of the feasibility report (the second stage) and the technical plan (the third stage) often involves professional companies and specific field experts to assist the government in the process. If the project is to be built by a contractor, the Guangdong provincial government has very specific rules about how the contractor should be selected, what the legal responsibilities of the contractor are, how the work should be monitored by different departments, and how funds should be apportioned to the contractor.

These regulations and monitoring systems have significantly improved the project management of infrastructure projects. For many years, the Guangdong provincial government faced some difficulties in ensuring that infrastructure projects could be finished according to schedule and that functional departments would not have a cost overrun. With the implementation of the three-stage approval process and the use of a third-party monitoring agent, those problems have been reduced considerably. Also, the finance department now requires that the functional department proposing the infrastructure project use its own accounts to cover any funding gap beyond the approved amount in the feasibility report. This creates an even greater incentive for the functional department to monitor the construction contractor more closely.

Recently, the provincial finance department has begun work to improve the management of infrastructure planning and budgeting. To bring an end to the practice of capital planning and budgeting being carried out without solid information about fixed assets, the finance department began in 2005 to conduct a comprehensive investigation into the types, ownership, and volume of fixed assets held by functional departments and then to separate business types of assets from other assets serving public goals. This creates a preliminary capital budgeting system. At present, this effort centers on assets used by administrative and service units, mainly covering buildings, vehicles, and large office facilities (Guangdong Provincial Government 2007). Hence, reforms are still needed to cover other government assets serving the public.

Remaining Issues

Despite the significant accomplishments discussed above, several problems remain to be resolved in the infrastructure decision-making process.

Fiscal Fragmentation and Lack of Transparency. The biggest challenge is a lack of transparency in the revenue and spending process. While budget reforms have strengthened the power of the finance department to control and monitor the revenues and spending of individual departments and have largely eliminated much extrabudgetary spending, certain financial activities (e.g., the operating profits of service units) continue to operate off budget to different degrees. New types of off-budgeting activities have developed to meet the need to finance infrastructure projects. Moreover, provincial and local governments lack a system of capital budgeting to integrate all types of infrastructure investment and to consider the consequences of infrastructure spending and policy decisions. Therefore, capital expenditures include a variety of expenditure items, including in-budgetary, extrabudgetary, and off-budgetary funds. Even within in-budgetary funds, capital expenditures can be dispersed across a variety of items.

This fiscal fragmentation generates much complexity and nontransparency in infrastructure investment. As discussed earlier, a large portion of infrastructure development is done through various self-fundraising mechanisms. The amount of spending supported by self-fundraising and the details of various self-fundraising sources are unknown, as there is no public record available.

Absence of transparency creates a problem of accountability. It also impedes the finance department from imposing effective fiscal control and improving allocation efficiency in infrastructure investment. Finally, it creates problems in understanding the fiscal health and liabilities of a provincial or local government. For example, it is difficult to know the amount of land-related revenues that have been generated by a local government, how a government's service units or investment companies help finance a project, and how much borrowing and contingency liabilities the service units or investment companies have created for the government. Even though the finance department may now have access to much better information about the government's total spending and revenue and can make better fiscal decisions on infrastructure planning, the public, private investors, local banks, and even the national government and the People's Bank of China do not have the same access to the information.

Indirect Borrowing, Contingent Liability, and Risk Management. Normative public finance theories suggest that because capital expenditures generate fixed assets whose benefits are extended for many years, it is equitable to borrow to finance infrastructure projects so that the financing burden of infrastructure projects can be spread among current and future taxpayers. However, according to Chinese budget law, subnational governments are not allowed to borrow, even though rapid economic growth, particularly in coastal provinces such as Guangdong, has generated tremendous demand for infrastructure development. As a result, provincial and local governments have to come up with a variety of innovative mechanisms to engage in indirect borrowing to meet their need for infrastructure investment.

This creates some serious problems, because indirect borrowing is often carried out in an environment without proper debt management systems and oversight. It is also awkward to institute because the creation of a formal branch of debt management within the finance department would imply that the government is openly violating the budget law. Consequently, indirect borrowing is prevalent, as borrowing authority is dispersed in the bureaucratic system. The lack of effective fiscal control over borrowing has greatly contributed to the expansion of contingent liabilities and imposed possible fiscal risks on many provincial and local governments in China, including Guangdong. How to manage these contingent liabilities has been a big challenge. For example, in 1998, Guangdong experienced a serious fiscal crisis when Guangdong International Investment Company went bankrupt. Hence, the Chinese government must urgently address this issue openly and develop a more effective system of debt and risk management.

Overdrawing and Off-Budget Management of Revenues from Lands. In many provinces, including Guangdong, local governments rely heavily on land-leasing revenues to finance infrastructure investment. This helps solve the immediate problem of the shortage of funds, but it also generates several problems. First, by using land leasing rather than a system of property tax, local governments have considerable incentives to overdraw revenue resources from land to address short-run fiscal problems. As a result, little may be left for future governments, especially because land is usually leased out for multiple decades. While property tax rates might increase, adjustment to long-term lease rates may present a problem.

Second, under the current system, land-related revenues are collected without transparency, then deposited in special fiscal accounts and used without external supervision. Neither the land-related revenues nor the spending of those revenues is included in the government budget, which must be submitted to the People's Congress. While most of the land-leasing revenues are used to invest in public infrastructure projects, it is quite impossible for the People's Congress at all levels of the government, let alone the public, to know where the government will spend or has spent these monies. This lack of transparency in the management and spending of land-related revenues, which are considerable, has made the government opaque despite the efforts of recent budget reforms.

Challenges in Developing a Multiyear Capital Improvement Plan. To achieve allocative efficiency in capital expenditures, it is important for the government to have a multi-year capital improvement plan. Currently, the Chinese government has regular five-year plans. However, the planning and budget functions have been granted to two different departments: The planning function is granted to the planning agency (DRC or DRD), while the budget function is granted to the finance department.

The effectiveness of a five-year plan depends largely on the coordination between the planning and budget agencies. This is especially true for the Guangdong provincial government, since, compared to other places, a small amount of budgetary funds are allocated to the planning agency. To effectively carry out projects included in the five-year plans, it is critical for the planning agency to gain support from the finance department. Undoubtedly, the finance department is likely to cooperate and is bound to allocate fiscal resources for infrastructure projects that have strong political support from the top leaders of the provincial polity. However, for other infrastructure projects, the finance department may not be so willing to cooperate with the planning agency, which can generate conflict between the two agencies.

One reason the finance department may sometimes conflict with the planning agency is that from the viewpoint of the finance department, the five-year plan compiled by the planning agency is ineffective in guiding resource allocation. This is because when the plan is being compiled, fiscal affordability is not fully considered by the planning agency. To resolve this problem, coordination between the planning agency and the finance department must be enhanced. However, the current system has failed to create an effective platform for the two to work together. In addition, the five-year plan is not adjusted to address changing socioeconomic situations after it is compiled in the first year. Consequently, after the first one or two years, it may be outdated and irrelevant for resource allocation.

Insufficient Information about Fixed Assets. Information is important for making reasonable decisions. This is especially true for infrastructure investment, which usually involves a large amount of money, complicated technical knowledge, and a long time span. Unlike capital budgeting practiced in other countries (e.g., local governments in the United States), Guangdong and all governments in China develop five-year plans and related capital spending plans without an annual evaluation of the current fixed assets. Without solid information about the amount and quality of current fixed assets, it is inevitable that priority setting in capital expenditures will often be arbitrary.

To address this problem, the Guangdong provincial government has pioneered an asset management system and has investigated the capital needs of the administrative and service units of the government. However, large challenges remain. First, the provincial government needs to extend the new system of asset management to other assets and then establish a system of asset pools including all assets built by public money. Second, the government needs to conduct a regular evaluation of current assets in order to provide useful information for priority setting. Third, the government must institutionalize the regular evaluation of assets as an indispensable part of the development of a capital improvement plan (or five-year plan) and capital expenditure decision making.

Complex Agency Relationships and Other Governance Problems. Infrastructure decision making, though showing considerable improvement since the budget reforms in the mid-1990s, continues to battle with some of the fundamental governance problems in the Chinese political system. While there is now a much improved decision-making process for infrastructure development in Guangdong, there are still too many horizontal and vertical command and control relationships governing individual departments. For example, while the finance department may have concerns about the long-term fiscal liabilities of the government and be hesitant to support a project, the functional department, such as education, transportation, or utilities, may be under a mandate from its superior at a higher level of the government to pursue certain policies and projects. Also, when the finance department wants to use land sales revenues to support a certain project, it may not have the full discretion to do so because land use is heavily regulated by the Provincial Department of Land and Resources and its local bureaus, which have their own multiyear plans and are subject to many regulations and policy targets established by the national government. Because of these horizontal and vertical agency relationships, it becomes very difficult for a provincial or local government to develop a long-term, comprehensive master plan for infrastructure development.

In addition, while many central government grants to provincial and local governments are distributed by individual ministries, the criteria are not well defined.

For example, many environmental protection projects should have been subsidized because of externality effects on other regions, but grants are not often given to coastal provinces based on that consideration.

What makes the problem worse is the culture of personal power in the Chinese bureaucracy. For example, if a top government or party leader wants to pursue a certain infrastructure project because it may benefit his or her personal career advancement in a few years, the project will usually be done, even though it may not fit well with the original long-term comprehensive plan and may negatively affect the long-term fiscal health of the government. Because the check-and-balance system within the Chinese political system is still not well developed, there is not much effective control of this practice. Since the career advancement of government and party officials often depends on the accomplishment of economic development targets and policies that show clear, visible results, government leaders have a lot of political incentives to come up with large-scale project ideas but very limited incentives to consider the cost-effectiveness of infrastructure projects. Again, because of these fundamental governance problems in the current Chinese political system, multiyear coherent planning for infrastructure development has been difficult.

Recommendations

This case study of Guangdong enables us to recognize not only certain weaknesses in the current decision-making process for infrastructure projects, but also problems at the level of the central government, as well as at the provincial and local levels. Therefore, the following recommendations are divided into two parts. The first part is for the central government level but is closely related to the capital expenditure management of subnational governments. The second part is directly related to the provincial and local sectors of the government.

Because China is a unitary state, the budgeting of subnational governments is carried out in the institutional environment set by the central government. Largely as a result of the 1994 fiscal reforms, subnational governments hold little budget autonomy in the formal legal framework. They lack the authority to initiate a new tax or to change the tax rate according to the local economic structure and fiscal status, nor can they budget according to their perceived local priorities. This is also true for Guangdong, a province with less fiscal dependency on the central government than some provinces. It is in this context that subnational governments such as Guangdong have been forced to rely on "self-fundraising" mechanisms to finance infrastructure projects.

To solve the problems associated with financing outside the budget, one option is for the central government to grant more budgetary autonomy to subnational governments. However, this seems quite unfeasible in the near future, as the central government has been extremely cautious about re-decentralizing fiscal authority to subnational governments since the 1994 fiscal reforms. Still, there are reforms that the central government might consider to enhance allocative efficiency and accountability in subnational governments' infrastructure investment.

Developing a Local Borrowing System

There are at least two alternatives for the central government to consider reforming the current loan management system. The first is to reform the current borrowing system, in which the national government borrows without considering subnational governments' needs and simply re-loans the debt to subnational governments. A new system needs to ensure that the national debt issued on behalf of subnational governments reflect their financial needs. This can be done by requiring subnational governments to submit their infrastructure plans before borrowing and before debt is assigned to them.

The second alternative is to revise the 1994 budget law to allow subnational governments to issue their own loans—that is, to create a local bond system, in which they would have direct access to loans—but are under greater scrutiny by the private bond market. Market forces would induce subnational governments to become more transparent, because they would have to disclose a lot of fiscal information, such as the government's current and foreseeable fiscal health, infrastructure plans, and the quality of its budgeting and financial management practices, to private bond investors. Of course, to control fiscal risks, the national government needs to specify clearly the legal use of local loans. Also, it may need to monitor and control the maximum debt level of each subnational government.

Municipal borrowing represents the most efficient, most transparent, and most equitable mechanism for the development of long-life public assets. With borrowing, the capital costs of infrastructure projects are recovered from the fiscal resources (either fees and charges or general current revenues) of the locality over the life of the asset. This is a businesslike approach that is standard for modern public financial management and subnational borrowing and successfully supports infrastructure development in many countries, from developed to developing and transition economies, throughout the world. This mechanism would ease the financing of infrastructure that supports pure public goods (general revenues available to the locality could support debt service), and, so long as the locality has sufficient revenue capacity, infrastructure could be added as merited by service demands. Of course, subnational governments should not be given borrowing authority without regulation, as has been clearly emphasized by many observers (Ahmad et al. 2005; Liu 2008; Plekhanov and Singh 2006).

However, if local borrowing is to be done on the free market (not through captive state banks or other financial intermediaries that have only limited ability to reject a subnational loan proposal), borrowers must provide much greater transparency with regard to their finances and maintain their financial data in accord with generally accepted reporting practices (separation of capital from current revenues, for instance). Lenders need a good understanding of the entities' financial situation before they would be willing to make loans. Currently available statistical reports fall far short of providing the information necessary for a diligent investor. Changes in financial reporting will bring greater consistency with international standards for public financial management, over and above any impact with regard to facilitating subnational borrowing.

Developing a Property Tax System Under Local Authority

As discussed before, subnational governments currently rely heavily on land lease revenues. To resolve the problems associated with this practice, such as overdevelopment of land resources and off-budgetary fiscal management, the central government may consider the possibility of creating a property tax system at the local level. This will provide an alternative to land lease revenues to address local fiscal needs. Since a property tax is assessed and collected annually, it can provide a stable source of revenue over time. Also, all tax revenues generated would be consolidated into the budget, thus enhancing the transparency of the budgetary system. Furthermore, a property tax can provide revenue for general government operations, thereby facilitating infrastructure investment in the provision of pure public goods that have no prospect for generating direct revenue. A tax limited to land value would be particularly attractive because of development impacts, but it might be more difficult to adopt in light of land holding rules.

Of course, to create this new system, China first needs to revise its current fragmented tax system involving a variety of property-related taxes, terminating several of those taxes and consolidating the rest into a new property tax. Moreover, to ensure tax equity, the new property tax must consider tax relief for homeowners who purchased houses before the implementation of the new property tax.[4]

Refining the Intergovernmental Relationship

The national government also needs to refine the current intergovernmental relationship. First, it needs to clarify the financing responsibilities among the different levels of government and clearly define which level will be responsible for what types of infrastructure investment. Second, the national government must reform the current intergovernmental transfer system, making it more transparent and giving subnational governments greater flexibility to adapt to local situations. Third, the central government ministries must restrain themselves from imposing unfunded mandates on subnational governments, as those mandates and sudden changes in policies generate huge uncertainties and difficulties for subnational governments in conducting long-term capital planning and budgeting.

While it is critically important for the Chinese national government to rethink some of its fiscal policies and the intergovernmental relationships that affect budgeting and financial management, it is equally important for provincial and local governments to take the initiative to reform some of their own current budgetary practices.

---

[4] Under the current system, some of the land lease fees and taxes on developers should have been "capitalized" into real estate prices and transferred to individual property users (not owners in China, since the government is the only owner of the land). If a property tax were to be introduced, it would be likely to depress property prices. As a result, current property users will not only need to bear a new tax burden annually, but will also be punished economically by the drop in real estate prices. Hence, some tax relief measures for these existing property users are necessary to guarantee equity and a smooth transition to the new tax system.

Consolidating Land Lease Revenues and Indirect Borrowing into the Budget

Before the national government makes any move to create a new borrowing system and a new property tax system, subnational governments, particularly provincial governments, need to consolidate land lease revenues and indirect borrowing into the budget. Information about these revenue sources, such as the amount of revenue received and how the money is used, should be submitted for approval not only to the finance department for administrative control purposes, but also to the People's Congress at the corresponding level of government in order to ensure some accountability in the use of these funds. Also, in reporting the information, specific details, not just the aggregate totals, should be given.

In the process of budgeting, both the finance department and the People's Congress must consider fiscal sustainability. It is critical to prevent the current administration from overdrawing land lease revenues. Perhaps a land revenue reserve fund from each year's land lease revenues could be created so that the use of the one-time land lease revenues could be kept available for future projects. With regard to indirect borrowing, it is critical at this point to conduct a comprehensive assessment of the implicit and contingent liabilities at each level of government. Then it is important to centralize all indirect borrowing activities under the control of the finance department and the supervision of the People's Congress. Moreover, it is crucial for the government and the People's Congress to assess the hidden risks associated with these indirect borrowing activities.

Implementing a Formal Capital Budgeting System

According to the budget law, the government budget must be composed of a current operating budget, a capital budget, a social security budget, and a budget for the operating activities of state-owned enterprises. However, for many years, the government budgets at all levels have failed to meet this legal requirement. It was not until 2008 that the national government finally began to include the operating activities of state-owned enterprises in the budget.

Given the progress made so far, provincial and local governments should experiment with capital budgeting. While inclusion of the operating activities of state-owned enterprises into the government budget will put those enterprises' capital expenditures under greater fiscal scrutiny, there is still a need to consolidate all public infrastructure projects financed by public funds into one budget to put them under greater budgetary control. This will help enhance accountability in public infrastructure spending. Also, by showing the information more systematically, policy makers may be able to see the big picture more clearly and enhance the allocative efficiency of public fund usage. However, to compile a meaningful capital budget, the government needs to (1) consolidate all capital expenditures for public infrastructures; (2) develop a capital improvement plan based on information from effective asset management; and (3) coordinate more effectively between the planning and the finance departments. Public infrastructure is currently developed in an extremely fragmented system. A formal structure would be more likely to provide an efficient and effective response to public demands.

Enhancing Coordination Between the Finance and Planning Departments

Capital planning and budgeting in China involve close coordination between two critical agencies: the planning department and the finance department. Indeed, even if there is no capital budget yet, these two agencies still need to work together more effectively to avoid policy conflicts and to ensure that capital project plans are financially feasible.

Such coordination is not easy in China. Currently, the authority to create and dissolve a governmental organization is highly centralized and controlled by the national government. Hence, even if a subnational government is willing to integrate the functions of the planning department into the finance department, it cannot do so unless the central government authorizes the initiative first. Given this constraint, the only feasible way to enhance coordination between the planning and finance departments is to involve them in each other's activities—that is, to let the finance agency play an important role in the development of the five-year plan and make the planning agency's authorization a necessary condition for approving a functional department's capital spending by the finance department. If all capital expenditures are to be consolidated into a single capital budget, a joint board composed of both agencies, whose establishment will not need approval from the upper-level government, could be used to review and approve all infrastructure projects.

Extending the Asset Management System

To improve allocative efficiency in infrastructure investment, provincial governments also need to establish an asset management system that includes all fixed assets funded by public money. That is, the asset management system should not only manage public infrastructure used by public units (e.g., office buildings), but also monitor and regulate those infrastructure projects serving public ends (e.g., public libraries). Moreover, the government must conduct regular assessments of these assets to provide useful information for the development of the five-year plan and the annual capital budget. If such a system is successfully developed at the provincial level, local governments may follow the model and create their own asset management systems to exercise better management and planning of all public infrastructure facilities.

Conclusion

For the past few decades, economic development in Guangdong Province has been stunning. It is now one of the largest regional economies in China, with the highest per capita GDP and the largest volume of world exports of all Chinese provinces. Such economic success is caused by many factors, but one of the key contributors has been Guangdong's willingness to invest in infrastructure to facilitate trade and to enhance the quality of residents' living conditions. Indeed, the expansion of many infrastructure facilities, such as highways, airports, seaports, roads and bridges, and sewage and sanitation, has been remarkable for the past two decades. Compared with other coastal provinces, Guangdong has demonstrated a greater and more consistent commitment to supporting infrastructure investment.

Such a commitment to finance and expand infrastructure does not come easily in the Chinese policy-making context. It requires strong leadership, effective coordination among departments, and a spirit of policy entrepreneurship to overcome many institutional and policy constraints. The rapid expansion of infrastructure investment in Guangdong also demonstrates the leadership and innovativeness of the finance departments of Guangdong provincial and local governments in utilizing diverse funding sources, including extrabudgetary revenues, land lease revenues, domestic bank loans, and public-private partnerships in financing. This allows Guangdong not only to access a wider pool of capital and lower its financing costs, but also to overcome the budgetary constraints imposed on subnational governments since the mid-1990s, with more budgetary resources centralized in the hands of the national government but subnational governments remaining responsible for many basic spending needs and support of economic development.

However, this chapter also points out several key problems in the current system of infrastructure financing. The use of land lease revenues and indirect borrowing lacks accountability and transparency; coordination between the planning and finance departments remains weak; "rule by man" remains very strong among the top leaders, who can arbitrarily initiate large-scale infrastructure projects; the bureaucratic structure remains fragmented due to the many vertical and horizontal lines of control; and the development of the capital assets management system is still in its infancy. As a result, the Chinese government still lacks a systematic approach to handling long-term capital improvement plans and to developing a regular, comprehensive capital budget.

We therefore recommend that the Chinese government rethink its current local debt policies, consider the possibility of introducing a new system of property taxes to reduce reliance on land lease revenues, and institute greater control and monitoring of indirect borrowing through quasi-governmental investment and development companies. Also, we see a need to develop a more comprehensive capital budgeting system, as required by the 1994 budget law, and a more effective capital assets management system so that the finance department can have more power and information to coordinate and monitor capital spending by all departments and quasi-public enterprises and institutions and more carefully manage the contingent liabilities problems that have already surfaced.

Finally, it is important to increase the transparency of capital budgeting decisions and the oversight power of the People's Congress at all levels of the government, so that the legislature can hold the government more accountable for infrastructure policies and spending decisions. We believe these steps are important so that in the long run, the rapid expansion of the economy and infrastructure facilities will not come at the expense of the long-term fiscal health of the Chinese government.

Acknowledgments

Janey Qian Wang, an Indiana University doctoral student now on the faculty of San Francisco State University, was the primary research assistant on this project. Also making significant contributions to the efforts of the Indiana University team were Renmin University doctoral students Yang He and Tao Lang (on leave) and Sun Yat-sen doctoral student Kai Kong. Assisting the Sun Yat-sen team were graduate students Ji Zhang, Shaolong Wu, Gang Chen, Yan Wu, Hui Shi, Yanhua Kuang, and Xiang Cai. All did valued work. The team gratefully thanks the Lincoln Institute of Land Policy for the support that made this project possible.

REFERENCES

Ahmad, Ehtisham, Maria Albino-War, and Raju Singh. 2005. Subnational public financial management: Institutions and macroeconomic considerations. Working paper No. WP/05/108. Washington, DC: International Monetary Fund.

Guangdong Finance Department. 1995, 1997, 2001, 2005, 2006, 2007. *Finance yearbook of Guangdong*. Guangzhou: Guangdong Economic Publishing House.

Guangdong Provincial Government. 2006. *Guangdong general report 2006: Challenges and solutions in current economy and social development*. Guangzhou.

———. 2007. Standing on reforming innovation for refining public expenditure management system. In *The practice and exploration of Guangdong provincial management innovation*, ed. General Office of Organization and Personnel Management, 120–123. Guangzhou: Department of Finance.

Guangdong Statistical Department. 1991, 1996, 1997, 2001, 2003, 2005, 2006, 2007. *Guangdong statistical yearbook*. Beijing: China Statistics Press.

Guangxi Zhuang Autonomous Region Statistical Department. 2001, 2003, 2005. *Guangxi statistical yearbook*. Beijing: China Statistics Press.

Guangzhou Statistical Department. 1991, 1996, 2001, 2006. *Guangzhou statistical yearbook*. Guangzhou: China Statistics Press.

Jiangxu Statistical Department. 2001, 2003, 2005. *Jiangxu statistical yearbook*. Beijing: China Statistics Press.

Liu, Lili. 2008. Creating a regulatory framework for managing subnational borrowing. In *Public finance in China: Reform and growth for a harmonious society*, eds. Jiwei Lou and Shuilin Wang. Washington, DC: World Bank.

Ma, Jun, and Yan Zhou. 2006. The investment decision-making system in the provincial government of China: A case study. Working Paper. Guangzhou, Guangdong: Sun Yat-sen University, Center for Public Administration Research.

Ministry of Construction of China. 2005. *China's urban construction statistical yearbook 2004*. Beijing: China Building Industry Press.

Ministry of Finance of China. 1995, 2002, 2005, 2006, 2008. *China finance yearbook*. Beijing: China Financial and Economic Publishing House.

Ministry of Land and Resources of China. 2006. *China land and resources almanac 2005*. Beijing: Geological Press.

National Bureau of Statistics of China. 1978–2007. *China statistical yearbook*. Beijing: China Statistics Press.

Plekhanov, Alexander, and Raju Singh. 2006. *How should subnational government borrowing be regulated? Some cross-country empirical evidence*. Staff Paper No. 53. Washington, DC: International Monetary Fund.

Shandong Statistical Department. 2001, 2003, 2005. *Shandong statistical yearbook*. Beijing: China Statistics Press.

Shi, Shaobin. 2007. Financing public goods through local debt: Conditions and effects. *Taxation & Economics* 2:24–28.
Sun, Ming. 2006. Five departments coordinated to stop parcel loan. *21st Century Business Herald*, May 11. http://finance.sina.com.cn/g/20060511/09562558887.shtml.
Zhejiang Statistical Department. 2001, 2003, 2005. *Zhejiang statistical yearbook*. Beijing: China Statistics Press.
Zhu, Guang-lei. 2005. *Contemporary Chinese government procedure*. Tianjin: Tianjin People's Press.

Local Revenue Sources

5

Provincial Tax Revenue

DONALD J. S. BREAN

This chapter presents an empirical overview of provincial taxation in China by examining the recent performance of seven specific provincial taxes in 31 provinces over the years 1999 to 2005. To enhance the comparability of revenue performance across provinces, each revenue source in each year is expressed on a per capita basis. Average annual growth rates of revenue flows are presented, along with standard measures of cross-section variance, again for each category of tax.

On the basis of 2005 GDP per capita, the 31 provinces are divided into three income groups—high, intermediate, and low income—to provide a focus for comparison of fiscal performance parallel to the provincial income disparity that is a serious concern in China today. Standard measures of fiscal buoyancy—the elasticity of per capita revenue with respect to GDP per capita—are computed for each tax for each province.

The provincial per capita GDP and tax database developed for this chapter allows calculation of a measure of interprovincial GDP disparity, as well as disparity in fiscal performance. The empirical work concludes with GDP per capita and each revenue item projected forward to 2015 and calculation of the GDP and tax disparity measures for that year. Given the structure of provincial taxation in China, the disparity of GDP per capita combined with the provincial cross-section disparity in GDP growth rates gives rise to eventually greater disparity in each tax per capita category.

The Structure of Taxation in China: Central-Local Perspectives

Beginning in 1978, which is the generally agreed-upon date of the inception of China's comprehensive economic reforms, the transition from central economic command to a decentralized market system inevitably and profoundly changed the fiscal relations between the center and the lower levels of government. Over the centuries, China had developed a sophisticated system of local government to raise revenues and to attend to local public needs. The tradition of local government with substantial revenue-generating authority in fact became stronger under Communist rule. Indeed, marshalling lower-level power was crucial to Mao Zedong during the revolution, while 30 years later Deng Xiaoping adopted similar political strategies to solidify support for economic reform.

China's challenge in fiscal reform, especially on the revenue side, was to replace the old command-style revenue sources with tax instruments that ensure adequate revenue within the new tax environment that is embedded in markets and that must be conducive to decentralized allocation of public-sector responsibilities. In the early days, when the market-based revenue system was finding its feet, a significant fiscal feature of the Chinese economic transition was the steep and protracted decline of government revenue relative to GDP with a corresponding rise in the fiscal deficit.

Table 5.1 illustrates the great national evaporation of revenue. It shows the decline in the revenue-to-GDP ratio in the years leading up to 1995 and the gradual reversal of the trend thereafter.

While revenue mobilization appeared feeble as the economic transition took root, another clear pattern was the migration of fiscal power and revenue from the center to the local governments. In the early 1980s, local governments turned as much as 26 percent of their collections over to the central government for national purposes. However, this share dwindled throughout the rest of the decade. By 1992 local governments, again all told, spent an amount equivalent to their collections while receiving a net transfer from the center equal to 2 percent of local expenditures.[1]

This fiscal phenomenon was to end in 1994 with a bang, not a whimper. Table 5.2 presents data on the central government's share of all (central plus local) revenue each year from 1978 to 2006. In the years immediately after 1978, the central share rose steadily, from 17 percent to 42 percent by 1984. Thereafter, however, the central share steadily declined, to 23 percent by 1993. The seismic shift that was to restore the central share was the comprehensive 1994 tax reforms. In the years leading up to the launch of those reforms, tax authorities in both the Ministry of Finance and the State Administration of Taxation had been carefully designing the features of the new tax regime, including special features that shape central-local fiscal relations to this day. The allocation of taxing responsibility dramatically shifted revenue collections in favor of the central government. The central share rose from 23 percent to 57 percent in the inaugural year of the reforms and has stayed in that range ever since.

Table 5.3 reports the 28-year history of total provincial tax to national GDP dating back to the launch of the economic reforms. The ratio of total provincial (i.e., noncentral) revenue to GDP declined steadily from 1978 to 1993, from 26 percent

---

[1] Under China's intergovernmental fiscal system rooted in the old regime, the central government's share of revenue was insufficient to meet central government expenditures. Historically, central revenues were considerably less than central expenditures, and the difference was made up by transfers from the local governments. For example, in 1984, local governments ran a "collections surplus" of about 17 billion yuan, while the central government ran a "collections deficit" of 23 billion. The net transfer was from local to center. However, between 1984 and 1989 the central share of tax collections fell steadily, from 42 percent to 32 percent. By 1989 the balance had tipped. As a result of the center's continuing responsibility for many local expenditure programs, but without corresponding revenue, the net transfer from the center to the subnational governments was equivalent to 19 percent of central collections.

TABLE 5.1
Total Tax (Central+Local) to GDP, 1978–2006 (percent)

1978	1979	1980	1981	1982	1983	1984	1985	1986	1987	1988	1989	1990	1991	1992	1993	1994	1995	1996	1997	1998	1999	2000	2001	2002	2003	2004	2005	2006
31	32	26	29	26	28	26	22	24	22	19	16	16	14	13	12	11	10	10	11	12	13	14	15	16	16	17	17	18

TABLE 5.2
Central Share of Total Tax Revenue, 1978–2006 (percent)

1978	1979	1980	1981	1982	1983	1984	1985	1986	1987	1988	1989	1990	1991	1992	1993	1994	1995	1996	1997	1998	1999	2000	2001	2002	2003	2004	2005	2006
16	21	25	27	29	37	42	39	38	35	35	31	34	30	28	22	56	52	49	49	50	51	52	52	55	55	55	52	56

TABLE 5.3
Total Provincial Tax to National GDP, 1978–2006 (percent)

1978	1979	1980	1981	1982	1983	1984	1985	1986	1987	1988	1989	1990	1991	1992	1993	1994	1995	1996	1997	1998	1999	2000	2001	2002	2003	2004	2005	2006
26	23	19	18	17	15	14	14	13	12	11	11	10	10	9	10	5	5	5	6	6	6	6	7	7	7	7	8	8

SOURCE: National Bureau of Statistics of China, *China Statistical Yearbook, 2006*, table 8-10.

to 10 percent, and then dropped even further in 1994. The provincial take as a percent of GDP has been quite steady, although rising slightly over the ensuing 13 years.

This chapter provides an empirical picture of provincial fiscal performance in the more recent years (1999–2006), a period when most structural and administrative features of the market-oriented tax reforms had taken hold. It is useful then to take a closer look at the policy objectives and structural features introduced in that reform package.

The 1994 Reforms

The objectives of China's 1994 tax reform were to establish a uniform tax system and to raise two fundamental ratios, the ratio of fiscal revenue to GDP and the ratio of central government revenue to total revenue. The 1994 tax regulations were announced as "unified regulation, justified burden, simplified process, and rationalized decentralization." The reforms were sweeping.

The 1994 reforms were designed to "recentralize" fiscal relations and to raise the long-run GDP elasticity of the revenue system. They comprehensively covered all taxes in the system, as well as introducing structural changes in tax administration and the tax-sharing system.[2] The intergovernmental fiscal problem was clear: While the declining power to tax at the center imposed a fiscal strain on the central government, the solution had to contend with an increasingly powerful and vocal faction of local authorities.

China's intergovernmental fiscal system is based on sharing rather than assignment. It is characterized by the following:

- All tax rates are determined centrally.
- Each provincial and local government is assigned a share of revenue collections within its boundaries.
- Tax administration is a shared responsibility between central and local governments.

In assigning revenue sources to different jurisdictional levels, the (central) government was guided by several practical principles. Tax instruments pertinent to national objectives such as macroeconomic policy and stabilization were assigned as *central taxes*. Taxes that could be viewed as more closely related to economic development and growth were assigned as *shared taxes*. Finally, those taxes that are most suited to being administered by local governments were assigned as *local taxes*.

The central-local tax assignment system following the 1994 reforms is outlined below:

Central taxes
- Tariffs and taxes on trade
- Income tax on central enterprise

---

[2] A thoughtful account of the revenue dimension of fiscal decentralization addressed by the 1994 reforms can be found in Bahl (1998). For a more recent review of the 1994 reforms with a special focus on tax-sharing features, see Zhang and Martinez-Vazquez (2003).

- Tax on revenues turned in by railways, banks, and insurance companies
- Income tax from financial enterprise licensed by the People's Bank of China
- Consumption tax
- Offshore oil resource tax

Shared taxes
- Value-added tax: central government 75 percent, local government 25 percent
- Stock transaction tax: central government 50 percent, local government 50 percent
- Resource tax other than offshore oil resource tax: mostly to local government

Local taxes
- Business tax, excluding those turned in by railways, banks, and insurance companies
- Income tax from local enterprises
- Personal income taxes
- Capital gains on land and property sales
- Estate duty
- Stamp duty

With a view to defining the fiscal rights and responsibilities of the center vis-à-vis local governments, which is the center's prerogative, Beijing opted to protect local interests by guaranteeing that their local tax revenue under the new system—through a complicated rebate scheme—would be no less than under the former arrangement. As a result, central revenues would increase only through general growth of revenue, although the center receives a larger share of the increase. As the economic and fiscal reforms took stronger hold, Beijing had the advantage of the larger share (75 percent) of the most income-elastic tax—the value-added tax, or VAT.

The 1994 reforms represented a significant improvement in the design of revenue assignments in China. Above all, it was much more amenable to China's burgeoning market economy than was the earlier "fiscal contract system." The reforms brought in a more modern structure of tax. Turnover taxes were replaced with a value-added tax. Excise taxes were taken out of local hands, immediately removing the incentive for local government to excessively encourage high-excise industries such as alcohol and tobacco. While reducing fiscal incentives for promoting local industry, the 1994 tax-sharing system meanwhile shifted incentives more toward commerce and trade by expanding the business tax on services and assigning it to local governments, where it has become an important revenue source that rivals the VAT. A short time later, in 1997, the provinces' fiscal arsenal was significantly strengthened with the introduction of the "contract tax," which has proven to be even more buoyant than the VAT.

The tax-sharing system introduced in 1994 effectively raised both the ratio of fiscal revenue to GDP and the ratio of central government revenue to total revenue. As shown in table 5.1, total government revenues (central plus local) to GDP rose from 11 percent in 1994 to 14 percent in the year 2000 and onward to 18 percent by 2006. Meanwhile, as shown in table 5.2, central revenues to total revenues rose sharply from 22 percent in 1993 to 52 percent in 1995, the same in 2000, and onward to 56 percent by 2006.[3]

With the foundation of the 1994 reforms along with subsequent adjustments through to 2000,[4] China entered the new millennium with an intergovernmental fiscal system that, on the revenue side at least, promised to be stable, less distortionary, and more income elastic.

Fiscal Performance of Local Governments

The remainder of this chapter presents an empirical analysis of the fiscal performance of local governments in China through the period 1999–2005. The focus is on seven major taxes administered by thirty-one local governments—twenty-six provinces, two autonomous regions, and three large cities.

The Data

The basic data are annual collections in each province of the following seven taxes: value-added tax, operations tax, company tax, individual income tax, resource tax, city construction tax, and contract tax. A number of smaller (in terms of revenue) taxes, some of which are being discontinued, were combined (under "All Other Taxes" in tables 5.8, 5.9, and 5.12). The sources of the data are the National Statistical Bureau of China and the China Internet Information Center. The data are yearly, 1999 to 2005. Some aggregated series reach 2006.

Each data point—for each tax and for accompanying variables such as GDP— has been transformed to a per capita value. Population data for each province for each year are from the National Statistical Bureau.

The per capita series allows for consistent and revealing interprovincial comparisons of the fiscal revenue mix, growth in total revenue and individual tax series, and tax elasticities. With the data in this form, we can also make projections of the stability of the structure and develop insight into the dynamics of income disparity among China's provinces.

Provincial Groups Ranked by GDP per Capita

Table 5.4 presents local GDP (in nominal yuan) per capita per annum for each of the 31 provinces, cities, and autonomous regions that are the focus of this study. Henceforth these will be referred to as "the provinces."

The provinces are ranked in descending order of GDP per capita for the year 2005. The overall group is divided into three categories—high income, intermediate income, and low income—with an approximately equal number of provinces in each group. There are 10 provinces in the high-income group, 11 in the intermediate group, and 10 in the low-income group. The cut-off GDP per capita between

---

[3] The enhanced central flow of revenue to the center provided the fiscal wherewithal to strengthen the equalization transfer system. The guiding principle in central-local fiscal relations seems to be to keep central's proportion in the neighborhood of 60 percent. With the local share being 40 percent, the central government can allocate about 20 percentage points of the consolidated budget to transfers.

[4] For a more complete discussion, see Wong and Bird (2005).

TABLE 5.4
Provincial GDP per Capita, 1999–2005 (yuan)

	1999	2001	2003	2005	Average Annual Growth (%)
High Income					
Shanghai	27,561	30,674	36,533	51,486	11.0
Beijing	17,452	20,576	25,152	51,419	19.7
Tianjin	15,152	18,328	24,203	35,452	15.2
Zhejiang	12,040	14,629	20,077	27,435	14.7
Jiangsu	10,718	12,933	16,826	24,489	14.8
Guangdong	11,850	13,681	17,130	24,327	12.7
Shandong	8,669	10,439	13,628	20,023	15.0
Liaoning	10,035	12,001	14,258	18,974	11.2
Fujian	10,762	12,365	15,000	18,583	9.5
Inner Mongolia	5,408	6,503	9,037	16,327	20.2
Group GDP	**12,965**	**15,213**	**19,184**	**28,851**	**14.3**
Intermediate Income					
Hebei	6,956	8,326	10,486	14,737	13.3
Heilongjiang	7,679	9,344	11,612	14,428	11.1
Jilin	6,315	7,553	9,330	13,329	13.3
Shanxi	4,750	5,440	7,412	12,458	17.4
Xinjiang	6,689	7,918	9,709	12,956	11.6
Chongqing	4,836	5,650	7,190	10,974	14.6
Hainan	6,258	6,859	8,278	10,804	9.5
Henan	4,913	5,903	7,291	11,287	14.9
Hubei	6,531	7,803	9,000	11,419	9.8
Ningxia	4,489	5,300	6,640	10,169	14.6
Qinghai	4,739	5,754	7,310	10,006	13.3
Group GDP	**5,832**	**6,895**	**8,569**	**12,052**	**12.9**
Low Income					
Shaanxi	4,137	5,040	6,501	9,881	15.6
Hunan	5,117	6,039	6,962	9,616	11.1
Jiangxi	4,684	5,198	6,653	9,410	12.3
Anhui	4,703	5,199	6,197	8,783	11.0
Guangxi	4,178	4,660	5,631	8,746	13.1
Yunnan	4,478	4,840	5,634	7,804	9.7
Xizang / Tibet	4,191	5,275	6,829	9,069	13.7
Sichuan	4,370	5,118	6,291	8,993	12.8
Gansu	3,700	4,165	5,011	7,456	12.4
Guizhou	2,493	2,856	3,504	5,306	13.4
Group GDP	**4,205**	**4,839**	**5,922**	**8,506**	**12.5**
Overall GDP per Capita	**7,111**	**8,421**	**10,560**	**15,413**	**13.8**

the high and intermediate groups is approximately 16,000 yuan per capita per annum; the cut-off between the intermediate and low groups is approximately 10,000 yuan per capita per annum.

The geographic distribution of the provinces in the three groups is closely in line with the well-known pattern of regional income disparity in China. The high-income group is composed for the most part of provinces located along the prosperous coast; the intermediate group is largely mid-nation; and the majority of the low-income group are farther west in China.

The three-part grouping of provinces according to GDP per capita, with a substantial number of provinces within each group, is a simple categorization that allows for comparison and contrast of the tax performance within and across these major groups.

Overall GDP per capita growth through this seven-year period was 13.8 percent per annum. The average annual growth was highest in the high-income group and lowest in the intermediate-income group.

Provincial Tax Revenue per Capita

Table 5.5 presents total tax revenue per capita—from all sources of tax revenue—collected by each province from 1999 to 2005. Tax collections per capita parallel the distribution of income per capita (in table 5.4) but not as closely as one might expect. The correlation between growth in GDP per capita and growth in tax collections per capita is 0.53.

Average annual growth of provincial tax revenue per capita was highest in the high-income group and lower in the intermediate-income group, again similar to the relative growth grouped by GDP per capita.

For the set of provinces as a whole, and for each of the income groups, average annual growth of tax revenue per capita exceeds the average annual growth of per capita GDP. At this highest level of aggregation, average annual tax revenue growth exceeds average annual GDP growth by 1.8 percent. However, while 15 individual provinces exhibit annual tax revenue growth greater than annual GDP growth, for the other 16 provinces tax revenue growth lags behind GDP growth. Issues of revenue growth versus GDP growth will be discussed further when revenue buoyancy is discussed.

Provincial Tax Revenue and GDP

Table 5.6 presents the ratio of provincial tax revenue—total, from all provincial taxes—to provincial GDP for each province for alternate years from 1999 to 2005. The ratio is consistently (over the years) highest for the high-income group and consistently lowest for the intermediate-income group. The low-income group presents a higher ratio than the intermediate group. Since the ratio of provincial tax revenue to provincial GDP is a rough measure of the average tax rate, this apparent violation of the most rudimentary principle of vertical equity in China is curious and potentially a matter of concern.

In table 5.6 group totals and the overall totals indicate that the ratio of provincial tax revenue to GDP has steadily increased since 1999.

TABLE 5.5
Provincial Tax Revenue per Capita, 1999–2005 (yuan)

	1999	2001	2003	2005	Average Annual Growth (%)
High Income					
Shanghai	3,017	3,802	5,048	7,609	16.7
Beijing	2,529	3,445	4,044	5,762	14.7
Tianjin	1,096	1,542	1,756	2,593	15.4
Jiangsu	438	722	933	1,481	22.5
Zhejiang	577	1,164	1,439	1,993	22.9
Guangdong	937	1,314	1,395	1,661	10.0
Liaoning	595	773	858	1,252	13.2
Fujian	496	698	722	1,010	12.6
Shandong	388	550	612	894	14.9
Inner Mongolia	298	351	447	867	19.5
Group Overall	**712**	**1,047**	**1,239**	**1,774**	**16.4**
Intermediate					
Hebei	268	328	377	574	13.5
Heilongjiang	389	487	528	647	8.8
Jilin	317	404	465	553	9.7
Shanxi	292	350	445	813	18.6
Xinjiang	351	446	542	710	12.4
Chongqing	211	292	381	633	20.1
Hainan	387	451	500	658	9.2
Henan	189	247	274	390	12.8
Hubei	253	318	342	497	11.9
Ningxia	283	431	421	617	13.9
Qinghai	224	298	356	505	14.5
Group Overall	**265**	**336**	**384**	**557**	**13.2**
Low Income					
Shaanxi	247	324	388	555	14.5
Hunan	178	233	280	423	15.5
Jiangxi	194	254	289	396	12.6
Anhui	221	269	276	400	10.4
Guangxi	203	301	302	409	12.4
Yunnan	348	391	421	553	8.0
Tibet	171	214	242	294	9.5
Sichuan	209	262	293	440	13.2
Gansu	193	242	276	355	10.7
Guizhou	165	213	241	368	14.3
Group Overall	**215**	**274**	**304**	**434**	**12.4**
Grand Overall	**396**	**554**	**645**	**944**	**15.6**

TABLE 5.6

Provincial Tax Revenue as Percent of Provincial GDP

	1999	2001	2003	2005
High Income				
Shanghai	10.95	12.39	13.82	14.78
Beijing	14.49	16.74	16.08	12.87
Tianjin	7.23	8.41	7.25	7.32
Zhejiang	4.80	7.96	7.17	7.26
Jiangsu	4.08	5.58	5.54	6.05
Guangdong	7.91	9.60	8.14	6.83
Shandong	4.48	5.27	4.49	4.46
Liaoning	5.93	6.44	6.02	6.60
Fujian	4.61	5.64	4.81	5.44
Inner Mongolia	5.50	5.40	4.95	5.31
Group Ratio	**6.38**	**7.89**	**7.31**	**7.25**
Intermediate				
Hebei	3.85	3.94	3.60	3.89
Heilongjiang	5.07	5.21	4.55	4.49
Jilin	5.02	5.34	4.99	4.15
Shanxi	6.14	6.44	6.01	6.53
Xinjiang	5.25	5.64	5.59	5.48
Chongqing	4.35	5.17	5.30	5.76
Hainan	6.19	6.57	6.04	6.09
Henan	3.85	4.19	3.75	3.45
Hubei	3.88	4.07	3.80	4.35
Ningxia	6.31	8.14	6.34	6.07
Qinghai	4.73	5.18	4.87	5.04
Group Ratio	**4.44**	**4.72**	**4.37**	**4.46**
Low Income				
Shaanxi	5.97	6.43	5.97	5.62
Hunan	3.48	3.85	4.02	4.11
Jiangxi	4.14	4.89	4.35	4.21
Anhui	4.69	5.18	4.45	4.55
Guangxi	4.87	6.46	5.35	4.68
Yunnan	7.76	8.09	7.48	7.09
Tibet	4.08	4.05	3.54	3.24
Sichuan	4.79	5.13	4.66	4.90
Gansu	5.22	5.80	5.51	4.76
Guizhou	6.64	7.46	6.89	6.94
Group Ratio	**4.97**	**5.54**	**5.07**	**4.97**
All Provinces	5.57	6.58	6.11	6.13
Coefficient of Variation				
High-income group	0.46	0.42	0.48	0.42
High-income group*	0.23	0.23	0.21	0.16
Intermediate-income group	0.18	0.22	0.19	0.19
Low-income group	0.24	0.23	0.23	0.23
Overall	0.39	0.40	0.44	0.40
Overall*	0.22	0.24	0.22	0.22

NOTE: "High-income group*" and "Overall*" exclude Beijing and Shanghai.

At the bottom of table 5.6, figures are presented for in-group coefficients of variation for the ratio of provincial tax revenue to GDP. This statistic provides an indication of diversity in fiscal performance within the income groups. The degree of in-group diversity is relatively small (especially when the two major cities are not included in the high-income group) and stable.

Tax Revenue per Capita by Tax Category and Province

Table 5.7 presents tax revenue per capita for each province across seven major categories of revenue. The operations tax, VAT, and company tax are substantial revenue sources. Combined, they represent more than 70 percent of provincial revenue.

Table 5.8 presents average annual rates of growth of revenues per capita for each individual in each province, as well as for income-group totals. Compared to the annual growth of all taxes combined through the 1999–2005 period, the VAT and the operations tax have above-average annual growth, whereas the company tax, the individual income tax, and the resource tax generally exhibit below-average annual growth. The most impressive annual revenue growth—across all three income groups—is in the contract tax, although that growth is of a relatively new and small base. For example, the 40.1 percent annual growth (per capita) of contract tax revenue for the intermediate-income group overall is not enough to keep that group out of third place (at 12.6 percent) in terms of overall revenue growth.

Revenue Elasticity by Tax Category and Province

Table 5.9 builds on several of the preceding tables. The revenue elasticity (or buoyancy) of the ith tax is the percentage change in the revenue of that i^{th} tax divided by the percentage change in GDP per capita over the same period. The calculation is

$$\text{Revenue Elasticity}_i = \{(R_{i,05} - R_{i,99})/[(R_{i,05} + R_{i,99})/2]\}/\{(Y_{05} - Y_{99})/[(Y_{05} + Y_{99})/2]\}$$

where $R_{i,99}$ = revenue per capita from the ith tax in 1999; $R_{i,05}$ = revenue per capita from the ith tax in 2005; Y_{99} = GDP per capita in the province in 1999; and Y_{05} = GDP per capita in the province in 2005.

Looking first at the extreme lower right-hand corner of table 5.9, we see that the revenue elasticity of all taxes (combined) across all provinces (combined) is 1.11. For example, at this highest level of aggregation, a 10 percent annual increase in GDP per capita gave rise to an 11.1 percent increase in tax revenue per capita for the same year.

Among the "big four" taxes—operations, VAT, company, and individual income—the first two exhibit elasticity that is substantially greater than unity with respect to GDP. This holds across all three income groups. On the other hand, the company tax and the individual income tax are less-than-unitary elastic, and this troubling relationship holds across all three income groups.

The city construction tax and the contract tax also exhibit above-unitary elasticity across all income groups. In the case of the former, which is a surtax-like levy on VAT and consumption tax (excises) paid, its elasticity is derivative of the elasticity of the VAT and the consumption tax. The impressive elasticity of the contract tax is likely spurious in view of the relatively short time since its inception.

TABLE 5.7
Per Capita Taxes by Category and Province, 2005 (yuan)

	VAT	Operations Tax	Company Tax	Individual Income Tax	Resource Tax	City Construction Tax	Contract Tax	All Other Taxes	Total
High Income									
Beijing	635	2,495	1,071	550	2	252	395	362	5,762
Shanghai	1,272	2,885	1,401	629	0	280	625	517	7,609
Tianjin	616	925	397	180	4	152	156	162	2,593
Jiangsu	355	459	238	89	4	95	108	135	1,481
Zhejiang	417	662	343	135	7	126	141	162	1,993
Guangdong	352	604	257	144	3	70	89	142	1,661
Liaoning	268	390	171	78	29	95	92	130	1,252
Fujian	207	352	154	78	6	52	59	102	1,010
Shandong	209	236	120	42	20	71	56	140	894
Inner Mongolia	203	328	81	42	28	60	19	107	867
Group Overall	**355**	**618**	**286**	**130**	**11**	**97**	**118**	**159**	**1,774**
Intermediate									
Hebei	177	154	78	41	16	43	22	44	574
Heilongjiang	223	156	49	41	29	72	23	55	647
Jilin	146	175	51	41	7	48	28	57	553
Shanxi	306	181	110	41	54	64	10	48	813
Xinjiang	214	237	38	46	30	68	22	54	710
Chongqing	120	251	50	38	11	47	51	65	633
Hainan	118	286	55	43	7	45	24	82	658
Henan	94	119	55	24	9	31	21	38	390
Hubei	115	160	68	31	6	42	26	48	497
Ningxia	147	264	44	37	4	51	26	44	617
Qinghai	144	184	47	19	26	43	11	31	505
Group Overall	**157**	**167**	**63**	**35**	**17**	**47**	**24**	**48**	**557**

Low Income									
Shaanxi	149	186	55	27	18	56	16	48	555
Hunan	93	149	35	26	2	40	31	48	423
Jiangxi	79	146	40	26	5	26	35	39	396
Anhui	94	128	49	20	7	33	29	38	400
Guangxi	84	147	40	31	4	28	24	51	409
Yunnan	126	152	75	27	7	66	19	81	553
Tibet	43	176	32	16	9	15	0	4	294
Sichuan	87	164	49	27	5	34	29	46	440
Gansu	98	122	33	20	8	36	9	30	355
Guizhou	84	124	43	24	5	35	9	44	368
Group Overall	**97**	**148**	**47**	**26**	**6**	**38**	**24**	**47**	**434**
Grand Overall	**206**	**320**	**136**	**65**	**11**	**62**	**57**	**87**	**944**
Coefficient of Variation									
High-income group	0.69	0.97	1.00	1.03	1.02	0.61	1.03	0.65	0.87
Intermediate-income group	0.36	0.26	0.33	0.22	0.81	0.24	0.43	0.26	0.18
Low-income group	0.29	0.14	0.27	0.17	0.59	0.38	0.54	0.43	0.19
Overall	1.01	1.49	1.73	1.64	0.98	0.84	1.75	1.06	1.34

TABLE 5.8
Tax per Capita, 2005: Average Annual Percentage Change by Category and Province, 1999–2005

	VAT	Operations Tax	Company Tax	Individual Income Tax	Resource Tax	City Construction Tax	Contract Tax	All Other Taxes	All Taxes
High Income									
Beijing	12.2	15.8	16.6	6.9	6.7	12.8	36.1	10.8	14.7
Shanghai	14.3	19.8	14.9	11.1	0.0	12.2	40.8	9.3	16.7
Tianjin	18.9	17.4	7.9	11.8	1.0	14.7	45.4	9.8	15.4
Jiangsu	19.7	26.5	21.1	16.5	20.7	21.8	45.3	17.0	22.4
Zhejiang	18.6	25.7	19.9	18.2	63.1	19.7	48.7	27.2	22.7
Guangdong	15.7	10.1	5.7	7.9	14.2	10.6	17.5	5.5	10.0
Liaoning	14.3	14.6	12.3	8.1	6.2	15.6	40.8	4.9	12.9
Fujian	16.9	14.2	13.4	2.7	20.6	12.1	26.7	5.2	12.4
Shandong	15.4	17.5	9.0	12.1	19.6	17.6	65.6	9.6	14.3
Inner Mongolia	25.2	29.9	15.3	16.1	16.6	22.7	54.4	2.0	18.4
Group Overall	**17.0**	**18.4**	**14.0**	**11.3**	**14.1**	**16.1**	**37.6**	**10.2**	**16.3**
Intermediate Income									
Hebei	18.3	15.7	8.2	11.6	15.5	16.5	44.7	0.1	12.9
Heilongjiang	13.9	10.5	10.7	12.6	−3.1	11.2	21.4	−4.9	9.1
Jilin	12.6	11.7	4.5	11.2	11.9	11.5	32.3	−1.1	9.5
Shanxi	27.2	15.9	21.9	6.1	24.4	21.8	49.3	−0.1	16.1
Xinjiang	20.2	13.9	3.8	4.8	13.9	15.2	46.2	−2.0	11.6
Chongqing	19.3	24.0	13.5	13.0	22.8	22.6	61.2	9.3	19.4
Hainan	24.6	12.3	6.7	−5.4	−4.2	19.8	18.8	−0.4	9.3
Henan	15.5	15.3	9.6	12.4	22.1	14.7	45.3	0.2	12.2
Hubei	14.7	16.3	11.1	12.0	17.6	15.3	43.1	−4.3	11.6
Ningxia	14.7	17.1	3.8	13.8	22.9	17.0	36.5	2.1	13.7
Qinghai	17.5	16.2	9.8	8.7	26.7	18.5	56.6	−1.6	12.9
Group Overall	**17.8**	**15.4**	**10.5**	**10.2**	**12.6**	**15.7**	**40.1**	**−0.9**	**12.6**

Low Income								
Shaanxi	21.1	15.5	13.0	17.8	35.1	20.7	44.4	-4.2	13.3
Hunan	16.8	20.5	11.2	10.5	12.5	15.6	50.7	3.2	15.4
Jiangxi	17.5	16.1	11.8	16.5	22.9	15.5	49.7	-6.3	12.3
Anhui	15.5	17.9	10.2	4.5	12.6	15.4	47.4	-9.6	10.1
Guangxi	13.1	17.1	6.4	9.8	25.5	16.5	46.6	1.7	12.1
Yunnan	9.0	10.9	13.0	10.8	22.0	6.4	34.4	-1.6	7.8
Tibet	7.5	17.6	-7.2	7.1	6.1	11.8		8.1	9.2
Sichuan	15.4	16.6	7.6	14.1	2.2	16.0	37.2	1.8	13.1
Gansu	14.1	13.0	3.5	18.3	14.7	14.6	35.3	-3.0	10.2
Guizhou	18.6	17.8	19.2	16.7	19.1	16.3	38.5	-1.3	13.9
Group Overall	**15.3**	**16.4**	**10.3**	**12.0**	**16.4**	**14.4**	**43.2**	**-1.9**	**12.0**
Grand Overall	17.3	18.1	13.6	11.8	13.8	16.0	39.5	5.2	15.3
Coefficient of Variation								
High-income group	0.20	0.31	0.35	0.41	1.02	0.25	0.30	0.68	0.25
Intermediate-income group	0.24	0.22	0.53	0.59	0.65	0.21	0.30	(14.35)	0.23
Low-income group	0.26	0.16	0.76	0.36	0.53	0.23	0.14	(4.35)	0.19
Overall	0.25	0.27	0.56	0.46	0.76	0.24	0.27	2.58	0.27

TABLE 5.9
Revenue Elasticity, Based on 1999–2005 Changes

	VAT	Operations Tax	Company Tax	Individual Income Tax	Resource Tax	City Construction Tax	Contract Tax	All Other Taxes	Total, All Taxes
High Income									
Beijing	0.75	0.94	0.98	0.45	0.44	0.79	1.66	0.68	0.89
Shanghai	1.26	1.63	1.30	1.01	—	1.10	2.55	0.86	1.43
Tianjin	1.19	1.11	0.56	0.80	0.07	0.97	2.02	0.68	1.01
Jiangsu	1.26	1.55	1.32	1.10	1.31	1.36	2.07	1.12	1.39
Zhejiang	1.21	1.53	1.27	1.19	2.31	1.26	2.13	1.59	1.41
Guangdong	1.19	0.81	0.48	0.65	1.10	0.85	1.30	0.46	0.81
Liaoning	1.24	1.25	1.09	0.74	0.58	1.33	2.51	0.46	1.15
Fujian	1.64	1.42	1.35	0.30	1.91	1.24	2.29	0.57	1.28
Shandong	1.02	1.14	0.64	0.83	1.24	1.14	2.29	0.68	1.00
Inner Mongolia	1.17	1.30	0.80	0.84	0.86	1.09	1.72	0.12	0.97
Group Elasticity	**1.17**	**1.25**	**1.00**	**0.83**	**1.01**	**1.13**	**1.99**	**0.76**	**1.14**
Intermediate Income									
Hebei	1.30	1.15	0.65	0.88	1.14	1.20	2.24	0.01	1.01
Heilongjiang	1.22	0.96	0.97	1.12	−0.31	1.01	1.72	−0.49	0.82
Jilin	0.96	0.90	0.37	0.87	0.91	0.88	1.92	−0.09	0.76
Shanxi	1.38	0.93	1.19	0.39	1.29	1.19	1.86	0.00	1.05
Xinjiang	1.57	1.16	0.35	0.44	1.17	1.26	2.55	−0.19	1.06
Chongqing	1.25	1.46	0.93	0.90	1.41	1.41	2.30	0.67	1.29
Hainan	2.17	1.25	0.73	−0.62	−0.48	1.86	1.78	−0.05	0.97
Henan	1.04	1.02	0.68	0.86	1.36	0.99	2.05	0.01	0.88
Hubei	1.43	1.56	1.12	1.20	1.66	1.48	2.91	−0.48	1.19
Ningxia	1.00	1.14	0.29	0.96	1.42	1.13	1.89	0.16	0.96
Qinghai	1.26	1.18	0.77	0.69	1.71	1.32	2.44	−0.14	1.08
Group Elasticity	**1.29**	**1.15**	**0.82**	**0.80**	**0.97**	**1.17**	**2.17**	**−0.07**	**1.01**

Low Income								
Shaanxi	1.26	0.99	0.85	1.11	1.75	1.25	1.96	−0.31	0.94
Hunan	1.29	1.51	0.92	0.87	1.01	1.22	2.51	0.28	1.21
Jiangxi	1.34	1.25	0.96	1.28	1.64	1.21	2.50	−0.57	1.02
Anhui	1.35	1.51	0.94	0.44	1.13	1.34	2.72	−0.97	0.95
Guangxi	1.00	1.25	0.52	0.77	1.68	1.21	2.31	0.14	0.95
Yunnan	0.94	1.11	1.29	1.10	1.97	0.68	2.62	−0.17	0.84
Tibet	0.58	1.23	−0.60	0.55	0.47	0.88	–	0.63	0.72
Sichuan	1.17	1.24	0.63	1.09	0.19	1.21	2.14	0.16	1.03
Gansu	1.11	1.05	0.30	1.38	1.16	1.15	2.14	−0.27	0.88
Guizhou	1.31	1.26	1.34	1.20	1.33	1.17	2.09	−0.11	1.05
Group Elasticity	**1.20**	**1.27**	**0.85**	**0.97**	**1.27**	**1.14**	**2.36**	**−0.17**	**1.00**
Grand Elasticity	**1.21**	**1.25**	**0.99**	**0.87**	**1.00**	**1.13**	**2.06**	**0.41**	**1.11**

Disparity in Provincial GDP per Capita: Now and Later

Table 5.10 presents a picture of the future rank order of provincial GDP per capita, taking explicit account of differential rates of GDP growth. From a base distribution of GDP per capita (the rank order in 2005), a projected distribution in 2015 is created by multiplying by a growth factor estimated by average annual growth rates for 1999–2005, viz.

$$[GDP/POP]_{i,15} = (GDP/POP)_{i,05} \times (1 + g_i^*)^{10}$$

where g_i^* is the average annual rate of GDP per capita growth in the ith province over the 1999–2005 period.

The growth differentials have substantial effect on the distribution of GDP per capita across the provinces. According to the projections 10 years out, some provinces move up in the GDP per capita ladder, while others, of course, fall back. Shaanxi and Hebei, for example, currently in the intermediate-income group, seem poised to move up to the high-income group, while Fujian is likely to move from the high-income to the intermediate group.

The Gini Index of Inequality was used to measure the disparity in provincial GDP per capita.[5] Based on projections of provincial GDP per capita, the Gini coefficient is estimated to rise (income disparity increases) from 0.33 to 0.40 by 2015.

Disparity in Provincial Tax per Capita: Now and Later

Table 5.11 presents the results of a 10-year projection of total tax per capita in each of the provinces from the base of 2005 and in view of the average annual provincial growth rates in each of the provinces 1999–2005.

Table 5.11 also presents the results of a novel perspective on provincial tax performance throughout China. The actual 2005 data and the projected figures for 2015 provided the basis for calculating provincial tax Gini coefficients. The same methodology used to compute GDP per capita Gini coefficients was applied to the national cross-section of provincial tax per capita. The results are presented at the bottom of table 5.11.

In table 5.12 the same approach applied to each of the seven specific categories of taxes of results in an across-the-board table of "provincial tax Gini coefficients."

The structure of provincial taxation in China gives a rationale to this form of analysis. There are thirty-one provinces (including the two autonomous regions and three cities) that have essentially a common tax structure with common definitions of tax base and similar rates. One might expect, for example, the Gini coefficient for GDP per capita to be comparable to the Gini coefficient of total tax per capita or perhaps even higher to the extent that the tax system is progressive.

---

[5] The Gini Index, or coefficient of inequality, is a common measure of inequality. The coefficient varies between 0, which reflects complete equality, and 1, which indicates complete inequality (in which one party has all the income or consumption; all others have none). A simple method to compute the Gini Index is based on the covariance of the income measure (Y) for each party in the distribution (individuals, households, or, in this case, China's provinces) and the rank (F) that the party occupies in the distribution of income (which takes a value between 0 for the poorest and 1 for the richest). Denoting mean income by y^*, the Gini Index is $Gini = 2 \, cov \, (Y, F)/y^*$

TABLE 5.10
Total Provincial GDP per Capita and Gini Coefficient, 2005 and 2015

	GDP per Capita 2005	Average Annual Growth 1999–2005	GDP per Capita Projected to 2015
High Income			
Shanghai	51,486	10.98	145,883
Beijing	44,774	19.73	271,129
Tianjin	35,452	15.22	146,188
Jiangsu	24,489	14.76	97,065
Zhejiang	27,435	14.71	108,261
Guangdong	24,327	12.74	80,674
Shandong	20,023	14.97	80,797
Liaoning	18,974	11.20	54,855
Fujian	18,583	9.53	46,184
Inner Mongolia	16,327	20.22	102,957
Group Overall	**28,187**	**14.26**	**106,919**
Intermediate Income			
Hebei	14,737	13.33	51,503
Heilongjiang	14,428	11.08	41,274
Jilin	13,329	13.26	46,302
Shanxi	12,458	17.43	62,129
Xinjiang	12,956	11.65	38,995
Chongqing	10,974	14.64	43,007
Hainan	10,804	9.53	26,843
Henan	11,287	14.87	45,156
Hubei	11,419	9.76	28,973
Ningxia	10,169	14.60	39,743
Qinghai	10,006	13.26	34,766
Group Overall	**12,052**	**12.86**	**40,401**
Low Income			
Shaanxi	9,881	15.62	42,169
Hunan	9,616	11.09	27,523
Jiangxi	9,410	12.33	30,103
Anhui	8,783	10.97	24,870
Guangxi	8,746	13.10	29,961
Yunnan	7,804	9.70	19,696
Xizang / Tibet	9,069	13.73	32,833
Sichuan	8,993	12.78	29,940
Gansu	7,456	12.39	23,969
Guizhou	5,306	13.42	18,686
Group Overall	**8,506**	**12.46**	**27,523**
Overall GDP per capita	**15,413**	**13.76**	**55,950**
Gini Coefficient, 2005	**0.33**		
Gini Coefficient, 2015	**0.40**		

TABLE 5.11

Total Provincial Taxes per Capita, 2005 Actual and 2015 Projected

	Total Taxes per Capita	Annual Growth 1999–2005	Projected Total Tax per Capita 2015
High Income			
Beijing	5,762	14.71	22,719
Shanghai	7,609	16.67	35,543
Tianjin	2,593	15.44	10,896
Jiangsu	1,481	22.42	11,196
Zhejiang	1,993	22.70	15,418
Guangdong	1,661	9.98	4,300
Liaoning	1,252	12.92	4,219
Fujian	1,010	12.42	3,259
Shandong	894	14.29	3,398
Inner Mongolia	867	18.43	4,710
Intermediate Income			
Hebei	574	12.88	1,927
Heilongjiang	647	9.13	1,551
Jilin	553	9.52	1,373
Shanxi	813	16.14	3,630
Xinjiang	710	11.57	2,122
Chongqing	633	19.42	3,731
Hainan	658	9.34	1,607
Henan	390	12.18	1,231
Hubei	497	11.63	1,493
Ningxia	617	13.68	2,227
Qinghai	505	12.89	1,697
Low Income			
Shaanxi	555	13.31	1,938
Hunan	423	15.43	1,778
Jiangxi	396	12.29	1,262
Anhui	400	10.10	1,046
Guangxi	409	12.07	1,279
Yunnan	553	7.79	1,171
Tibet	294	9.19	709
Sichuan	440	13.13	1,513
Gansu	355	10.23	939
Guizhou	368	13.87	1,349
Provincial Tax Gini Coefficient, 2005		**0.52**	
Provincial Tax Gini Coefficient, 2015		**0.61**	

Over time, to the extent that the elasticity of total tax to GDP is greater than unity, we could expect the provincial tax Gini coefficient to behave like the GDP per capita Gini coefficient, which, as we have seen, increases in value (cross-provincial disparity increases) as GDP per capita is projected 10 years into the future based on historical growth rates.

TABLE 5.12
Provincial Tax Gini Coefficients, 2005 Actual and 2015 Projected

	VAT	Operations Tax	Company Tax	Individual Income Tax	Resource Tax	City Construction Tax	Contract Tax	All Other Taxes	All Taxes
2005	0.44	0.55	0.64	0.60	0.50	0.38	0.65	0.46	0.52
2015	0.47	0.61	0.73	0.59	0.71	0.39	0.67	0.72	0.61

Table 5.12 shows that for every individual tax item—as well, of course, as the total—the provincial tax Gini coefficient is higher in the (projected) year 2015 than for 2005. Given the structure of taxation in China, the disparity of GDP per capita combined with the cross-section disparity in GDP growth rates gives rise to eventually greater disparity in each tax-per-capita category.

Conclusion

This chapter presents an empirical overview of provincial taxation in China, focusing on the recent performance of seven specific provincial taxes in thirty-one provinces. To enhance the comparability of revenue performance across provinces, each revenue source in each year is expressed on a per capita basis. Average annual growth rates for the revenue flows are presented, along with standard measures of cross-section variance, again for each category of tax.

The 31 provinces are divided into three income groups on the basis of 2005 GDP per capita—high income, intermediate income, and low income. This categorization provides a basis for the comparison of fiscal performance in parallel to the provincial income disparity that is a serious concern in China today.

Standard measures of fiscal buoyancy—the elasticity of per capita revenue with respect to GDP per capita—are presented for each tax for each province.

The provincial per capita GDP and tax data base developed for this chapter allowed calculation of a measure of interprovincial GDP disparity, as well as disparity in fiscal performance. GDP per capita and each revenue item were projected forward to 2015, followed by calculation of GDP and tax disparity measures for that year. Given the structure of provincial taxation in China, the dispersion of GDP per capita combined with the provincial cross-section variance in GDP growth rates gives rise to eventually greater disparity in each tax-per-capita category.

REFERENCES

Bahl, Roy. 1998. Central-provincial-local fiscal relations. In *Taxation in modern China*, ed. D. J. S. Brean. New York: Routledge.
National Bureau of Statistics of China. 2006. *China statistical yearbook*. Beijing: China Statistics Press.
Wong, Christine P. W., and Richard Bird. 2005. China's fiscal system: A work in progress. International Tax Program Paper No. 0515. Toronto: Institute for International Business, Rotman School of Management, University of Toronto.
Zhang, Zhihua, and Jorge Martinez-Vazquez. 2003. The system of equalization transfers in China. International Studies Program Working Paper No. 0312. Atlanta: Georgia State University, Andrew Young School of Policy Studies.

Tax Structure and Economic Growth

JOYCE YANYUN MAN AND XINYE ZHENG

In the past few decades, there have been numerous empirical studies that attempt to address the question of what determines an economy's long-term growth. The theoretical growth literature defines distortionary taxes as those that affect the price of an accumulated factor of production, such as physical capital, human capital, or technology. Thus, increases in distortionary taxation lower the growth rate of output.

The exogenous (or neoclassical) growth theory of the 1950s and 1960s developed by Solow (1956) and Swan (1956) was based on a production function that capital and labor (measured in man-hours) stimulates growth. Under the assumption of constant returns to scale and diminishing marginal productivity of both inputs, growth occurs in the model through the accumulation of capital; but there is a natural limit to the level of consumption per capita due to the limited supply of labor and the diminishing marginal productivity of capital. There exists an optimal output for the economy, and no amount of investment will ever allow consumption to exceed the maximum attainable level of consumption per capita. Capital accumulation influences only the transitional growth rate since steady-state growth is determined by exogenous technological progress and population growth. In this model, labor or capital or both inputs become more productive over time through exogenous factors summarized as "technical progress." As a result, the "growth engine" is exogenous, and the rate of economic growth cannot be affected by policy. In the neoclassical model of economic growth (Cass 1965; Koopmans 1965), fiscal policy changes affect the equilibrium level of GDP and have only transitional growth effects. Turnovsky (1996) shows that increases in marginal tax rates on physical and human capital lower the transitional growth rate instead of the steady-state growth rate.

The endogenous growth models argue that long-term steady-state economic growth is driven by the accumulation of reproducible capital such as physical and human capital. Increases in physical and human capital accumulation, public infrastructure, and innovation lead to faster steady-state growth rates. Such models (Barro, Mankiw, and Sala-i-Martin 1992; Lucas 1988) suggest that if the production function has constant returns to scale in human capital and physical capital jointly, investment in both inputs can raise output without limit. In this model, output depends on labor use and a range of other inputs. Technological progress either introduces new inputs into the production function or enhances the quality of inputs, stimulating economic growth (Aghion and Howitt 1992; Romer 1987; 1990). Romer (1986) also argues that sustained growth can be achieved under the assumption that there are externalities between firms. The new knowledge and techniques invested by one firm can flow to other firms, raising productivity and the entire economic output.

In models of endogenous growth, any tax policy that distorts the incentives to accumulate physical and human capital will permanently reduce the growth rate. Rebelo (1991) shows that increases in marginal tax rates on physical and human capital lower the steady-state growth rate. Furthermore, endogenous growth theories predict that different taxes affect growth in diverse ways. In addition, all taxes may not be equally distorting, and therefore the tax mix can be an important determinant of economic growth. If labor supply is highly inelastic, a consumption tax or a flat tax on labor income does not distort an individual's intertemporal consumption choice and so does not affect the individual's incentives to accumulate capital and consequently has no impact on economic growth (Rebelo 1991). On the other hand, taxes on capital and capital accumulation, such as personal and corporate income taxes, may have adverse growth effects.

However, the empirical growth literature typically does not distinguish between taxes paid on income, consumption, or property, but rather lumps all distortionary taxation into one or two overall tax rates. Koester and Kormendi (1989) and Easterly and Rebelo (1993a; 1993b) include one overall measure of tax distortion in their growth regressions. Mullen and Williams (1994) and Becsi (1996) include one estimate of the total effective marginal tax rate in their growth regressions in their studies of U.S. states. According to Katz, Mahler, and Franz (1983), Koester and Kormendi (1989), and Agell, Lindh, and Ohlsson (1997), the average tax rate, defined as the total tax revenue share of GDP, has no effect on economic growth. However, Engen and Skinner (1992) report a significant negative effect, and Cashin (1995) finds the log of the average tax rate negatively correlated with growth per worker.[1] These conflicting results may come from divergent specifications; different estimation methodologies; or the choices of the regression's control variables, data used, or other factors.

This chapter attempts to analyze the effects of overall average tax rate and disaggregated taxes on economic growth using fixed effect and random effect models and the 2SLS estimation method for Chinese provincial data from 1998 to 2006. It aims to make a contribution to the existing literature in the following ways:

---

[1] Katz, Mahler, and Franz (1983) include the statutory income tax rates in the highest income bracket in their cross-sectional income tax rates and find that the average income tax rate does not significantly correlate with economic growth. Koester and Kormendi (1989) find that the average marginal tax rate has a negative correlation with the level of income but not with economic growth.

1. It analyzes the growth model using panel data for Chinese provinces between 1998 and 2006 to provide empirical evidence on the effects of taxation on economic growth.
2. It uses both overall average tax rate and different tax rates to test whether all taxes have equal effects on economic growth.
3. It distinguishes the effects of taxation on the level of output and the rate of growth of output. As a result, it may provide empirical evidence of whether an exogenous or endogenous model can better explain the economic growth in China. The exogenous model predicts only level effects of a change in policy; the endogenous growth model suggests both level and growth effects.
4. It employs and compares both fixed effect and random effect models in an attempt to test and control for possible omitted variable problems and regional effects.
5. It investigates the possible effects of taxes on land and property to provide much needed policy implications for the fiscal reform and local tax restructuring efforts in China.

Models and Specification Issues

This chapter explores the relationship between various tax structure indicators and economic growth in China. It assumes that government policy—tax policy, in particular—has an impact on economic growth. It follows the work of Barro and Sala-i-Martin (1995) and others in the regional growth literature and estimates the following equations:

$$LnGDP_{it} = \alpha_0 + \beta_m T_{it} + \delta_z Z_{it} + \mu_i + \lambda_t + \varepsilon_{it} \quad (1)$$

$$GDPRATE_{it} = \alpha_0 + \beta_m T_{it} + \delta_z Z_{it} + \mu_i + \lambda_t + \varepsilon_{it} \quad (2)$$

where GDP_{it} is the per capita GDP in province i at the time t, and $GDPRATE_{it}$ is the annualized growth rate of per capita GDP. T is the vector of tax structure variables. Z is the set of other variables that are believed to affect GDP or $GDPRATE$. λ_t and μ_i are the time- and jurisdiction-specific fixed (province) effects. According to much previous research (e.g., Helms 1985), it is necessary on statistical grounds and desirable on logical grounds to treat μ_i and λ_t as fixed effects rather than as stochastic error terms in this cross-section and time series growth model.

Past empirical studies have found that government policy variables and economic growth are simultaneously determined and interdependent. This suggests that changes in taxation may affect economic growth, but economic performance may also lead to changes in tax policies. Thus, the 2SLS estimation method has been applied to control for possible simultaneity bias due to the interdependent relationship between tax policy and economic growth.

Data and Hypotheses

Equations (1) and (2) are estimated using annual panel data for the period 1998 through 2006 for 30 provinces in China.[2] Allowing for the necessary lags ($GDP_{i, t-1}$

---

[2] Due to a lack of data on land-related taxes, Tianjin was excluded from the data set for the regression analysis.

and lagged variables used as instruments), a total of 240 observations (for eight years) are thus available. The data were taken from the National Bureau of Statistics of China, *Chinese Statistical Abstracts*, State Administration of Taxation, *China Taxation Abstracts*, the Ministry of Finance, and the 2000 Economic Census.

The dependent variable is measured as per capita GDP in logarithm in equation (1) and annual growth rate of per capita in equation (2).

The explanatory variables fall into three categories: (1) taxes and other revenues; (2) demographic and labor force characteristics, urbanization rate, and industrial composition (see table 6.1); and (3) public expenditures and the level and quality of public services. Tax variables are measured as per capita total tax revenue or the ratio

TABLE 6.1
Descriptive Statistics of Selected Variables

Variable	Variable Names	Mean	SD	Min.	Max.
Dependent Variables					
LN (GDP per capita)	LGDP	9.15	0.61	7.81	10.96
GDP growth rate	GDPRATE	0.12	0.06	−0.06	0.38
Explanatory Variables					
Average tax rate	TAXRATE	0.07	0.02	0.04	0.15
Tax rate per capita	TAX	930.00	121.00	180.00	868.00
Land and property tax rate	PTAXRATIO	0.00	0.00	0.00	0.01
Land and property tax per capita	PTAX	40.00	60.00	0.00	450.00
VAT tax as a ratio to GDP	VATRATIO	0.01	0.00	0.00	0.03
VAT tax per capita	VAT	160.00	190.00	30.00	149.00
Business tax as a ratio to GDP	BTAXRATIO	0.02	0.01	0.01	0.06
Business tax per capita	BTAX	280.00	480.00	50.00	308.00
Income tax as a ratio to GDP	ITAXRATIO	0.00	0.00	0.00	0.02
Income tax per capita	ITAX	70.00	120.00	10.00	720.00
Literacy rate	LITERACY	0.84	0.09	0.41	0.96
Population growth rate	POPRATE	0.01	0.02	−0.11	0.11
Manufacturing share in GDP	MANU	0.43	0.08	0.20	0.58
Fixed capital growth rate	FIXCAPITAL	0.42	0.12	0.25	0.79
Fixed capital per capita	FIXCAPITALPC	486.00	386.00	840.00	21,490.00
Infrastructure as a ratio to GDP	INFRARATIO	0.02	0.04	0.00	0.33
Infrastructure spending per capita	INFRA	25.20	37.82	2.59	220.10
Education spending as a ratio to GDP	EDURATIO	0.02	0.01	0.01	0.08
Education spending per capita	EDU	250.00	180.00	60.00	1,130.00

SOURCES: National Bureau of Statistics of China, *Chinese Statistical Abstracts*, *Urban Statistical Abstracts*, Economic Census.
NOTE: SD = standard deviation.

of total tax revenue to GDP as a measure of overall average tax rate. Alternatively, the tax variables are disaggregated into value-added tax (VAT), business tax, corporate and personal income tax, and land and property tax per capita or with respect to GDP.

Ideally, we would like to have a measure of various effective tax rates per se. However, any attempt to use statutory tax rate schedules in constructing a measure of effective rates across Chinese provinces over time is problematic because of the substantial nonuniformity of enforcement practices and variations in rate structures of some taxes across regions in China. As an alternative, tax revenues from various taxes as a share of GDP in each province are used as tax rate proxies. One may correctly point out that the use of GDP in the denominator of tax rate measures would lead to a spurious correlation with the dependent variable under certain circumstances. Thus, a 2SLS method has been used to control for such simultaneity.

In the second categories of explanatory variables, per capita government expenditures on infrastructure and education are included in the regression equations of economic level and growth. Other variables include the literacy rate, urbanization rate, population growth rate, and share of manufacture sector in each jurisdiction's economy to measure demographic and labor force characteristics and industrial composition.

The tax variables TAXRATE and TAX are measured as the ratio of total tax revenue to GDP and per capita GDP in a jurisdiction, respectively. They are used to measure the level of an over average tax rate or tax burden. VAT is a tax on a number of specified taxable items with a rate of 13 percent or 17 percent. VAT is administered by the State Administration of Taxation (the import VAT is collected by the customs on behalf), and the revenue from it is shared between the central government (75%) and local governments (25%). VAT is the major source of fiscal revenue for the government of China, particularly the central government. Business tax is a tax payable against turnover by all enterprises and individuals undertaking the following business activities: providing taxable services, including communication, transport, construction, finance and insurance, telecom, culture, entertainment and service industries; transferring the provision of intangible assets; and selling immovable properties. The basic formula is: tax payable = turnover × tax rate. The property tax variable is a combination of three types of taxes levied on land and real property, including the urban land tax, real estate tax, and land value-added tax (see chapter 1, this volume). The urbanization rate is defined as the share of urban population in the total population as a proxy for the degree of urbanization in a jurisdiction. The regression results are discussed in the following section.

Empirical Results

The economic growth theories were tested using regression analysis based on panel data for Chinese provinces between 1998 and 2006 to allow for time- and jurisdiction-specific effects to control for variations over time, business cycle fluctuations, and time invariant regional characteristics.

Table 6.2 reports fixed effect and random effect regression results where tax variables are defined as per capita total tax revenue and per capita various tax indicators. It shows that overall total tax revenue per capita has a statistically significant and

TABLE 6.2
Estimation Results Under Alternative Specifications of Tax Variables for per Capita GDP

	Specification (1) Per Capita Tax and Growth		Specification (2) Tax Structure and Growth	
	Fixed Effect	Random Effect	Fixed Effect	Random Effect
TAX	−0.151	−0.138	—	—
	(7.02)**	(6.58)**		
LITERACY	0.476	0.635	0.277	0.554
	(2.27)*	(3.15)**	(−1.37)	(2.85)**
EDU	1.751	1.655	1.711	1.506
	(9.87)**	(9.25)**	(9.87)**	(8.42)**
FIXCAPITAL	0.048	0.052	0.049	0.058
	(8.08)**	(8.39)**	(8.36)**	(9.07)**
INFRA	−0.185	−0.181	−0.172	−0.189
	(4.47)**	(4.19)**	(4.43)**	(4.47)**
MANU	2.914	2.439	2.267	1.752
	(9.58)**	(8.70)**	(7.33)**	(6.00)**
POPRATE	−1.00	−0.895	−0.827	−0.703
	(2.77)**	(2.35)*	(2.45)*	−1.89
URBAN	0.404	0.453	0.432	0.514
	(5.87)**	(6.24)**	(6.72)**	(7.27)**
PTAX	—	—	−1.975	−2.436
			(3.86)**	(4.55)**
VAT	—	—	0.86	0.784
			(4.13)**	(3.55)**
BTAX	—	—	−0.447	−0.428
			(5.46)**	(4.87)**
ITAX	—	—	0.046	0.897
			−0.15	(3.09)**
Constant	6.884	6.925	7.248	7.186
	(38.11)**	(40.90)**	(39.61)**	(43.11)**
Observations	240	240	240	240
R-squared	0.58		0.79	

NOTE: Dependent variable is per capita GDP in logarithm. Absolute values of z statistics are in parentheses: * = significant at 5%; ** = significant at 1%.

negative relationship with economic growth. When the tax variable is defined as total tax revenue with respect to GDP as a proxy of the overall average tax rate, as in table 6.3, Specification (3), the negative relationship between the tax and economic growth is noticeable and consistent. These results provide empirical evidence that taxation has a distortionary effect on the economy and that a higher overall tax burden leads to lower economic growth. Results in table 6.3 also reveal that various tax indicators do not have equal effects on economic growth. This supports the argument made by Widmalm (2001) that different taxes have different growth effects.

The variable of primary interest, the tax on land and real property in China, has a statistically significant negative relationship with economic growth. Such a negative impact is consistent with different specifications of the models at various mea-

TABLE 6.3
Estimation Results Under Alternative Specifications of Tax Variables as Ratio to GDP

	Specification (3) Tax Burden and Growth		Specification (4) Tax Structure and Growth	
	Fixed Effect	Random Effect	Fixed Effect	Random Effect
TAXRATE	−9.914	−3.733	—	—
	(3.59)**	−1.89		
LITERACY	0.661	1.124	0.237	0.919
	(2.47)*	(4.26)**	(−1.05)	(3.53)**
EDURATIO	21.121	5.373	16.817	0.627
	(6.24)**	(2.03)*	(5.88)**	−0.23
FIX CAPITAL	0.082	0.087	0.078	0.093
	(10.94)**	(12.60)**	(13.59)**	(12.50)**
INFRARATIO	−0.715	−0.438	−0.431	−0.346
	(−1.47)	(−0.79)	(−1.05)	(−0.61)
MANU	3.847	2.001	3.004	1.348
	(9.92)**	(6.00)**	(7.37)**	(2.96)**
POPRATE	−1.816	−1.028	−1.125	−0.899
	(3.76)**	(1.98)*	(2.89)**	−1.7
URBAN	0.264	0.518	0.441	0.703
	(2.92)**	(5.31)**	(5.35)**	(6.37)**
PTAXRATIO	—	—	−53.685	−90.828
			(2.97)**	(3.75)**
VATRATIO	—	—	23,726.89	15,003.42
			(3.10)**	−1.71
BTAXRATIO	—	—	−13,846.56	−1,479.93
			(2.63)**	−0.24
ITAXRATIO	—	—	−8,812.65	30,881.75
			−0.9	(3.13)**
Constant	6.693	6.902	6.937	7.1
	(26.84)**	(27.79)**	(31.52)**	(25.30)**
Observations	210	210	210	210

NOTE: Dependent variable is per capita GDP in logarithm. Absolute values of z statistics are in parentheses: * = significant at 5%; ** = significant at 1%.

sures of this variable as indicated in tables 6.2 and 6.3. Property tax per capita (PTAX) and property tax ratio with respect to GDP (PTAXRATIO) both have negative coefficient estimates and are significantly different from zero. It indicates that higher taxes on land and real property lead to lower economic growth, everything else being the same. This result provides empirical evidence supporting the theoretical prediction that property taxation lowers the return on reproducible physical capital and on nonreproducible land. Thus, increases in land and property tax rates will reduce growth in investment, output, and productivity. This demonstrates that land and property taxes, measured as either per capita tax revenue or the tax burden, result in a decline in economic growth across time and jurisdictions in China.

Taxes on business income are also negatively correlated with economic growth, as predicted by the fixed effect models. This result is in line with the theoretical prediction that taxes on capital and the accumulation of capital, such as corporate income taxes, have adverse growth effects. The findings from this study support the argument that taxes on capital income generated by enterprises lower the return on reproducible capital and thus decrease investment, which in turn decreases the growth rate of output, labor, and productivity. These results are consistent with the findings of Xu (1994) and Turnovsky (1996) that increases in marginal tax rates on income lower the growth rates of output, average productivity, investment, and labor. Income tax rates lower the return on reproducible capital and thus decrease investment.

However, consumption tax as measured by per capita VAT revenue has a statistically significant and positive correlation with GDP. That result may indicate that the VAT may have captured the economic and tax capacity of the residents in a jurisdiction instead of the tax burden borne by individuals. As a result, such variables are positively associated with economic growth. This finding also supports Wildmalm's (2001) results suggesting that the consumption tax is growth enhancing and is consistent with the results of Stokey and Rebelo (1995), which suggest that under most circumstances a consumption or sales taxation does not affect the return on capital and thus has no effect on investment, output, or productivity.

Due to a limited use and selective enforcement of personal income tax in China, the personal income tax variable does not produce a statistically significant effect on growth, because the fraction of this tax with respect to GDP is small. Thus, no clear conclusion can be drawn about the impact of personal income tax from the empirical analysis here.

As shown in tables 6.2 and 6.3, the strong positive coefficient estimate of FIXCAPITAL suggests that fixed capital investment has a significant positive effect on economic growth. Investment in fixed capital is one of the major determinants of GDP growth. Previous studies have predicted that quality of education services and government spending in education result in a more productive labor force and thus a higher economic growth rate. In this study, per capita education spending (EDU) and the share of education spending with respect to GDP (EDURATIO) are both positively correlated with economic growth. Not surprisingly, the quality of the labor force measured by the literacy rate of the jurisdiction has a correct positive sign in tables 6.2 and 6.3, indicating the productive effect of a high-quality labor force. In addition, the higher ratio of the manufacturing sector in the economy and the higher degree of urbanization lead to faster economic growth, as predicted by the empirical models. However, population growth leads to lower per capita economic performance.

The empirical results also support the hypothesis that the economies of the more industrialized (MANU) and urbanized jurisdictions would have a higher growth rate, everything else being equal. Only infrastructure per capita has a wrong sign. That may have been caused by including the fixed capital variable in the model. The negative sign of the population growth rate (POPRATE) on per capita GDP is inconsistent with previous research findings.

To test whether the empirical results are sensitive to the definition of economic growth variable, an alternative measure of dependent variable was employed as the annual growth rate of per capita GDP. Table 6.4 shows the estimation results for the

TABLE 6.4
Estimation Results Under Alternative Specifications of Tax Variables for Annual Growth Rate of per Capita GDP

	Specification (5) Average Tax Rate and Growth		Specification (6) Tax Structure and Growth	
	Fixed Effect	Random Effect	Fixed Effect	Random Effect
TAXRATE	−1.103	−0.991	—	—
	(2.28)*	(4.32)**		
LITERATE	0.038	0.152	−0.017	0.144
	−0.32	(2.28)*	−0.14	(2.15)*
EDURATIO	1.722	1.844	0.618	1.51
	−1.18	(2.79)**	−0.41	(2.02)*
FIXCAPTIAL	0.202	0.228	0.21	0.195
	(3.03)**	(5.79)**	(3.00)**	(4.44)**
INFRARATIO	−0.282	−0.439	−0.214	−0.414
	−1.32	(2.70)**	−1	(2.40)*
MANU	0.401	0.08	0.213	0.107
	(2.22)*	−1.58	−1.02	−1.28
POPRATE	0.115	−0.011	0.205	0.081
	−0.54	−0.06	−0.95	−0.41
URBAN	0.195	0.134	0.201	0.138
	(5.02)**	(4.63)**	(4.61)**	(4.12)**
PTAXRATIO	—	—	−13.689	−5.766
			(−1.97)**	−1.38
VATRATIO	—	—	5.849	−2.468
			−1.85	−1.4
ITAXRATIO	—	—	−2.587	−5.206
			−0.75	(2.18)*
BTAXRATIO	—	—	−0.769	0.675
			−0.4	−0.68
Constant	−0.203	−0.154	−0.136	−0.151
	(2.47)*	(2.55)*	−1.52	(2.32)*
Observations	240	240	240	240
R-squared	0.44		0.45	

NOTE: Dependent variable is annual growth rate of GDP. Absolute values of z statistics are in parentheses: * = significant at 5%; ** = significant at 1%.

effects of average tax rate and various taxes as a ratio to GDP on the annual growth rate of per capita GDP. Not surprisingly, the results shown in table 6.4 are consistent with those predicted by the model using the log of the per capita GDP.

To control for reverse causation between the level of per capita GDP and the various tax variables, the 2SLS estimation method was used to provide more consistent and robust estimation results. Table 6.5 reports the regression results after accounting for a possible simultaneity bias. Such a correction did not lead to noticeable changes in the sign of the variables of our primary interest, indicating that the empirical results of this study are statistically stable and consistent and are not sensitive to different definitions of the variables or alternative specifications of the models.

TABLE 6.5
2SLS Estimation Results Under Alternative Specifications of Tax Variables for per Capita GDP in Logarithm

	Specification (7) Per Capita Tax and GDP		Specification (8) Tax Structure and GDP	
	Fixed Effect	Random Effect	Fixed Effect	Random Effect
TAXPC	−0.062	−0.04	—	—
	(3.09)**	−1.69		
LITERACY	0.426	0.971	0.237	0.919
	−1.91	(4.00)**	−1.05	(3.53)**
EDURATIO	18.023	5.69	16.817	0.627
	(6.35)**	(2.18)*	(5.88)**	−0.23
FIXCAPITALPC	0.075	0.084	0.078	0.093
	(12.19)**	(11.71)**	(13.59)**	(12.50)**
INFRARATIO	−0.77	−0.449	−0.431	−0.346
	−1.83	−0.86	−1.05	−0.61
MANU	3.687	2.225	3.004	1.348
	(10.37)**	(6.60)**	(7.37)**	(2.96)**
POPRATE	−1.252	−0.99	−1.125	−0.899
	(3.25)**	(2.05)*	(2.89)**	−1.7
URBAN	0.382	0.528	0.441	0.703
	(5.30)**	(5.81)**	(5.35)**	(6.37)**
PTAXRATIO	—	—	−53.685	−90.828
			(2.97)**	(3.75)**
VATRATIO	—	—	23.727	15.003
			(3.10)**	−1.71
BTAXRATIO	—	—	−13.847	−1.48
			(2.63)**	−0.24
ITAXRATIO	—	—	−8.813	30.882
			−0.9	(3.13)**
Constant	6.382	6.713	6.937	7.1
	(33.43)**	(30.17)**	(31.52)**	(25.30)**
Observations	210	210	210	210

NOTE: Dependent variable is per capita GDP in logarithm. Absolute values of z statistics are in parentheses: * = significant at 5%; ** = significant at 1%.

Conclusions

This chapter analyzes the interdependent relationship between taxation and economic growth using data from Chinese provinces between 1999 and 2006. The role of the average tax rate and tax structure on economic growth was empirically tested, and empirical evidence produced that the average tax rate has a negative relationship with per capita GDP, after controlling for variables on public expenditure, size of fixed capital investment, demographic and social economic characteristics, and industrial composition, as well as time- and jurisdiction-specific fixed effects. These results support the endogenous growth model, in which tax policy has a permanent effect on level and growth of local and regional economies.

Separating the effects of land and property taxes, business income taxes, personal income taxes, and value-added taxes suggests that not all taxes have equal effects on the economy. The taxes on land and property and business capital income are consistently negatively related to economic growth, but the consumption tax measured by VAT has a positive impact on GDP. It may well be that VAT is a proxy for the tax capacity instead of a tax burden in China; thus, the use of this tax does not negatively affect the return of capital or have any negative impact on economic growth. The personal income tax also does not produce a noticeable negative effect on economic growth. That may indicate that labor supply in China is very inelastic or that the use of such a tax is limited in China and as a result does not alter the labor-leisure choices of individuals or reduce economic activities as in other countries, such as the United States, as studies of U.S. tax policy indicate.

The results of this study demonstrate that the composition of the tax system is as important as the absolute level of taxation for economic growth. The study provides empirical evidence that the tax mix matters and that the overall average tax rate has adverse growth effects in China. It particularly reveals that the taxes on land and property and on business income are distortionary. Increases in such distortionary taxation lower the growth rate of output. This suggests that sustained growth in China could be achieved by lowering the tax burden and overall tax collection; reducing taxes on capital income, physical capital, and land; and mobilizing tax resources with efficient administration and enforcement. Redesign of the tax system through fiscal reform is likely to exert a cumulatively important influence on long-term growth rates and economic development.

REFERENCES

Agell, J., T. Lindh, and H. Ohlsson. 1997. Growth and the public sector: A critical review essay. *European Journal of Political Economy* 13 (1):33–52.

Aghion, P., and P. Howitt. 1992. A model of growth through creative destruction. *Econometrica* 60(2):65–94.

Barro, R. J., N. G. Mankiw, and X. Sala-i-Martin. 1992. Capital mobility in neoclassical models of growth. Paper No. 655. New Haven, CT: Yale University, Economic Growth Center.

Barro, R. J., and X. Sala-i-Martin. 1995. *Economic growth*. New York: McGraw-Hill.

Becsi, Zsolt. 1996. Do state and local taxes affect relative state growth? *Economic Review* (March/April):18–36.

Cashin, P. 1995. Government spending, taxes, and economic growth. IMF Staff Paper 42(2). Washington, DC: International Monetary Fund.

Cass, D. 1965. Optimum growth in an aggregative model of capital accumulation. *Review of Economic Studies* 32:233–240.

Easterly, W., and S. T. Rebelo. 1993a. Fiscal policy and economic growth. *Journal of Monetary Economics* 32:417–458.

———. 1993b. Marginal income tax rates and economic growth in developing countries. *European Economic Review* 37(2):409–417.

Engen, Eric M. and Jonathan Skinner. 1992. Fiscal policy and economic growth. NBER Working Papers 4223. Washington, DC: National Bureau of Economic Research, Inc.

Helms, L. Jay. 1985. The effect of state and local taxes on economic growth: A time series–cross section approach. *Review of Economics and Statistics* 67(4):574–582.

Katz, C. J., V. A. Mahler, and M. G. Franz. 1983. The impact of taxes on growth and distribution in developed capitalist countries: A cross-national study. *American Political Science Review* 77:871–886.

Koester, Reinhard B., and Roger C. Kormendi. 1989. Taxation, aggregate activity and economic growth: Cross-country evidence on some supply-side hypotheses. *Economic Inquiry* 27(3): 367–386.

Koopmans, T. 1965. On the concept of optimal economic growth. In *The econometric approach to development planning*. Chicago: Rand McNally.

Lindh, Thomas, and Henry Ohlsson. 1996. Self-employment and windfall gains: Evidence from the Swedish lottery. *Economic Journal* 106(439):1515–1526.

Lucas, Robert E. 1988. On the mechanics of economic development. *Journal of Monetary Economics* 22:3–42.

Mullen, J. K., and M. Williams. 1994. Marginal tax rates and state economic growth. *Regional Science and Urban Economics* 24:687–705.

Rebelo, S. 1991. Long-run policy analysis and long-run growth. *Journal of Political Economy* 99:500–521.

Romer, P. M. 1986. Increasing returns and long-run growth. *Journal of Political Economy* 94(5): 1002–1037.

———. 1987. Growth based on increasing returns due to specialization. *American Economic Review* 77(2):56–63.

———. 1990. Human capital and growth: Theory and evidence. *Carnegie-Rochester Conference Series on Public Policy* 32:251–286.

Solow, Robert M. 1956. A contribution to the theory of economic growth. *Quarterly Journal of Economics* 70(1):323–351.

Stokey, N. L., and S. T. Rebelo. 1995. Growth effects of flat-rate taxes. *Journal of Political Economy* 103:519–550.

Swan, T. W. 1956. Economic growth and capital accumulation. *Economic Record* 32:334–361.

Turnovsky, S. J. 1996. *Methods of macroeconomic dynamics*. Cambridge, MA: MIT Press.

Widmalm, F. 2001. Tax structure and growth: Are some taxes better than others? *Public Choice* 107:199–219.

Xu, B. 1994. Tax policy implications in endogenous growth models. IMF Working Paper No. 94/38. Washington, DC: International Monetary Fund.

Fiscal Reform and Land Public Finance: Zouping County in National Context

SUSAN H. WHITING

Land has become a key source of fiscal revenue for local governments in China. As the value of land has increased with urbanization and economic development, local governments have sought to exploit their control over land in order to generate both on- and off-budget revenue. Scholars and policy makers have come to refer to this phenomenon as "land public finance." This chapter argues that land public finance is in large part an outgrowth of trends in central-local fiscal relations.

During the course of China's transition from a planned to a market economy, central-local fiscal relations have undergone a series of fundamental reforms. Current challenges grow out of a number of features of the Chinese political economy, the most important of which is the mismatch between the allocation of revenues and the assignment of expenditure responsibilities across levels of government. Local governments—county governments in particular—often lack adequate revenues within the formal fiscal system to finance the wide range of public goods and services they are mandated by higher levels to provide. The mismatch between revenues and expenditure responsibilities leads to heavy reliance on intergovernmental fiscal transfers that, nonetheless, have not yet effectively redressed revenue inadequacy or the high levels of inequality that have emerged in the context of economic reform. This fiscal gap drives additional problems, including the growth of hidden government debts and off-budget funds at the local level. In order to shrink the gap between available revenue and expenditure needs, many local governments rely on the taxes and fees they can generate through their control over the conversion of agricultural land to nonagricultural purposes.

This chapter draws links between these broader trends in the fiscal system and the phenomenon of land public finance. The first section provides background on the evolution of the fiscal system since the initiation of economic reform. The second section examines the nature of revenue and expenditure assignments, intergovernmental fiscal transfers, and the implications of these features of the fiscal system for coping with revenue inadequacy at the local level and equalization across locales. The third section introduces some political factors exacerbating problems in central-local fiscal relations. Finally, the fourth section develops a case study of one of China's "top 100" counties in order to examine how it has exploited land to promote revenue generation in the context of the mismatch between fiscal revenue and expenditure.

Background: Evolution of the Fiscal System

Since the initiation of economic reform in the late 1970s, the fiscal system in China has evolved to better suit the needs of a market economy. At the end of the Maoist era, the fiscal system was characterized by unified incomes and expenditures: Subnational governments turned virtually all tax receipts and profits from state-owned enterprises over to the central government and then looked to the center to meet their expenditure needs (Oksenberg and Tong 1991). In the 1980s, a fiscal contracting system emerged in which local governments handed a fixed quota of tax revenues over to higher levels, while retaining a larger share of above-quota revenues. Local governments gained control of much of their own tax revenues, and, at the same time, the central government devolved responsibility for financing many public goods to local governments (Wong 1991). Several features of this system, in place until 1994, are noteworthy: High marginal revenue retention rates encouraged local governments to promote economic activity within their jurisdictions; periodic renegotiations of the tax quota prompted local governments to hide revenues by shifting them off budget; and the central government sacrificed control over a large share of fiscal revenue. These points are evident in the decline in the central share of budgetary revenue to a low of 22 percent in 1993, and in the rapid growth of extrabudgetary funds as a share of total government expenditure. Revenue mobilization also suffered in the shift from a planned to a market economy, with budgetary revenue as a share of GDP falling to a low of about 11 percent by the mid-1990s.[1] See table 7.1.

Tax and fiscal reforms, implemented beginning in 1994, were designed to address these weaknesses of the transitional fiscal system. The reforms entailed revamping of major tax types, establishment of new institutions to collect taxes, and redistribution of control over revenue between central and local governments.

Centralization and Decentralization in a Unitary State

This section describes the institutions of the current fiscal system and highlights the challenges that have emerged in central-local fiscal relations following implementation of the 1994 reforms. It focuses in particular on the combination of relatively more centralized control over fiscal revenue and highly decentralized expenditure responsibility for many public goods and services. This combination of

---

[1] Corporate income taxes replaced profit remittances by state-owned enterprises as a source of budgetary revenue, but the profits of state-owned enterprises were increasingly competed away by new, nonstate market entrants (Naughton 1995). At the same time, the state's capacity to collect corporate income taxes from new private firms was just beginning to develop (Whiting 2001).

TABLE 7.1
The "Two Ratios," 1984–2005 (percent)

	Revenue as a Share of GDP	Central Share of Total Revenue
1984	22.8	40.5
1985	22.2	38.4
1986	20.7	36.7
1987	18.2	33.5
1988	15.7	32.9
1989	15.7	30.9
1990	15.7	33.8
1991	15.7	29.8
1992	14.5	28.1
1993	12.3	22.0
1994	10.8	55.7
1995	10.3	52.2
1996	10.4	49.4
1997	11.0	48.9
1998	11.7	49.5
1999	12.8	51.1
2000	13.5	52.2
2001	14.9	52.4
2002	15.7	55.0
2003	16.0	54.6
2004	16.5	54.9
2005	17.3	53.1

SOURCE: Ministry of Finance, 2007.

features means that many local governments lack adequate revenue and resort to a range of "creative financing" practices in order to meet their responsibilities.

Decentralization

As a continent-sized country with provinces the size of some European states, China is, of necessity, relatively decentralized. There are five tiers of government, reaching from the center through 32 provincial-, 333 municipal-, 2,861 county- and district-, and 43,255 town- and street-level units, the latter two with an average population of roughly 30,000 people as of 2004. See figure 7.1. Moreover, staffing levels suggest that the real work of governance takes place well below the center. Nearly 60 percent of civil service employees work at the county or township level.[2]

Revenue Assignments and Control

China remains a unitary state, however, in which only the center has the right to legislate taxes. There is a hierarchy of authoritative rules and laws issued by the center: Most authoritative, in principle, are the laws—including tax and budget

---
[2] Xi Liu, *Chinese Civil Service System* (2002), p. 29, as cited in OECD (2005), p. 60.

FIGURE 7.1
China's Government Structure

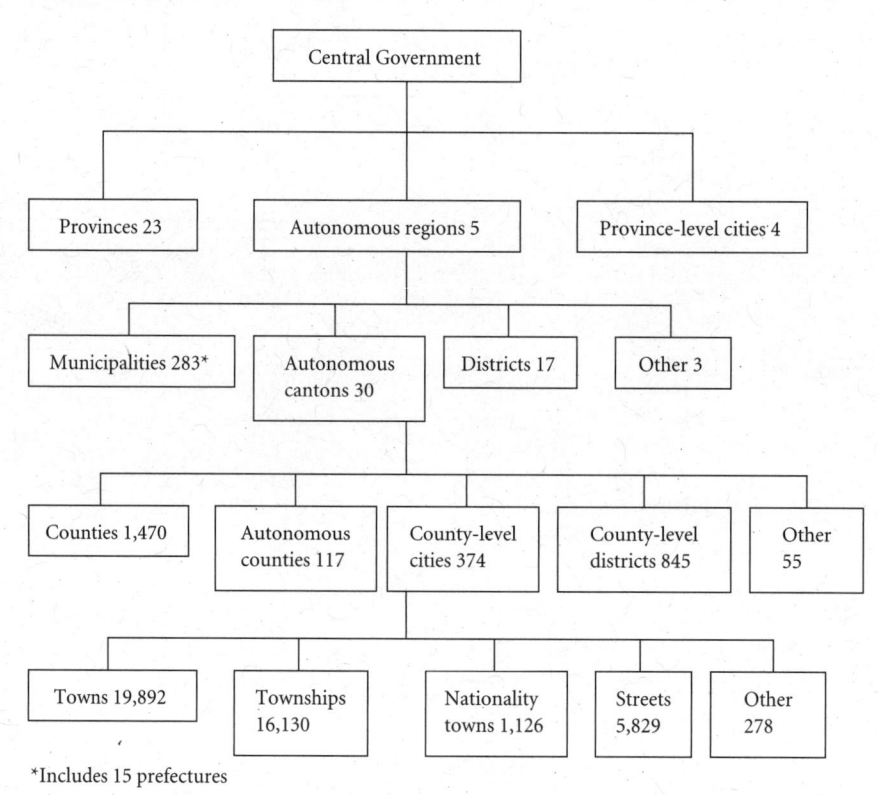

```
                          Central Government
        ┌──────────────────────┼──────────────────────┐
   Provinces 23        Autonomous regions 5    Province-level cities 4
        ┌──────────────┬───────┴───────┬──────────────┐
  Municipalities   Autonomous      Districts 17     Other 3
     283*          cantons 30
   ┌──────────┬──────────┬──────────────┬──────────┐
 Counties  Autonomous  County-level  County-level   Other
  1,470    counties    cities 374    districts     55
             117                      845
   ┌──────────┬──────────┬──────────────┬──────────┐
  Towns    Townships   Nationality    Streets      Other
 19,892     16,130     towns 1,126     5,829        278
```

*Includes 15 prefectures

laws—passed by the National People's Congress (NPC), followed by regulations promulgated by the State Council and rules put out by ministries like the Ministry of Finance (MOF) and then central agencies like the State Administration of Taxation (SAT). Tax bases and rates are set by the central government; local governments have only limited authority to adjust certain tax rates within a certain range in a few instances (OECD 2006). Thus, where formal taxes are insufficient to meet expenditure needs, local governments resort to "creative financing," as illustrated in the later section, "Reliance on Extrabudgetary and Off-Budget Funds."

The center used its authority to implement a new tax-sharing system (TSS) beginning in 1994. This system was designed to recentralize control over revenue following the dissolution of central control during the preceding fiscal contracting regime. As a result, revenue control is now significantly more centralized than expenditure responsibility, since the 1994 reforms left expenditure responsibilities largely unchanged. Under the TSS, taxes are divided into central, local, and shared categories, with major revenue earners controlled primarily by the central government (table 7.2). For example, in 1994, a revamped and expanded value-added tax (VAT) replaced the turnover taxes of the planned economy as a key revenue source; the center assigned the VAT to the shared category, retaining 75 percent and returning 25

TABLE 7.2
Revenue Assignments: Central, Local, and Shared as of 2002

Central	Local	Shared
Tariffs	Business tax (except financial institutions and railroads)	VAT (75% central–25% local)
Consumption taxes	Contract tax	Stamp tax (97% central–3% local)
Income taxes of centrally owned SOEs	Urban land use tax	Corporate and individual income taxes (60% central–40% local)
Import-related consumption taxes and value-added taxes	Urban maintenance and development tax (except financial institutions and railroads)	Resource taxes (offshore oil–central; remainder–local)
Taxes on financial institutions and railroads	Fixed asset investment adjustment tax	
Profits from centrally controlled SOEs	Profits from locally controlled SOEs	
	Housing property tax	
	Agriculture-related taxes	
	Tax on use of arable land	
	Tax on land value increase	

SOURCE: Adapted from OECD, 2006.

percent to the localities. The reallocation of revenue drove the center's share of budgetary funds from 22 percent in 1993 to more than 50 percent since 1994. See table 7.1.

To improve revenue mobilization and to counter incentives for local governments to hide tax revenues from the center, a National Tax Service (NTS) was established as part of the reforms. The NTS has offices at all levels of government and collects both central and shared taxes. The Local Tax Service (LTS), which has offices at the provincial level and below, collects local taxes. These institutional changes were a contributing factor in the reversal of the trend of falling revenues as a percentage of GDP. Budgetary revenue as a share of GDP increased from 10.8 percent in 1994 to 17.3 percent in 2005 (table 7.1). Even so, the center allocates less than 10 percent of GDP—"a relatively low figure for a large and diversified country that faces many major expenditure needs" (Wong 2005a, 13).

Subsequent changes have further centralized control over revenue and reduced local revenues, which are only partially compensated for by increasing intergovernmental fiscal transfers. In 2002, the central government reassigned corporate and individual income taxes from the local to the shared category, with the center taking 50 percent in the first year and 60 percent thereafter. Hubei Province provides an example, where locally controlled income taxes fell from 5.32 billion yuan in 2001 (23 percent of local revenues) to 3.75 billion yuan (15 percent of local revenues) in 2002 (Li 2006).

In 2006, the center abolished the agriculture tax, culminating a series of changes in taxes and fees on rural residents, including the abolition of collective revenues for villages and townships.[3] In Hubei, 3.3 billion yuan from the four agriculture taxes constituted 11 percent of local revenues in 2004 (Li 2006). The complete abolition of the two primary agriculture taxes—again, only partially compensated for by new intergovernmental fiscal transfers—has put a further revenue squeeze on local administrations at the lowest levels of the government hierarchy.

The trend has been toward concentrating fiscal revenues at the highest levels of the system, while expenditure shares have remained roughly the same. Between 1993 and 2003, central and provincial shares of total revenue increased from 35 percent to 66 percent, while their shares of total expenditure increased from 45 percent to only 49 percent (Wong 2006).

The 1994 budget law and subsequent regulations leave subprovincial revenue sharing arrangements largely to the discretion of governments at the provincial level and below, allowing for significant variation across provinces. World Bank (2002) data from 1999 illustrate this diversity. See table 7.3. In the sample provinces, with the exception of Gansu, revenue control shifted upward—a situation referred to as "having a head but no feet" (Li 2006). To address this problem, some provinces have implemented reforms involving direct provincial oversight of county public finance.

Expenditure Responsibilities

From the perspective of expenditure responsibilities, by contrast, China is among the most decentralized countries in the world; nearly three-quarters of all government expenditure takes place at subnational levels. Elsewhere, the average level of subnational expenditure throughout the 1990s was 14 percent for developing countries, 26 percent for transition countries, and 32 percent for OECD countries. Comparable figures among countries with relatively more decentralized fiscal systems were 61 percent for Japan and 46 percent for India (Wong 2005a). Education and health in particular are shouldered to an unusual degree by local governments in China. Estimates of the average share of these expenditures borne by the lowest-level governments (counties and townships) range from 60 percent to 70 percent for education and from 55 to 60 percent for public health (Wang 2006). Two provinces provide more extreme local examples; the county and township levels accounted for 70.5 percent and 74.2 percent of education expenditures in Gansu and Hunan, respectively, in 1999 (Wong 2005b, 12–13).

In recent years, the State Council has promoted a policy of increasing the importance of the county vis-à-vis the township, although—even at the county level—expenditures remain highly decentralized. With the 2001 State Council "Decision on the Reform and Development of Basic Education," for example, payment of rural teachers' salaries is now handled at the county level. Subsequent reforms in the treasury system have similarly shifted the disbursement of salaries of other public

---

[3] Collective revenues include the "three deductions," for public reserve funds, public welfare funds, and management fees, and the "five charges," for rural education, family planning, militia training, rural road construction, and subsidies to entitled groups like disabled veterans. Report on the Work of the Government (2006).

TABLE 7.3
Distribution of Revenues across Subnational Governments as of 1999 (percent)

	China	Hebei	Gansu	Hunan	Jiangsu
Province	21.2	20.6	16.5	13.6	16.2
Prefecture	35.4	23.4	24.9	27.8	43.8
County (joint)	43.4	35.8	39.9	35.2	40.0
Township		20.2	18.7	23.4	0.0
Total	100.0	100.0	100.0	100.0	100.0

Change in Distribution of Revenues Since 1994–1995

	China	Hebei	Gansu	Hunan	Jiangsu
Province	4.1	0.9	−1.4	−0.4	11.3
Prefecture	−5.6	−1.9	−3.0	3.3	−1.8
County (joint)	1.5	2.5	0.6	0.8	−9.5
Township		−1.5	3.8	−3.6	0.0

SOURCE: World Bank, 2002.

employees to the county level (Wong 2005b, 25). As a result, the township level of public finance is becoming "hollowed out."

Ran Tao and Ping Qin (2007, 27–28) write, "Although many townships in rural China have been merged both before and after the rural tax reform, downsizing local bureaucracy has so far been unsuccessful ... even once townships have merged, most of the cadres from the previous townships have kept their posts." Where alternative sources of employment are scarce, local governments may find political risks in downsizing.

The Fiscal Gap

The disjuncture between revenue assignments and expenditure responsibility has left a substantial fiscal gap facing subnational governments. Local taxes and the local portion of shared taxes cover only about 40–45 percent of local fiscal needs. This fiscal gap has generated a relatively high degree of dependence by lower-level governments on fiscal transfers, which grew from 239 billion yuan in 1994 to 1,041 billion yuan in 2004 (Sun 2006). Since the consolidation of the TSS, the central government has dedicated roughly 70 percent of its revenues to fiscal transfers, providing between 40 and 50 percent of local governments' budgetary expenditures. With 40–50 percent of fiscal needs covered by intergovernmental fiscal transfers and another 40–45 percent covered by local and shared taxes, 5–10 percent of fiscal needs remain unmet (Wang 2006). As a result of the existing division of expenditure responsibilities, fiscal deficits are effectively pushed onto lower levels. Local governments, in turn, employ a variety of means to cover their expenditure responsibilities.

Reliance on Extrabudgetary and Off-Budget Funds

One of the most prominent ways local governments cope with revenue inadequacy is by generating revenue outside the formal budget system in the form of extrabudgetary and off-budget funds (Liu and Tao 2007, 167). Extrabudgetary funds are surtaxes, levies, and user charges collected and spent by government agencies in performing duties delegated to them by higher levels (OECD 2006, 19); in recent years, the MOF has begun to exert greater oversight over these funds. In principle, all extrabudgetary funds are public fiscal revenues approved at the central or provincial level and deposited in special fiscal accounts (OECD 2006, 143). In addition, pooled pension funds and unemployment insurance funds are registered and managed as extrabudgetary funds in social security accounts.[4] Extrabudgetary, social security, and government bond expenditures add approximately 7 percent of GDP to official expenditure.

Off-budget funds, by contrast, exist outside effective MOF oversight. There exist no comprehensive data for those funds, but they are reported to rival or even exceed the size of the formal budget for many local governments. The sources of off-budget funds reflect both available revenue "handles"—places where revenue opportunities exist to exploit—and gaps in effective MOF oversight. These sources have shifted over time from enterprise fees to highway fees to land transfer fees and sale of government assets.

According to one study of land fees conducted in 2004, Guangdong, Shandong, Hunan, Zhejiang, and Jiangsu provinces generated the most off-budget funds from land transfers (Ping 2007, 9). Nationwide, these funds were estimated to total 615 billion yuan in 2004, equivalent to roughly 3–4 percent of GDP; they have become a primary source of income for many local governments (p. 9). A MOF study of local land revenues (including primarily land transfer fees) shows that they increased at nearly 70 percent per year on average nationwide between 2000 and 2004 (Zhang 2007). By 2004, county-level governments accounted for 28 percent of revenue and 34 percent of expenditures from this source. Zhang Yanlong concludes that "revenue from land transactions has become a critical revenue source for local governments" (p. 20). Moreover, because these funds lack MOF oversight, they easily shade into corruption; real estate developers, for example, may provide kickbacks to local government officials who make land available at low prices, shortchanging the farmers who lose access to the land in the process. These funds also support legitimate government expenditures, however. According to Li (2006, 42), for example, in Hubei Province the funds derived from land transfer fees are "almost without exception" dedicated to basic infrastructure development. Ping Xinqiao (2006) finds that, compared with budgetary funds, off-budget funds tend to have positive effects on spending for infrastructure and administration but negative or neutral effects on spending for education, agriculture, and other public

---

[4] In 1993, funds belonging to state-owned enterprises, formerly classified as extrabudgetary funds (EBF), were excluded from the definition of EBF. In 1994, 83 types of EBF were redefined as budgetary revenue in a first step toward unifying budgetary and extrabudgetary funds into a single budget. In 1996, 13 major EBF, including vehicle purchase fees, road maintenance fees, road construction funds, were similarly subjected to formal budgetary control (Whiting 1999).

goods. Furthermore, outlays tend to be employed inefficiently—in particular, for increasing the number of administrative staff.

One problem with off-budget funds—including land transfer fees—is that these funds, which constitute an important supplement to budgetary revenues, are most abundant in wealthier areas with the greatest access to budgetary revenues.

Transfer Dependence and Inequality

The fiscal system has failed to address significant and growing regional inequality. The central and western regions enjoyed only 55 and 75 percent, respectively, of the fiscal capacity of the eastern region in 1994, but those figures declined to 43 and 48 percent by the year 2000 (MOF 2007). Such disparities reflect not only the impact of disproportionate growth in the coastal region but also the effect of the TSS. Since the end of the last decade, however, equalization policies have become a higher priority for government policy makers. Resources dedicated to equalization have increased, as the following paragraphs show. Nevertheless, data on per capita budgetary expenditures for the year 2002 reveal a ratio of 8.1:1 for the richest and poorest provincial-level units, with expenditures of 5,307 yuan per capita in Shanghai and 655 in Guizhou (Wong 2005a, 13).[5] Alternative calculations for 2005 indicate per capita budgetary expenditures of 8,008 yuan in Shanghai and 908 in Henan, giving a ratio of 8.8:1 for the richest and poorest provinces (Wang 2006).

Changes in the system of intergovernmental fiscal transfers have slowed the trend toward greater disequalization but have not reversed it. Intergovernmental fiscal transfers are multi-stranded, and only some of the strands are effectively equalizing. The largest element in central government transfers are tax rebates. The main tax rebate, pegged to the growth of VAT and consumption taxes, was negotiated between the center and the provinces in 1993. It was intended to safeguard the immediate interests of powerful localities by preventing any severe decline in revenue after the TSS was implemented. Therefore, it accrues to the benefit of the wealthier provinces (Sun 2006). However, the rebate reflects a shrinking portion of total transfers; it accounted for about three-quarters of central transfers during the mid-1990s, less than half as of 2002, and roughly one-third—or 375.8 billion yuan—in 2005 (Wong 2005a; OECD 2006, 74).

Another large element of intergovernmental fiscal transfers is in the category of earmarked transfers, which totaled 351.7 billion yuan in 2005 (MOF 2007). This category is increasingly broad, reflecting many different government policy initiatives and encompassing funds for such things as major infrastructure development, agricultural development, and development of underdeveloped areas (Song and Shao 2005). With the implementation of the Western Regional Development Initiative beginning in 1999, these funds have been targeted increasingly toward projects in the poorer western and inland regions of the country. A potentially disequalizing element in these transfers is the requirement for local matching funds from local governments in order to access many of these grants.

---

[5] Note that this calculation excludes Tibet.

A wide array of other special transfer funds are also intended to meet specific purposes. For example, the MOF separately reports an earmarked transfer for minority areas, which has risen from 2.5 billion yuan in 2000 to 15.9 billion yuan in 2005, channeling more funds into potentially equalizing uses. Many special transfer funds reflect central government attempts to compensate local governments for the adverse effects of reforms. Social security subsidies include bailouts for local social security schemes as well as subsidies to support payments to laid-off or unemployed workers, which reached or exceeded 50 billion yuan in 2001 and 2002 (Wong 2005a, 15). A wage adjustment subsidy was introduced in 1998 to offset the cost of centrally mandated wage increases for public employees, which has resulted in the doubling of civil servant salaries. Wage adjustment subsidies reached 99.4 billion yuan in 2004 and remained at that level in 2005, according to MOF figures. Elsewhere, this category is reported to have reached 187.3 billion yuan by 2004 (Wong 2005a, 14). "Both the wage increase subsidies and subsidies to social security and welfare programs are transfers aimed at bailing out local governments: meeting payroll, and keeping social security and unemployment schemes from defaulting" (Wong 2005a, 15). This kind of ad hoc public financing has certain attendant weaknesses. As Wong points out, "Rudimentary budgeting practices that allocate subsidies on a per-staff basis continue to encourage adding staff despite national campaigns calling for downsizing the civil service" (p. 15).

With rural tax and fee reform, another special transfer was established to increase the resources of local governments adversely affected by the reforms, providing funds for the payment of primary and middle school teachers' salaries. This rural-tax-and-fee-reform transfer fund has increased rapidly from 8 billion yuan in 2001 to 66.1 billion yuan in 2005 (MOF; Tao and Qin 2007, 21). In 2005, it was supplemented by a special program to aid counties and townships in difficulty. This program operates on the basis of "awards" or "bonuses," allocating 15 billion yuan in 2005 to counties and townships meeting certain criteria—namely increasing tax revenues, reducing government staff, increasing grain production, and running a clean government. These special transfers went primarily to the central (8.31 billion, yuan or 55 percent) and western (5.2 billion yuan, or 35 percent) regions, with only 1.45 billion, yuan or 10 percent, going to the eastern region (MOF 2007).

In 2005, general purpose transfers, intended to be equalizing, totaled 112 billion yuan, with 48 percent going to the western, 47 percent to the central, and 5 percent to the eastern region (MOF 2007). An important element in the rule-based calculation of this transfer is the number of civil servants on the official government payroll, which introduces a bias away from population-based measures of need for public services and reinforces incentives to add to already high government staffing levels (Jieyun Li 2006, 27; Wong 2005a). The impact of general purpose transfers is limited by their small size compared to rebates and earmarked transfers.

In sum, only certain intergovernmental fiscal transfers are equalizing in their effect. Moreover, even with reliance on multi-stranded, intergovernmental fiscal transfers to supplement their own revenues, local governments face a fiscal gap. Localities where land values are higher—the same areas where overall revenue capacity is greater—have the greatest opportunity to engage in land public finance.

As the following section demonstrates, local officials also face political pressures to generate revenues to meet expenditure responsibilities.

Political Factors in Central-Local Fiscal Relations

Several features of the Leninist political system contribute to the tensions and challenges in central-local fiscal relations discussed above. First, top party and government officials at each level of the state hierarchy (e.g., Chinese Communist Party [CCP] secretaries, mayors, county executives) are accountable not to the citizens they govern but rather to the party-state apparatus at the next higher level, which bears the responsibility for both appointing them and evaluating their job performance (Whiting 2004). The performance of leading cadres is monitored and evaluated on the basis of specific performance targets set for them by their superiors in the administrative hierarchy and strongly linked both to monetary incentives in the form of bonuses and to promotion prospects.

These criteria reflect the priorities and concerns of political elites and not necessarily those of the community members. Performance targets often include GDP growth, employment levels, fiscal revenue, exports, and utilization of foreign direct investment (Wu 2006, 11). In some locales, targets more closely mirror the expenditure responsibilities of local cadres, with targets assessing agricultural procurement levels, realized investments in infrastructure, completion rates for nine-year compulsory education, and population growth rates. Cadres pursue targets with a relatively short time horizon—annual evaluation and a three-year term of office for government executives (five years for party secretaries) (Whiting 2004). These features of the political system lead to counterproductive behaviors such as channeling government investment into wasteful, high-profile projects selected for their short-term impacts (Wang 2006; Wu 2006; Ping 2006). This system also creates pressure to go off-budget or incur debt to meet performance targets when budgetary revenues are inadequate.

There are inadequate mechanisms for citizen oversight of their officials. Although citizens participate in the direct election of local People's Congress deputies at the township and county levels, the nomination process is tightly controlled by the CCP. Once in office, local deputies are only nominally involved in the appraisal of government cadres. The role of the People's Congress remains largely symbolic to date—form without substance in the view of some Chinese scholars (Wu 2006, 14). Local governments are agents of higher levels; even in collecting taxes and allocating scarce public resources, their actions reflect the priorities of their superiors—shaped by the mechanisms of cadre evaluation—rather than those of local residents.

Case Study of a "Top 100 Economic Performer"

As one of the top-performing 100 counties in China, in the top 5 percent of counties nationwide in terms of a range of indicators as of 2004–2005, Zouping County in Shandong Province is a model county (NBS 2006).[6] Yet, as recently as 1998, the

---

[6] This case study is based on published sources, cited in the text, and interviews conducted by the author in July 2007. All interviewees were guaranteed anonymity and are cited as "author's interviews" in the text.

county was considered "unexceptional in either the pace and nature of change over the past fifteen years or in its historical or geographic endowments" (Walder 1998, 2). This section indicates that what has changed is the county's ability to exploit land as a resource for economic growth and fiscal revenue. Its location along the new major highway linking the provincial capital of Jinan and the port city of Qingdao has been a boon to the county. Other top-performing counties like this one are concentrated in the coastal provinces of Zhejiang, Jiangsu, Guangdong, and Shandong, where urbanization is progressing at a rapid pace (NBS 2006). According to Peking University scholar Ping Xinqiao (2006, 618), also concentrated in these provinces are government land requisitions, which, in turn, are a major source of on-budget and off-budget revenue and a focus of recent central government policy directives.[7] The following paragraphs examine fiscal practices in Zouping County in light of central policy.

The County in Context

As of 2004, in Shandong Province, the county-level economy with the highest GDP per capita achieved 46,669 yuan, while the lowest reached only 3,457 yuan. Disparity is apparent even within wealthy coastal provinces like Shandong. Consistent with the analysis above, two-thirds of counties in Shandong face difficulties meeting wage obligations, and, following the abolition of the agriculture tax, many townships are described as hollow, relying primarily on intergovernmental fiscal transfers (Zhu 2007).[8] Zouping County is advancing rapidly in this context: 2004 GDP per capita was 21,999 yuan, increasing to 38,029 yuan by 2006. Per capita budgetary expenditure reached 2,365 yuan in 2006, up from 722 yuan in 2002 (Zouping County Statistical Bureau).

Zouping County is located in Binzhou Municipality of Shandong Province, where the county level accounts for the bulk of the economic activity, including 78 percent of GDP and 85 percent of local fiscal income (Zouping County Statistical Bureau). County public finance is under the guidance of the municipal and provincial levels. The local share of corporate income taxes (40 percent) is divided, with 8 percent going to the province and 32 percent going to the county. According to a representative of the county public finance bureau, the province takes 15 percent of the local share (40 percent) of individual income taxes, while the county gets 25 percent (author's interview 2007). The distribution of the business tax is 20 percent to the

---

[7] Similarly, Liu Mingxing and Tao Ran (2007, 169) find that "in richer regions, local governments, especially those at the county and township level, are generally able to provide decent public goods and services to residents and businesses, since they not only enjoy higher tax revenues coming from the development of non-agricultural sectors, but can draw on additional high income from the sale of rights to develop local land...."

[8] In Zouping County, the provincial and municipal levels provided subsidies of 30 million yuan and the county itself added 20 million yuan in subsidies linked to the abolition of the agriculture taxes and collective revenues that left some grassroots areas in fiscal difficulty. As of 2001, there were 13,000 active government employees whose salaries were paid through the county budget; by 2006, the number had increased to nearly 15,000. At the township level, the number of active government employees paid with budgetary funds had decreased from 8,582 in 2001 to 7,535 in 2006, of whom 1,091 were paid by budgetary grants and 6,644 were paid with budgetary subsidies, including 4,865 teachers. As noted above, it may be easier for townships in wealthier counties to downsize, as there may be greater opportunities for alternative pursuits. In 2006, Zouping began paying township public employees directly; however, there remain a small number of township public employees and health care providers who are paid by the township directly.

province, 20 percent to the municipality, and 60 percent shared between the county and township levels according to the level at which the tax-paying enterprise is registered (author's interview 2007). Moreover, the county aggressively competes for ear-marked transfers and provides matching funds from the county level.

The ongoing centralization of control over revenue (such as corporate and individual income taxes) and the abolition of agriculture taxes has affected Zouping, but the effects were smaller in Zouping than in many other counties, in part because of Zouping's ability to readily exploit the value of its land. Locally controlled income taxes accounted for 57 percent of local budgetary revenue in 2001, dropping to 27 percent in 2002, following centralization (table 7.4). The reallocation caused a drop in total revenue in 2002, but by 2003 the county had already recovered, exceeding 2001 local budgetary revenue by nearly 100 million yuan (table 7.5). This rapid recovery was due to the dramatic growth in local VAT and business tax revenues, as well as urban maintenance and construction tax revenue (table 7.6). (See the discussion relating land and taxes, in the section entitled Land Public Finance, below.)

TABLE 7.4
Sources of Budgetary Revenue (percent share of total)

Year	Value-added Tax	Business Tax	Direct Land Taxes*	Income Taxes	Agriculture Taxes	Urban Maintenance and Construction Taxes	Fines	Administrative Fees	Other**	Total
2001	18	8	2	57	4	3	1	2	6	100
2002	26	11	3	27	12	4	1	3	13	100
2003	26	13	4	19	9	8	4	3	14	100
2004	26	13	9	13	3	9	7	3	17	100
2005	34	10	13	9	0	8	1	3	22	100
2006	31	9	16	10	0	6	14	3	10	100

NOTES: *Direct land taxes: urban land use tax, arable land occupation tax, and deed tax. **Other: residual category.

TABLE 7.5
Sources of Budgetary Revenue (level, million yuan)

Year	Value-added Tax	Business Tax	Direct Land Taxes*	Income Taxes	Agri-culture Taxes	Urban Maintenance and Construction Taxes	Fines	Administrative Fees	Other**	Total
2001	62.20	26.00	5.42	196.15	12.68	11.24	3.01	8.13	21.45	346.28
2002	82.52	35.17	10.43	85.62	39.61	14.41	2.61	10.80	41.63	322.80
2003	116.18	56.75	16.61	81.44	39.17	34.59	19.16	12.49	62.15	438.54
2004	151.30	77.57	54.63	75.25	19.70	54.84	38.66	15.96	103.14	591.05
2005	337.77	100.45	125.56	86.25	0.00	81.07	13.02	35.01	224.34	1003.47
2006	435.63	131.32	221.25	140.66	0.00	80.73	201.71	48.21	142.36	1401.87

NOTES: *Direct land taxes: urban land use tax, arable land occupation tax, and deed tax. **Other: residual category.

TABLE 7.6
Sources of Budgetary Revenue (percent increase)

Year	Value-added Tax	Business Tax	Direct Land Taxes*	Income Taxes	Agriculture Taxes	Urban Maintenance and Construction Taxes	Fines	Administrative Fees	Other**	Total
2002	32.7	35.3	92.4	−56.3	212.4	28.2	−13.3	32.8	94.1	−6.8
2003	40.8	61.4	59.3	−4.9	−1.1	140.0	634.1	15.6	49.3	35.9
2004	30.2	36.7	228.9	−7.6	−49.7	58.5	101.8	27.8	66.0	34.8
2005	123.2	29.5	129.8	14.6	0.0	47.8	−66.3	119.4	117.5	69.8
2006	29.0	30.7	76.2	63.1	0.0	−0.4	1449.2	37.7	−36.5	39.7

NOTES: *Direct land taxes: urban land use tax, arable land occupation tax, and deed tax. **Other: residual category.

In Zouping, the county stopped collecting the agricultural special products tax and the slaughter tax after 2002 and the agriculture tax after 2004. In 2004, however, the agriculture tax accounted for only 3.3 percent of county budgetary revenues; thus, the impact was more minimal than in less industrialized localities, where agriculture taxes constituted a larger share of local revenue.

The increase in VAT and other taxes also reflects the growth of the Weiqiao Group, located in Zouping and owner of one of the largest textile plants worldwide. Weiqiao has also diversified into aluminum processing in the county. Overall, it employs approximately 150,000 workers and occupies more than 310 hectares of land in the region in and around Zouping (author's interviews 2007). According to a representative of the National Tax Service, it is the single-largest source of taxes in the county, providing 50–60 percent of tax revenues. In addition, as of 2007, the conglomerate had attracted a large number of related enterprises to the county, including seven additional firms with output valued at over 100 million yuan, 16 with output over 10 million yuan, and 87 with output over 1 million yuan. The growth of the Weiqiao Group is related to the expansion of local development zones (termed "zone fever") occurring in Zouping, as elsewhere (Cartier 2001; see also Liu and Tao 2007, 176).

Land Public Finance

One way local governments—particularly in wealthier, peri-urban areas—cope with revenue inadequacy is by generating revenue through their ability to requisition land "in the public interest" (Land Management Law, Article 2). Local officials cite the creation of job opportunities and new revenue-generating economic activity through conversion of agricultural land to industrial or commercial purposes as a motivation for land transfers. Such land requisitions can generate revenue in at least four ways (Zhang 2007, 24). First, as highlighted during a 2007 Shandong Province state land resources meeting, local governments can use low-priced land to attract investors in industry as a means of increasing GDP growth and taxes. Second, they can promote rapid real estate development, which also generates taxes and other financial opportunities for local governments. Third, county governments can generate land transfer fees. Fourth, they can use land as collateral for loans.

Using Land to Attract Industry

One of multiple land public finance strategies adopted in Zouping is using land to attract core industries. According to several officials interviewed (author's interview 2007), "attracting investment" was a key performance criterion in the county, and "exempting land transfer fees as a preferential policy" was a common measure employed to meet that goal. At the same time, the 2007 Shandong Province State Land Resources Meeting highlighted precisely the problem of local governments reducing or exempting land transfer fees in the name of attracting investment. The meeting called for strict implementation of minimum standards for transfer of land for industrial uses. The same point was made ten years earlier in the 1997 Shandong provincial government's "Notice Regarding Strengthening Collection Management of Transfer Fees for Use Rights over State Land." Article 4 of the notice emphasizes that local governments may not reduce or exempt land transfer fees. However, other local officials in Zouping highlight the "great flexibility" of county policies with respect to land as well as water and electricity (author's interview 2007). These practices and the trends in tax revenue across types are consistent with a strategy of using land to attract industry. Following marked increases in requisitioned land in the early 2000s (table 7.7), Zouping experienced more than a doubling of VAT revenues in 2005 (table 7.6). VAT revenue climbed from 62 million yuan in 2001 (18 percent of total budgetary revenue) to 338 million yuan in 2005, when it accounted for fully one-third of total budgetary revenue (tables 7.4 and 7.5).

Promoting Land Development to Generate Taxes. Like many other counties, Zouping has developed and expanded an industrial park and a development zone. Originally part of the township-level unit of Gaoxin, the development zone is a county-level entity, and the county controls the tax revenue (author's interview 2007). Development began in 2002, from land transferred originally from local farmers. Data on the area of farm land requisitioned is available only from 2004. These data show that from 2004 to 2006, at least 3–5 percent of the county's arable land was requisitioned each year, and that, in each of those years, 80–95 percent of that land came from Gaoxin (table 7.7). A major expansion of the county development zone began with land from Gaoxin (township level) using land transferred from local farmers (author's interview 2007). At the same time, there were reports of frequent protests by affected farmers in the county (Guy Alitto, University of Chicago, personal communication, 2008).

TABLE 7.7
Land Requisitioned at Zouping and Gaoxin, 2004–2006

Year	Zouping Land Requisitioned (mu)	Percent of Arable Land Requisitioned	Gaoxin Land Requisitioned (mu)	Gaoxin Percent of Requisitioned Land
2004	28,249	3.0	26,784	94.8
2005	41,654	4.4	33,193	79.7
2006	45,727	4.8	36,973	80.9

SOURCE: Zouping County Statistical Bureau, *Zouping Statistical Yearbook* (2001–2006).

Economic activity in the development zone already accounted for half the county's fiscal income as of 2007 (author's interview 2007). With respect to direct land tax revenue in Zouping, the urban land use tax, farmland occupation tax, and deed tax together grew from 1.6 percent of local budgetary revenue in 2001 to more than 15 percent in 2006 (table 7.4). Taken together, these taxes exhibited an average annual growth rate of 110 percent from 2001 to 2006 (table 7.6). In terms of revenue sources indirectly linked to land and land development, the construction and real estate sectors alone accounted for nearly 50 percent of all business taxes in 2005 and 2006, the only years for which data are reported for Zouping. One interviewee highlighted the extent to which taxes from the construction industry followed land management policies, policies to attract investment, and the speed of urban construction (author's interview 2007).

Generating Land Transfer Fees. In principle, county governments must use competitive bidding, auctions, or public listings to ensure that land transfers take place at market levels. These policies were laid out in a stream of central documents, including State Council Document 2001 No. 15, State Land Resources Ministry 2002 No. 11, State Land Resources Ministry and Supervision Ministry 2004 No. 71 (Ministry of Land Resources). In 2004 the deadline was set as 31 August, after which local governments were instructed to end negotiated pricing for land for industrial use and implement competitive bidding.

As noted above, according to one study of land transfer fees, conducted in 2004, Guangdong, Shandong, Hunan, and Jiangsu provinces generated the most off-budget funds from land transfers (Ping 2006). The Zouping County land management bureau officially reported stable land transfer fees of about 100 million yuan annually, equivalent to less than 10 percent of 2006 budgetary revenue. However, a special study commissioned by the State Council in another economic "top 100" county found 1.18 billion yuan from land trades in 2003 alone, equivalent to nearly one-quarter of budgetary revenue (Zhang 2007).

Moreover, land transfer fees are supposed to be subject to official fiscal management. Indeed, in 1997, the Shandong provincial government emphasized that the public finance bureau should collect all fees, including all funds over and above compensation for farmers (Shandong Provincial Government 1997). However, in Zouping, officials report that the public finance bureau has no control over these funds (author's interview 2007). In 2006, the State Council Office issued document No. 100, "Notice Regarding Standardizing Management of Income and Expenditures from the Transfer of State Land Use Rights," and the Shandong Provincial Government (2007) followed in June with guidelines for implementation. According to these central and provincial guidelines, income from land transfers may be used for (1) compensation for land takings; (2) land development; (3) supporting agriculture, including social security for farmers; (4) urban infrastructure construction; and (5) other expenditures, including the state land benefit fund (to finance land bank purchases). The guidelines emphasize that the public finance bureau and the land resources bureau are intended to cooperate in submitting land transfer fees for public finance oversight and treasury management.

Since agricultural land must first be converted to state land before being put to nonagricultural uses, and since there is frequently a large gap between the valuation of land for compensation to farmers and the valuation of land for transfer to developers, local cadres can generate and control significant revenues as middlemen in the land transfer process. They subsequently become party to disputes with villagers when villagers raise concerns about the procedures by which land was transferred or about the amount of compensation they receive.

Using Land as Collateral for Debt

The use of banked land as loan collateral for development projects is a fourth important part of land public finance (Zhang 2007, 24). According to Yanlong Zhang (2007, 24), "Land banking centers were built as institutions through which ... governments could monopolize commercial land trades and maximize financial gains." In 2001 Shandong Province authorized the establishment of land banks at the county level and above, following a State Council (2001) directive to strengthen land management. These centers—like Zouping's Land Bank Exchange Center of the Land Resources Bureau—control not only idled urban land but also requisitioned farm land. Fock and Wong (2008, 26) show that "local governments are increasingly taking out loans using requisitioned land as collateral through the creation of such 'land banks,' and these loans have become an even greater source of funds than the land-use right transfer fees in many areas."

In Zouping, land and new debt are linked at the township level, but not only as straightforward collateral as suggested in many contemporary policy discussions. For example, the county promoted new school construction at the township level but provided "policies not money" to finance construction (author's interview 2007). In 2006, one town invested more than 20 million yuan (total town budgetary expenditures were 19 million in 2006) in a four-building middle school campus. The construction company in essence loaned funds equivalent to the cost of construction to the town, which the town intends gradually to repay. The special policy provided by the county is to allow the town to move all middle school students to the new campus and allow the town to control the land transfer fees from current and future transfers of land from the old school sites. In 2007 the town transferred part of the land to finance some current expenditures, but it is holding the majority of the land in anticipation of appreciating land values as the urban core expands. The town plans to repay the construction loan once it realizes the value of the land from the old school sites.

Summary

The survey of official revenue sources and expenditure responsibilities at the center of this chapter highlights how centralization of control over fiscal revenue has created a wide fiscal gap between revenue and expenditure for many local governments. The gap is only partially addressed by growing intergovernmental fiscal transfers, leaving local governments to engage in a range of "creative financing" approaches, focused increasingly on land. The case study of one county in Shandong

Province shows how a favorably located county has used land to generate revenues to close the fiscal gap. At the same time, the discussion notes that the ability to generate off-budget revenues—from land and other sources—is unevenly distributed, leaving less favorably situated counties struggling to pay salaries and provide public goods and services.

Acknowledgments

The author would like to thank the participants in the Conference on Local Public Finance and Property Taxation in China, organized by the Lincoln Institute of Land Policy, especially Yu-Hung Hong and Joyce Man. The first sections of this chapter are drawn from work done for the International Conference on Intergovernmental Fiscal Relations in China, organized by the National Committee on U.S.-China Relations and Renmin University of China, as reported in Susan H. Whiting, "Central-Local Fiscal Relations in China," *China Policy Series* (No. 22), April 2007, and used with permission.

REFERENCES

Brandt, Loren, Scott Rozelle, and Matthew A. Turner. 2004. Local government behavior and property rights formation in rural China. *Journal of Institutional and Theoretical Economics* 160(4):627–662.
Cartier, Carolyn. 2001. "Zone fever," the arable land debate, and real estate speculation: China's evolving land use regime and its geographical contradictions. *Journal of Contemporary China* 10(28):445–469.
Fock, Achim, and Christine Wong. 2008. Financing rural development for a harmonious society in China. World Bank Policy Research Working Paper No. 4693. Washington, DC: World Bank (August).
Land Management Law of the People's Republic of China, adopted 1986, amended 1998. http://www.china.org.cn/english/environment/34345.htm.
Li, Bo. 2006. Tax jurisdiction division between central and local government: Hubei Province as an example. Unpublished manuscript. School of Public Finance and Taxation, Zhongnan University of Economics and Law, Wuhan.
Li, Jieyun. 2006. Looking at intergovernmental fiscal relations from the perspective of local public finance. Unpublished manuscript. Guangxi Province Public Finance Bureau.
Liu, Mingxing, and Ran Tao. 2007. Local governance, policy mandates and fiscal reform in China. In *Paying for progress in China: Public finance, human welfare, and changing patterns of inequality*, eds. Vivienne Shue and Christine Wong, 166–189. London: Routledge.
Ministry of Finance (MOF). 2007. http://www.mof.gov.cn/zhengwuxinxi/caizhengshuju/index_9.htm (in Chinese).
Ministry of Land and Resources. *Regulations on the invitation of bids, auction, or listing for transfer of use rights over state land*. Beijing.
National Bureau of Statistics (NBS) of China. 2005. *China statistical yearbook*. Beijing: China Statistics Press.
———. 2006. 2005 Top 100 counties nationally basically stable but rankings of top 10 change. http://www.stats.gov.cn/tjfx/fxbg/t20060930_402355417.htm.
Naughton, Barry. 1995. *Growing out of the plan: Chinese economic reform, 1978–1993*. New York: Cambridge University Press.
OECD (Organisation for Economic Co-operation and Development). 2005. *Governance in China*. Paris: OECD Publishing.

———. 2006. *Challenges for China's public spending: Toward greater effectiveness and equity.* Paris: OECD Publishing.

Oksenberg, Michel, and James Tong. 1991. The evolution of central-provincial fiscal relations in China, 1971–1984: The formal system. *China Quarterly* 125 (March):1–32.

Ping, Xinqiao. 2006. An estimate of the scale of "Land Public Finance" in China. *Peking University Chinese Economy Research Center Bulletin* 56.

———. 2007. China's local budget system. *China Development Research Foundation Report*, 30.

Report on the Work of the Government delivered by Premier Wen Jiabao at the Fourth Session of the Tenth National People's Congress. March 5, 2006. http://english.gov.cn/2006-03/14/content_227247.htm.

Shandong Provincial Government. 1997. Notice regarding strengthening collection management of transfer fees for use rights over state land. http://www.southcn.com/law/fzzt/fgsjk/200511140115.htm.

———. 2001. Methods for Banking State Land. http://shandong.gov.cn/art/2005/11/14/art_9194_84.html.

———. 2007. Opinion Regarding Implementation of State Council Office 2006 Notice No. 100, http://www.law110.com/law/32/shandong/law1102006222134.htm.

Song, Chao, and Shao Zhi. 2005. Research on the question of the scale of intergovernmental fiscal transfer in China. *Local Public Finance Research* 1 (in Chinese).

State Council. 2001. Notice on strengthening the management of state-owned land assets. No. 15.

State Council Office. 2006. Notice regarding standardizing management of income and expenditures from state land use rights transfers. No. 100.

Sun, Kai. 2006. Intergovernmental fiscal transfer payment system in China: Issues and reforms. Paper presented at the International Conference on Intergovernmental Fiscal Relations in China, Renmin University, Beijing (July 10–11).

Tao, Ran, and Ping Qin. 2007. How has rural tax reform affected farmers and local governance in China? *China & World Economy* 15(3):19–32.

Walder, Andrew. 1998. *Zouping in transition.* Cambridge, MA: Harvard University Press.

Wang, Yongjun. 2006. Improving the division of revenues among levels of government. Paper presented at the International Conference on Intergovernmental Fiscal Relations in China, Renmin University, Beijing (July 10–11).

Whiting, Susan H. 1999. The institutionalization of fiscal reform in China: The problem of extra-budgetary funds. Presented at the Annual Meeting of the Association for Asian Studies, Boston (March 11–14).

———. 2001. *Power and wealth in rural China: The political economy of institutional change.* New York: Cambridge University Press.

———. 2004. The cadre evaluation system at the grassroots: The paradox of party rule. In *Holding China together,* eds. Barry Naughton and Dali Yang. New York: Cambridge University Press.

Wong, Christine P. W. 1991. Central-local relations in an era of fiscal decline: The paradox of fiscal decentralization in post-Mao China. *China Quarterly* 128 (December): 691–715.

———. 2005a. Can China change development paradigm for the 21st century? German Institute for International and Security Affairs Working Paper FG 7. Berlin: German Institute for International and Security Affairs (April).

———. 2005b. Decentralization and governance in China: Managing across levels of government. Paper prepared for the OECD, revised. Paris: OECD (August).

———. 2006. Central-local fiscal relations in China. Presented at the International Conference on Intergovernmental Fiscal Relations in China, Renmin University, Beijing (July 10–11).

World Bank. 2002. China: National development and sub-national finance report No. 22951-CHA, Washington, DC, (April).

Wu, Hao. 2006. Reform of governance and transformation of functions of local governments in China. Unpublished manuscript. Jilin University, Changchun.

Zhang, Yanlong. 2007. Urban entrepreneurialism. Unpublished manuscript. Duke University, Durham, NC.
Zhu, Konglai. 2007. Problems of and approaches to county economic development in Shandong Province. *Macro-Economic Management*, 57–61.
Zouping County Statistical Bureau. 2001–2006. *Zouping statistical yearbook*.

8

The Path to Property Taxation

JOHN E. ANDERSON

The Chinese fiscal system has undergone major changes in recent years and continues to foment. A major policy issue currently focuses on the potential move away from a system of taxes and fees, often applied at the point of development, to a unified ad valorem property tax levied on an annual basis. This chapter examines the implications of such a policy regime change and presents an analysis of the effects of real estate taxes and fees on urban land and housing development using a dynamic framework of analysis developed in Anderson (1986; 2005) and Turnbull (1988; 2005a; 2005b). Investment incentive effects of taxes and fees are analyzed as they affect both when and how urban development occurs. The case of a land value tax and the case of an improvements tax are considered. Policy insights based on the analytic results for both fees and taxes are provided for the current Chinese situation. The final section of the chapter includes policy implications of alternative real estate tax and fee regimes, with special emphasis placed on the transition path involved in moving from a regime of ad hoc real estate taxes and fees to a unified property tax regime.

Chinese Transitions

With the founding of the socialist centrally controlled economic system in China in 1949, urban land was nationalized and controlled by the state. Land transactions were illegal. Local governments allocated land as a productive input to producers and did so via directives. There was no reliance on market allocation or attention paid to prices. Under strict socialist principles urban land was not considered a commodity, no individual property rights were recognized, and no economic transactions involving land were permitted. In 1988, however, the constitution was amended to legalize the transfer of land use rights. Starting at that time, the land market in China began to develop as leasehold property rights were recognized.

Reforms and Attitudes About Land

According to Zhu (2005), since 1978 there have been three distinct eras of economic reform and accompanying attitudes toward land: (1) from 1978 to 1987 land was treated as a free good, as a necessary but unpriced productive input required to meet central plan output targets; (2) from 1988 to 1992 greenfield land sites were developed extensively, and land was considered a valuable commodity; and (3) from 1993 to the present time brownfield land sites have been brought into market allocation by Chinese work units called *danwei*.

Since 1988, when the National People's Congress approved a constitutional amendment recognizing the right of transferring land use under the law, market principles have potentially played a role in allocating land among competing users. Public land leasing is now legal and common as municipal governments lease land to developers and land users for a fixed time period in exchange for a payment.

In the Chinese system, leaseholds can be acquired through tender, auction, or negotiation. Many leases are granted via negotiation rather than competitive tenders or auctions, however. As a result, competitive market prices for land are still not pervasive. Zhu (2005) cites the example of the fast-growing city of Shenzhen over the period 1988–1999, in which 36.4 square kilometers of land were allocated through leasing. Of that total land area, 97.7 percent was allocated by negotiation, 2.0 percent by tender, and just 0.3 percent by auction. Zhu's conclusion is that "the old system of free allocation of land survives in the guise of land leasing by negotiation" (p. 1373). In an economic efficiency sense, it is important that land leasing and land allocation processes be improved in order to capture welfare improvements in the Chinese economy. Deng (2002; 2005) has analyzed the effect of land leasing in the Chinese context and demonstrated that leasing can be welfare improving. He uses a full-blown theoretical model of an urban economy in the Chinese setting in developing his results. In addition, he argues that land leasing can play an important role in the endogenous evolution of urban institutions essential to urban development in an advanced economy.

Transition to Market Allocation of Real Estate

Currently in China many aspiring families find it difficult to purchase a private home to improve their living situation. Housing prices have been high and rising rapidly. Affordability has been a major concern. Popular news accounts such as Xu (2004) identify the cause of high housing prices as the government's requirement that home buyers pay all taxes and fees at once, including land-leasing fees, at the time the house is purchased. Developers incorporate these taxes and fees into the purchase price of the house. In Beijing, for example, the result is that the price of a 60-square-meter apartment unit is 360,000 yuan (US$43,373), which is more than 10 times the average annual income for an ordinary family. In response, the government has proposed a policy switch to levy a single unified real estate tax as a replacement for the present system of taxes and fees—a concept introduced at the Third Plenary Session of the 16th Central Committee of the Chinese Communist Party in October of 2003.

Of course, if there were well-developed capital markets, the inclusion of lump-sum taxes and fees at the time of a house purchase would not necessarily be problematic. It would simply mean that the buyer would finance a larger amount to buy the house and pay it off over time. With efficient capital markets we would not expect any difference in the present value of the house price. In the Chinese context, however, there is an absence of well-developed financial markets. Credit-constrained families are priced out of the housing market altogether.

While market reforms are transforming China in many ways, in the real estate sector reforms are not yet complete. A little more than a decade ago, Walker and Hin (1994) wrote that China's economic modernization had led to the emergence of an embryonic real estate market. Li (1997) describes how the initiation of private land use rights in China caused rapid changes in land markets. Within the context of market principles beginning to allocate land, however, there is a land allocation legacy left by the socialist practice of planned allocation. The application of market principles where the initial conditions reflect planned allocation, rather than market allocation, yields a hybrid result. Han (1998) has emphasized that during the transition from a planned economy to a market-oriented system, the relevant economic agents have been enterprises, businesses, and organizations—not individuals.

The stock of traditional state-owned properties is shrinking as the stock of private market properties grows, but the transition has not yet yielded a mature housing market. Zhang (2001) describes how the government hopes to completely introduce a market mechanism into the housing sector, but at present most housing is still purchased by work units. They purchase homes at market prices and then resell the homes to their employees at affordable prices. In this way, the work units affect both the housing and the labor markets, altering the market outcomes. Zhang maintains that the most obvious structural change needed for further progress of the Chinese housing market is the development of a mortgage finance system. Newell et al. (2005) demonstrates that over the period 1995–2002 Chinese office markets and real estate companies underperformed other asset classes on a risk-adjusted basis.

Due to the high and rapidly rising house prices, the Chinese government has attempted to cool down the real estate market. For example, Areddy (2006) reports that new rules have been implemented to slow foreign investment in local real estate markets. The rules were issued jointly by six government agencies, including the central bank. Foreign property buyers are now required to provide at least 50 percent of the capital (increased from 35 percent previously) up front for investments of at least $10 million. In addition, purchases of apartments are limited to overseas nationals who actually live in China. While foreign purchases of property in China only amounted to $3.4 billion in 2005, according to Chinese government data cited by Areddy, foreign spending has been growing. Beijing is apparently worried that foreign investment is pricing many Chinese families out of the housing market, causing house price inflation. China's government also reportedly believes that in implementing these new rules, it is encouraging long-term investment in a controllable way, rather than chaotic short-term investment. Concern for the development of free real estate markets is justified on the basis of the statement by President Hu that the government must "thoroughly control" fixed-asset investment.

China's emerging real estate market is not a robust free market in which the invisible hand allocates resources. Rather, it is an emerging market situation where at present ambiguities in the definition and enforcement of property rights limit the full development of markets. Despite the nascent character of real estate market development in China, there is clear evidence that market forces are at work. For example, Bao, Glasock, and Zhou (2007) report empirical evidence of an emerging land market in Beijing that follows the traditional urban economic models to a large extent. Recent popular news reports, such as that of the UPI (2007), indicate that the primary motivation for China's consideration of property tax adoption is to control skyrocketing housing prices, especially in Beijing. The property tax is scheduled to be adopted on a trial basis in some regions and major cities. Interestingly, the UPI story quotes a report from the National Economic Research Institute, China Reform Foundation, saying that the variety of taxes levied on developers in the past have been passed on to purchasers when the properties were sold. The current policy debate in China is focused on how potentially to transform the current system of up-front fees and taxes into a unified property tax system.

Reforms and Taxes

Parker and Thornton (2007) characterize fiscal developments in modern China as groping toward a fiscal system capable of providing a coherent framework for improving accountability of the government's use of public funds. This process has involved a period of decentralization in the 1980s, followed by a recentralization regime that began in 1995. Decentralization reforms permitted local governments to keep marginal increases in tax revenue, providing incentives to pursue economic growth policies. Subsequent recentralization of revenue sources, while retaining decentralized expenditures, resulted in large fiscal gaps. Subsequent reform of the fiscal transfer system confronted local governments with hard budget constraints in order to resolve this problem.

Tao and Liu (2005) provide an overview of taxation in China, including estimates of both rural and urban residents' tax burdens over the period of the 1990s. They find that for urban households the main tax burden came from indirect taxes based on consumption of goods and services. Personal income taxes contributed a very small additional burden. For rural households, they found that the main components of the tax burden were from direct taxes, including the agricultural tax, local fees, and education charges. They also found that while rural household income and consumption were much lower than those of urban households, rural households were taxed more heavily relative to their incomes. Furthermore, they estimated that the taxes paid by rural households were much more regressive than those paid by urban households.

In part to solve the problem of rural farmers' tax burdens, the Chinese government introduced a rural tax reform in 2002 that was intended to remove all informal fee charges by local governments while retaining the formal agricultural tax. Those fees were eliminated in 2006. Along with the elimination of local fees came an increase in transfers from the central government to local governments. In 2005 Premier Wen Jiabao made a promise at the People's Congress Annual Meeting to remove all agricultural taxes over a three-year period. The effect of such a reform, if implemented fully, would be to make local governments more reliant on the central government for transfers. This situation perpetuates the current growth-centered development strategy, according to Liu and Tao (2004), that imposes central government development policy mandates on local governments.

Tax-for-Fee Reform

Chinese fiscal reforms have emphasized local government investment in infrastructure. Luo et al. (2007) and Lin, Tao, and Liu (2006) describe a series of reforms that have attempted to provide a solid basis for the rural economy's fiscal system. In the early 1980s a decentralization reform occurred, under which a fiscal contracting system was promoted. The core idea of this reform effort was to improve incentives for revenue generation at the local level. As this reform effort advanced in the late 1980s and early 1990s, however, the share of central government revenues fell sharply as local government revenues rose. With that development, a second round of reform was implemented, known as the recentralization reform. Under this regime the system of tax sharing was strengthened. The central government share of revenues rose dramatically under this reform. Problems remained, however, in the fiscal system. In particular, neither of these reform efforts addressed the issue of local government fees. With mandates to improve infrastructure and a declining share of revenues in the recentralization reform, local governments were under pressure to find revenues elsewhere. Tao and Liu (2005) demonstrate that local fees grew during this time, accounting for a rising share of the per capita income of rural residents. By the late 1990s the situation became untenable. The response was a third round of reform, known as the tax-for-fee reform.

The tax-for-fee reform effort attempted to put in place a standardized tax system to replace the system of various local fees imposed on farmers. In exchange for losing local fee revenue, villages were supposed to use the tax revenues provided to invest in local infrastructure. Indeed, villages were mandated to invest in infrastructure using the county-level government transfers. After a pilot program in 2001 testing this reform effort in Anhui Province, the 2002 tax-for-fee program was officially launched. Luo et al. (2007) report that the program reduced local fees from 30 yuan per capita in 2000 to 0 yuan per capita in 2004. Transfers from higher-level governments down to the village level only replaced about half of the lost local government fees, however. Revenue from transfers rose from 5 yuan per capita in 2000 to 22 yuan per capita in 2004. At the same time, there has been increased demand for investment in public goods by farmers. Luo et al. (2007) report that the most common village infrastructure projects are for (1) roads and bridges; (2) school construction; (3) irrigation and drainage; (4) drinking water; (5) community public address systems; (6) recreation centers; and (7) health clinics.

Current System of Real Estate Taxation

China's State Administration of Taxation (SAT) provides a catalog of the various taxes that currently apply to real estate. Among the 26 taxes levied in China the following taxes apply to real estate:

- Value-added tax.
- Land appreciation tax.
- Farmland occupation tax.
- Transfer tax.
- House property tax.
- Urban and real estate tax.
- City maintenance and construction tax.
- Stamp tax.
- Income tax.

In addition, local governments apply various fees to real estate transactions. For example, in Shanghai there are real estate fees, including (1) transaction handling and registration fees, applying to the purchase of new commercial housing, real property transactions, rental property, and property exchange; (2) public notary and land measurement fees; and (3) other fees such as appraisal broker, auction, and exchange fees. In Beijing, the Local Taxation Bureau describes 20 forms of taxation in its overview of the Chinese tax system.

Presently, the property tax on houses is applied in cities, county capitals, townships, and industrial and mining districts. The tax liability is computed as 1.2 percent of the original value of the property less an exemption amount ranging between 10 and 30 percent. For rental houses, the tax liability is 12 percent of rental income. There are many exemptions to the property tax, including houses owned by individuals for nonbusiness use (e.g., an owner-occupant exemption). The urban real estate tax applies only to property owned by foreign enterprises or Chinese enterprises with foreign investment. The tax is computed either as 1.2 percent of the value of the house or as 18 percent of the rental income of the house. Newly constructed houses are exempt from the tax for three years. The land appreciation tax is applied at progressive rates ranging from 30 to 60 percent at the time of land transfer transactions.

While there are many specific questions of interest regarding the current array of taxes applied to real estate, we will focus on two fundamental issues: What are the economic impacts of fees and property taxes on housing development, and what would likely happen in a policy regime switch from up-front fees to property taxes?

A Model of Land Leasing and Urban Development

Basic Land Lease

As the above review indicated, many local government units in China are financing the provision of public goods and the expansion of urban infrastructure by leasing land. By leasing government-owned land to developers, the local government entity generates a revenue stream that can be used to pay for infrastructure projects in the community. As practiced in China, there is usually no direct link between the lease required for a given plot of land and the infrastructure provided for that plot (e.g., streets, water, lighting, curbs and gutters). Typically, the local government leases the land for a fixed term of 50 years.

Suppose that the government decides to lease a plot of land at a fixed lease payment w per year for a total of T years. The value V of the stream of lease payments over time can be expressed as follows,

$$V(T) = \int_0^T w e^{-rt} dt, \qquad (1)$$

where w is the periodic lease payment required, r is the discount rate, e is the exponential function, and T is the fixed term of the lease. Solving equation (1) provides the following expression for the value of the lease,

$$V(T) = \left(\frac{w}{r}\right)[1 - e^{-rT}]. \qquad (2)$$

This expression indicates that the value of the lease is the capitalized value of the annual payment stream as if it were a perpetuity (w/r), scaled down by the term to account for the finite lease term T. Consider a case where the discount rate is $r = .03$, the term of the lease is $T = 50$ (typical lease term), and $w = 1$. Given these parameter values, the value of the lease is $V = 25.9$. That is, for each yuan required in annual lease payment w, the value of the lease V is 25.9 yuan. Obviously, the present discounted value of the lease payment stream is less than the nominal value of the payments ($wT = 50$). Simple leases such as this are being used pervasively by Chinese local governments to generate revenue.

We know that Chinese local governments often lease land at below-market rates, which results in a reduced revenue stream. If the annual market lease rate is w_m and the corresponding value of the lease is V_m, we can write the lost revenue expression as,

$$V_m(T) - V(T) = \frac{(w_m - w)}{r}[1 - e^{rT}]. \qquad (3)$$

Notice that a below-market rate lease price simply scales down the value in a linear fashion. For example, if $w = .1 w_m$, reflecting the situation where the local government is leasing the land for one-tenth of its market lease price on an annual basis, the government is foregoing nine-tenths of the lease value.

While a simple lease such as this generates a payment stream over time, describing the lease in this way does not answer two fundamental questions: (1) what determines the annual lease payment w? and (2) what determines the choice of lease contract length T? At present, Chinese local governments are not using optimal policies in the choice of either parameter, as discussed above. Hence, they are not optimizing, in terms of maximizing the value of the lease, and consequently, they are not capturing the full potential of financing to fund infrastructure improvements. Of course, they may not want to capture the full value of the property if they wish to move away from government ownership of land.

Miceli, Sirmans, and Turnbull (2001) have shown that the legal design of a lease contract affects the value of the leased asset. Furthermore, they have shown that an efficiently designed lease involves elements of both property and contract law. As a result, in common law countries the law of leases typically falls into the nexus between these two areas of common law. Empirical evidence on the link between lease terms and asset prices can be found in the literature. For example, Janssen

(2003) has demonstrated that when governments lease land to developers for income-producing urban apartment buildings, as opposed to selling the land with freehold tenure, there is a negative impact on the price of the apartment buildings. His evidence from Stockholm, Sweden, confirms that the market is quite systematic in its approach to pricing in this regard. We expect that the fewer land rights retained by the government and the more likely the lease is to be renewed, the smaller will be the land lease price discount. Grenadier (2005) provides a unified equilibrium analysis for the valuation of commercial real estate leases, including explicit land value expressions.

The choice of lease term T is also an important issue. At present, when local governments in China grant leases they are for $T = 50$ years in exchange for a stream of lease payments. In this way, the government retains ownership of the land but earns a revenue stream that it can use to fund public infrastructure improvement or pay operating expenses. Since this practice is relatively new, little analysis has been performed on its consequences.

Grenadier (2005) has developed a lease model that provides closed-form solutions for equilibrium land values, building values, and the term structure of the lease. His model demonstrates that the slope of the term structure of T depends crucially on the extent of competition among developers. For a given lease term T, the more competitors in the industry, the lower is the equilibrium rent. For a given number of competitors, the term structure of the lease T may be upward sloping ($n = 4$ case), single-humped ($n = 6$ case), or downward sloping ($n = 20$ case). His model results are intuitive based on an expectations hypothesis. Long-term lease rates must be structured to leave both landlords and tenants indifferent between two alternatives: (1) signing a long-term lease; and (2) the expected outcome of rolling over a series of short-term leases. With just a few competitors there is a weak supply response to increased rents, permitting short-term rents to rise with demand. With an intermediate number of competitors expected, short-term rents can rise, but competitive pressure leads to increased supply eventually. With a high degree of competition, expected short-term lease rates cannot rise very much due to rent increases being met by increased construction.

Optimal Development: Basic Model

We begin with a basic model of optimal development in which we assume that the local government owns the land and acts as the developer or leases the land to a developer.[1] The developer must decide both when to convert the undeveloped land to a developed use and how best to develop the land. The two decisions that have to be made are the time at which to develop and the structural density (measured in units of capital per unit of land) of the development. We begin describing the model by defining the essential variables and functions involved in these two decisions.

Let S be the structural density for developed land, where density is measured in units of capital per acre of land. The function $R(S,t)$ is the land rent function, which represents the upper envelope of bid rents for competing land uses at time t with

---

[1] The basic model here is adapted from Anderson 2009.

structural density S. The rent function is assumed to be (1) increasing in $S(R_S > 0)$; (2) concave in $S(R_{SS} < 0)$; and (3) increasing in $t(R_t > 0)$. The land rent at time t for undeveloped land is w, the discount rate is r, and T is the time at which the land is developed. Development is costly, as captured by the cost function $C(S)$, where cost is a function of the structural density S. We assumed this function is increasing in structural density ($C_S > 0$) and weakly convex ($C_{SS} \geq 0$).

With these basic assumptions, we can write the present value of the return to a parcel of land as the sum of two components: (1) the land rent earned prior to development; (2) the land rent earned subsequent to development, given that development occurs at time T and structural density S, less (3) the present value of the development cost $C(S)$:

$$V(S,T) = \int_0^T we^{-rt}dt + \int_T^\infty R(S,t)e^{-rt}dt - C(S)e^{-rt} \qquad (4)$$

The developer's problem is to maximize $V(S,T)$ by choosing the optimal structural density S and time of development T. This optimization problem has two first-order conditions corresponding to the optimal choices of S and T. First, we have the optimal structural density condition:

$$\int_T^\infty R_S(S,t)e^{r(T-t)}dt = C'(S) \qquad (5)$$

This condition for the optimal structural density requires that the discounted present value of the added rent due to greater density equal the marginal cost of the added density. Second, we have the optimal timing condition:

$$rC(S) + w = R(S,T). \qquad (6)$$

This condition for the optimal development timing requires the developer to wait until the annualized cost of development plus the opportunity cost of the land equals the land rent from development. The left-hand side of equation (6) is the marginal benefit (*MB*) of waiting to develop, including both the interest cost of development and the opportunity cost of the land given by its undeveloped land rent. The right-hand side of (6) is the marginal cost (*MC*) of waiting to develop, which is the forgone developed rent.

Figures 8.1 and 8.2 illustrate the choice of both S and T. The upper panel of each figure illustrates the optimal timing condition with the choice of T depending on the *MB* and *MC* of waiting an additional period. *MB* is the cost of capital $rC(S)$ plus the income earned in agricultural or predevelopment land use w. According to Turnbull (2005b), the slope of *MB* depends on the sign of S', or the slope of the *dd* curve. If competing demands for alternative land uses result in a lower (higher) current structural density than will be the case with future best use, then $R_{St} > 0$ ($R_{St} < 0$) and the density demanded (*dd*) curve is rising (falling) over time. The *MB* curve is upward sloping as shown in figure 8.1 when *dd* is rising and downward sloping as shown in figure 8.2 when *dd* is falling. *MC* is the forgone developed rent $R(S,T)$. So the optimal time to develop is that time T where *MB* = *MC*. We assume that the second-order condition also holds.

FIGURE 8.1

Effect of an Increase in the Marginal Cost of Waiting on Development Timing and Density When Density Demanded (*dd*) Is Rising Over Time

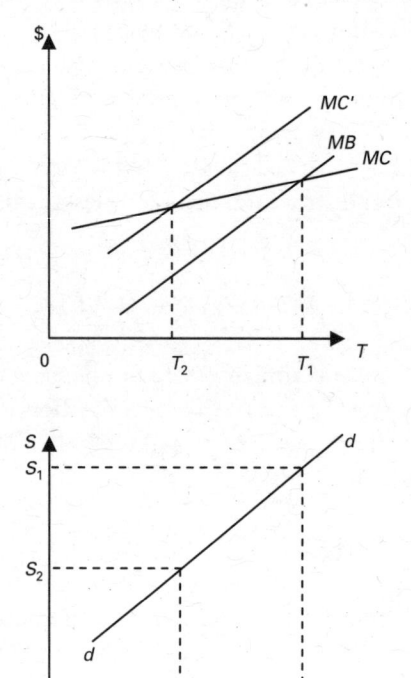

Both figures 8.1 and 8.2 show the impact of an increase in *MC*, as would be the case if the land user had to bear the full market cost of holding the land. In the Chinese context, if the municipal government holds the land or leases it to a land user at a rate below the market rate, the *MC* curve will not rise to *MC'*. In a market situation where real estate prices are rapidly rising, as in a rapidly growing Chinese municipality, the forgone developed rent (*MC*) of waiting to develop is rising, as illustrated. The effect of a rising *MC* is to speed development timing from T_1 to T_2 and to change the structural density from S_1 to S_2. Structural density decreases in a growing city, as in figure 8.1, where *dd* is rising, and increases in a declining city, as in figure 8.2, where *dd* is falling. The effect of a municipality not shifting *MC* up fully, by charging a below-market lease price for the land, is slowed development and increased structural density in a growing city (or reduced structural density in a declining city).

Optimal Development: Model with Taxes on Land and Structures

Now assume that we have a property tax rate applied at the rate τ to the land and a tax of θ applied to land improvements. Using the results of Anderson (2005), we

FIGURE 8.2
Effect of an Increase in the Marginal Cost of Waiting on Development Timing and Density When Density Demanded (*dd*) Is Falling Over Time

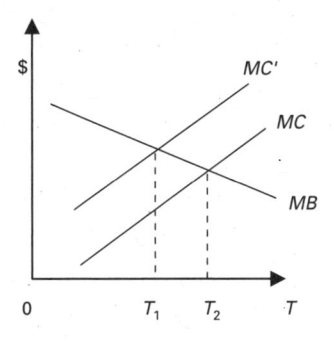

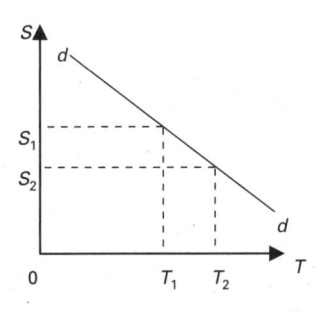

can show that the first-order conditions (5) and (6) are modified as follows. The optimal structural density condition becomes

$$\int_0^T R_S(S,t)e^{r(T-t)}dt = \frac{(r+\theta)}{(r+\tau)}C'(S) \tag{7}$$

and the optimal timing condition becomes

$$(r+\theta)C(S) + w = R(S, T) \tag{8}$$

If we compare these two conditions to equations (5) and (6), we see that both the optimal development timing and the structural density may be affected.

Table 8.1 provides a summary of the comparative static effects of changes in the tax rates, depending on the slope of the *dd* curve. In the case where *dd* slopes upward, an increase in the land tax rate applied before development causes structural density to be reduced and development timing to be accelerated. An increase in the land tax rate applied after development has uncertain effects on both structural density and development timing. Increasing the improvements tax rate has uncertain effects on both structural density and development timing. If *dd* is

TABLE 8.1
Comparative Static Effects of Taxation on Structural Density and Development Timing

	Slope of *dd* curve	Effect on *S*	Effect on *T*
Before-development land tax τ	+	−	−
	−	+	−
After-development land tax τ	+/−	?	?
Improvements tax θ	+	?	?
	−	−	+

downward sloping, an increase in the before-development land tax rate increases structural density and accelerates the timing of development. An increase in the after-development land tax rate has uncertain effects, whereas an increase in the improvements tax rate reduces structural density and postpones the time of development.

Tax on Land Only. Taxing land only is a policy approach rooted in the socialist reality of collective ownership of the land. Municipal governments may grant land leases that are nearly equivalent to ownership (either a long-term lease or a series of short-term leases with automatic and costless renewals) and apply a tax on the value of the land to generate revenues. This policy approach retains nominal ownership of land by the municipal government while simultaneously granting effective ownership rights to developers.

Using the first-order necessary conditions from above, set $\theta = 0$ to remove the tax on improvements. The modified first-order conditions for structural density and timing in this special case are then

$$\int_0^T R_S(S,t)e^{(r+\tau)(T-t)}dt = \frac{(r)}{(r+\tau)}C'(S) \tag{9}$$

and

$$rC(S) + w = R(S,T). \tag{10}$$

Comparing these two equations to equations (7) and (8), we see that the land value tax has a distinct set of influences on development timing and structural density. In the timing condition (10) the marginal benefit of waiting is reduced due to the absence of the tax on improvements. That causes development to speed up.[2] In the density equation (9) the marginal cost of density is reduced, which results in greater density.

---

[2] This result violates the known neutrality property of a land tax. If land is taxed in a way that is unrelated to the current use of the land, the tax has no effect on development timing. In this model, the value of land being taxed is directly related to its current use, resulting in a timing effect.

Tax on Structures Only. In the special case of a tax on structures only, we let $\tau = 0$ in order to remove the tax on land, leaving only a tax on improvements at the rate θ. The first-order conditions for structural density and timing are then

$$\int_0^T R_S(S,t)e^{r(T-t)}dt = \frac{(r+\theta)}{(r)}C'(S) \tag{11}$$

and

$$(r+\theta)\,C(S) + w = R(S,T). \tag{12}$$

We can use these two conditions as benchmarks as we consider the effects of development fees and examine the effect of an annual ad valorem tax on structures only, as compared with a one-time development fee.

Optimal Development: Model with Development Fee

Our focus is the transition from ad hoc up-front development fees to annual ad valorem real estate taxes, so we must begin with a consideration of the impact of a development fee in the model. We begin by assuming that there are no property taxes applied to land or structures. Then we can examine what happens if the municipality applies a development fee. Think about two types of development fees: (1) a lump-sum development fee; and (2) a development fee that is positively related to structural density of development.

Lump-Sum Development Fee. Suppose we have a lump-sum development fee F included in the cost of development in equation (4). First, note that there is a reduction in the value of the property. The value of the property is reduced by the present value of the development fee.

Beyond that, a lump-sum development fee has no direct effect on the structural density equation (5), but it does have an indirect effect that alters the timing of development. Since the fee is lump-sum, it does not affect $C'(S)$ in the structural density equation (5). So structural density is unaffected by the development fee directly. The fee does appear in the timing condition (6), however, and it will affect the timing of development. The development fee affects the *MB* of waiting to develop, shifting it upward in figures 8.1 and 8.2, so the optimal time to develop is delayed. As a result, the development fee has the effect of slowing development. That delay in development has an indirect effect on the optimal structural density, which depends on whether *dd* is rising or falling. With a rising (falling) *dd* curve, that delay in development timing has the effect of increasing (decreasing) structural density once it does occur. Consequently, a lump-sum development fee will reduce the value of the property, slow development, and alter structural density in a way that depends on the slope of the *dd* curve.

Development Fee Increasing with Structural Density. Now suppose that the development fee is directly related to the structural density of development. Suppose that the fee is $F(S)$, with $F' > 0$. The fee then acts in the same way as a one-time tax on buildings. The right-hand side of equation (5) becomes $C'(S) + F'(S)$, and the structural density condition is

$$\int_T^\infty R_S(S,t)e^{r(T-t)}dt = C'(S) + F'(S). \tag{13}$$

With this modification the MC of density rises. The MB of density (the left-hand side of the equation) must equal the MC of added density plus the marginal development fee. As a result, the fee causes the optimal density to be lower, other things being equal. This causes the dd curve to shift downward in figures 8.1 and 8.2, which, in turn, has an effect on the timing of development. The development timing condition becomes

$$r[C(S(T)) + F(S(T))] + w = R(S(T), T). \tag{14}$$

There are two offsetting effects in this condition. The MB of waiting to develop the land is increased by the fee on the left-hand side, but with lower optimal structural density the MB may be reduced. If we assume that the development fee increases MB more than the lower structural density reduces MB, the net effect is an upward shift in MB and slower development. Reduced density also has the effect of reducing the MC, shifting down the MC curves in figures 8.1 and 8.2. The combined effect on development timing and structural density is ambiguous.

If the dd curve is rising over time, as we would expect in a rapidly growing Chinese municipality, the development fee unambiguously delays the optimal time to develop. The reason is that for a given MB the fee shifts the MC curve downward, which thereby increases the optimal T. For a given MC the upward shift in MB also causes T to increase. If the introduction of a development fee has the net effect of raising the MB, development is delayed. The impact of a development fee on structural density is ambiguous, however, if the dd curve is rising over time. The effect will depend on the size of the shift in dd. A delay in the optimal time to develop causes structural density to rise, but the dd curve shifts downward, which results in a lower optimal density at any point in time. If dd is falling over time, a development fee has the unambiguous effect of delaying the optimal time to develop and reducing the optimal structural density.

So the introduction of a development fee that is directly related to structural density has the effect of (1) reducing the value of the property; (2) reducing the structural density of development; and (3) slowing the development process. Table 8.2 summarizes the comparative static effects.

Policy Options

There are various policy options for Chinese municipalities. The tax-for-fees policy is currently being implemented in rural China, but other policy paths could start with fees that act as a tax on structures, moving toward either a traditional property tax or a land value tax.

TABLE 8.2
Comparative Static Effects of Development Fees on Structural Density and Development Timing

	Slope of dd curve	Effect on S	Effect on T
Lump-sum fee F	+	+	+
	−	−	+
Fee increasing in structural density	+	?	?
	−	−	+

Switch from Development Fees to Property Tax. An essential issue to consider, given the tax-for-fee reform policy in China, is the economic impact of conversion from a development fee to some form of property taxation. Suppose we begin with a system in which there is a preexisting development fee levied in a lump sum at the time of development. Given the analysis presented above, we know that the fee has the impact of slowing development, with an effect on structural density that depends on the slope of the density-demanded curve.

In the case where density demanded is rising over time, as we would expect for a growing Chinese municipality, a development fee causes the structural density to increase. Removal of a fee speeds development and reduces density. Introduction of a unified property tax, including both a tax on land and an improvements tax, would speed development via the effect of the predevelopment land tax but would have uncertain effects on timing due to the post-development land tax and the tax on improvements. The effect on structural density is negative due to the predevelopment land tax but uncertain due to the post-development land tax and the tax on improvements. In the case where density demanded is falling over time, as would be the case in a declining municipality, a development fee causes structural density to be lower and development timing to be delayed. Removal of a fee speeds development and increases structural density. Introduction of a property tax would speed development timing via the effect of the predevelopment land tax but slow development via the improvements tax. The effect on structural density would also be uncertain, as the predevelopment land tax would increase density, but the improvements tax would reduce density.

The net result is that a policy change from a lump-sum development fee to a unified property tax would touch off a complex set of interacting effects influencing both the timing and the density of development, with very uncertain consequences. There are no simple answers to be provided on the impacts of this type of policy regime switch.

Transition Path to Property Taxation. If we think about the Chinese path to property taxation as beginning with a tax on structures and moving toward either a graded tax system that places a higher tax on land than structures or equal taxation of structures and land, we need to consider the potential tax trade-off. The potential path to be followed is certainly not linear.

Brueckner (1986) has examined the long-run effects of a movement to a two-rate tax system in an equilibrium urban housing market with exogenous house prices. Housing is homogeneous and is produced with constant returns to scale technology by profit-maximizing developers operating in a competitive market. The assumption of exogenous housing prices is relevant to a situation where we are analyzing the short-run implications of a tax policy change, or where the policy is implemented in a portion, but not the entirety, of a metropolitan area. Such conditions are likely to be the case in the early stages of property tax reform in China.

The Brueckner model indicates that the trade-off in tax rates is given by the following expression:

$$\frac{\partial \theta}{\partial \tau} = -\left[\frac{1}{rS}\right] \frac{1}{\left[1 - \frac{(1+\tau)\theta\sigma}{(1+\theta)\mu_l}\right]} \quad (15)$$

where r and i are the net-of-tax rental prices of capital and land, respectively; S is the structural density or ratio of capital per acre of land ($S = K/L$); σ is the elasticity of substitution; and μ_l is land's factor share. Bruecker has shown that the sign of this derivative is "almost certainly negative." Hence, there is a trade-off in the tax rates applied to structures and land that depends on a set of key parameters identified above. For values of the elasticity of substitution that are sufficiently small, this derivative will be negative. Consequently, as the land tax is increased, the improvements tax can be decreased while holding revenue constant. The trade-off is nonlinear, however, as the second derivative $\partial^2\theta/\partial\tau^2$ has been shown to be negative. The trade-off between the tax rates becomes more severe as a community moves toward heavier reliance on either one of the taxes.

Figure 8.3, adapted from Anderson (1999), illustrates the nonlinear trade-off in tax rate space. The ray from the origin labeled $\tau = \theta$ represents the traditional property tax where land and structures are taxed at equal rates. The level of property taxation rises as we move outward along the ray. The downward sloping line segment from θ_3 to τ_3 represents a linear trade-off in tax rates that occurs in the special case where the elasticity of substitution is zero, $\sigma = 0$. In that case the slope of the trade-off is a constant:

$$\frac{\partial \theta}{\partial \tau} = -\frac{i}{rS}. \quad (16)$$

This expression is simply minus the relative returns to land and capital. As the land tax is increased and revenue rises by the amount of the tax increase applied to the amount of land in the city, the reduction in the improvements tax is simply determined by the value of improvements in the city.

In the more general case, however, where the elasticity of substitution is not zero, the iso-revenue trade-off available to a community is the bowed curve below that line segment. The slope of that curve reflects the derivative in the equation above. Suppose that we start at the point $(0,\theta_2)$ in figure 8.3, where we have the tax rate θ_2 applied to structures and a zero tax rate applied to land. We can follow the nonlinear iso-revenue tax rate trade-off downward in a southeasterly direction.

FIGURE 8.3
Land and Improvements Tax Rate Options

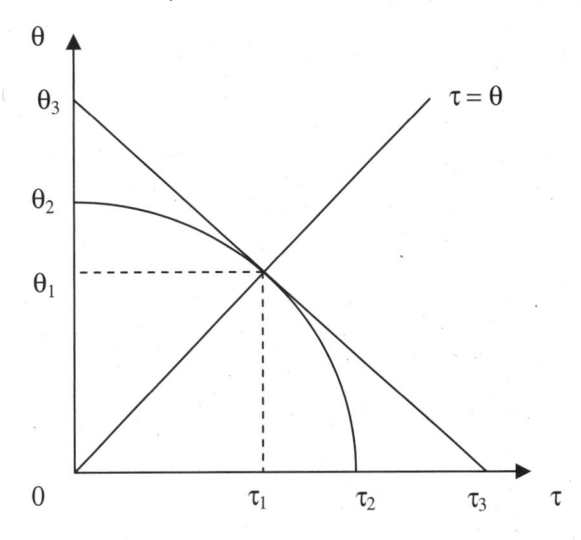

The traditional property tax point with equal tax rates applied to land and structures is labeled (τ_1,θ_1). Going beyond that point, we could move up to a graded tax system that applies a higher rate of taxation to land than to structures, eventually ending at the point where we have a pure land tax at $(\tau_2,0)$.

Thinking analytically about the menu of policy options available to a community, as mapped out by the curve in figure 8.3, we should also examine the efficiency issue. Minimizing the excess burden of taxation is a fundamental objective in considering what combination of tax rates should be used. We can write the combined excess burden of taxing land and structures as

$$EB_T = EB_\tau(\tau) + EB_\theta(\theta) \tag{17}$$

We are assuming no interaction between the two taxes, yielding the simple relationship that the total excess burden of taxation is the sum of the excess burdens due to the two taxes.

Totally differentiating the excess burden expression and solving for the slope of the iso-excess burden function yields

$$\frac{d\theta}{d\tau} = -\frac{\dfrac{dEB_\tau}{\partial \tau}}{\dfrac{\partial EB_\theta}{\partial \theta}} \tag{18}$$

Hence, the slope of the iso-excess burden contour in tax space is minus the ratio of the marginal excess burdens of the two tax rates. The reduction in the improvements tax with an increase in the land tax while holding the excess burden constant, simply reflects the relative marginal excess burdens of the two tax rates. It is well known that the land tax is relatively more efficient as compared to the improvements tax. Consequently, we know that the marginal excess burden of the land tax is smaller than that of the improvements tax. As a result, the slope of the iso-excess burden contour is relatively flat and thus a corner solution will be optimal. A community wishing to minimize the excess burden of taxation will tax land only.

Summary and Conclusions

Recent proposals in China for urban land development and housing construction tax and fee reforms focus on the possibility of converting the existing system of multiple real estate taxes and fees paid at the time of development into a unified ad valorem real estate tax. Such a policy regime change would have potential impacts on housing prices and the patterns of housing development that are important to consider. The practice of developers turning taxes and fees into up-front housing costs has impacts on housing prices and development patterns that are also worthy of further consideration. Correspondingly, it is important to analyze the potential impacts of changing the practice of requiring home buyers to pay all taxes and fees at once upon purchase of a home, spreading the taxes and fees over time instead.

This chapter summarized the major economic impacts of development fees and ad valorem property taxes with applications to the contemporary policy setting of China, where fiscal reform plans are following a path to property taxation. Dynamic models of the development process indicate that the policy switch from a lump-sum fee to a property tax would have a complex set of effects on both development timing and structural density—with uncertain effects. Moreover, the differential incidence of the two financing methods is important to consider. There are no simple answers regarding the impacts of such a policy regime switch. In order to advance research on this topic, more work is necessary to develop appropriate models of the transition from a land-leasing regime to a quasi-ownership regime with taxes or fees used to fund local government provision of public goods.

REFERENCES

Anderson, Gordon, and Ying Ge. 2004. Do economic reforms accelerate urban growth? The case of China. *Urban Studies* 41(11):2197–2210.

Anderson, John E. 1986. Property taxes and the timing of urban land development. *Regional Science and Urban Economics* 16(4):483–492.

———. 1999. Two-rate property tax effects on land development. *Journal of Real Estate Finance and Economics* 18(2):181–190.

———. 2005. Taxes and fees as forms of land use regulation. *Journal of Real Estate Finance and Economics* 31(4):413–427.

———. 2009. Financing urban development in China. *Chinese Economy* 42(2):48–62.

Areddy, James T. 2006. China restricts foreign spending on real estate. *Wall Street Journal*, July 25.

Bao, Helen X. H., John L. Glasock, and Sheery Z. Zhou. 2007. Land value determination in an emerging market: Empirical evidence from China. Unpublished Working Paper. Cambridge, U.K.: Cambridge University, Department of Land Economy.

Beijing Local Taxation Bureau. Overview of China's tax system. http://english.tax.861.gov.cn/zgszky/zgszky.htm.

Brueckner, Jan. 1986. A modern analysis of the effects of site value taxation. *National Tax Journal* 39(1):49–58.

Deng, F. Frederic. 2002. Ground lease–based land use system versus common interest development. *Land Economics* 78(2):190–206.
———. 2005. Public land leasing and the changing roles of local government in urban China. *Annals of Regional Science* 39(2):353–373.
Grenadier, Steven R. 2005. An equilibrium analysis of real estate leases. *Journal of Business* 78(4):1173–1219.
Han, Sun Sheng. 1998. Real estate development in China: A regional perspective. *Journal of Real Estate Literature* 6(2):121–133.
Janssen, Christian T. L. 2003. Estimating the effect of land leases on prices of inner-city apartment buildings. *Urban Studies* 40(10):2049–2066.
Li, Ling Hin. 1997. Privatization of the urban land market in Shanghai. *Journal of Real Estate Literature* 5(2):161–168.
Lin, Justin Yifu, Ran Tao, and Mingxing Liu. 2006. Rural taxation and local governance reform in China's economic transition: Evolution, policy responses and remaining challenges. Paper presented at the Economic Policy Reform in Asia conference, organized by the Stanford Center for International Development and the Stanford Institute for Economic Policy Research, Palo Alto, CA (May 31–June 2).
Lin, Shuanglin. 2000. The decline of China's budgetary revenue: Reasons and consequences. *Contemporary Economic Policy* 18(4):477–490.
Lin, Shuanglin, and Shunfeng Song. 2002. Urban economic growth in China: Theory and evidence. *Urban Studies* 39(12):2251–2266.
Liu, Mingxing, and Ran Tao. 2004. Regional competition, fiscal reform and local governance in China. Paper presented at the conference Paying for Progress: Public Finance, Human Welfare, and Inequality in China, Institute for Chinese Studies, Oxford, UK (May 21–23).
Luo, Renfu, Linxiu Zhand, Jikun Huang, and Scott Rozelle. 2007. Elections, fiscal reform and public goods provision in rural China. *Journal of Comparative Economics* 35(3):583–611.
Miceli, Thomas J., C. F. Sirmans, and Geoffrey K. Turnbull. 2001. The property-contract boundary: An economic analysis of leases. *American Law and Economics Review* 3(1):165–185.
Newell, Graeme, K. W. Chau, S. K. Wang, and Keith McKinnell. 2005. Dynamics of the direct and indirect real estate markets in China. *Journal of Real Estate Portfolio Management* 11(3):263–279.
Parker, Elliot, and Judith Thornton. 2007. Fiscal centralization and decentralization in Russia and China. *Comparative Economic Studies* 49(4):514–542.
State Administration of Taxation (SAT). 2010. Tax Law. July 7, 2010. http://www.chinatax.gov.cn/n6669073/n6669088/index.html.
Tao, Ran, and Mingxing Liu. 2005. Urban and Rural Household Taxation in China: Measurement, comparison and policy implications. *Journal of the Asia and Pacific Economy* 10(4):486–505.
Turnbull, Geoffrey K. 1988. Property taxes and the transition of land to urban use. *Journal of Real Estate Finance and Economics* 1(4):393–403.
———. 2005a. Introduction: The dynamic perspective in urban land use policy. *Journal of Real Estate Finance and Economics* 31(4):351–356.
———. 2005b. The investment incentive effects of land use regulations. *Journal of Real Estate Finance and Economics* 31(4):357–396.
UPI (United Press International). 2007. China considers property tax. October 17.
Walker, Anthony, and Li Ling Hin. 1994. Land use rights reform and the real estate market in China. *Journal of Real Estate Literature* 2(2):199–211.
Xie, Qingshu, A. R. Ghanbari Parsa, and Barry Redding. 2002. The emergence of the urban land market in China: Evolution, structure, constraints and perspectives. *Urban Studies* 39(8):1375–1398.
Xu, Dashan. 2004. Tax plan to slash housing prices. *China Daily*, March 15. http://www.chinadaily.com.cn/english/doc/2004-03/15/content_314765.htm.
Yeoh, Emile Kok-Kheng. 2007. China's de facto fiscal federalism: Challenges and prospects. Working Paper No. 2007-7. Kuala Lumpur: University of Malaya, Institute of China Studies.

Zhang, Zing Quan. 2001. Risk and uncertainty in the Chinese housing market. *Journal of Real Estate Literature* 9(2):161–172.

Zhu, Jieming. 2004. From land use right to land development right: Institutional change in China's urban development. *Urban Studies* 41(7):1249–1267.

———. 2005. A transitional institution for the emerging land market in urban China. *Urban Studies* 42(8):1369–1390.

Integrating the Proposed Property Tax with the Public Leasehold System

9

YU-HUNG HONG AND DIANA BRUBAKER

Tremendous efforts have been put into reintroducing property taxation to countries in transition (see Bird and Slack 2004; 2006; Malme and Youngman 2001; Šulija and Šulija 2005). Aside from other personal and immobile property taxes collected at the time of transfer, policy makers and analysts are particularly attentive to the levy on the possession of real estate. In most cases, an ad valorem property tax that is applied to both land and buildings is treated as the standard model. Although creating such a property tax system seems proper in transition countries where fiscal decentralization and restitution of private property are progressing rapidly, its implementation is not without problems. Challenges abound.[1] Using China as a case, this chapter examines an important, yet often overlooked, topic related to real property taxation in transition countries: taxing public leasehold land. Public leaseholds are common land tenure systems found in many transforming economies. The state owns a majority of the land and assigns development and use rights to private entities through long-term leases.

Taxing public leaseholds is particularly relevant to China because since 2002, Chinese policy makers have been experimenting with a proposed property tax system that would replace three existing real property taxes—the urban land use tax, building tax, and urban real estate tax.[2] The proposed property tax is an ad

---

[1] At a conference co-organized by the Lincoln Institute of Land Policy and the State Council Research Development Center of China in 2005, Professor Roy Bahl highlighted seven challenging issues for the proposed real property tax reform in China: (1) restructuring intergovernmental fiscal relations; (2) assimilating the proposed property tax into the existing fiscal system; (3) revising public accounting procedures and regulations; (4) coordinating cooperation among different public agencies for information exchanges; (5) nurturing a positive public attitude toward property taxation; (6) assessing impacts of property taxation on land resources allocation and utilization; and (7) designing a property tax system that is in accord with the existing land tenure arrangements. The final point is the subject here, and Professor Bahl should be credited for bringing this insight to our attention.

[2] See Hong (2003) and the Development Research Center of the State Council (2005) for detailed discussions of the structure of the proposed property tax.

valorem tax that would impose a uniform tax rate on an assessed value of land and buildings. It would be levied in urban areas only, not in rural townships.

The new tax scheme was supposed to be adopted in 2008, but implementation has been postponed without a further specific deadline. The State Administration of Taxation is currently testing the property tax assessment system in ten pilot areas—four independent cities and six areas located within provinces: Tianjin, Beijing, Shenzhen, Chongqing, central Henan, eastern Anhui, eastern Fujian, northeastern Liaoning, eastern Jiangsu, and northwestern Ningxia (Naughton 2007). The new property tax is expected to resolve the unsustainability of the current urban fiscal systems, which rely heavily on lease revenues from a dwindling supply of urban land.

Although there were proposals to abolish the current land-leasing fees after the adoption of the proposed property tax, the central government decided that local governments should collect both levies in the future. Key questions about integrating the property tax scheme with the current land-leasing system are then as follows:

1. Would the proposed property tax be complementary to or compete with the land-leasing fee in generating revenues for local governments? In China, where the government is the landowner, if the economic tax incidence of the property tax would fall mostly on local governments in terms of lower land-leasing revenues, why would local officials be willing to implement a new tax system that may at best have neutral and at worst negative impacts on their budgets?
2. Should existing land users who have already paid their leasing fee for using land be liable for additional property tax payments?
3. If the proposed property tax lowers land value and, in turn, property prices, why would interest groups, such as property owners, banks, and public and private real estate developers, support such a policy initiative?

Answers to these questions can affect the legitimacy and operations of the proposed property tax scheme, which in turn determine its implementation, administrative, and compliance costs.

Because the new property tax has yet to be implemented, data are unavailable to answer the above questions definitely. Instead, this chapter has four objectives: (1) because leasehold fee collection and property taxation are matters related to land value allocation, discussing how apportionment may differ between public leasehold and freehold systems; (2) projecting four scenarios for property tax impacts on leasehold revenue and land value; (3) applying those scenarios to China utilizing ideas of tax and public spending capitalization into property prices and estimating capitalization of property tax liabilities and public goods provision using a random effects regression model and panel data from 1999–2006; and (4) suggesting potential policy implications for the implementation of the proposed property tax reform in China.

Land Value Allocation Under Public Leasehold

Western conceptualization of real property taxation is usually founded on the premise that land and buildings are privately owned. The property tax is seen as an instrument to reserve a portion of the increase in private property value for the public (Youngman and Malme 2004). This perspective makes sense in situations where private property is the predominant mode of real estate ownership. Yet to what extent could this be applied to countries where real estate, especially land, is publicly owned?[3] Thus far, the Chinese government has showed no intention to fully privatize land. The major change that the government made was in 1987, when it allowed private individuals to lease land use rights from local governments for a definite time and with the payment of a land-leasing fee. In 1988 the Chinese National People's Congress amended the constitution to legally acknowledge the transferability of land use rights between private entities (Development Research Center of the State Council 2005, 37). Another amendment to the Chinese constitution was made in 2004, legally recognizing buildings erected on leasehold land as private property (Constitution of the People's Republic of China 1982, chapter 1, article 13). Hence, a person who possesses a piece of real estate in China is by legal definition the owner of the house (or apartment) but only the user of the land.

Residential land is leased for 70 years, commercial for 50, and industrial for 40. Initially, local governments had to share lease revenue with the national government, but the central government's share was gradually scaled back until in 1994 municipalities eventually were allowed to retain all of the lease revenues (Peterson 2006). Lease revenue is paid in an up-front lump sum. When municipalities want to lease a parcel of land to a private entity, they generally use one of three methods: private negotiation, public tender, or auction. In July 2002 the central government allowed cities to lease land to private developers only through public tender or auction, but cities did not completely obey. For example, Beijing did not instruct its own city officials to lease land through public auction until 2004. In 2003 central statistics indicated that 33 percent of land leases were conducted through public auction (Peterson 2006), and that share has risen in recent years. Lin and Ho (2005), however, report that public auctions are often manipulated by local governments.

Given these unique property relations in countries where land is leasehold, policy makers who try to tax land should in principle be able to delineate the different portions of land value and allocate them to the varied parties involved in land development. Figure 9.1 shows conceptually the different components of land value and their corresponding beneficiaries. In reality, however, the precise separation of these elements is very difficult, rendering property taxation and the collection of other land-related levies controversial.

Land value comprises at least four components. The first is the intrinsic land value, which reflects the productivity or economic use value of the land determined

---

[3] Undoubtedly, some governments in Eastern Europe have been privatizing state assets. It remains common, however, that most land is still state owned. For example, in Russia, where the state is supportive of land privatization, only selected cities, such as Novgorod, Tver, and Saratov, have a large portion of their land sold to private individuals (Krupa, Mikesell, and Zorn 2006). In fact, out of all the land being privatized, about 90 percent is located in just one city—Saratov (ibid., 8).

FIGURE 9.1

Components of Land Value and Corresponding Beneficiaries Under Public Leasehold Systems

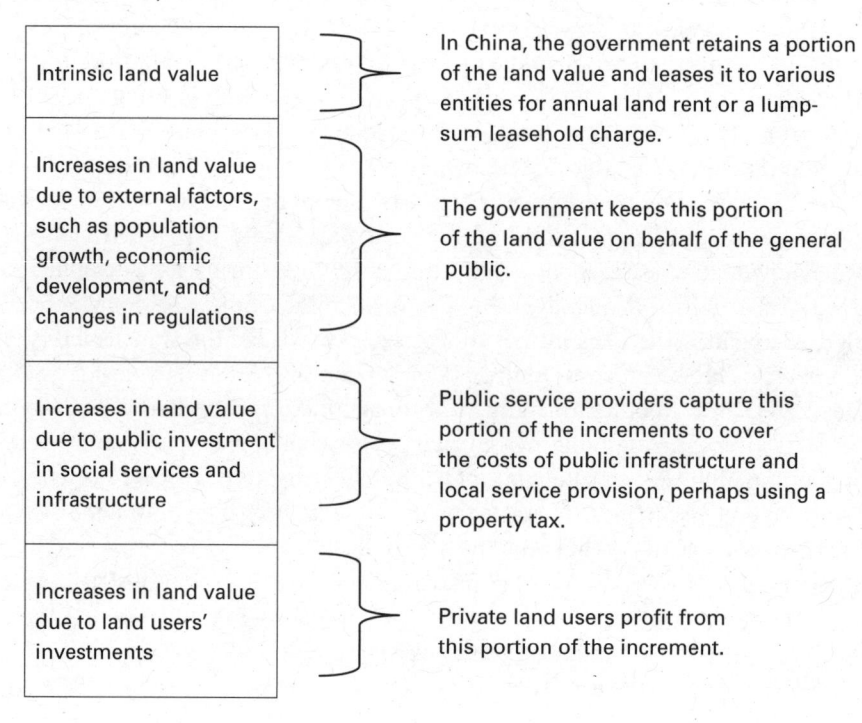

Land Value Component	Beneficiary
Intrinsic land value	In China, the government retains a portion of the land value and leases it to various entities for annual land rent or a lump-sum leasehold charge.
Increases in land value due to external factors, such as population growth, economic development, and changes in regulations	The government keeps this portion of the land value on behalf of the general public.
Increases in land value due to public investment in social services and infrastructure	Public service providers capture this portion of the increments to cover the costs of public infrastructure and local service provision, perhaps using a property tax.
Increases in land value due to land users' investments	Private land users profit from this portion of the increment.

by its development potential, location, soil type, and other factors. Under a freehold system, a landowner who pays for or inherits the land should possess this portion of the land value. When land is publicly owned, the government acts as the custodian of the asset on behalf of the people. Both private and public landowners can lease the right to use land to a third party. To obtain a reasonable return on land investment, the landowner (public or private) will collect rent from the lessee and retain any after-tax capital appreciation if she decides to sell the asset.

Second, land value can be generated by external factors, such as population growth, economic development, and changes in land use regulations. These factors are not related to the investment or labor of the landowners or users. Hence, this portion of the land value (sometimes referred to as *surplus land value*) should be captured by the government for the purposes of income redistribution or other public investment (George 1962). Under a private property system, the government can recoup this portion of the land value by imposing a capital gains tax or other property tax on private landowners. Under a leasehold system, because the government that collects the capital gains tax is also the landowner, in theory there would be no need to collect such a tax. Real practices, however, are more complicated than what the theory prescribes. Normally, land users are allowed to transfer their leasehold rights to another entity before the end of the lease and are able to profit from increases in the value of the land use right (Hong and Bourassa 2003). Unless the government has the first right of refusal in land transactions, a mechanism for capturing surplus land value is needed.[4]

Third, land value can also rise due to increases in local infrastructure investment and social services. Improvements in amenities, such as schools, roads, water and sewage, and public parks, can increase housing demand in a neighborhood, thus inflating the value of a property. Because this land value increment is caused by public spending, public service providers should retain this benefit to cover the costs of infrastructure investment and local services. Many benefit-tax scholars argue that the property tax is an efficient instrument for capturing this portion of land value, acting as a price for a bundle of public goods provided by local governments (Fischel 2001; Oates 1969). When land is freehold, the rationale for allocating this portion of the land value to public service providers, albeit technically complex, is easy to understand for taxpayers, who are the consumers of public goods. Yet under a public leasehold system in which the government lessor and property tax collectors are perceived as one entity, lessees may be confused as to why they need to pay property taxes in addition to leasing fees for using public land.

Scholars and practitioners in general perceive the leasing fee and the property tax as not the same. The former is a payment to the landowner, the state, under a public leasehold system, for leasing the land use rights to a private individual. The latter is considered a payment for local services and infrastructure provided by the government. The amount of land rent that lessees pay to a government lessor should be determined by the supply and demand of land use rights; and the amount of a property tax should be based on the quality and quantity of local services received. This is similar to a situation in which a private owner lets her property to a renter and collects a monthly rent for allowing the tenant to occupy the premises. It would be unreasonable to argue that the tenant should not pay rents to his landlord if the government levies a tax on the use of the property. But this is precisely what many analysts in China advocate. They believe that the government should abolish the leasing fee after the adoption of a new property tax. These two levies are interrelated with each other, but they are far from being the payments for an identical service. As will be demonstrated later, collections of leasing fees and property taxes are not mutually exclusive.

Fourth, private land improvements undertaken by owners or users can also enhance land value. Undoubtedly, the party who invests in the land and assumes the risk should benefit from the land value increment. As stated earlier, although it is theoretically sensible to delineate and allocate the different portions of land value according to the value generators, there is no consensus on how to accomplish this. Hence, whenever there is a proposed change to an allocation method, such as a property tax reform, confusion as to how the interest of involved parties may be affected is inevitable.

---

[4] See Hong (1998) and Hong and Bourassa (2003) for discussions of land value capture under public leasehold systems.

Land Rent, Property Tax, and Tax Incidence

In designing a new tax system, the most fundamental issue is its economic incidence—that is, who actually bears the burden of the tax, as opposed to who is legally liable to make the payment. Four scenarios follow in which adoption of a property tax under a public leasehold system may affect land value allocation to different parties. To simplify the scenario analysis, we assume that only a land tax is in question and that the supply of land (or land use rights) is inelastic.

Scenario 1

We make two more assumptions for scenario 1: (1) property tax collections are not invested in public infrastructure or local services (or the expansion of infrastructure investment is constrained by one or more fixed inputs in the short run); and (2) property tax liabilities are fully capitalized in land value—that is, capital and labor are relatively mobile and perfectly informed about a proposed property tax reform. The standard argument of tax incidence under such a situation is that the landowner (the government) will bear the large portion, if not all, of the economic burden even if the statutory incidence falls on the land users. The reason is that the new tax imposes additional costs (future tax liabilities) on land users and, ceteris paribus, will lower the demand for land use rights. As illustrated in figure 9.2, the demand curve will shift from D to D'. As the land value decreases from LV_0 to LV_1, the amount of lease revenue that the government can charge lessees for leasing land will fall if leasing fees are determined by the market. In other words, lessees are able to transfer the economic incidence of the new tax to the government, represented by the shaded rectangle in figure 9.2. The total cost of using land will increase moderately from LV_0 to $LV_1(1+t)$, where t is the property tax rate. This scenario implies that any new tax collections generated through property taxation may be equaled by a decrease in lease income. As shown in figure 9.2, the amount of lease revenue collected before the implementation of the new property tax system ($LV_0 * Q_0$) is lower than the combined collections from land leasing and property taxation ($LV_1 [1+t] * Q_1$) after the new system is adopted.

If tax capitalization occurs fully and instantaneously, taxing public leasehold land could lead to three outcomes. First, there could be a reduction in the total revenue for local governments because property tax collections are unlikely to fully compensate for the loss of lease income caused by the decrease in land value. If this occurs, what fiscal incentive would central authorities have for local governments to undertake the heavy capital and labor investment needed for property tax reform?

Second, the tax system could shift control over land-related revenues from one branch of local government to another. In some countries, central and local land bureaus are normally the government units that monitor land resource allocation and are therefore responsible for leasing public land and the collection of lease payments. Tax policy and collection, however, usually fall within the jurisdiction of ministries of finance and tax administrative agencies. If a land tax converts a portion of the land-leasing fee into tax payments, it could redistribute the power over local

FIGURE 9.2
Relationship Between Land Value and Property Tax Under Scenario 1

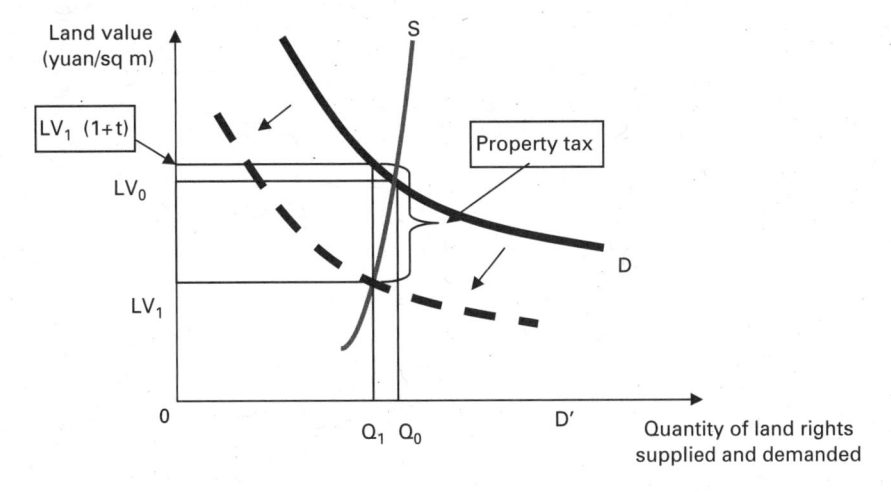

[Figure: Graph showing Land value (yuan/sq m) on vertical axis and Quantity of land rights supplied and demanded on horizontal axis. Curves labeled S, D, D'. Horizontal levels marked $LV_1(1+t)$, LV_0, and LV_1. Vertical quantities marked Q_1 and Q_0. A bracketed region labeled "Property tax".]

revenues from the land bureaus to the tax agencies. Depending on how important the lease income is in government budgets, this change could create rivalry between agencies.

A land tax could also alter fiscal relations between the central and local governments or between different levels of subnational government. Suppose further that tax collections would have to be shared between different levels of government, whereas the lease income would not. If the lease revenue were treated as an off-budget item, local officials could retain 100 percent of the funds for local uses. If local governments have to surrender a portion of the property tax collections to higher levels of government, they might concentrate their efforts to generate public funds through land leasing, thus rendering the implementation of tax reform arduous.

Third, if leasehold charges are paid up front in a lump sum, taxing leasehold land would defer a portion of the immediate lease payments to later years due to the capitalization of tax liabilities into leasehold values. This postponement implies that the current government would have less revenue to defray local spending, at least in the beginning of the reform. If the lease revenue accounts for a major share of local government budgets, officials would not be enthusiastic about taxing leasehold land. One potential solution is to allow local governments to borrow funds from public or private financial intermediaries to cover any fiscal shortfalls, using future property tax collections as collateral. Tax payments could be deposited into a special fund account to ensure that they would be used to repay the related debts.

Scenario 2

So far, our analysis has not considered another type of capitalization that may occur when a government levies a property tax. The aim of collecting the tax is to raise public funds for financing local infrastructure and services. In scenario 2, we assume that property tax collections are fully invested in public goods and that

FIGURE 9.3
Relationship Between Land Value and Property Tax Under Scenario 2

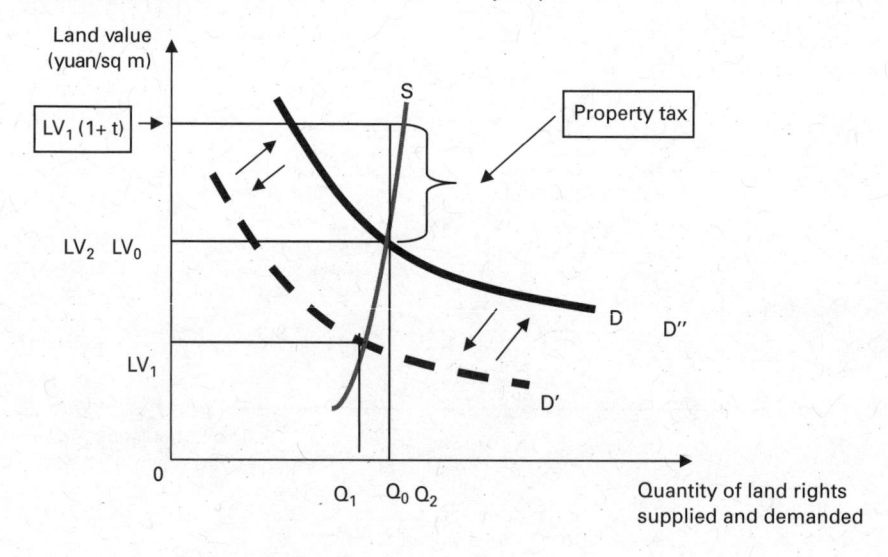

these investments are not constrained by any fixed inputs. Public investments can improve neighborhood amenities and boost property prices.

As shown in figure 9.3, the demand shifts curve from D' to D'', which raises the land value from LV_1 to LV_2. This assumes that the increase in public expenditures, holding other factors constant, has a capitalization effect that offsets entirely the impact of property tax liabilities on leasehold values. In reality, the net capitalization effect may not necessarily be zero. Whether the net effect will keep leasehold values the same will depend on many factors, such as the homogeneity of residents within a community with respect to demands for local public services, the mobility of the residents, the location-dependence of residents' income, and the variety of local government services available to satisfy diverse tastes (Mieszkowski and Zodrow 1989; Tiebout 1956). These preconditions may be attainable through binding zoning (Hamilton 1975; 1976).

Suppose that the net capitalization effect is zero, in which case property tax collections would no longer be generated at the expense of lease income. Land value and lease revenue would rise back up to the pre-reform level due to the increase in public expenditures. Tax collections would become an additional income for financing new public goods. As stated earlier, many proponents of the benefit view of property taxation treat the property tax as a payment for public services received (Fischel 2001; Oates 1969). When property tax revenue is reinvested in local infrastructure and services, those benefits will be capitalized into property prices. This mechanism for financing public goods in theory would have no effect on housing consumption (Zodrow 2001; 2006).[5]

---

[5] The benefit view is certainly not the only perspective on the effect of property taxation on housing consumption. The alternative is the "new" or "capital tax" view, which argues that the property tax is a tax on the use of capital and thus can create distortions by reallocating investment from high-tax to low-tax jurisdictions. According to this view, the property tax will reduce per capita housing consumption as taxpayers attempt to avoid the tax (Zodrow 2006).

The validity of the above argument is based not only on the degree to which capitalization of tax liabilities and public spending will take place but also on the timing of the two processes. Assume that tax capitalization occurs immediately after the government announces the new scheme, whereas a corresponding increase in public expenditures would be capitalized into land values only upon completion of a proposed project, which might take a long time. All else being equal, the government would receive a smaller amount of lease revenue in the beginning, owing to lower leasehold values caused by the capitalization of tax liabilities, as predicted in scenario 1. Not until the increase in public expenditures induces higher leasehold values could property tax collections be considered extra revenue for financing public services.

Another issue related to the timing of capitalization is that a new land tax could create horizontal inequity in the initial stage of reform. Existing lessees who leased land in the past might have paid the entire leasehold charges up front without anticipating the possibility of paying a new property tax. Those lessees did not have a chance to adjust their leasing fees downward, so as to account for the extra tax liabilities for using land. For lessees who plan to lease land after the reform, the situation will be different. Knowing that they will have to pay property taxes in the future, new lessees will lower their offers for leasing public land, so as to compensate for future tax expenditures. In other words, these new lessees will pay lower leasehold charges than did existing land users.

This problem can be mediated if the government collects an annual land rent instead of the entire leasehold charges up front. Under a land rent system, the government can adjust the rental level annually according to changes in the fair-market value of land. This way, both existing and new lessees would be charged at the same rental level regardless of when they acquired their leasehold rights.

If collecting a land rent is not a viable option, the government could minimize this horizontal inequity by pledging to use the property tax revenue for specific infrastructure projects (similar to the tax increment financing [TIF] schemes in the United States). If the government convinced land users that improvements in land would be implemented in the near future, new lessees might be willing to pay a higher leasing fee for the land use rights, thereby narrowing the discrepancy in leasehold charges before and after the tax reform. Certainly, this method will work only if the government has a good reputation of keeping its promises and the demonstrated competency to actually execute the planned investment. In an environment where taxpayers are not fully informed about how their tax contributions are used or what benefits they can expect from paying taxes, it is hard to imagine that new lessees would be willing to pay a higher leasing fee for promises that may not materialize. Trust in the government can shape expectations and the capitalization rate of public spending.

Scenario 3

Scenario 3 is similar to scenario 2, except that the assumption of increasing returns to scale of public infrastructure investment is added. A proportional change in production inputs causes a greater than proportional change in output of public goods.

The usual explanation for this type of production structure is the existence of capital costs that are large compared to variable costs. If capital costs in the long run do not increase as fast as output, a larger output would allow the fixed costs to be spread over more units, causing a decrease in per unit cost of production. This situation often applies to public utilities such as communications, water, sewer, highway, and transit services, all of which have large capital requirements.

If a doubling of public spending would cause output of public goods to more than double, the cost per person serviced would fall as the number of consumers rises. Again, if there is full capitalization of public spending and tax liabilities, public investments with increasing returns to scale might lead to a big increase in land value, outweighing the downward pressure on land value caused by tax capitalization. As depicted in figure 9.4, increases in public spending would shift the demand curve from D' to D'', causing land value to rise from LV_1 to LV_2. The higher land value would increase lease revenue. Property tax collections would become an additional revenue source for local governments. Property prices would increase due to stronger housing demand.

Scenario 4

The last three scenarios are under the restrictive assumptions that full capitalization of higher taxes and public spending occurs. According to Palmon and Smith (1998), there has not been a consensus on tax capitalization rates in the United States. For instance, some researchers find little significant property tax capitalization effects on prices (Gronberg 1979; Wales and Wiens 1974), while others document varying degrees of partial, full, and overcapitalization (Ihlanfeldt and Jackson 1982; King 1977; Oates 1969). Because data for measuring the capitalization rates for property tax liabilities and public spending are hard to obtain, scenario 4 pres-

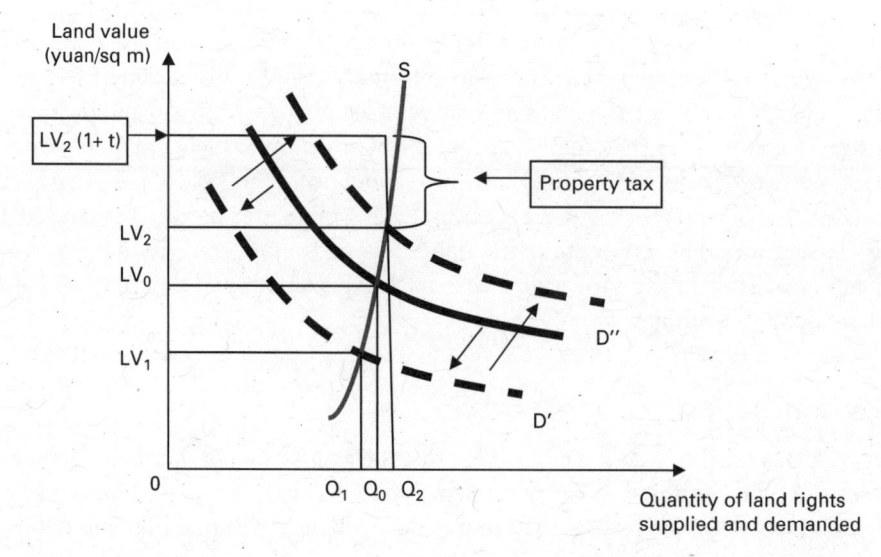

FIGURE 9.4

Relationship Between Land Value and Property Tax Under Scenario 3

FIGURE 9.5
Relationship Between Land Value and Property Tax Under Scenario 4

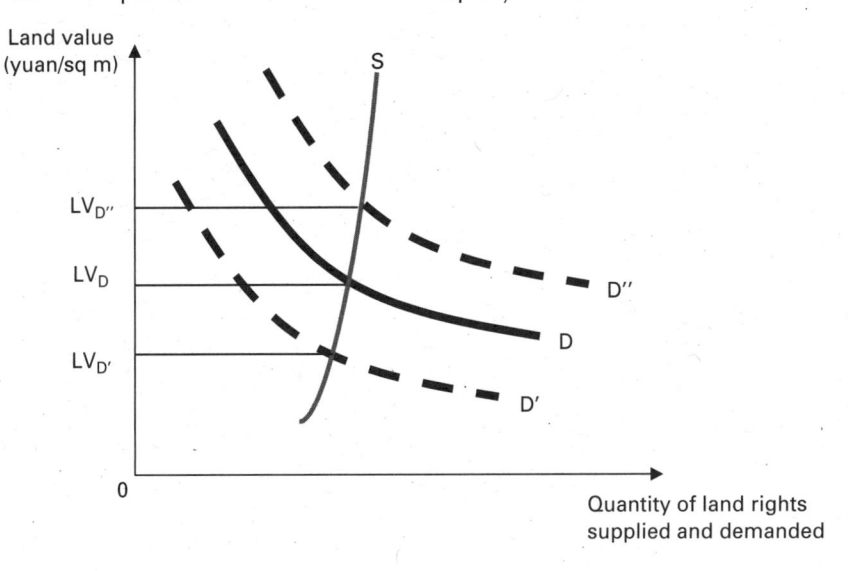

[Figure: Graph with Land value (yuan/sq m) on y-axis and Quantity of land rights supplied and demanded on x-axis. Shows supply curve S (vertical) and three demand curves D', D, D'' with corresponding land values $LV_{D'}$, LV_D, $LV_{D''}$.]

ents a set of more ambiguous outcomes, with all the same assumptions for scenarios 1–3, except for full capitalization of tax liabilities and public spending.

Figure 9.5 illustrates an array of outcomes that depend on the net effect of tax and spending capitalization. If the rate of tax capitalization is higher than that of public spending, land value would fall between LV_D and $LV_{D'}$, because benefits of the increase in public good provision financed by property taxes would not be able to offset the added cost of using land. The demand curve D would shift to the left but not all the way to D', due to incomplete tax capitalization. The economic tax incidence would not fall mostly on the government lessor but would partly shift forward to the land user. In contrast, if the rate of tax capitalization is lower than that of public spending, land value will rise between LV_D and $LV_{D''}$ due to the increase in the demand for land. The demand curve D will shift to the right but not beyond D'' because tax and spending capitalization is not full. The tax incidence will transfer entirely to the land user.

The Chinese Case

To examine the potential of the above four scenarios for the proposed property tax reform in China, three factors related to the assumptions of each scenario will be analyzed: (1) local government incentive to collect the new property tax; (2) the utilization of property tax collections; and (3) the capitalization of public goods investment and tax liabilities into land and housing prices.

Local Government Incentive

How will local governments respond to the central government's mandate to implement the proposed property tax? Lin and Ho (2005) and Gong (2006) document the tendency for local officials to disobey central government regulations regarding public finance and land revenues. Local officials in China have also often been noted for their entrepreneurial activities and mindsets (Oi 1998). The proposed property tax mandated by the central government might be viewed by local officials as a fortuitous decision that allows them to collect more funds. Or, because land revenues are now accounted for in extrabudgetary records, local governments may be hesitant to implement the tax if it competes with land-leasing revenues. The same is true regarding the perception of property taxes competing with user fees. The new property tax is supposed to replace some user fees, which are currently off-budget items. Because the property tax revenue will be recorded in the formal budget, some local governments may believe that it is in their best interest to continue to charge user fees and exactions.

In 1994 the central authorities directed local governments to collect a capital gains tax on home sellers (referred to in China as a land appreciation tax). Many local governments effectively did not comply. In 2006 and 2007, the central government issued several circulars ordering local governments to strengthen their collections of the land value-added tax and specifying how it should be collected (State Administration of Taxation 2007a; 2007b; Ministry of Finance and State Administration of Taxation 2007). It is often difficult for the center to control local governments, especially if they perceive the new property tax as interference in local economic growth. Central policy makers should be aware of local governments' incentives in designing the new property tax system. If local governments are reluctant to collect the property tax, reform objectives will not be realized. As postulated by scenarios 2 and 3, if the new tax raises land value and in turn increases lease revenues, that would provide the needed incentive for local governments to carry out the reform.

Utilization of Property Tax Revenue

Analysis of local government accounts data shows that local own-source revenues have been consistently lower than spending on local services and infrastructure. Table 9.1 shows the buoyancy of expenditures on local public goods (LPGs) in relation to local own-source revenues of four prefecture-level cities.[6] Between 2000 and 2006, LPG expenditures relative to own-source revenues were not buoyant. The last two columns compare the percent changes of the share of revenues spent on total expenditures to the share of revenues spent on local public goods from 2000 to 2006. The −8 percent average in both columns indicates that over this

---

[6] Designation of which expenditures are LPG expenditures was made by the authors. The following expenditure items were excluded from the LPG expenditure category: geological prospecting; agriculture; forestry; supporting underdeveloped areas; and operating expenses of agriculture, forestry, water conservancy, and meteorology departments were all excluded because they occur in rural areas, where households will not be subjected to the proposed property tax. Expenditures for national defense, foreign affairs, and armed police troops were not included because they do not benefit specific localities. Expenditures for pensions and relief funds for social welfare, retirement payments for persons from administrative departments, and subsidies to social security programs were not included on the grounds that social security benefits are provided at the province or prefecture-city level, are tied to an individual's province, and cannot be obtained if one moves to a different locality. Expenditures for interest on debts and special items were also excluded. All other items were included. See National Bureau of Statistics, *China Statistical Yearbook*, 2001–2007, tables 8–15, for details.

TABLE 9.1
Revenues and Expenditures of Prefecture-Level Cities (billions of yuan)

City	Year	Total Expenditures	Total Expenditures on LPGs[a]	Total Own-Source Revenues	Ratio of Revenues Expended	Ratio of Revenues Spent on LPGs[a]	Change in Percent of Revenue Expended	Change in Percent of Revenues Spent on LPGs[a]
Beijing	2006	129.7	106.3	111.7	1.16	0.95	−8	−8
	2003	73.5	61.4	59.3	1.24	1.04	−4	−7
	2000	44.3	38.2	34.5	1.28	1.11		
Tianjin	2006	54.3	44.8	41.7	1.30	1.08	−22	−21
	2003	31.2	26.2	20.5	1.53	1.28	13	11
	2000	18.7	15.7	13.4	1.40	1.18		
Chongqing	2006	59.4	41.7	31.8	1.87	1.31	−24	−19
	2003	34.2	24.3	16.2	2.11	1.50	−4	−1
	2000	18.8	13.2	8.7	2.15	1.52		
Shanghai	2006	179.6	158.3	157.6	1.14	1.00	−9	−11
	2003	108.8	98.9	88.6	1.23	1.12	−3	−4
	2000	60.9	56.1	48.5	1.25	1.16		
Average		67.8	57.1	52.7	1.47	1.19	−8	−8

SOURCE: National Bureau of Statistics, *China Statistical Yearbook*, 2007, 2004, 2001.

NOTE: Revenues reported in this table are all local government own-source revenues and do not include extrabudgetary revenues. [a] "Local public goods" expenditures here refer to expenses on local public services and infrastructures. Please see footnote 6 for an explanation of which expenditures are included in local goods.

period, as the share of own-source revenues contributed to total expenditures decreased, the share spent on LPGs decreased at the same rate. All the selected cities experienced continuous reductions in the share of revenues spent on LPGs during this period.

The buoyancy of LPG expenditures related to overall expenditures and revenues is an important indicator for the success of property tax benefit capitalization. Public spending cannot eventually raise home prices if the property tax revenues are not spent on LPGs. In addition, local governments generally spend much of land-leasing revenues, which are nonbudgetary revenue items, on capital infrastructure investment (Peterson 2006). Aside from lease revenues, debt financing secured by future land lease revenues is the other major source of funding for infrastructure projects (Peterson 2006). Table 9.1 suggests that the new property tax revenues must be spent entirely on LPGs, because local own-source revenues have not been sufficient to cover all LPG expenditures. Clear laws that mandate the utilization of property tax revenues on LPGs may be needed. Yet providing local government with guidelines to collect the new property tax and spend the revenue will not be enough to ensure fiscal success. Market forces will also determine the capitalization rate of property tax liabilities and public spending into housing and land prices, which in turn affect the land-leasing income of local governments.

Capitalization of Tax Liabilities and Public Spending

Several hedonic regressions analyzing housing markets in China suggest that some local government expenditures are being capitalized into property prices. In a study of 900 apartment complexes in Beijing, Kahn and Zheng (2008) found positive and statistically significant effects on housing prices for units that are closer to (1) subway lines; (2) parks; (3) top high schools; (4) a university; and (5) areas with better air quality. Using time series data of prices and features of 709 apartments throughout Beijing, Gu and Zheng (2008) also found positive and statistically significant effects on housing prices for units that were closer to subway stops. Wen, Jia, and Guo (2005) studied the Hangzhou housing market with 2,473 observations in 290 housing community and found that traffic conditions, community management, environment, and entertainment facilities have significant effects on housing prices. Table 9.2 summarizes the findings of these studies.

The question of whether property tax liabilities are being capitalized into housing prices in China is difficult to answer. As far as we know, there is no existing study on this topic. To complicate matters further, the proposed property tax has not yet begun, although it has been widely reported in the mass media. All the publicity could affect home buyers' anticipation of future housing prices, leading to decreases in property values. It is difficult to measure the effects of the announcement of property tax reform, however, since they are not easily distinguished from the numerous other contemporaneous efforts of the government to cool down the property markets such as increases in the required mortgage down payments on investment purchases and limits on foreign purchases of apartment units.

To separate the tax capitalization effect from other influences that affect property prices, we compiled panel data based on information from the *China Statistical*

TABLE 9.2
Summary of Results of Three Hedonic Regression Studies

	Dependent Variable Is Log (House Price)		Dependent Variable Is Log (House Price)		Dependent Variable Is Log (Land Price)	
Independent Variable	Coefficient	Source	Coefficient	Source	Coefficient	Source
Log (distance to an inner subway in km)	−0.108*** (−3.8)	Kahn and Zheng (2008)	−0.08*** (−6.9)	Gu and Zheng (2008)	−0.108*** (−5.8)	Gu and Zheng (2008)
Log (distance to an outer subway in km)	0.023 (−1.11)	Kahn and Zheng (2008)	−0.03*** (−3.5)	Gu and Zheng (2008)	0.002 (−0.2)	Gu and Zheng (2008)
Log (distance to Grade A high school in km)	−0.054*** (−2.45)	Kahn and Zheng (2008)	−0.07 (−5.7)	Gu and Zheng (2008)	−0.168*** (−8.1)	Gu and Zheng (2008)
Distance to West Lake in km	−0.154*** (−39.5)	Wen et al. (2005)				
Log (distance to a park in km)	−0.057 (−2.06)	Kahn and Zheng (2008)				
Traffic conditions	0.056	Wen et al. (2005)				
Community management	0.044	Wen et al. (2005)				
Entertainment	0.02	Wen et al. (2005)				
Environment	0.041	Wen et al. (2005)				
Bad air quality	−0.005*** (−5.85)	Kahn and Zheng (2008)				

NOTE: ***,** and * indicate statistical significance at the 1, 5, and 10% levels, respectively. T-statistics are in parentheses below the coefficient value.

Yearbook (National Bureau of Statistics 2001–2007). The panel data are composed of cross-sectional time series information about average commercial property prices, estimated total effective tax rates of three property taxes (urban and township land use tax, building tax, and real estate tax), measures of local public goods provision, and other related factors in twenty-seven provinces and four provincial-level cities (see table 9.3 for details). We used fixed and random effects regression techniques to estimate the tax capitalization effect on commercial property prices in China. There were two reasons for choosing this approach.

First, due to the lack of district-level information, we could not employ the commonly used hedonic price modeling to assess the tax capitalization effect on housing prices in a specific market. Instead, we focused on commercial property markets

TABLE 9.3
Descriptive Statistics of Variables

Variable	Description	Obs.	Mean	SD	Min.	Max.	Expected Sign
Dependent variable							
Avg_price (yuan per sq m)	Average commercial property price: In using average prices, we assume a high level of homogeneity of commercial properties within each province.	242	3,246.82	2,340.31	843.26	13,554.71	
Independent variable							
Tax_rate (percent)	Effective tax rate: Total tax revenue collected from three property-related taxes divided by the estimated total commercial building value	240	0.567%	0.560%	0.04%	2.27%	Negative
VAT/GRP	The ratio between value-added tax collections and gross regional product	248	0.040	0.052	0.002	0.254	Negative
Unemp (percent)	Unemployment rate	242	3.79%	0.75%	1.2%	6.5%	Positive
Sewage (cm per capita)	Volume of daily sewage treated, divided by total population	238	0.060	0.069	0.0002	0.560	Positive
Patent (percent)	Patents granted as a percent of the national total	248	2.93%	3.85%	0.01%	21.5%	Positive
Electricity (10,000 kwh per person)	Electricity consumption per capita	240	0.171	0.107	0.046	0.626	Positive
Paved_roads (sq km per person)	Paved roads per capita	248	9.920	3.640	3.900	31.830	Positive
H_degree	University degrees granted per capita	248	0.00125	0.00103	0.00028	0.00671	Positive

NOTE: Obs. = Observations; SD = standard deviation.

across 31 provinces because provincial-level data were available. Our assumption was that, aside from other considerations, businesses do take into account the differential effective property tax rates across regions in making location decisions. Conversely, individuals are less likely to move from one province to another simply because of lower property taxes. Thus, in our regression analysis, we estimated the tax capitalization effect on commercial properties only. In fact, most nonluxury residential properties are exempt from the current property taxes on buildings. For example, nonbusiness buildings owned by local citizens are exempt from the building tax. The urban real estate tax is levied only on properties possessed by foreign entities. Thus, the exclusion of residential housing markets from our analysis should not lead to a significant loss of information.

Second, while it was possible to use ordinary least-square (OLS) multiple regression techniques to estimate tax capitalization in a single housing market, it was not optimal for our study, which examined both longitudinal and time series data. Differences in commercial property markets across provinces potentially create an omitted variable bias that is hard to control for in OLS models. The problem was mediated by using the fixed and random effects regression techniques. The fixed effects regression allowed us to control for omitted variables that differed between provinces but were constant over time. These variables included, for example, the unique geographical characteristics of each province, its natural resource endowment, and its local culture. We also used a random effects model to control for some variables that were fixed between cases but varied over time and other omitted variables that were constant over time but differed between cases. An example of the first type of variables includes regulations that the central government imposes on all commercial real estate markets across regions. These national regulations are applied equally to all provinces but can change over time. The panel data and these two regression techniques enabled us to control for both types of omitted variables that affected the dependent variable. Our fixed and random effects regression model is as follows:

$$\log(\text{Avg\_price}_{i,t}) = \alpha_i + \beta_1 * \log(\text{Tax\_rate}_{i,t}) + \beta_2 * \log(\text{VAT/GRP}_{i,t}) \\ + \beta_3 * \log(\text{Unemp}_{i,t}) + \beta_4 * \text{Sewage}_{i,t} + \beta_5 * \log(\text{Patent}_{i,t}) \\ + \beta_6 * \log(\text{Electricity}_{i,t}) + \beta_7 * \log(\text{Length\_road}_{i,t}) \\ + \beta_8 * \log(\text{H\_degree}_{i,t}) + u_i + \varepsilon_{i,t}$$

where

Avg_price$_{i,t}$ = average price per square meter of floor area of commercial property in province i at period t

Tax_rate$_{i,t}$ = effective property tax rate in province i at period t

VAT/GRP$_{i,t}$ = value-added tax revenue as a ratio of gross regional product in province i at period t

Unemp$_{i,t}$ = unemployment rate in province i at period t

Sewage$_{i,t}$ = daily disposal volume of sewage in centimeters per capita in province i at period t

Patent$_{i,t}$ = percent of patents granted of the national total in province i at period t

Electricity$_{i,t}$ = electricity consumption per capita in province i at period t
Paved_roads$_{i,t}$ = length of paved road per capita in province i at period t
H_degree$_{i,t}$ = number of higher degrees granted per capita in province i at period t
u_i = random effects
$\varepsilon_{i,t}$ = error term

Table 9.4 shows the regression results derived from the random effects regression. Estimated coefficients of public goods are consistent with previous studies mentioned earlier. Variables for measuring capitalization of public infrastructure, such as sewage treatment (Sewage) and transportation (Paved_roads), are all positive and statistically significant. Investment in science and technology measured in terms of patents granted as a percent of the national total (Patent) is also significant. Yet education measured in terms of per capita university degrees given annually (H_degree) does not have a significant impact on price. Other instrumental variables measuring labor market conditions (Unemp) and economic development level (Electricity) are significant. We also used value-added tax (VAT) revenue as a ratio of gross regional product (VAT/GRP) to control for the influence of VAT on commercial property price. The regression estimates that a 1 percent increase in the VAT rate will reduce commercial property prices by 0.05 percent.

TABLE 9.4

Capitalization Estimates of Property Tax and Public Goods [dependent variable: log(avg_price)]

Independent Variable	Estimated Coefficient
Constant	6.703***
	(0.720)
log(Tax_rate)	−0.167***
	(0.0251)
Sewage	2.684***
	(0.580)
log(Paved_roads)	0.139**
	(0.074)
log(Patent)	0.068***
	(0.028)
log(H_degree)	0.068
	(0.058)
log(Unemp)	−0.350***
	(0.118)
log(Electricity)	0.412***
	(0.062)
log(VAT)	−0.051***
	(0.016)
R^2	0.732
No. of observations	235

NOTE: *** and ** indicate statistical significance at the 1 and 5% levels, respectively. Standard errors are in parentheses below the coefficient value.

The effective property tax rate (Tax_rate) has a statistically significant negative impact on commercial property price. As shown in table 9.4, a 1 percent increase in the effective property tax rate would lead to a 0.16 percent decrease in average price, holding all other factors constant. This finding might surprise some observers because property tax rates in China have not been high. The urban and township land use tax (LUT) is an area-based tax, and local governments divide their jurisdictions into different taxing zones according to population size or land use. Land in different zones is taxed at an array of tax rates preset by the central government, ranging from 0.2 to 10 yuan per square meter (1 yuan = US$0.143). The building tax (BT) and urban real estate tax (URET) are value-based taxes levied on the assessed capital value (or the purchasing cost for the BT) of the property. The tax rate is 1.2 percent for the BT and 1.5 percent for the URET. If an estimated rental value is used instead, the tax rates for the BT and URET will be 12 and 15 percent, respectively. In some locales, like Beijing, if actual rental value is available because individual property owners rent their dwellings to another party at the market rate, the BT will be calculated at 4 percent of gross rental income of the property.

Chinese officials have admitted that the tax rates for the LUT are set too low; hence they assert that the collections of that tax are not a major revenue source for local governments. According to table 9.5, the three property taxes that were included in our regression analysis accounted for only a small percentage of the total own-source revenue for local government. In 2006 the URET and LUT taxes were 3.78 percent of total local revenue. Percentages found in more prosperous cities, such as Beijing, Tianjin, Shanghai, and Chongqing, were not higher than the national figure (see the last two columns in table 9.5).

Although property tax revenues are not large, they may still affect taxpayer behavior. The current two value-based property taxes (BT and URET) are heavily focused on taxing commercial and foreign-owned residential properties. Thus, the two taxes are collected from specific sectors of the economy that may shoulder

TABLE 9.5

Land-Related Taxes, 2006 (yuan billions)

	Urban Real Estate Tax	Urban and Township Land Use Tax	City Maintenance and Construction Tax	Stamp Tax	Land Value-Added Tax	Total Own-Source Local Government Revenue	First 2 Taxes as Percentage of Total Local Own-Revenues	All 5 Land-Related Taxes as a Percentage of Total Local Own-Revenues
All local governments	51.48	17.68	93.34	20.26	23.15	1,830.36	3.78	11.25
Beijing	4.33	0.40	4.52	1.35	0.57	111.72	4.23	10.00
Tianjin	1.26	0.11	1.92	0.50	0.36	41.70	3.29	9.95
Shanghai	4.27	0.26	5.30	2.69	3.57	157.61	2.87	10.20
Chongqing	0.66	0.45	1.55	0.32	0.44	31.77	3.47	10.72

SOURCE: National Bureau of Statistics, *China Statistical Yearbook* (2007), tables 8–14.
NOTE: Data in the table refer to budgetary data.

the majority of the tax burden. It will require less-aggregate-level studies to verify this assertion. Unfortunately, data limitation prohibited us from examining this issue.

The key result of this provincial-level analysis is that there is evidence to support capitalization of tax liabilities and public services in commercial real estate markets in China. The relationship between tax and spending capitalization is important because it implies that commercial real estate developers and investors desire to get what they pay for. If they pay property taxes, they demand better local infrastructure and public services. Certainly this does not mean that the Tiebout idea is in full swing. The assumptions that benefits accrue only to property tax payers, that everyone is perfectly mobile, and that jurisdictions are composed of residents with like income and tastes encounter problems in China. Labor and capital are relatively immobile due to government policies and the hukou (household registration) system (Boyreau-Debray and Wei 2004; Huang and Wei 2001). The implication of the findings is that there seems to be sorting in commercial property markets according to government spending and taxation.

Conclusions

To conclude, we return to the three questions posed in the beginning of this chapter. Our answers are speculative and incomplete. As to whether the new property tax would complement or compete with the land-leasing fee, we found evidence of tax capitalization into commercial real estate prices in our study. If the new tax lowers prices, land value will fall. Local governments may in turn receive lower income from leasing public land. In other words, scenario 1 may occur if we do not consider the benefit side of property taxation. There is, however, evidence to support capitalization of public spending into property prices, as well. Hence the assumption of having no public goods investment effect on prices is unrealistic. If additional funds raised from the new tax were invested in public goods, property prices should increase. We do not have the information to show how the interaction between capitalization of tax liabilities and public spending may finally affect prices. Yet it is reasonable to argue that scenario 1 is unlikely in the Chinese case. There is no evidence to indicate full tax and spending capitalization into property value. Estimating the rate of return on infrastructure investment is also beyond the scope of this paper. Thus, the possibility of scenarios 2 and 3 remains an open question, and additional research is needed.

Scenario 4 seems to be most probable. It suggests that if the rate of tax capitalization is stronger than that of public goods investment, land value will fall. But the drop in land value would not be drastic if local governments increased their spending on public services. If investors and home buyers respond more positively toward government spending than toward the new tax, property and land values may even rise. Lease revenue would increase because of higher land prices. The idea that the proposed property tax scheme might increase lease revenue should be conveyed carefully to local officials who are worried about the fiscal impacts of the new tax. The effect may depend on how they utilize the additional tax collections.

If property owners and buyers are indeed willing to pay for what they want, as implied by our analysis, the new tax could be an efficient way to finance additional public investment. This information may help convince local officials to cooperate fully with the central government in the upcoming property tax reform. It may also encourage them to increase their investment in public goods.

If there is an incentive for local government to invest the extra funds in public goods, existing land users may be able to see the new property tax as merely payment for additional services. This may in turn mediate their concern about paying both leasehold charges and property taxes. Besides, if real estate developers and bankers see the positive impact of the new tax on the value of their assets and investment portfolios, they may also be willing to support the reform. That said, the data used in this study are highly aggregate. They are from a secondary source that the statistical methods, coverage, and definitions may vary from year to year. Hence, our estimates may only indicate trends and characterize major differences rather than offering precise quantitative measures. Readers are urged to consider these limitations in interpreting our findings. As stated earlier, more research is needed to estimate the capitalization rates of tax and spending. Disaggregate data and analyses are also required.

REFERENCES

Bird, Richard M., and Enid Slack, eds. 2004. *International handbook of land and property taxation*. Cheltenham, U.K.: Edward Elgar.

———. 2006. Taxing land and property in emerging economies: Raising revenue . . . and more? Paper presented at the Conference on Land Policies for Urban Development, Cambridge, MA (June 5–6).

Constitution of the People's Republic of China. 1982. http://english.people.com.cn/constitution/constitution.html.

Development Research Center of the State Council. 2005. China's real estate taxation system. Working Paper No. WP06CT1. Cambridge, MA: Lincoln Institute of Land Policy.

Fischel, William A. 2001. Municipal corporations, homeowners, and the benefit view of the property tax. In *Property taxation and local government finance*, ed. Wallace E. Oates. Cambridge, MA: Lincoln Institute of Land Policy.

George, Henry. [1879] 1962. *Progress and poverty*. New York: Robert Schalkenbach Foundation.

Gong, Tina. 2006. Corruption and local governance: The double identity of Chinese local governments in market reform. *Pacific Review* 19(1):85–102.

Gronberg, Timothy J. 1979. The interaction of markets in housing and local public goods: A simultaneous equations approach. *Southern Economic Journal* 46(2):445–459.

Gu, Yizhen, and Siqi Zheng. 2008. The impacts of suburb rail transit on property value and development intensity: The case of No. 13 line in Beijing [in Chinese]. Working Paper.

Hamilton, Bruce W. 1975. Zoning and property taxation in a system of local government. *Urban Studies* 12(2):205–211.

———. 1976. Capitalization of intrajurisdictional differences in local tax prices. *American Economics Review* 66(5):743–753.

Hong, Yu Hung. 1998. Transaction costs of allocating the increased land value under public leasehold systems: Hong Kong. *Urban Studies* 35(9):1577–1595.

———. 2003. The last straw: Reforming local property tax in The People's Republic of China. Report for the David C. Lincoln Fellowship Program. Cambridge, MA: Lincoln Institute of Land Policy.

Hong, Yu-Hung, and Steven C. Bourassa. 2003. Why public leasehold? Issues and concepts. In *Leasing public land: Policy debates and international experiences*, eds. Steven C. Bourassa and Yu-Hung Hong. Cambridge, MA: Lincoln Institute of Land Policy.

Huang, Ling, and Shang-Jin Wei. 2001. One China, many kingdoms? Understanding local protection using individual price data. IMF Paper. Washington, DC: International Monetary Fund.

Ihlanfeldt, Keith, and John Jackson. 1982. Systematic assessment error and intrajurisdictional property tax capitalization. *Southern Economic Journal* 49:417–427.

Kahn, Matthew, and Siqi Zheng. 2008. Land and residential property markets in a booming economy: New evidence from Beijing. *Journal of Urban Economics* 63:743–757.

King, A. Thomas. 1973. Estimating property tax capitalization: A critical comment. *Journal of Political Economy* 85(2):425–431.

Krupa, Olha, John L. Mikesell, and C. Kurt Zorn. 2006. Land value taxation for local government finance in the Russian Federation: A case study of Saratov Oblast. Working Paper No. WP06KZ1. Cambridge, MA: Lincoln Institute of Land Policy.

Lin, George C. S., and Samuel P. S. Ho. 2005. The state, land system, and land development processes in contemporary China. *Annals of the Association of American Geographers* 95(2): 411–436.

Malme, Jane H., and Joan M. Youngman. 2001. *The development of property taxation in economies in transition: Case studies from central and eastern Europe*. Washington, DC: World Bank.

Mieszkowski, Peter, and George R. Zodrow. 1989. Taxation and the Tiebout model: The differential effects of head taxes, taxes on land rents, and property taxes. *Journal of Economic Literature* 27:1098–1146.

Ministry of Finance and State Administration of Taxation. 2007. Circular on the policy relating to land value-added tax on ordinary standard residential premises. *China Law & Practice* :1.

National Bureau of Statistics. 2001–2007. *China statistical yearbook*. Beijing: China Statistics Press.

Naughton, Fergus. 2007. China expanding property tax pilot project ahead of 2008 introduction. *Forbes AFX News Limited*, October 16.

Oates, Wallace E. 1969. The effects of property taxes and local public spending on property value: An empirical study of tax capitalization and the Tiebout hypothesis. *Journal of Political Economy* 77(6):956–961.

Oi, Jean. 1998. The evolution of local state corporatism. In *Zouping in transition: The process of reform in rural north China*, ed. Andrew Walder, Cambridge, MA: Harvard University Press.

Palmon, Oded, and Barton A. Smith. 1998. New evidence on property tax capitalization. *Journal of Political Economy* 106:1099–1111.

Peterson, George E. 2006. Land leasing and land sale as an infrastructure-financing option. World Bank Policy Research Working Paper No. 4043. Washington, DC: World Bank (November). http://ssrn.com/abstract=940509.

State Administration of Taxation. 2007a. Circular on issues relevant to the administration of the settlement of land value-added tax on real property developers. *China Law and Practice* (February):1.

———. 2007b. Land appreciation tax is not a newly levied tax. January 8. http://202.108.90.130/n6669073/n6669118/6940866.html

Šulija, Vytautas, and Gintautas Šulija. 2005. Reform of the property tax and problems of real estate appraisal for taxation purposes in transitional economies of central and eastern Europe. Working Paper No. WP05VS1. Cambridge, MA: Lincoln Institute of Land Policy.

Tiebout, Charles M. 1956. A pure theory of local expenditures. *Journal of Political Economy* 64(5):416–424.

Wales, T. J., and Elmer G. Wiens. 1974. Capitalization of residential property taxes: An empirical study. *The Review of Economics and Statistics* 56(3):329–333.

Wen, Hai-Zhen, Sheng-Hua Jia, and Xiao-Yu Guo. 2005. Hedonic price analysis of urban housing: An empirical research on Hangzhou, China. *Journal of Zhejiang University* (Science) 6A(8):907–914.

Youngman, Joan, and Jane Malme. 2004. The property tax in a new environment: Lessons from international tax reform efforts. Paper presented at the Andrew Young School Fourth Annual Conference on Public Finance Issues in an International Perspective: Challenges of Tax Reform in a Global Economy, Stone Mountain, Georgia (May 24–25).

Zodrow, George R. 2001. Reflections on the new view and the benefit view of the property tax. In *Property taxation and local government finance*, ed. Wallace E. Oates. Cambridge, MA: Lincoln Institute of Land Policy.

———. 2006. Who pays the property tax? And what does capitalization tell us about who pays? *Land Lines* (April):14–19.

Intergovernmental Transfers

10

The Determinants of Intergovernmental Transfer

LI ZHANG AND XINYE ZHENG

In China in recent years there has been an increasing interest in the intergovernmental transfer system, among other issues. Nonetheless, compared with other aspects of the economy, the intergovernmental transfer system receives relatively less attention, partly owing to the unavailability of data.

Literature on the transfer system in China has mainly dwelt on the role of transfers in achieving the objective of equalization across localities (Persson and Eriksson 2006) and whether different layers of subnational government structures enforce or offset the goal of the central governments (Bahl and Wallace 2003; Martinez-Vazquez and Timofeev 2006). The question we are interested in is what factors determine the number of transfers each locality receives. In other words, what criteria does the central government or other higher-level government follow in allocating transfers to lower-level government? Are nationally designated poverty counties (NDPCs) receiving transfers based on factors different from those for non-NDPCs?[1]

Not until recently has the literature started to explore the transfer system in this direction. However, the limited research so far seems to put the emphasis on political factors instead of economic factors. For example, Persson and Eriksson (2006) attribute the trend of transfers becoming equalized to the desire of the central government to achieve social stability. Wang (2005) also sees transfers as tools used by Chinese politicians to please their constituents or neutralize potential threats.[2]

However, economic conditions also play an important role, one usually more significant than the political roles. China has been adopting the mechanisms of a market economy, and the relevant reforms conducted in various sectors, including fiscal relations, have put more and more emphasis on economics. Thus, it is imperative to analyze the determinants of transfers in China from an economic perspective.

---

[1] There are now 591 NDPCs, based on income level, status, and other similar factors. Supposedly the center implements special fiscal policies toward these counties, including more transfers.

[2] Treisman (1996) also explains intergovernmental transfers in Russia by political factors.

Most of the literature on the transfer system in China has been restricted to provincial data, mainly due to availability. Now with our data set, analysis can be extended to the county level for 1997–2003. We are hoping that the county-level data will allow us to capture more of the variations in transfers across counties and explain the determinants of transfer allocations or actual transfers with more precision. Our empirical results show that the total effect of the transfer is not equalizing, even though the transfer without the tax rebate is equalizing. The effect of the tax rebate, which is pro-rich, is dominating. Although China has established an objective of equalization, the actual policy consequence shows that the objective has not yet been fulfilled.

This chapter reviews the economics behind the intergovernmental transfer: why higher-level governments make transfers to lower-level governments. Special focus is on the transfer system in China: how it has evolved and what is included in the current transfer system. Then an empirical analysis is conducted using our county-level data set to examine how transfers are allocated to each county. The total transfer is used, as well as the two broad categories of transfers. The sample is eventually divided into two subgroups, NDPCs and non-NDPCs, which are compared, and then the whole sample is divided into urban counties and rural counties.

Economics of Transfer and the Transfer System in China

In countries with multiple levels of government, intergovernmental transfers have been an important instrument for higher-level governments to correct for the horizontal and vertical imbalances among local governments. Local governments, due to the difference in their natural endowments, economic conditions, and demographic characteristics, have different capacities for raising revenues and also differ in their public expenditure needs. This inevitably results in a horizontal imbalance in needs and capabilities. Assignments of revenues and expenditures could put more responsibilities on lower-level governments without giving them enough revenue sources, which would lead to a vertical imbalance. Intergovernmental transfers from higher-level governments to lower-level governments can mitigate both imbalances. When local governments are reluctant to provide public services at an adequate level due to the spillover of the benefits, the central government can correct this by issuing some kind of transfer. Or when local governments implement national programs on behalf of the central government, the latter should at least provide funds via intergovernmental transfers.

Intergovernmental transfers are present in almost all the countries. And depending on whether they have a specific purpose, they can usually be classified into two broad categories: conditional and unconditional. The many types of transfers in China can generally be fit into these two categories.

The intergovernmental transfer system in China has been criticized for its lack of transparency, its ad hoc and discretionary instead of rule-based methods (Ahmad, Singh, and Fortuna 2004). In view of the huge disparities across regions and the mismatch between expenditure responsibilities and revenue sources, transfers have taken on very important roles in intergovernmental relations in China over the years. Local governments, especially those in poor regions, rely on transfers

FIGURE 10.1
Division of Expenditure Responsibilities for Central and Local Governments

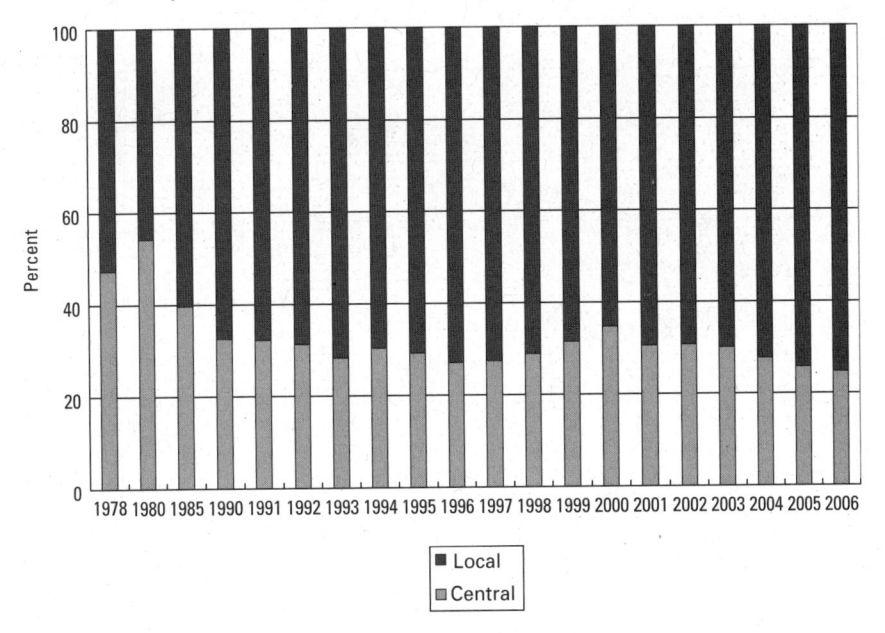

from higher-level governments more and more. In figure 10.1, we can see that local governments spent more than twice that of the central government in most of the years represented.

In figure 10.2 we can see that the center is taking up higher and higher shares in total revenue and leaving less and less to local governments, especially after the 1994 tax reform. Having such low revenue shares while being responsible for more public services, local governments are certainly in great need of intergovernmental transfers.

Currently there are many types of transfers in China. Even though they can be grouped into either conditional or unconditional, they have specific names and are generally for different purposes. According to the classification of the Ministry of Finance (MOF), there are four major categories: tax rebates, institutional transfers, equalization purpose transfers, and special transfers.[3] There are some subcategories in each of those. For example, equalization purpose transfers include the general purpose transfer, transfer for minority regions, transfer for wage adjustments for civil servants, and transfer for agricultural tax reform. From the names, it is obvious that most of these have specific purposes. Basically, only the general purpose transfer is an unconditional one. But all of these are aimed either at addressing the vertical imbalance or at helping poor regions and can be roughly grouped into equalization purpose transfers. To look at the equalization effects, we divide the total transfers into two parts. One is tax rebates, and the other is equalization transfers, which include the equalization purpose transfer and the remaining two categories.

---

[3] According to the international definition, tax sharing is part of the intergovernmental transfer. However, the definition adopted by the Chinese government usually does not include tax sharing, and in this chapter we follow the Chinese definition.

FIGURE 10.2
Division of Revenue Between Central and Local Governments

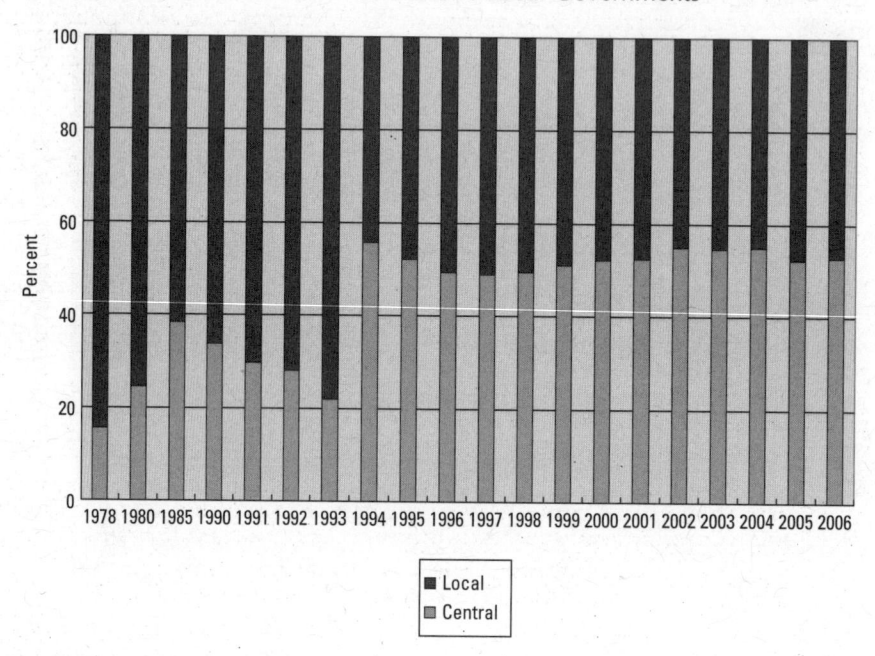

FIGURE 10.3
Transfer Categories over Years

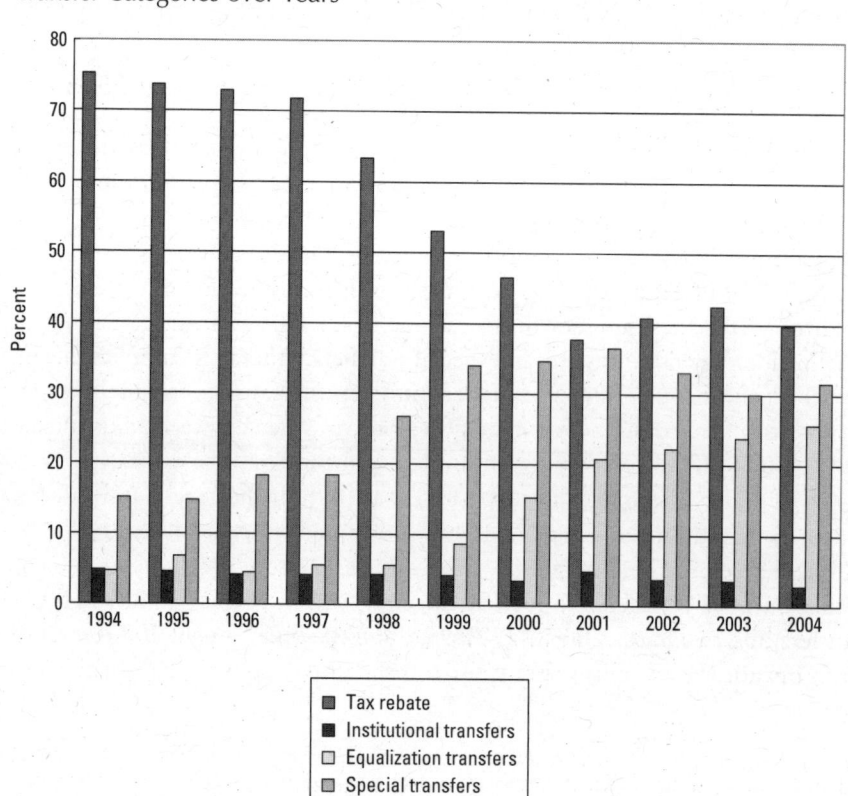

Tax rebates started with the 1994 tax reform, when the central government wanted to give incentives to local governments to accept the tax reforms. It guaranteed keeping the interests of local governments as of 1993 intact, which was basically a compromise between the interests of the center and the interests of local governments. In other words, local governments could at least keep their interests after the 1994 tax reform.[4] Therefore, the reforms were pro-rich at the beginning: Rich provinces would obtain more in tax rebates, while poor provinces would obtain less. The institutional transfers and the special transfers are not always for equalization purposes, and including the two in our equalization transfer category will undoubtedly exaggerate the extent of equalization outcomes of the transfer system. Nonetheless, even with equalization transfers inflated, we can see that they could not outweigh the effects of the tax rebates. As illustrated in figure 10.3, until 2004, even though tax rebates had been decreasing over the years, they made up the highest share of total transfers.

Economic Factors Determining Transfers in Chinese Counties

Our empirical analysis is based on the sum of all categories of transfers; it is also divided between tax rebates and all other transfers, mostly for the purpose of equalization.[5] The results of the fixed effects regressions are shown in table 10.1. From this table we can see that the higher the per capita GDP level, the lower the per capita equalization transfers but the higher the tax rebates a county gets. For total transfers, the relationship is again positive, which means the effects of the tax rebate dominate the effects of the equalization transfers. All results are highly significant.

From another variable, per capita own revenue, the coefficients are positive for both tax rebates and total transfers, but negative for equalization transfers, with all results significant at the 1 percent level. The amounts of per capita equalization transfers counties get are negatively correlated with per capita own revenue, while per capita own revenue is positively correlated with tax rebates per capita. When these two counteracting forces are summed, the effects of tax rebates are again dominant.

On the other hand, when we look at the lag of per capita expenditure, things are reversed. The lag of per capita expenditure is positively correlated with transfers whether or not we take into consideration tax rebates: The higher the expenditure in a period, the higher the transfers allocated to the county in the next period. However, when it comes to tax rebates per capita, the relationship becomes negative and significant. Since tax rebates are calculated based on the formula denoted above, this negative relationship should not be interpreted as meaning the lower the expenditure last year, the higher the rebate this year.

In addition, the population variable has a negative sign except for rebates, but none of them is significant. However, the share of rural population in total is positive and significant for equalization transfers, meaning that the higher the proportion of rural population, the more equalization transfers are allocated. This confirms that equalization transfers are pro-poor. But the effects are not present in the case of tax rebates; in regression (4) the sign even becomes negative. Fortunately,

---

[4] There is a detailed explanation of the history of as well as the formula for tax rebates in Zhang and Martinez (2002).
[5] For this reason, the term *equalization transfers* is used here for all transfers except tax rebates.

TABLE 10.1
Transfer Results for All Counties

	Equalization Transfer	Equalization Transfer	Tax Rebate	Tax Rebate	Total Transfer	Total Transfer
Per capita GDP	−0.001 (2.21)**	−0.001 (2.75)***	0.007 (46.61)***	0.006 (44.54)***	0.006 (19.54)***	0.006 (17.90)***
Population	−0.221 (1.54)	−0.220 (1.57)	0.045 (0.63)	0.115 (1.64)	−0.176 (1.13)	−0.106 (0.69)
Lag of per capita exp.	0.241 (39.91)***	0.244 (40.15)***	−0.019 (6.27)***	−0.011 (3.70)***	0.221 (33.73)***	0.233 (35.37)***
Share of rural population	1.323 (4.68)***	1.214 (4.29)***	0.090 (0.63)	−0.129 (0.91)	1.412 (4.59)***	1.086 (3.54)***
Share of public employee/pop.		591.989 (3.89)***		1,428.969 (18.90)***		2,020.958 (12.27)***
Per capita own revenue	−0.035 (5.28)***	−0.039 (5.75)***	0.172 (51.16)***	0.164 (49.14)***	0.137 (18.83)***	0.126 (17.24)***
Total fiscal dependents	−0.000 (0.65)	—	0.001 (2.03)**		0.000 (0.35)	
Year dummies	Yes	Yes	Yes	Yes	Yes	Yes
Constant	174.474 (7.32)***	159.247 (6.72)***	3.802 (0.32)	−22.236 (1.89)*	178.276 (6.86)***	137.010 (5.34)***
Observations	14,433	14,433	14,433	14,433	14,433	14,433
Number of counties	2,703	2,703	2,703	2,703	2,703	2,703
R^2	0.45	0.45	0.46	0.48	0.52	0.53

SOURCE: Ministry of Finance, *China fiscal statistics for prefectures, cities, and counties, 1998–2004.*
NOTE: *$p < 0.1$, **$p < 0.05$, ***$p < 0.01$.

this time the pro-poor feature from the equalization transfer is dominant, since for total transfers the rural population share is again positive and significant.

From the time dummies, we can see that the amounts of equalization transfers and total transfers are both increasing over the years, while tax rebates did not exhibit an increasing trend until 2002.

Therefore, the results of our regressions show that the central government does try to engage in equalization efforts, as exemplified by the equalization transfers. However, those efforts have been more than offset by tax rebates. The overall effect of the transfer system is pro-rich. The objective of the policy has not been fulfilled.

Extension

Transfers to NDPCs and non-NDPCs. The whole sample was then divided into two subgroups: NDPCs (nationally designated poverty counties) and non-NDPCs. The regressions were run separately for the two groups, and the results are shown in table 10.2.

TABLE 10.2
Regression Results for NDPCs and Non-NDPCs

	NDPCs			Non-NDPCs		
	Total	Equalization	Rebate	Total	Equalization	Rebate
Per capita GDP	0.001	0.001	0.000	0.005	−0.001	0.006
	(0.83)	(0.67)	(0.83)	(16.40)***	(2.40)**	(37.92)***
Population	−0.120	−0.105	−0.014	−0.122	−0.255	0.132
	(0.66)	(0.58)	(0.43)	(0.66)	(1.51)	(1.45)
Lag of per capita exp.	0.862	0.845	0.017	0.208	0.215	−0.007
	(51.42)***	(49.83)***	(5.41)***	(29.01)***	(32.89)***	(1.95)*
Share of rural population	2.076	2.145	−0.069	0.367	0.823	−0.456
	(4.97)***	(5.07)***	(0.89)	(1.03)	(2.54)**	(2.61)***
Share of public employee/pop.	−35.172	−61.411	26.238	2,018.946	533.217	1,485.729
	(0.15)	(0.26)	(0.60)	(10.70)***	(3.10)***	(16.05)***
Per capita own revenue	−0.518	−0.640	0.122	0.142	−0.019	0.161
	(10.79)***	(13.19)***	(13.79)***	(18.19)***	(2.75)***	(42.20)***
Year dummies	Yes	Yes	Yes	Yes	Yes	Yes
Constant	−66.645	−90.952	24.307	−67.004	−44.273	−22.732
	(1.72)*	(2.33)**	(3.40)***	(2.30)**	(1.67)*	(1.59)
Observations	3,326	3,326	3,326	11,268	11,268	11,268
Number of counties	590	590	590	2,124	2,124	2,124
R^2	0.81	0.79	0.30	0.50	0.39	0.48

SOURCE: Ministry of Finance, *China fiscal statistics for prefectures, cities, and counties, 1998–2004.*
NOTE: *p < 0.1, **p < 0.05, ***p < 0.01

From the table we can see that for NDPCs things are significantly different from the case with the whole sample. First, the per capita GDP doesn't exhibit any systematic relationship to the two categories of transfers or to total transfers. The signs of the coefficients of the equalization transfers and the tax rebates are the same as in the whole sample; however, the sum of the two effects takes the sign of the equalization transfers instead of the tax rebates, which means the former is dominant in the case of NDPCs. The share of rural population also shows that the effects of equalization transfers overrule those of the tax rebates. In addition, the lower the per capita own revenue and the higher the share of rural population, the more transfers an NDPC county gets.

For non-NDPCs, things are almost the same as in the whole sample, except for the share of rural population in the total population. Here significantly higher tax rebates go to non-NDPCs with lower rural population shares. This relationship is so strong that it outweighs the positive and significant relationship between rural population share and equalization transfers; the positive and significant results shown for the whole sample in the case of NDPCs don't replicate here.

Thus, our results show that the central government does try to implement different policies for the NDPCs and make transfers more pro-poor. However, since

China has only 590 NDPCs nationwide, making up only 20 percent of the total number of counties, the overall effects become pro-rich instead.[6]

Transfers to Rural Counties vs. Urban Counties. To divide the whole sample into rural counties and urban counties, we first had to determine which was which. If rural population exceeded 85 percent of the total population of a county, we denoted that county rural; if the share of rural population was lower or equal to 85 percent, we denoted the county urban. We ran the regressions separately for rural counties and urban counties; the results are in table 10.3.[7]

We can see from table 10.3 that for urban counties, things are almost the same as for the whole sample. However, for rural counties, we can see from per capita GDP that total transfers have the same sign, negative, as that of equalization transfers, which means they are pro-poor, instead of the sign of tax rebates, which is pro-rich.

TABLE 10.3
Results for Rural Counties and Urban Counties

	Rural Counties			Urban Counties		
	Total	Equalization	Rebate	Total	Equalization	Rebate
Per capita GDP	−0.004	−0.007	0.003	0.004	0.001	0.003
	(3.77)***	(7.11)***	(15.99)***	(11.02)***	(1.88)*	(17.09)***
Population	−3.420	−2.605	−0.816	0.198	−0.339	0.537
	(2.85)***	(2.16)**	(3.24)***	(0.73)	(1.42)	(3.62)***
Lag of per capita exp.	0.547	0.510	0.037	0.199	0.222	−0.023
	(30.16)***	(28.04)***	(9.70)***	(27.34)***	(34.60)***	(5.86)***
Share of rural population	1.123	1.132	−0.009	0.631	0.208	0.423
	(0.68)	(0.69)	(0.03)	(1.42)	(0.53)	(1.74)*
Share of public employee/pop.	−729.463	−798.691	69.228	6,542.811	3,183.153	3,359.658
	(3.43)***	(3.75)***	(1.55)	(22.93)***	(12.63)***	(21.49)***
Per capita own revenue	0.014	−0.004	0.018	0.149	−0.123	0.272
	(1.42)	(0.40)	(8.65)***	(14.20)***	(13.24)***	(47.26)***
Year dummies	Yes	Yes	Yes	Yes	Yes	Yes
Constant	94.001	41.042	52.959	−224.839	−62.499	−162.340
	(0.58)	(0.25)	(1.55)	(6.59)***	(2.07)**	(8.68)***
Observations	6,357	6,357	6,357	8,076	8,076	8,076
Number of counties	1,385	1,385	1,385	1,769	1,769	1,769
R^2	0.50	0.45	0.25	0.59	0.48	0.58

SOURCE: Ministry of Finance, *China fiscal statistics for prefectures, cities, and counties, 1998–2004.*
NOTE: *p < 0.1, **p < 0.05, ***p < 0.01

---

[6] NDPCs make up only one-fifth of total counties, but these poor counties are also much less important in terms of overall economic conditions compared with those of non-NDPCs.

[7] The selection of 85 percent as our criterion is because, at this level, the division of urban and rural counties are more consistent with reality.

The Impact of Rural Tax-for-Fee Reform. Another issue we are interested in is the impact of the rural tax-for-fee reform on the components of transfers. The reform was initiated in Anhui Province in 1999 and extended to all other provinces in 2002; it has been the most profound reform since the tax-sharing reform in 1994. The objective of the reform was to alleviate farmers' heavy burdens by reducing and finally eliminating agriculture-related taxes. In order to capture its impact, we used a dummy variable, which takes the value of 1 when a specific region starts the rural reform in that year, 0 otherwise. We don't have a complete list of when and where the reform started and was extended. We use the presence of a special form of transfer as a criterion: the transfer for rural reform.[8] When the value of the transfer for rural reform is greater than 0 in a region in a certain year, we take it to mean that the reform started in that region, and therefore the dummy takes the value of 1. We also include the impact of rural reform, constructed by interacting the share of rural population in the total population with the reform dummy in some of the specifications.

First we look at the whole sample in table 10.4. In general, the results changed little compared with the results without the reform dummies. The total transfer is pro-rich, even though the equalization is pro-poor. For the first three regressions, when the impact measure is not included, we can see from the coefficients on the reform dummy that the impact of reform on equalization transfer is positive and significant, while negative and significant for the tax rebate. These counteracting components make the impact of the reform negative but insignificant on the total transfer. But in the three regressions (4) through (6), when the impact of reform on rural population is included, the reform dummy in general becomes negative and significant for both tax rebate and total transfer, while the impact on rural population is significantly positive for the equalization transfer as well as the total transfer.

Table 10.5a shows the difference of impacts on urban counties and rural counties, following the procedure shown in table 10.3, except that the reform dummy is included.

These results show that the impact of the tax reform is significantly negative on equalization transfer, tax rebate, and total transfer for rural counties. It also negatively affects tax rebate and total transfer, but not equalization transfers, for urban counties. When the interaction of reform dummy and rural population share is included, the impact on rural population generally shows positive and significant effects; the impact of the tax rebate on urban counties is negative but insignificant. These results seem to suggest that the tax reform negatively affects the transfers received by counties where rural tax reform is implemented in relative terms, but the impacts on the counties with a higher rural population share are relatively smaller. The results conform to the reality, since the center allocates more transfers for rural reform to compensate for the loss in agriculture taxes. Counties with a

---

[8] In Anhui Province, where the reform was initiated as early as 1999, there were no such transfers before 2002, when the reform was broadened to many other provinces. We have a list of counties where the experiment was first conducted in 1999, and since it was extended to the whole province in 2000, we let the dummy take the value of 1 for all the counties in Anhui in 2000 and 2001. This way of constructing the dummy may not be precisely accurate; but it is the best we could do with current information, and it should serve our purpose.

higher rural population share suffer from a higher loss in agriculture taxes, and therefore they are entitled to higher transfers in compensation.

Alternatively, table 10.5b shows the results if we don't include the interaction term. We can see that the reform dummy is insignificant for total transfer to urban counties, even though it is significantly positive for equalization transfers and negative for tax rebates, the same as for the whole sample. For rural counties, the impacts are negative in all three regressions; only the tax rebate has a significant result.

Why does the rural tax-for-fee reform have such negative impacts on transfers, and even more significant consequences for rural counties? One possible explanation lies in the relationship between different layers of governments in China. The data we are using are county-level data. It is possible that the higher-level govern-

TABLE 10.4
Impact of Tax-for-Fee Reform on Different Components of Transfers (all observations included)

	Total	Equalization	Rebate	Total	Equalization	Rebate
Per capita GDP	0.006	−0.001	0.006	0.006	−0.001	0.006
	(17.88)***	(2.70)***	(44.66)***	(17.99)***	(2.54)**	(44.58)***
Population	−0.108	−0.214	0.106	−0.111	−0.217	0.106
	(0.71)	(1.52)	(1.52)	(0.73)	(1.54)	(1.52)
Lag of per capita exp.	0.232	0.246	−0.014	0.232	0.246	−0.014
	(35.14)***	(40.40)***	(4.67)***	(35.16)***	(40.42)***	(4.67)***
Share of rural population	1.087	1.211	−0.125	0.993	1.112	−0.119
	(3.54)***	(4.28)***	(0.89)	(3.22)***	(3.90)***	(0.85)
Share of public employee/pop.	2,028.516	571.847	1,456.668	2,033.910	577.542	1,456.367
	(12.31)***	(3.76)***	(19.37)***	(12.34)***	(3.80)***	(19.37)***
Per capita own revenue	0.124	−0.036	0.160	0.125	−0.036	0.160
	(17.02)***	(5.32)***	(48.07)***	(17.07)***	(5.27)***	(48.06)***
Reform dummy	−11.873	31.642	−43.516	−35.962	6.208	−42.170
	(1.49)	(4.30)***	(11.95)***	(2.93)***	(0.55)	(7.53)***
Impact of reform	(2.58)***	(2.96)***	(0.32)	31.350	33.101	−1.751
Year dummies	Yes	Yes	Yes	Yes	Yes	Yes
Constant	148.905	127.547	21.358	155.954	134.990	20.964
	(5.54)***	(5.15)***	(1.74)*	(5.78)***	(5.42)***	(1.70)*
Observations	14,433	14,433	14,433	14,433	14,433	14,433
Number of counties	2,703	2,703	2,703	2,703	2,703	2,703
R^2	0.53	0.45	0.49	0.53	0.45	0.49

SOURCE: Ministry of Finance, *China fiscal statistics for prefectures, cities, and counties, 1998–2004*.
NOTE: *p < 0.1, **p < 0.05, ***p < 0.01

ments, be they provincial governments or even prefecture governments—under pressure from the central government to implement rural tax reform and ensure the special transfers for tax reform—reduce the amount of the other part of transfer to the counties.

Summary

The total transfers are pro-rich due to the effects of the tax rebate. However, if we look at equalization transfers, we can see that that category of transfer is indeed meant to equalize, especially for the poor areas and rural areas.

TABLE 10.5A
Different Impacts of Rural Tax-for-Fee Reform on Urban and Rural Counties

	Urban Counties			Rural Counties		
	Total	Equal	Rebate	Total	Equal	Rebate
Per capita GDP	0.004	0.001	0.003	−0.004	−0.007	0.003
	(11.12)***	(1.84)*	(17.43)***	(3.80)***	(7.11)***	(15.90)***
Population	0.194	−0.320	0.514	−3.464	−2.639	−0.826
	(0.72)	(1.34)	(3.49)***	(2.89)***	(2.19)**	(3.28)***
Lag of per capita exp.	0.198	0.224	−0.026	0.542	0.506	0.036
	(27.16)***	(34.80)***	(6.48)***	(29.79)***	(27.73)***	(9.39)***
Share of rural population	0.544	0.124	0.420	1.032	1.045	−0.013
	(1.22)	(0.31)	(1.73)*	(0.63)	(0.63)	(0.04)
Share of public employee/pop.	6,561.944	3,148.614	3,413.330	−720.656	−795.453	74.796
	(22.98)***	(12.50)***	(21.93)***	(3.39)***	(3.73)***	(1.68)*
Per capita own revenue	0.147	−0.117	0.265	0.014	−0.003	0.018
	(13.84)***	(12.50)***	(45.63)***	(1.46)	(0.35)	(8.64)***
Reform dummy	−31.320	7.807	−39.128	−69.944	−44.789	−25.155
	(2.15)**	(0.61)	(4.92)***	(2.75)***	(1.76)*	(4.73)***
Impact of reform	29.342	36.540	−7.198	57.017	43.401	13.617
	(1.71)*	(2.42)**	(0.77)	(2.57)**	(1.95)*	(2.93)***
Year dummies	Yes	Yes	Yes	Yes	Yes	Yes
Constant	−219.017	−58.337	−160.680	105.347	51.319	54.028
	(6.39)***	(1.93)*	(8.61)***	(0.65)	(0.32)	(1.59)
Observations	8,076	8,076	8,076	6,357	6,357	6,357
Number of counties	1,769	1,769	1,769	1,385	1,385	1,385
R^2	0.59	0.48	0.59	0.50	0.45	0.26

SOURCE: Ministry of Finance, *China fiscal statistics for prefectures, cities, and counties, 1998–2004.*
NOTES: *p < 0.1, **p < 0.05, ***p < 0.01

TABLE 10.5B
Different Impacts of Rural Tax-for-Fee Reform on Urban and Rural Counties (without considering impact of reform)

	Urban Counties			Rural Counties		
	Total	Equal	Rebate	Total	Equal	Rebate
Per capita GDP	0.004	0.001	0.003	−0.004	−0.007	0.003
	(11.07)***	(1.75)*	(17.48)***	(3.80)***	(7.11)***	(15.89)***
Population	0.191	−0.324	0.515	−3.419	−2.604	−0.815
	(0.71)	(1.36)	(3.50)***	(2.85)***	(2.16)**	(3.24)***
Lag of per capita exp.	0.198	0.224	−0.026	0.547	0.510	0.037
	(27.16)***	(34.79)***	(6.48)***	(30.16)***	(28.04)***	(9.70)***
Share of rural population	0.624	0.224	0.401	1.151	1.135	0.016
	(1.41)	(0.57)	(1.66)*	(0.70)	(0.69)	(0.05)
Share of public employee/pop.	6,558.912	3,144.839	3,414.073	−724.028	−798.019	73.991
	(22.96)***	(12.48)***	(21.93)***	(3.41)***	(3.74)***	(1.66)*
Per capita own revenue	0.147	−0.118	0.265	0.014	−0.004	0.018
	(13.82)***	(12.53)***	(45.64)***	(1.39)	(0.40)	(8.56)***
Reform dummy	−12.914	30.730	−43.643	−13.256	−1.639	−11.617
	(1.31)	(3.52)***	(8.09)***	(1.05)	(0.13)	(4.40)***
Year dummies	Yes	Yes	Yes	Yes	Yes	Yes
Constant	−223.987	−64.526	−159.461	91.428	40.724	50.704
	(6.56)***	(2.14)**	(8.57)***	(0.56)	(0.25)	(1.49)
Observations	8,076	8,076	8,076	6,357	6,357	6,357
Number of counties	1,769	1,769	1,769	1,385	1,385	1,385
R^2	0.59	0.48	0.59	0.50	0.45	0.25

SOURCE: Ministry of Finance, *China fiscal statistics for prefectures, cities, and counties, 1998–2004.*
NOTE: *p < 0.1, **p < 0.05, ***p < 0.01

REFERENCES

Ahmad, Ehtisham, Raju Singh, and Mario Fortuna. 2004. Toward more effective redistribution: Reform options for intergovernmental transfers in China. IMF Working Paper No. 04/98. Washington DC: International Monetary Fund.

Bahl, Roy, and Sally Wallace. 2003. Fiscal decentralization: The provincial-local dimension. In *Public finance in developing and transitional countries: Essays in honor of Richard Bird*, eds. Jorge Martinez-Vazquez and James Alm. Northampton, MA: Edward Elgar.

Martinez-Vazquez, Jorge, and Andrey Timofeev. 2006. Regional-local dimension of Russia's fiscal decentralization. Working Paper No. 06-16. Atlanta: Georgia State University, Andrew Young School of Policy Studies, International Studies Program (May).

Ministry of Finance. n.d. *China fiscal statistics for prefectures, cities, and counties.* Beijing.

Persson, Petra, and Anna Eriksson. 2006. From blind pursuit of growth to balanced development? An analysis of the political logic of fiscal intergovernmental transfers in China, 1998–2003. Dissertation. Stockholm: Stockholm School of Economics.

Wang, Shaoguang. 2005. The political logic of fiscal transfers in China. In *China's west region development: Domestic strategies and global implications*, eds. Ding Lu and William A. W. Neilson. Singapore: World Scientific Publishing.

Central Government Transfers: For Equity or for Growth?

SHUANGLIN LIN

In principle, the main purposes of central government transfers to local governments should be the correction of externalities and the redistribution of resources among regions. According to Break (1967, 105), the basic economic reason for U.S. federal functional grants-in-aid is to subsidize the widespread, and ever increasing, spillover of benefits from some of the most important state and local expenditure programs. However, Inman (1988) argued that offsetting spillovers may not be an important objective of federal grant policy in practice. He showed that U.S. federal grants and the variables that might capture the potential of spillovers are not significantly related. In contrast, he found support for the idea that a main purpose of federal grants is to bring more equal distribution of resources and more equitable distribution of public goods. He showed that federal aid is always inversely related to the level of state income. Fisher (2007, 222) found a correlation between per capita grants and per capita income, even without controlling other factors that affect the interstate distribution of grants, although a bit weaker than that found by Inman (1988). This chapter analyzes central and local fiscal disparity and the factors determining the central government transfers by using data for 31 Chinese provinces from 1995 to 2004.

Fiscal capability is reflected by per capita government revenue and per capita government spending. Regional fiscal disparity shows the difference in fiscal capability among different regions. The 1994 tax reforms in China have greatly increased the revenue share of the central government in total revenue and decreased the revenue share of local governments. Since the tax reform, every province in every year has had fiscal deficits, and the central government has run surpluses every year (although the overall budget has been in deficit). As a result, local governments have become heavily dependent on the central government for transfers. There are two types of transfers from the central government, grants and value-added tax (VAT) rebates. Grants, including general grants and matching grants, are given to local governments mainly based on need. VAT is the most important tax in China, accounting for 37.5 percent of total tax revenue in 2005 (National Bureau of Taxation 2006). According to the law, VAT is shared by the central and local governments at a ratio of 75 percent to 25 percent. However, the central government rebates a part of the increment of the VAT to provinces based on tax revenue growth rate. This provides enormous incentives for local governments to increase their output.

The huge central government's budget surpluses, severe local fiscal difficulties, and substantial fiscal disparities among local governments place the central government transfers to the local governments in a decisive position. The shortage of government revenues in China's less developed regions has resulted in inadequate expenditures on public education, public health care, poverty relief, and environmental protection and has caused illegal fee collections. What determines the central government transfers to local governments? Is the current transfer system effective in reducing regional fiscal disparity? These are crucial issues related to China's fiscal reforms.

Many prior studies have focused on the decline in total government revenue in the 1990s, and studies on central government transfers are still limited. Bahl and Wallich (1992, 20), Stiglitz (1998), Brean (1998), Wong, Heady, and Woo (1995, 6), and Lin (2000) analyzed the decline in government revenue share in GDP and called for increasing government budgetary revenues. Central-local fiscal disparity became an important issue after the 1994 tax reforms. In 1995 the central government received 52.2 percent (52.3 percent in 2005) of total government revenues but covered only around 29.2 percent (26 percent in 2005) of total expenditures in 1995. Local governments have relied on extrabudgetary revenues from fee collections. Wu (1997), Fan (1998), and Jia (2000) analyzed local fiscal difficulties and local governments' various fee collections. With income inequality increasing, fiscal disparities among local governments have recently become a focal point. Hofman and Guerra (2005) analyzed the size and the importance of fiscal disparities in East Asia. Using China's county-level data from 1994 to 2000, Tsui (2005) and Yu and Tsui (2005) showed the importance of local tax system, intergovernmental transfers, and institutional factors in determining county-level fiscal disparities. Since about 40 percent of local government expenditures are financed by central government transfers now, and central government transfers are essential for local governments, studies of China's transfer system become crucial (National Bureau of Statistics 2006).

This chapter shows the fiscal disparity among Chinese provinces by examining per capita government spending and per capita government spending on education and health care. The fiscal disparities between the rich provinces and the poor provinces are substantial. The chapter also examines the central government transfers to local governments, which consist of tax rebates and grants. Grants are mainly equity promoting—that is, poor provinces are supposed to receive more than rich provinces. Through detailed analysis, the chapter will show that the VAT rebate system is growth stimulating, that fast-growing provinces have received more tax transfers than slow-growing provinces.

Using the data from 31 provinces for the period 1995–2004, this chapter also tests a number of interesting hypotheses. It turns out that provinces with a higher level of income received more per capita transfers from the central government than provinces with a lower level of income; and provinces with a higher growth rate received more per capita transfers than provinces with a lower rate of growth. Thus, tax rebates dominate the equity-promoting grants in the central government transfer system, and the current government transfer system is ineffective in reducing the regional fiscal disparity. Minority regions and western regions also received more transfers from the central government than other regions. Minority and western regions are among the slow-growing, poor regions in China. Thus, the nonminority and nonwestern slow-growing regions seem to be in an unfavorable position in the current transfer system.

Central-Local and Regional Fiscal Disparities

The 1994 tax reform greatly strengthened the central government's fiscal power and weakened local governments' fiscal power. Table 11.1 shows budgetary revenues and expenditures of central and local governments from 1978 to 2005. From 1978 to 1984, local governments as a whole ran huge surpluses every year, although the surpluses were decreasing year by year. From 1985 to 1993, local government budgets were basically balanced every year. As a result of the tax reform, the central government share of total revenue increased from 22 percent in 1993 to 52.3 percent in 2005. Meanwhile, the central government expenditure share actually declined from 28.3 percent in 1993 to 26.0 percent in 2005. Since the tax reform in 1994, every provincial government has run a budget deficit every year. Local governments of all regions in China rely heavily on the central government transfers to finance their expenditures.

Table 11.2 shows the central government's share of total government revenue, the central government's share of total government expenditures, the ratios of central government expenditures to central government revenue, and the ratio of central government transfers to central government revenue for selected countries. It can be seen that, of all the countries listed, China's central government share of total government spending was the smallest, only 27.7 percent in 2004, compared to 89.9 percent in Thailand, 83.4 percent in Chile, 80.8 percent in France, 72 percent in the United Kingdom, 61 percent in Germany, and 53.2 percent in the United States. Thus, in China, local governments mainly undertake the provision of public services. China's ratio of central government expenditures to revenue is the lowest among the countries listed, with 52.2 percent in 2004, compared to 99.5 percent in Germany, 97.9 percent in France, 108.4 percent in the United States, 84 percent in the United Kingdom, 77.9 percent in Thailand, and 76.5 percent in Chile. That means that nearly half of China's central government revenues were not spent directly by the central government; instead, they were transferred to the local governments. Finally, the ratio of China's central government transfers to its budgetary revenue was the largest in the selected group of countries: 68.9 percent in 2004, compared to 8.6 percent in Germany, 9.9 percent in France, 20.9 percent in the United States,

TABLE 11.1
Budgetary Revenues and Expenditures of Central and Local Governments

Year	Revenue National	Revenue Central	Revenue Local	Proportion Central (%)	Expenditure National	Expenditure Central	Expenditure Local	Proportion Central (%)	Local Government Self-Sufficiency Rate (%)
1978	1,132.26	175.77	956.49	15.5	1,122.09	532.12	589.97	47.4	162.1
1979	1,146.38	231.34	915.04	20.2	1,281.79	655.08	626.71	51.1	146.0
1980	1,159.93	284.45	875.48	24.5	1,228.83	666.81	562.02	54.3	155.8
1981	1,175.79	311.07	864.72	26.5	1,138.41	625.65	512.76	55.0	168.6
1982	1,212.33	346.84	865.49	28.6	1,229.98	651.81	578.17	53.0	149.7
1983	1,366.95	490.01	876.94	35.8	1,409.52	759.6	649.92	53.9	134.9
1984	1,642.86	665.47	977.39	40.5	1,701.02	893.33	807.69	52.5	121.0
1985	2,004.82	769.63	1,235.19	38.4	2,004.25	795.25	1,209.00	39.7	102.2
1986	2,122.01	778.42	1,343.59	36.7	2,204.91	836.36	1,368.55	37.9	98.2
1987	2,199.35	736.29	1,463.06	33.5	2,262.18	845.63	1,416.55	37.4	103.3
1988	2,357.24	774.76	1,582.48	32.9	2,491.21	845.04	1,646.17	33.9	96.1
1989	2,664.90	822.52	1,842.38	30.9	2,823.78	888.77	1,935.01	31.5	95.2
1990	2,937.10	992.42	1,944.68	33.8	3,083.59	1,004.47	2,079.12	32.6	93.5
1991	3,149.48	938.25	2,211.23	29.8	3,386.62	1,090.81	2,295.81	32.2	96.3
1992	3,483.37	979.51	2,503.86	28.1	3,742.20	1,170.44	2,571.76	31.3	97.4

1993	4,348.95	957.51	3,391.44	22.0	4,642.30	1,312.06	3,330.24	28.3	101.8
1994	5,218.10	2,906.50	2,311.60	55.7	5,792.62	1,754.43	4,038.19	30.3	57.2
1995	6,242.20	3,256.62	2,985.58	52.2	6,823.72	1,995.39	4,828.33	29.2	61.8
1996	7,407.99	3,661.07	3,746.92	49.4	7,937.55	2,151.27	5,786.28	27.1	64.8
1997	8,651.14	4,226.92	4,424.22	48.9	9,233.56	2,532.50	6,701.06	27.4	66.0
1998	9,875.95	4,892.00	4,983.95	49.5	10,798.18	3,125.60	7,672.58	28.9	65.0
1999	11,444.08	5,849.21	5,594.87	51.1	13,187.67	4,152.33	9,035.34	31.5	61.9
2000	13,395.23	6,989.17	6,406.06	52.2	15,886.50	5,519.85	10,366.65	34.7	61.8
2001	16,386.04	8,582.74	7,803.30	52.4	18,902.58	5,768.02	13,134.56	30.5	59.4
2002	18,903.64	10,388.64	8,515.00	55.0	22,053.15	6,771.70	15,281.45	30.7	55.7
2003	21,715.25	11,865.27	9,849.98	54.6	24,649.95	7,420.10	17,229.85	30.1	57.2
2004	26,396.47	14,503.10	11,893.37	54.9	28,486.89	7,894.08	20,592.81	27.7	57.8
2005	31,627.89	16,535.94	15,092.04	52.3	33,708.12	8,775.73	24,932.39	26.0	60.5

SOURCES: Ministry of Finance, 1997; National Bureau of Statistics, 2005, 2006.

NOTE: The figures in this table do not include the revenues from issuing internal and external debt, and do not include interest payments on internal and external debt and basic construction expenditures financed by foreign debt.

TABLE 11.2
Shares of Central Government Revenue and Expenditure for Selected Countries, 2004 (percent)

Country	Central Government Share of Total Revenue	Central Government Share of Total Expenditure	Central Government Share of Total Revenue (excluding social contributions)	Ratio of Central Government Expenditure to Its Revenue	Ratio of Central Government Transfers to Its Revenue
Argentina	61.9	58.9	57.5	87.2	13.4
Australia	73.8	55.4	73.8	71.2	25.4
China	57.2	27.7	57.2	52.2	68.9
Chile	89.7	83.4	89.1	76.5	4.0
Czech Republic	85.3	76.6	76.0	91.8	16.5
Denmark	64.6	36.5	63.6	55.4	39.9
France	87.1	80.8	79.8	97.9	9.9
Germany	66.9	61.0	45.2	99.5	8.6
Hungary	85.8	75.6	80.2	93.8	17.7
Italy	81.1	69.0	73.8	87.2	18.4
Netherlands	88.8	62.2	83.3	72.5	30.9
Poland[a]	87.0	77.8	80.0	96.1	15.6
Portugal	91.5	87.0	88.2	99.0	6.7
Russia	68.0	60.9	60.7	70.9	8.8
Spain[a]	82.6	70.7	73.9	77.3	17.4
Thailand	92.3	89.9	92.0	77.9	9.5
U.K.	90.7	72.0	88.4	84.0	23.9
United States	54.3	53.2	40.5	108.4	20.9

SOURCE: International Monetary Fund, *Government Finance Statistics Yearbook*, 2005.
[a] Data are for 2003, as data for 2004 are unavailable.

23.9 percent in the United Kingdom, 9.5 percent in Thailand, and 4.0 percent in Chile.[1] Thus, the Chinese central government transferred much more of its revenues to local governments than any other country in this group.

Fiscal capacity is also largely unequal among regions in China. In China local governments (province, prefecture, county, and township governments) do not have the right to issue debt; their budgets must be approved by the central government and must be balanced after government transfers. Thus, uneven fiscal capacities among regions in China are reflected by the differences in per capita government expenditures. Three of the four municipalities directly under central government, Beijing, Shanghai, and Tianjin, lead all other regions in per capita government expenditures. Figure 11.1 illustrates the per capita government expenditure in 2000 and 2005 for 31 provinces, ranked from the lowest to the highest in terms of per capita government expenditures in 2005. In 2000, per capita government expenditure in Shanghai was 3,709 yuan, and in Henan it was only 468 yuan; in 2005 per capita government expenditure in Shanghai was 9,259 yuan, and in Henan it was

---
[1] Note that the transfers include funds raised though issuing government bonds.

FIGURE 11.1
Per Capita Government Expenditure by Region, 2000 and 2005

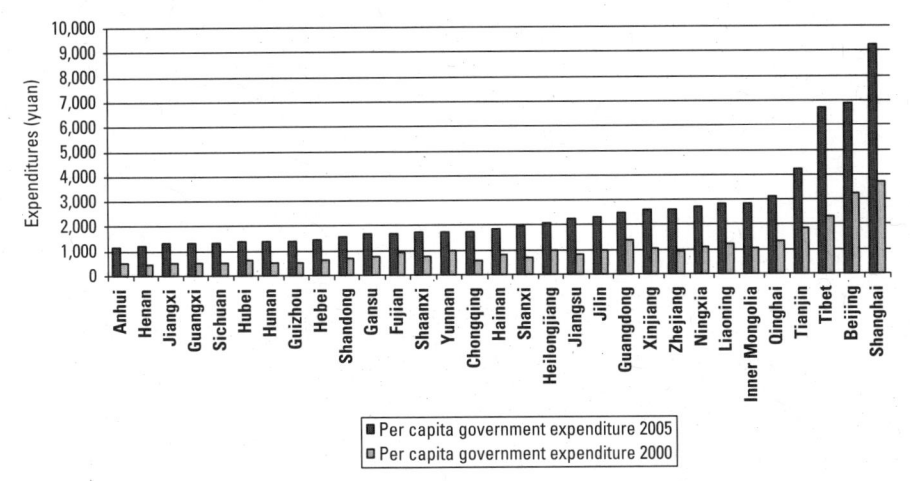

1,190 yuan. Shanghai's per capita expenditure in 2005 was nearly eight times larger than that of Henan (National Bureau of Statistics 2006).

Minority regions also have higher per capita government expenditures. These regions have been less developed in China. The central government has made great efforts in recent years to increase the public goods and services provisions in minority regions to stimulate economic development and to prevent separatist movements in these regions. In 2005 per capita government expenditure for Tibet was 6,697 yuan, below only Shanghai and Beijing; meanwhile, per capita government expenditures for Qinghai, Inner Mongolia, Ningxia, and Xinjiang were 3,127 yuan, 2,858 yuan, 2,690 yuan, and 2,582 yuan, respectively. The Guangxi Autonomous Region, of the Zhuang nationality, was an exception, with a per capita government expenditure of only 1,312 yuan among the lowest government per capita expenditures. The Zhuang nationality is a smaller minority group, compared to Man (Manchurian), Meng (Mongolian), Hui (Muslim), and Zang (Tibetan).

The government has recently increased the per capita expenditure in the northeastern three provinces, Liaoning, Jilin, and Heilongjiang, following a strategy of reviving the old industrial base. These three provinces were the base of China's heavy industries, with many state enterprises. After economic reforms, they fell behind due to the bad performance of state enterprises.

Among the provinces unable to enjoy special government subsidy policies, Zhejiang, Guangdong, and Jiangsu led the way in government spending, with per capita government spending of 2,584 yuan, 2,490 yuan, and 2,239 yuan, respectively, in 2005. The provinces in the central part of China have lower government spending than other provinces. For example, Anhui's per capita government expenditure was only 1,165 yuan in 2005, the lowest in the nation.

Table 11.3 provides information on the per capita total government expenditure, education expenditure, health care expenditure, and welfare expenditure in 31 provinces in 1995 and 2005. The per capita education expenditure was

TABLE 11.3
Per Capita Regional Government Expenditures (yuan)

Region	Per Capita Government Expenditure 1995	Per Capita Government Expenditure 2005	Per Capita Education & Health Care Expenditures 1995	Per Capita Education Expenditure 2005	Per Capita Health Care Expenditure 2005	Per Capita Welfare Expenditure 1995	Per Capita Welfare Expenditure 2005	Population (10,000 persons) 1995	Population (10,000 persons) 2005
Beijing	1,234	6,881	306	948	427	39	208	1,251	1,538
Tianjin	991	4,239	225	644	182	17	83	942	1,043
Hebei	297	1,429	88	249	66	10	41	6,437	6,851
Shanxi	367	1,993	108	304	84	12	59	3,077	3,355
Inner Mongolia	447	2,858	117	330	87	9	62	2,284	2,386
Liaoning	669	2,853	137	337	81	17	107	4,092	4,221
Jilin	466	2,324	130	273	76	14	85	2,592	2,716
Heilongjiang	472	2,062	108	279	73	9	62	3,701	3,820
Shanghai	1,837	9,259	405	1,029	293	18	140	1,415	1,778
Jiangsu	359	2,239	114	345	100	10	58	7,066	7,475
Zhejiang	417	2,584	126	473	132	11	63	4,319	4,898
Anhui	226	1,165	66	192	41	6	42	6,013	6,120
Fujian	530	1,679	131	315	73	11	48	3,237	3,535
Jiangxi	272	1,308	74	204	51	8	58	4,063	4,311
Shandong	317	1,585	93	269	59	9	44	8,705	9,248
Henan	228	1,190	62	200	45	6	38	9,100	9,380
Hubei	281	1,364	81	208	55	7	60	5,772	5,710
Hunan	272	1,381	73	194	39	7	50	6,392	6,326
Guangdong	765	2,490	188	358	90	11	45	6,868	9,194
Guangxi	309	1,312	83	226	64	7	34	4,543	4,660
Hainan	585	1,827	152	292	79	11	58	724	828
Chongqing	282	1,742	83	217	54	7	62	1,520	2,798
Sichuan	249	1,318	71	171	60	6	46	11,162	8,212
Guizhou	243	1396	67	250	69	6	41	3,508	3,730
Yunnan	589	1,722	130	275	101	15	46	3,990	4,450
Tibet	1,453	6,695	248	736	257	32	97	240	277
Shaanxi	292	1,718	85	267	58	8	52	3,514	3,720
Gansu	334	1,655	88	260	69	8	45	2,438	2,594
Qinghai	599	3,126	154	374	163	16	93	481	543
Ningxia	448	2,689	123	328	91	7	60	513	596
Xinjiang	580	2,582	183	361	129	7	56	1,661	2,010

SOURCE: National Bureau of Statistics, *China Statistical Yearbook, 1996*; *China Statistical Abstract, 2006.*

substantially different among regions. In both years, the region with the highest government expenditure was Shanghai, and the region with the lowest government expenditure was Anhui. In 1995, Anhui's per capita government expenditure was 226 yuan, while Shanghai's was 1,837 yuan, 8.13 times as high as Anhui's; in 2005, Anhui's per capita government expenditure was 1,165 yuan, while Shanghai's was 9,259 yuan, 7.95 times as high as Anhui's. Per capita education expenditures for Shanghai and Beijing were 1028.9 yuan and 948.5 yuan, respectively, while for Anhui and Henan they were only 191.9 yuan and 199.7 yuan, respectively (National Bureau of Statistics 2006). Figure 11.2 illustrates the per capita government expenditure on education, health care, and welfare in 2005, ranking provinces from the lowest to the highest.

Similar to the education expenditure, the health care expenditure is higher in rich regions than in poor regions (see table 11.3). For example, the per capita health care expenditure was 427 yuan for Beijing and only 39 yuan for Hunan and 41 yuan for Anhui. Three of the four municipalities directly under the central government—Beijing, Shanghai, and Tianjin—and minority regions have higher per capita government health care expenditures than other regions. The poor nonminority regions in the central part of China ranked at the bottom.

Welfare expenditure includes expenditures on compensation for bereaved family, social welfare, and poverty relief. Ironically, the rich regions had higher levels of per capita welfare expenditure than the poor regions. For example, in 2005, the per capita welfare expenditure for Shanghai was 140 yuan, more than three times higher than that of Henan (only 38 yuan).

FIGURE 11.2

Per Capita Government Expenditure on Education, Health Care, and Welfare, by Region, 2005

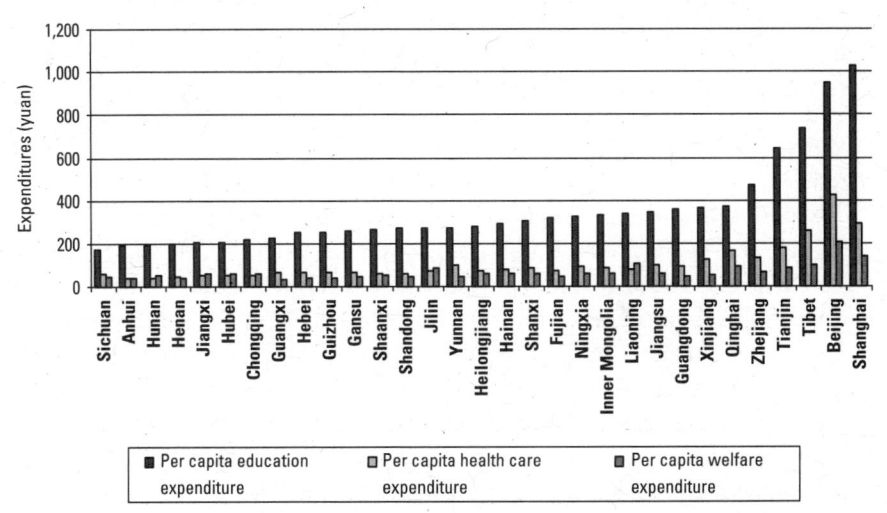

Central Government Transfers to Local Governments

In China, the central government transfers funds to local governments through various channels: appropriations for special projects (*matching grants*), which require the recipient government to match each grant with a given amount of money; general transfers (*general grants*), which have few restrictions on the recipients; fixed subsidies, or submissions (*lump-sum grants*), which were determined under the old system; budgetary subsidies; and, most important, tax rebates. In 2000, the central government transfer to local governments was 466.53 billion yuan, of which tax rebates were 226.75 billion yuan, or 48.6 percent of total transfers; fixed subsidies were 12.5 billion yuan, or 2.7 percent of total transfers; general transfers were 83.25 billion yuan, or 17.8 percent of total transfers; and project subsidies and others were 144.03 billion yuan, or 30.9 percent of total transfers.

Appropriations for special projects include expenditures for price subsidies, supporting undeveloped areas, basic construction, education, and agricultural development. General transfers started as transition period transfers. In 1995, the Chinese government instituted a regulation called the Transfer Mechanism during the Transition Period (*guoduqi zhuanyi zhifu banfa*), which specified the principles of the transition period transfers. Transition period transfers are small in volume and mainly given to the poor areas. In 2001, the State Council issued the Promulgation of the Plan for Sharing the Individual Income Tax (*guanyu yinfa suode shui fenxiang gaige fangan de tongzhi*), which required local governments to submit a portion of their personal income tax to the central government. In 2002, the central government began transferring all the revenue from personal income tax to local governments as a general transfer, and the name "transition period transfers" was no longer used. The formula for general transfers is as follows:

$$\text{general transfers} = (\text{standard expenditures for the region} - \text{standard revenues for the region}) \times \text{transfer coefficient for the region}.$$

If standard revenue is greater than standard expenditures, then no transfer is made.

Fixed subsidies, or submissions under the old system (*yuan tizhi ding e buzhu jin shangjie*), were created to reduce resistance to the 1994 tax reform. Before the 1994 tax reform, the central government subsidized local governments in poor regions and received submitted revenues from rich regions under the fiscal responsibility system. After the 1994 reform, the subsidies and submissions continued. Before 1995 the quantity of revenue submission was determined by quota or calculated using a growth formula. In 1995 the central government set new quotas for all revenue-submitting provinces.

Budgetary subsidies (*juesuan buzhu*) are made to balance local government budgets. At the end of each year, the central government and local governments recalculate local expenditures, revenues, and intergovernmental transfers. The gap between local governments' budgeted expenditures and final expenditures is filled by the central government. Normally, the difference between budget and final figures is not large; thus, this type of subsidy is small.

Tax rebates are the most important component of central government transfers. In 1994, total government tax rebates were 179.9 billion yuan, accounting for 75.4 percent of total central government transfers. Since then the share of tax rebates has declined, although the absolute value of the rebates is still increasing. In 2002, tax rebates were 41 percent, while grants and subsidies were 54.7 percent, of which the share of general grants was 22 percent; the share of project grants was 32.7 percent.[2] To reduce resistance to the tax reform plan and to keep the local vested interest, the central government rebated to the local governments all of the net tax revenue due to the tax reforms in 1993. The tax rebate in the base year of 1993 was

tax rebate in 1993 = consumption tax (100 percent) + VAT (75 percent)
— transfers from the central government

The tax rebate in 1993 becomes the base for tax rebate in subsequent years. Letting 1993 be year 0 and the tax rebate in year t be R_t, the tax rebate follows the following formula (Liu 2003):

R_t = tax rebate in 1993 × (1 + 30 percent × the growth rate of VAT and consumption tax in year 1)
× (1 + 30 percent × the growth rate of VAT and consumption tax in year 2)
× ···
× (1 + 30 percent × the growth rate of VAT and consumption tax in year $t-1$)
× (1 + 30 percent × the growth rate of VAT and consumption tax in year t).

If R_0 is the tax base in 1993 and ϕ_t is the growth rate of VAT and the consumption tax, the tax rebate in year t is

$$R_t = R_0 \prod_{n=1}^{t}(1+0.3\phi_n) = R_0(1+0.3\phi_1)(1+0.3\phi_2)\Lambda(1+0.3\phi_t), t \geq 1.$$

Assume that $\phi_t = \phi$ is a constant. Thus,

$$R_t = R_0 (1+0.3\phi)^t, t \geq 1. \tag{1}$$

If $\phi = 20$ percent, and the tax rebate in 1993 (the base year) is $R_0 = 10{,}000$, then tax rebates in years 1, 2, and 3, respectively, will be

$$R_1 = 10{,}000 \times (1+0.06) = 10{,}600$$
$$R_2 = 10{,}000 \times (1+0.06)^2 = 11{,}236$$
$$R_3 = 10{,}000 \times (1+0.06)^3 = 11{,}910.16$$

---

[2] See the Ministry of Finance Web site: http://www.mof.gov.cn/news/up˚loadfile/2002nianzhongyangcaizheng˚˚yusuan.juesuanshouzhi.xls.

Let's examine the relationship between tax rebates and the growth rate of VAT and the consumption tax. The differentiating equation (1) with respect to ϕ gives the following:

$$\frac{dR_t}{d\phi} = 0.3 R_0 t (1+0.3\phi)^{t-1} > 0, \quad t \geq 1, \tag{2}$$

$$\frac{d^2 R_t}{d\phi^2} = 0.09 R_0 t(t-1)(1+0.3\phi)^{t-2} > 0, \quad t > 1. \tag{3}$$

That is to say, the tax rebate from the central government increases as the growth rate of VAT and the consumption tax increases, and the increase is at an increasing rate.

Let R_t^r and R_t^p be the tax rebates of the rich and the poor areas, respectively; ϕ^r and ϕ^p be the growth rate of VAT and the consumption tax, respectively; and L_t^r and L_t^p be the population of the rich and the poor areas, respectively. Based on equation (1), the difference between the tax rebates of the rich and the poor regions is as follows:

$$\frac{R_t^r}{L_t^r} - \frac{R_t^p}{L_t^p} = \frac{R_0^r}{L_0^r}(1+0.3\phi^r)^t - \frac{R_0^p}{L_0^p}(1+0.3\phi^p)^t.$$

In China, rich provinces have grown faster than the poor provinces, and thus, the gap between tax rebates will expand. If the growth rate of VAT and the consumption tax are equal—that is, $\phi = \phi^r = \phi^p$—and the population in each province does not change, the gap between the rebates in the rich and the poor provinces becomes

$$\frac{R_t^r}{L^r} - \frac{R_t^p}{L^p} = \left(\frac{R_0^r}{L^r} - \frac{R_0^p}{L^p}\right)(1+0.3\phi)^t. \tag{4}$$

It can be seen that if $\frac{R_0^r}{L^r} - \frac{R_0^p}{L^p} > 0$ and $\phi > 0$, then

$$\lim_{t \to \infty} \left(\frac{R_t^r}{L^r} - \frac{R_t^p}{L^p}\right) = \left(\frac{R_0^r}{L^r} - \frac{R_0^p}{L^p}\right)(1+0.3\phi)^t \to \infty. \tag{5}$$

That is to say, even though the growth rates of VAT and the consumption tax in two provinces are equal, the difference between the rebates of the rich and the poor will become infinitely large as time goes on.

We next analyze the relationship between the tax rebate and the growth rate and the value added. Assume that R_t / L_t is the per capita tax rebates a province gets from the central government and $\dot{y}_t$ is the growth rate of value added. Note that if the tax rate is constant, the growth rate of the value added is equal to the growth rate of the tax revenue—that is, $\dot{y}_t = \phi$. Thus, we have the following:

$$\frac{R_t}{L_t} = \frac{R_0}{L_t}(1+0.3\dot{y})^t = \frac{R_0}{L_0} \frac{L_0}{L_1} \frac{L_1}{L_2} \times \cdots \times \frac{L_{t-2}}{L_{t-1}} \frac{L_{t-1}}{L_t}(1+0.3\dot{y})^t$$

$$= \frac{R_0}{L_0}\left(\frac{1}{\dot{L}_1+1} \frac{1}{\dot{L}_2+1} \times \cdots \times \frac{1}{\dot{L}_{t-1}+1} \frac{1}{\dot{L}_t+1}\right)(1+0.3\dot{y}_t)^t. \tag{6}$$

Assume that the population growth rate is constant—that is, $\dot{L}_i = \dot{L}$, for $i = 1, \ldots, t$. Thus, equation (6) becomes

$$\frac{R_t}{L_t} = \frac{R_0}{L_0}\left(\frac{1}{\dot{L}_1 + 1}\right)^t (1 + 0.3\dot{y}_t)^t. \tag{7}$$

Differentiating R_t / L_t with respect to R_0 / L_0, $\dot{y}$, and $\dot{L}$ gives

$$\frac{\partial (R_t / L_t)}{\partial (R_0 / L_0)} = \left(\frac{1}{\dot{L}+1}\right)^t (1 + 0.3\dot{y}_t)^t > 0; \tag{8}$$

$$\frac{\partial (R_t / L)}{\partial \dot{y}_t} = 0.3\left(\frac{1}{\dot{L}+1}\right)^t \frac{R_0}{L_0}(1+0.3\dot{y})^{t-1} > 0; \text{ and} \tag{9}$$

$$\frac{\partial (R_t / L)}{\partial \dot{L}} = 0.3(-t)\left(\frac{1}{\dot{L}+1}\right)^{t+1} \frac{R_0}{L_0}(1+0.3\dot{y})^{t-1} < 0. \tag{10}$$

That is to say, for a given growth rate of value added and a given rate of population growth, per capita rebate is higher if the initial rebate is higher; for a given initial per capita rebate and the growth rate of the population, the higher the growth rate of output, the higher the per capita tax rebate will be; and for a given initial per capita rebate and the growth rate of output, the higher the growth rate of the population and the lower the per capita tax rebate will be.

Clearly, the current transfer system is not in favor of the poor or the slow-growing provinces. Every province intends to get more transfers from the central government. Every province wants more transfers from the central government. The poor provinces, such as Jiangxi and Gansu, want the central government to help the poor (*fupin*) (Guo 2003; Zhang 2003), while the rich provinces, such as Jiangsu and Shandong, want the central government to reward the rich (*cujiu*) (Li 2003; Sun 2003). All local governments want to get a larger share of tax revenues. For example, Yunan Province depends on tobacco industries for tax revenues, and the government collects a consumption tax on cigarettes and other tobacco products. Right now, the central government gets all the consumption tax revenue. Yunan wants the central government to give 25 percent of the consumption tax revenue back, as the VAT. Yunan also wants the central government to give 50 percent of the increase in the VAT revenue back to the province, instead of the current 30 percent (Ouyang 2003). To obtain more freedom in disposing of the transferred funds, many provinces ask the central government to increase general grants and reduce project grants, which specify the use of the funds and require local governments to provide matching funds. The poor provinces also ask the central government to increase the rate of the tax rebate (see, for example, Zhang 2003).

In China the minority regions are poor regions. The central government has been transferring more to minority regions for the purpose of social and political stability. Also, in recent years the government has intended to help the poor western region by initiating the western development project.

Empirical Analyses of Government Transfers

This section examines the determinants of the Chinese intergovernmental transfers by using the panel data from 31 Chinese provinces for the period 1995–2004.

Data and Hypotheses

The data are mainly from various issues of the *China Statistical Yearbook* and the *Government Finance Yearbook of China*. As mentioned earlier, the new tax system and tax rebate system were established in 1994. However, the data on transfers for all provinces start only in 1995. Also, the Chinese government adjusted China's GDP figures and other statistics in 2005, and the recent data do not match the earlier data. Thus, our sample period starts in 1995 and ends in 2004, making it the largest internally consistent data set available. We have to split the data for Sichuan and Chongqing for 1995 and 1996, because Chongqing is independent from Sichuan and became a municipality directly under central government control in 1997.

Transfers from the central government, from the *Finance Yearbook of China*, 1996–2005, published by the Ministry of Finance, are shown in table 11.4. Real transfer per capita is obtained by dividing a province's total transfers by its population and price index.

The data for gross domestic product (GDP) by region are from the *China Statistical Yearbook* 1998, 1999, 2001, and 2005, published by the National Bureau of Statistics of China. The GDP of Sichuan in 1995 is the value of Sichuan minus the value of Chongqing; the *China Statistical Yearbook* of 1998 provides the GDP in 1996 for both Sichuan and Chongqing, so we used the data directly from the book. Per capita real GDP is obtained by dividing a province's total GDP by its population and price index.

The data on population are from the *China Statistical Yearbook*, 1995–2006, published by the National Bureau of Statistics. The population and GDP of Chongqing in 1995 and 1996 are from the *China Compendium of Statistics 1949–2004*. The adjusted population for Sichuan in 1995 and 1996 is calculated by deducting Chongqing's population from Sichuan's unadjusted population.

The data of the retail price index (RPI) are compiled based on two data sets, the *China Regional Economy: A Profile of 17 Years of Reform and Opening Up* and the *China Compendium of Statistics 1949–2004*. The former provides retail price indices from 1994 to 1995 (1978 = 100), and the latter provides data for the growth rate of retail prices from 1995 to 2004 (price of preceding year = 100). In our price index, 1978 is the base year. Since the price index for Tibet is not provided by the data source, we used the national retail price index (RPI) as an approximation. In addition, we adopted the RPI of Sichuan to approximate that for Chongqing for 1995 and 1996.

Table 11.5a shows the basic statistics of per capita real transfer, per capita real GDP, real GDP growth rate, and the population growth rate. The mean of per capita real transfer per year from 1995 to 2000 was 101.68 yuan (at 1978 constant prices), with Tibet having the maximum of 446.48 yuan (followed by Shanghai, Tianjin,

TABLE 11.4

Provincial per Capita Transfers from the Central Government, 1995–2005 (current yuan)

Region	1995	1996	1997	1998	1999	2000	2001	2002	2003	2004	2005
Beijing	746	709	766	856	1,048	826	1,156	1,058	1,268	1,356	1,286
Tianjin	699	624	641	676	739	846	990	1,153	1,285	1,496	1,514
Hebei	146	155	159	177	228	270	357	449	506	621	701
Shanxi	165	172	175	200	271	345	494	591	675	872	957
Inner Mongolia	276	315	340	402	492	677	1,008	1,209	1,143	1,634	1,730
Liaoning	380	384	309	438	551	656	802	845	979	1,135	1,244
Jilin	250	278	322	356	517	597	769	897	1,088	1,296	1,534
Heilongjiang	257	235	252	331	486	582	716	817	845	1,189	1,351
Shanghai	1,385	1,378	1,395	1,481	1,551	1,453	1,411	1,725	1,906	2,257	1,975
Jiangsu	231	236	244	268	282	293	319	399	452	587	534
Zhejiang	266	276	229	310	327	346	366	530	590	773	628
Anhui	104	120	123	160	213	270	359	401	458	548	655
Fujian	212	207	180	227	249	264	296	381	432	554	520
Jiangxi	124	136	141	219	264	286	399	486	526	672	780
Shandong	150	159	127	179	196	210	231	311	361	450	497
Henan	113	117	121	146	186	223	274	345	405	511	638
Hubei	156	168	172	231	275	303	462	487	518	673	814
Hunan	138	155	151	212	255	296	382	469	493	685	796
Guangdong	281	253	222	275	287	265	32	495	557	666	531
Guangxi	145	159	162	183	214	278	384	452	490	621	766
Hainan	184	202	213	237	291	365	474	584	768	932	1,051
Sichuan	117	130	124	146	188	276	389	473	468	619	745
Guizhou	142	153	162	194	259	352	463	547	558	724	893
Yunnan	348	354	365	400	462	541	682	717	791	914	980
Tibet	1,328	1,279	1,397	1,649	2,237	2,427	3,750	4,912	4,945	4,962	6,915
Shaanxi	147	156	168	211	285	469	585	662	676	941	1,040
Gansu	192	214	230	284	362	495	666	460	816	1,065	1,197
Qinghai	396	447	501	599	852	1,064	1,773	1,860	1,785	2,370	2,805
Ningxia	316	343	369	511	666	864	1,277	1,527	1,275	1,728	2,067
Xinjiang	315	386	398	459	540	620	1,008	1,146	1,230	1,457	1,709
Chongqing	117	130	185	229	292	388	510	672	624	761	951

SOURCE: Ministry of Finance, 1999–2006.

TABLE 11.5A
Summary of Statistics of Variables

Variable	Obs.	Mean	SD	Min.	Max.	Max./Min.
Per capita real transfer 1995–2000 (yuan at the 1978 price)	31	101.68	0.8906	40.78	446.48	10.95
Per capita real transfer 2000–2004 (yuan at the 1978 price)	31	223.50	1.9054	98.43	1,099.25	11.17
Per capita real transfer 1995–2004 (yuan at the 1978 price)	31	158.29	1.3484	72.53	754.50	10.40
Per capita real GDP 1995–2000 (yuan at the 1978 price)	31	1,706.33	10.4734	584.86	5,655.21	9.67
Per capita real GDP 2000–2004 (yuan at the 1978 price)	31	2,712.03	17.4059	876.14	8,971.12	10.24
Per capita real GDP 1995–2004 (yuan at the 1978 price)	31	2,168.96	13.6746	714.22	7,179.33	10.05
Real GDP growth rate 1995–2000	31	0.1011	0.0168	0.0569	0.1383	2.43
Real GDP growth rate 2000–2004	31	0.1269	0.0195	0.0939	0.1609	1.71
Real GDP growth rate 1995–2004	31	0.1126	0.0137	0.0853	0.1399	1.64
Population growth rate 1995–2000	31	0.0116	0.0104	−0.0024	0.046	—
Population growth rate 2000–2004	31	0.0071	0.0075	−0.01	0.0255	—
Population growth rate 1995–2004	31	0.0096	0.0054	0.0033	0.0231	7

NOTE: Obs. = observations; SD = standard deviation.

Beijing, Qinghai, and Ningxia) and Sichuan having the minimum of 40.78 yuan (followed by Guangxi and Hunan). The gap between the top and the bottom was 10.95 times. The mean of per capita real transfer per year from 2000 to 2004 was 223.50 yuan, with Tibet having the maximum of 1,099.25 yuan (followed by Shanghai, Qinghai, and Ningxia) and Shandong having the minimum of 98.43 yuan (followed by Fujian). The gap between the top and the bottom was 11.17 times. The mean of per capita real transfer per year for the whole sample period from 1995 to 2004 was 158.29 yuan, with Tibet having the maximum of 754.5 yuan (followed by Shanghai with 398.1 yuan, Qinghai with 281.6 yuan, and Tianjin with 268.9 yuan) and Hunan having the minimum of 72.5 yuan (followed by Sichuan with 73.44 yuan). The gap between the top and the bottom was 10.4 times. For the period of 1995 to 2004, the maximum real per capita GDP per year was 7,179.33 yuan for Shanghai (followed by Tianjin with 5,153.03 yuan and Beijing with 4,086.77 yuan), and the minimum real per capita GDP per year was 714.22 yuan for Guizhou (followed by Gansu with 1,071.9 yuan), with a gap of 10.05 times. The gap in real per capita GDP between the rich provinces and the poor provinces increased from 9.67 times to 10.24 times. China's growth rate of GDP increased between 1995 and 2004, with the mean of the growth rate being 10.11 percent for the period of 1995 to 2000 and 12.69 percent for the period of 2000 to 2004. Some provinces experienced negative population growth. For example, the growth rate of population from 2000 to 2004 was −0.997 percent for Guangdong, −0.175 percent for Jilin, and −0.124 percent for Liaoning. Shanghai, Guangdong, and Beijing led the nation in population growth from 1995 to 2004, at 2.31 percent, 2.11 percent, and 1.965 percent, respectively, due to migration.

Table 11.5b shows the correlation coefficients of the variables. The correlation coefficient between the variable *minority* and the variable *west* is 0.55. This is because all of the minority regions are in the west part of China. The correlation coefficient of per capita real GDP and the growth rate of real GDP is 0.42, indicating that rich provinces grew faster than poor provinces.

Our testable hypotheses are based on the analyses in the last section. The regression equation is as follows:

$$q_{it} = a_0 + a_1 y_{it} + a_2 \dot{y}_n + a_3 \dot{L}_{it} + a_4 west + a_5\ minority + u_{it} \qquad (11)$$

where q_{it} is per capita real transfer, y_{it} is per capita real GDP, $\dot{y}_{it}$ is the growth rate of real GDP, $\dot{L}_{it}$ is the population growth rate, *west* is the dummy variable for western regions, *minority* is the dummy variable for minority regions, and u_{it} is the error term. Per capita real transfer is obtained by dividing the total transfers to each province in each year by the population and price index of the province. The total transfer for each province in each year was taken from the *Finance Yearbook of China* (1996–2005). The population data is from the *China Statistical Yearbook* (1996–2005).

The explanations of the independent variables and discussion of the hypotheses follows.

Per capita GDP. One of the major objectives of the intergovernmental transfers is to redistribute the interregional income and to make the provision of public goods

TABLE 11.5B
Correlation Coefficients of Variables

	Per Capita Real Transfers	Per Capita Real GDP	Real GDP Growth Rate	Population Growth Rate	Western Regions	Minority Regions
Per capita real transfers	1					
Per capita real GDP	0.3303	1				
Real GDP growth rate	0.3556	0.4194	1			
Population growth rate	0.0555	0.0711	0.088	1		
Western regions	0.2238	−0.4034	−0.1114	0.0379	1	
Minority regions	0.3515	−0.2037	−0.0182	0.0505	0.5518	1

more equitable among regions. Thus, the government is supposed to transfer more to provinces with less per capita income. Evidence shows that central governments, including the federal government in the United States, indeed make more transfers to low-income regions (see Fisher 2007; Inman 1988). However, as discussed previously (see equation 6), China's tax rebate system was formulated to transfer more to the regions with higher per capita income. Thus, the provinces with higher initial per capita income have a higher per capita transfer from the central government.

Growth rate of real GDP. Growth rate of real GDP = ln(*real GDP in period t + n*) − ln(*real GDP in period t*). As mentioned earlier, the tax rebate is an important ingredient of the central transfer. Based on the analyses in the preceding section (see equations 6 and 7), the higher the per capita GDP growth is, the more transfers the local government will receive, with other things being equal. On the other hand, the government has intended to help the slow-growing poor regions. If the policy of rewarding the rich dominates, the coefficient of $\dot{y}$, a_2, will be positive; if the policy of helping the poor dominates, the coefficient of $\dot{y}$, a_2, will be negative.

Population growth rate. The data for population is from various issues of the *China Statistical Yearbook*. $\dot{L}_{it} = [\ln(\textit{population in period } t+n) - \ln(\textit{population in period } t)] / n$ where n is the difference between the two time periods. From the earlier analysis of the VAT rebate system, we know that the faster the population growth rate is, the lower the per capita tax rebate will be. Since tax rebate is an important part of transfers, we believe that the population growth rate and per capita transfer should be negatively related.

Western region. By the official definition, the western region consists of the following 12 provinces: the municipalities of Chongqing, Sichuan, Guizhou, Yunan, Shaanxi, Gansu, and Qinghai and the autonomous regions of Ningxia, Inner Mongolia, Guangxi, Xinjiang, and Tibet. The western region is poor, and the central government is supposed to transfer more to this region to support its development. Particularly, in 2000 the State Council issued a document announcing a series of favorable policies for western region development, including more fiscal transfers to the region (State Council 2000). Thus, there should have been a substantial increase in transfers to the western region after 2000.

Minority regions. The government has for years emphasized the development of the minority regions, which mainly include Guangxi, Inner Mongolia, Ningxia, Tibet, and Xinjiang.[3] Thus, minority areas should receive more transfers on average. It should be mentioned that the central government has other favorable policies toward minority regions, as well. For example, China adopted the policy of one child per family at the end of the 1970s. However, all minorities are not covered by that policy; some people can have two children per family. China has 56 nationalities, with the Han nationality being the largest and the remaining 55 all being minorities.

---

[3] There are also autonomous prefectures and autonomous counties for minorities in China. Since provincial data are used in this chapter, the smaller minority areas are not considered here.

Regression Analyses

Panel regressions are performed to test the testable hypotheses discussed in the last subsection. With two dummy variables, western region (*west*) and minority regions (*minority*) included, we have to utilize the random effects models in our regressions. The fixed effects model does not work in this case.[4]

Regressions are based on the data from the whole sample period (1995–2004), as well as on two subsample periods (1995–2000 and 2000–2004). Table 11.6a shows the regression results based on the data from 1995 to 2004. It can be seen that per capita real transfers from the central government to a province are positively related to per capita real GDP in the province. That is to say, the province with a higher level of per capita real GDP had a higher level of per capita real transfers from the central government (see regression 1). This relationship still holds when other explanatory variables are included in the regression equation (see regressions 3 and 5). The level of significance is at 1 percent in all three regressions.

Output growth is positively related to per capita transfers at a 1 percent statistically significant level in all regressions (regressions 2–5), indicating that provinces with higher output growth rates have higher per capita real transfers from the

TABLE 11.6A
Regressions of Real per Capita Transfers from the Central Government, 1995–2004

Variables	(1)	(2)	(3)	(4)	(5)
y_{it}	0.068		0.054		0.057
	(0.006)***		(0.006)***		(0.006)***
$\dot{y}_n$		13.798	7.745	13.907	7.482
		(1.642)***	(1.631)***	(1.643)***	(1.607)***
$\dot{L}_{it}$		−4.938	−2.744	−4.949	−2.679
	(2.851)*	(2.558)	(2.852)*	(2.521)	
west				0.214	1.023
				(0.490)	(0.502)**
minority				1.479	1.366
				(0.648)**	(0.653)**
constant	0.118	0.114	−0.402	−0.219	−1.066
	(0.274)	(0.285)	(0.283)	(0.316)	(0.319)***
Observations	310	310	310	310	310
R^2 overall	0.1091	0.1182	0.1436	0.2504	0.3636

NOTE: Number of panel regressions and standard errors are in parentheses. * = statistically significant at the 10% level; ** = statistically significant at the 5% level; *** = statistically significant at the 1% level.

---

[4] The fixed effects model controls for unmeasured province characteristics and time factors via province- and time-specific effects, whereas the random effects model treats these as components of the error term. There are general arguments supporting the random effects model. Mundlak (1978) argues that we should always treat individual effects as random. The fixed effects model is simply analyzed conditionally on the effects present in the observed sample. Greene (1997) points out that from a purely practical standpoint, the dummy variable approach is costly in terms of degrees of freedom lost, and in a wide, longitudinal data set, the random effects model has some intuitive appeal.

central government. As discussed earlier, transfers include tax rebates, which depend on the increase in value-added taxes, and therefore, the increase in output. However, the grants are designed to help the slow-growing poor provinces. Our results indicate that the tax rebates dominate the grants in the central government transfer system.

The rate of population growth is negatively related to per capita transfer. However, the coefficient is significant at the 10 percent level in regressions 2 and 4 only.

The dummy variable, the western region, is statistically significant at 1 percent of significance when per capita GDP is controlled in regression 5, indicating that the western region received more per capita transfers from the central government.

The dummy variable, minority regions, is highly significant—that is, the minority regions have received more per capita transfers from the central government than other regions. This relationship is robust in all of the regressions when the dummy variable is included (regressions 2–5).

To see the determinants of the transfers in different time periods, we ran regressions using the data for the period from 1995 to 2000 and for the period from 2000 to 2004. The results concerning the relationship between per capita transfer and per capita GDP remains unchanged—that is, provinces with high per capita GDP received more per capita transfers from the central government, while provinces with less per capita GDP received fewer per capita transfers from the central government. The results are statistically significant at the 1 percent level in all the regressions when per capita GDP is included.

The coefficient of output growth has a positive sign in all the regressions in the two subsamples. It was statistically significant at the 1 percent or 5 percent level in regressions 2–5 in tables 11.6a and b, in which the data for the period 1995–2004 were used. Although it is statistically significant at the 1 percent or 5 percent level in regressions 2–4, it becomes insignificant in regression 5 in table 11.6c, in which the data for the period 2000–2004 were used.

The coefficient of the rate of population growth still has a negative sign in tables 11.6b and 11.6c but is not statistically significant. The dummy variable, minority regions, is statistically highly significant, indicating that the western region received more per capita transfers from the central government.

The dummy variable, the western region, is not statistically significant in any regression in table 11.6b, which uses data for the period 1995–2000. However, it is statistically significant at 1 percent in all regressions in table 11.6c, which includes regression results for the period 2000–2004. The results are not hard to explain. Before 2000, the western region did not receive special attention from the central government. In 2000 the central government adopted a western development strategy and began to increase financial aid to the west. Our regression results indicate that the western region indeed received more per capita transfers from the central government after the western development strategy was adopted.

As mentioned earlier, the government adjusted the statistics on GDP in 2005. The revised data go back only to 2001. We ran regressions using the revised data for the period 2001–2005 and obtained similar results. Particularly, per capita real

TABLE 11.6B
Regressions of Real per Capita Transfers from the Central Government, 1995–2000

Variables	(1)	(2)	(3)	(4)	(5)
y_{it}	0.050		0.049		0.052
	(0.006)***		(0.006)***		(0.006)***
$\dot{y}_n$		2.598	1.807	2.672	1.860
		(0.902)***	(0.764)**	(0.910)***	(0.760)**
$\dot{L}_{it}$		0.011	−1.411	0.021	−1.520
		(1.382)	(1.174)	(1.393)	(1.168)
west				−0.074	0.535
				(0.334)	(0.317)*
minority				0.898	0.806
				(0.442)**	(0.409)**
constant	0.171	0.760	0.026	0.636	−0.380
	(0.181)	(0.171)***	(0.188)	(0.197)***	(0.214)*
Observations	186	186	186	186	186
R^2 overall	0.1814	0.0516	0.1835	0.1483	0.4211

NOTE: Number of panel regressions and standard errors are in parentheses. * = statistically significant at the 10% level; ** = statistically significant at the 5% level; *** = statistically significant at the 1% level.

TABLE 11.6C
Regressions of Real per Capita Transfers from the Central Government, 2000–2004

Variables	(1)	(2)	(3)	(4)	(5)
y_{it}	0.063		0.052		0.059
	(0.008)***		(0.009)***		(0.009)***
$\dot{y}_n$		11.390	4.550	11.318	3.606
		(2.117)***	(2.238)**	(2.112)***	(2.187)*
$\dot{L}_{it}$		−4.115	−0.950	−4.095	−0.532
		(2.221)*	(2.058)	(2.217)*	(2.001)
west				0.318	1.442
				(0.737)	(0.763)*
minority				2.145	2.036
				(0.976)**	(0.983)**
constant	0.516	0.857	0.257	0.397	−0.699
	(0.411)	(0.420)**	(0.423)	(0.463)	(0.479)
Observations	155	155	155	155	155
R^2 overall	0.0288	0.0772	0.0399	0.2641	0.3214

NOTE: Number of panel regressions and standard errors are in parentheses. * = statistically significant at the 10% level; ** = statistically significant at the 5% level; *** = statistically significant at the 1% level.

transfers are positively related to per capita real GDP, as well as to the growth rate of real GDP.[5] Thus, the results that we have obtained appear robust.

Summary

The fiscal disparity between China's central and local governments has been substantial. After the 1994 tax reforms, the central government share of total government revenue increased, while its expenditure share has remained unchanged. The ratio of local government revenues to their expenditures was 60.5 percent in 2005, implying that near 40 percent of local government expenditures need to be financed by central government transfers. Fiscal disparities among provinces, measured by per capita government expenditures, are also substantial, with the top being about 10 times as large as the bottom. Since local governments have little power to establish their own taxes and no right to issue bonds, central government transfers become crucial for reducing local fiscal inequality.

Central government transfers, consisting of tax rebates and grants, are supposed to reduce the fiscal disparities among provinces. While grants are mainly equity promoting, the tax rebate system encourages provinces to create more tax revenues for the central government. The empirical evidence based on panel data from 1995 to 2004 for 31 provinces shows that the tax rebates dominate the equity-promoting grants in central government transfers; provinces with a higher level of income received more per capita transfers from the central government than those with a lower level of income; and provinces with a higher growth rate received more per capita transfers than provinces with a lower rate of growth. Thus, the current transfer system is ineffective in reducing the regional fiscal disparity.

To obtain more revenues, local governments have actively pursued economic growth, resulting in periodic economic overheating and environmental deterioration. As the country faces persistent regional income and fiscal disparities, reforming the transfer system has become imperative. One option is to eliminate the growth-stimulating tax rebate system and increase the local government share of VAT revenues.

Acknowledgments

Part of the research for this chapter was done while the author was a visiting senior research fellow at the East Asian Institute of the National University of Singapore. The author appreciates the helpful comments made by the participants of the conference and thanks Jackie Lynch, Miaomiao Yu, Yi Zheng, and Jing Su for their excellent research assistance. Any remaining errors are the author's responsibility.

REFERENCES

Bahl, Roy, and Christine Wallich. 1992. Intergovernmental fiscal relations in China. Working Paper No. WPS 863. Washington, DC: World Bank, Country Economics Department.

---

[5] The results are available on request.

Break, George F. 1967. *International fiscal relations in the United States.* Washington, DC: Brookings Institution.
Brean, Donald. 1998. Financial perspectives on fiscal reform. In *China's tax reform options*, eds. Trish Fulton, Jinyan Li, and Dianqing Xu, 47–56. Hackensack, NJ: World Scientific.
Fan, Gang. 1998. Market-oriented economic reform and the growth of off-budget local public finance. In *Taxation in modern China*, ed. Donald Brean, 209–227. New York and London: Routledge.
Fisher, Ronald C. 2007. *State and local government finance*, 3rd ed. Mason, OH: Thomson South-Western.
Greene, William H. 1997. *Econometric analysis*, 3rd ed. Upper Saddle River, NJ: Prentice Hall.
Guo, Jiangzhong. 2003. Analysis of the tax-sharing system in Gansu and policy recommendations [In Chinese]. In *China and overseas experts on fiscal transfers*, ed. Research Department of the Budgetary Committee, Standing Committee of the National People's Congress, 272–283. Beijing: China Financial and Economic Publishing House.
Hofman, Bert. 1993. An analysis of Chinese fiscal data over the reform period. *China Economic Review* 42(2):213–230.
Hofman, Bert, and Susana Cordeiro Guerra. 2005. Fiscal disparities in East Asia: How large and do they matter? In *East Asia decentralizes: Making local government work*, ed. World Bank, 67–83. Washington, DC: World Bank.
Inman, Robert P. 1988. Federal assistance and local services in the United States: The evolution of a new federalist fiscal order. In *Fiscal federalism: Quantitative studies*, ed. Harvey Rosen. Chicago: University of Chicago Press.
International Monetary Fund. 2005. *Government finance statistics Yearbook.* Washington, DC.
Jia, Kang. 2000. Problems and solutions of transforming from fees to taxation. In *Converting fees into taxation*, ed. Gao Peiyong. Beijing: Economic Science Publishing House.
Li, Ping. 2003. The situation of fiscal transfers in Jiangsu Province and some suggestions [In Chinese]. In *China and overseas experts on fiscal transfers*, ed. Research Department of the Budgetary Committee, Standing Committee of the National People's Congress, 183–187. Beijing: China Financial and Economic Publishing House.
Lin, Shuanglin. 2000. The decline of China's budgetary revenue: Reasons and consequences. *Contemporary Economic Policy* 18:477–490.
Liu, Ying. 2003. The problems with China's fiscal transfer system [In Chinese]. In *China and overseas experts on fiscal transfers*, ed. Research Department of the Budgetary Committee, Standing Committee of the National People's Congress, 25. Beijing: China Financial and Economic Publishing House.
Lu, Quanlian. 2003. Deepening the reforms of China's intergovernmental transfer system [In Chinese]. In *China and overseas experts on fiscal transfers*, ed. Research Department of the Budgetary Committee, Standing Committee of the National People's Congress, 162–170. Beijing: China Financial and Economic Publishing House.
Min, Chunhui. 2003. The situation of fiscal transfers in Liaoning and suggestions [In Chinese]. In *China and overseas experts on fiscal transfers*, ed. Research Department of the Budgetary Committee, Standing Committee of the National People's Congress, 162–170. Beijing: China Financial and Economic Publishing House.
Ministry of Finance. 1996–2006. *China finance yearbook.* Beijing: China Financial and Economic Publishing House.
Mundlak, Yair. 1978. On the pooling of time series and cross-sectional data. *Econometrica* 46: 69–86.
National Bureau of Statistics. 1996–2006. *China statistical yearbook.* Beijing: China Statistics Press.
———. 1997. *Seventeen years' regional statistics after reforms and opening-up.* Beijing: Publishing House of China's Bureau of Statistics.
———. 2005. *China compendium of statistics, 1994–2004.* Beijing: China Statistics Press.
———. 2006. *China statistical abstract.* Beijing: China Statistics Press.

National Bureau of Taxation. 2006. *Tax yearbook of China*.
Ouyang, Guobin. 2003. Comments and suggestions on further reforms on the central-local government transfer system [In Chinese]. In *China and overseas experts on fiscal transfers,* ed. Research Department of the Budgetary Committee, Standing Committee of the National People's Congress, 254–261. Beijing: China Financial and Economic Publishing House.
State Council. 2000. *Circular of the State Council on adopting the policies of the Western Region Development.* Document No. 33. Beijing: China Publishing House of Taxation.
Stiglitz, Joseph. 1998. China's reform strategies in the second stage: A speech at Peking University. *People's Daily*, November 13.
Sun, Taishan. 2003. The situation of transfers from the provincial government to under-provincial governments in Shandong Province [In Chinese]. In *China and overseas experts on fiscal transfers,* ed. Research Department of the Budgetary Committee, Standing Committee of the National People's Congress, 201–207. Beijing: China Financial and Economic Publishing House.
Tsui, Kai-yuen. 2005. Local tax system, intergovernmental transfers and China's local fiscal disparities. *Journal of Comparative Economics* 33:173–196.
Wong, Christine P. W., Christopher Heady, and Wing T. Woo. 1995. *Fiscal management and economic reform in the People's Republic of China.* Hong Kong: Oxford University Press.
Wu, Shi-an. 1997. *China's fee collection research.* Beijing: China Financial and Economic Publishing House.
Yang, Changyong. 2005. Research on the fairness of China's fiscal transfer system [In Chinese]. Memo. Beijing: Department of Public Finance, Peking University.
Yu, Qing, and Kai-yuen Tsui. 2005. Factor decomposition of sub-provincial fiscal disparities in China. *China Economic Review* 16:403–418.
Zhang, Zhenqiu. 2003. The basic situation of transfers in Jiangxi Province [In Chinese]. In *China and overseas experts on fiscal transfers,* ed. Research Department of the Budgetary Committee, Standing Committee of the National People's Congress, 197–200. Beijing: China Financial and Economic Publishing House.

12
Fiscal Reform and Rural Public Finance

RICHARD BIRD, LOREN BRANDT, SCOTT ROZELLE, AND LINXIU ZHANG

China's rural sector is important. Despite the rapid out-migration of recent decades, over 650 million people still live in its 750,000 villages. China's highly successful economic reforms began in its rural sector. In the long run, both the path its future development takes and the social, economic, and political consequences of that growth will continue to depend in key ways upon how the rural sector is treated. The continuing outflow of people from the rural sector in itself makes it important for national development to ensure that rural individuals, both those who leave and those who remain, are provided with at least minimal local public services. But if China's many remaining villages (and the townships in which they are situated) are to become more viable, accountable, and at least moderately effective in providing such services, they need a more sustainable fiscal basis than they now have. Growing disparities in income, wealth, and public services between the urban and rural sectors, between different regions of the country, and within the rural sector will increase the stress on the political system over time.

For all these reasons, rural public finance issues have attracted considerable recent attention in China (Fock and Wong 2005; Li 2006; Tao and Liu 2005; World Bank 2005). The same concerns have also prompted significant reforms affecting the rural public sector at both the township and village levels. Collectively referred to as *feigaishui*, or the tax-for-fee reforms, they include the elimination of regular fee assessments imposed on rural households, the removal of the long-standing agricultural tax, a change in the management of village fiscal accounts, and increased investment efforts by upper-level governments in the rural sector. Although villages are not an official level of government in China, in key respects they constitute (together with townships) the most important level of the public sector in terms of building rural infrastructure and providing a solid fiscal foundation for the provision of rural local public services.

Assessment of these important reform initiatives has been limited, however, largely because of a scarcity of comprehensive fiscal data at both the village and township levels. Drawing on a unique survey designed and carried out by several of its authors, this chapter provides a summary analysis of the changes in township and village finance between 2000 and 2004, a period that spans the implementation of key reforms.[1] This survey, which was carried out in March-April 2005, extends to one hundred villages in fifty townships in twenty-five counties in five provinces (Jilin, Hebei, Shaanxi, Sichuan, and Jiangsu). Even though the counties, townships, and villages in each province were selected to provide a representative cross section, China is so vast and varied a country that the entire story cannot be told here.[2] It is also important to keep in mind that by the end of 2004, the full effect of these reforms had not likely played out. Follow-up survey work completed in the spring of 2008 will soon allow our analysis to be updated.

Tax-for-Fee Reform and Village Finance

Table 12.1 provides a broad summary of the major changes in village finance that emerge from a detailed analysis of these data. It includes data for 2000 and 2004 at the provincial level, as well as for those villages in the richest and poorest quintiles in our sample, and focuses on several key aggregates: village per capita measures of fiscal revenue, expenditure (current as well as capital), fiscal balance (deficit or surplus), and total public goods investment.

At the risk of oversimplification, the overall effect of the tax-for-fee reform on village finances appears to be mixed. Revenues increased only modestly with the elimination of the regular fee for assessments on farmers (*tiliu*), but total expenditures grew by more than 20 percent, largely because of increasing village capital expenditures. As a result, by 2004 a growing number of villages were running deficits. Moreover, the increase in transfers from higher levels of government covered only about 40 percent of the revenue loss. Other sources of revenue—notably revenue from the contracting out of village land and enterprises, and from village land and asset sales—made up the balance, with the result that total revenues were almost the same in 2004 as in 2000. The other revenue sources that helped villages temporarily narrow the spending gap are almost certainly not sustainable; this is discussed in more detail later in the chapter.

Considering all sources of finance over this period, villages experienced a nearly fourfold increase in total public goods investment, from 48.4 yuan per capita to 191.3 yuan per capita. Much of this increase was in roads, and about 75 percent of it was financed by increased transfers. Despite the fact that capital expenditures from higher-level transfers to poor areas were larger than those to richer areas, the net result was a slight increase in the inequality of fiscal expenditure at the village level.

---

[1] More detailed description and analysis of these data at the village and township levels can be found in two reports prepared for the World Bank (Zhang et al. 2005; Zhang et al. 2006).

[2] The sample provinces cover each of China's five major agro-ecological zones. Within each province, we randomly selected counties, towns, and villages. The village data are based mainly on interviews with village accountants, who, in most of the villages, used accounting records as a basis for their answers. Township data are based largely on official accounting books supplemented by interviews with officials concerned with accounting.

TABLE 12.1
Summary Table of Village Fiscal Balance, 2000 and 2004 (yuan per capita)

	2000									2004								
	Total	Jiangsu	Sichuan	Shaanxi	Jilin	Hebei	Rich	Poor		Total	Jiangsu	Sichuan	Shaanxi	Jilin	Hebei	Rich	Poor
Revenues	78.7	103.5	32.9	31.2	154.8	40.6	143.1	75.2		82.1	109.8	22.9	48	156	41.2	145	133.9
Total expenditure (1)	70.4	89.6	26.2	42.2	98.8	79.5	138.7	56.1		70.3	107.8	28.6	38.5	104.3	39.9	125.5	77.9
current expenditure	44.8	65.8	20.3	23.3	68.3	28.5	75.8	42.8		40.1	62.1	19.6	26.5	53.8	21.9	70.9	37.6
capital expenditure (1)	14.6	17.1	2.3	4.3	2.4	45.8	45.1	6.2		17.3	36.9	1.1	4.4	16.8	14.2	37.8	11.8
repayment of principle	11	6.7	3.6	14.6	28.1	5.2	17.8	7.1		12.9	8.8	7.9	7.6	33.7	3.8	16.8	28.5
Total expenditure (2)[a]	78.5	98.2	30.8	73	99.5	84.2	141.5	94.1		95.3	167.5	55.8	51.9	104.3	49.7	187.9	84.7
capital expenditure (2)	22.7	25.7	6.9	35.1	3.1	50.5	47.9	44.2		42.3	96.6	28.3	17.8	16.8	24	100.2	18.6
Deficit/surplus surplus (1)[b]	8.3	13.9	6.7	−11	56	−38.9	4.4	19.1		11.8	2	−5.7	9.5	51.7	1.3	19.5	56
Deficit/surplus surplus (2)	0.2	5.3	2.1	−41.8	55.3	−43.6	1.6	−18.9		−13.2	−57.7	−32.9	−3.9	51.7	−8.5	−42.9	49.2
Total public goods investment	48.4	58.6	52.4	69.4	6.6	60.1	63.4	65.8		191.3	352.7	214.5	156.4	78.2	63.4	317.2	170.5

[a] Total expenditure (2) is the sum of the current expenditure and repayment of principle as listed above. The only difference between total expenditure (1) and (2) is that capital expenditure (2) includes the amount financed by debt as listed in the table. [b] Deficit/surplus (1) is revenue minus total expenditure (1); deficit/surplus (2) is revenue minus total expenditure (2).

Richer villages were able to derive sufficiently more revenue from their own sources, which more than offset the redistributive effect of transfers.

This aggregate picture conceals significant heterogeneity across provinces and even within provinces. Furthermore, even if the fiscal health of China's villages did not deteriorate too much as a result of the reform, other evidence, discussed later, suggests that this outcome may well have come at the expense of the fiscal health of China's townships, the next level up in China's administrative hierarchy.

Village Revenues

Table 12.2 provides a more detailed summary of village per capita revenues in 2000 and 2004. In 2000, village revenue per capita was 78.7 yuan. Assessments on farmers (38.1 percent) were the most important source of village revenue, with nearly three-quarters of villages reporting revenue from tiliu. Next in importance were revenues from land and asset sales (20 percent), followed by payments for contracting out of village land and enterprises (17.7 percent). Transfers from higher levels of government accounted for only 5.9 percent of all village revenue, with slightly less than half of all villages reporting revenue from these sources.

In 2000, we can observe significant differences across provinces in revenue per capita on the order of 5:1.[3] Fiscal resources were most abundant in Jilin and Jiangsu, with per capita revenues of 154.8 and 103.5 yuan, respectively. In contrast, Sichuan and Shaanxi had much less revenue. These disparities mainly reflect differences in land-based revenues. For example, in Jilin revenue earned from the contracting of village land and assets was especially important. Interestingly, the difference between the richest and poorest village quintiles was much less, on the order of magnitude of only 2:1.

Between 2000 and 2004, per capita village fiscal revenues increased only by about 5 percent, from 78.7 to 82.1 yuan. This percentage increase was much lower than the rise in per capita rural incomes (National Bureau of Statistics 2006). The elimination of tiliu of 30 yuan per capita was offset by increased revenue from transfers from above (13.2 yuan), land and asset sales (7.7), contract payments for land and from enterprises (6.0), and a surtax rebate from the agricultural tax introduced in 2002 (4.5).[4] Despite their significant increase, in 2004 transfers from above still provided only about a fifth of total village revenue. On average, other village sources of revenue covered half of the loss of revenue from the abolition of

---

[3] The details by province and also in terms of the richest and poorest quintiles may be found in Zhang et al. (2005).

[4] This rebate was supposed to be the main source of income to replace tiliu. In place of most fees that farmers were paying, a single agricultural tax assessment (in theory to be set at 8.5 percent of the local agricultural GDP) was collected from farmers. Although the entire amount was remitted to the township government, part of this amount (1.5 percentage points) was supposed to go back into the village's account as current revenue. This funding source is what we label the "surtax rebate from the agricultural tax." In 2004, however, the government began a three-year program to eliminate the agricultural tax, with local governments being required to reduce the agricultural tax by 3.5 percent in 2005 and an additional 2.5 percent in each of 2006 and 2007. In some provinces, provincial and local officials accelerated the government's program and eliminated the tax completely in 2005. As a result, only 58.3 percent of villages collected the surtax rebate in 2004. This amount is supposed to be replaced by direct transfers from above.

TABLE 12.2
Per Capita Fiscal Revenue: Sources of Funding (yuan and percent)

Revenue Category	2000 Mean	2000 SD	2000 Percent >0	2000 Percent of Total Revenue	2004 Mean	2004 SD	2004 Percent >0	2004 Percent of Total Revenue
Transfers from above	4.6	7.5	48.5	5.9	17.8	37.4	82.2	21.7
Regular fee assessments from farmers (tiliu)	30.0	39.0	73.3	38.1	0.2	1.5	1.0	0.2
Surtax rebate from agriculture tax	0.2	1.3	1.0	0.2	4.7	5.5	58.4	5.7
Contract payment for land	8.1	16.3	50.5	10.3	12.0	31.2	51.5	14.6
Contract payment for enterprises	5.8	31.8	17.8	7.4	7.9	44.2	12.9	9.6
Land and asset sales	15.8	55.1	18.8	20.0	23.5	85.2	32.7	28.6
Other revenues[a]	14.3	24.9	54.5	18.2	16.0	24.9	59.4	19.5
Total revenues	**78.7**	**93.4**	**99.0**	**100.0**	**82.1**	**123.4**	**100.0**	**100.0**

NOTE: SD = standard deviation.

[a] Other revenues include such items as administration fees from enterprises, profits from village-owned enterprises, and income from fines.

tiliu and grew in importance. Revenue from village land and asset sales, for example, increased from 18.8 percent in 2000 to 28.6 percent in 2004, with a third of all villages reporting income from this source.

The effects again differed from province to province (not shown). In three provinces (Jiangsu, Jilin, and Hebei) the changes in average per capita revenue were nominal. In Shaanxi, however, there was actually an increase of more than half. In contrast, in Sichuan there was a reduction of nearly a third. Some of this heterogeneity reflects differences in how villages made up the shortfall in revenue caused by the elimination of tiliu. In Jilin, for example, most of the shortfall was made up by an increase in transfers from above. In Jiangsu, a third came from transfers from above, half from an increase in contract payments for land and from enterprises, and the rest was largely from the surtax rebate from the agricultural tax. In Hebei, the surtax rebate from the agricultural tax was the most important source of the offset, followed by transfers from above and land and asset sales. In Shaanxi, the reduction in the tiliu was offset partly by a small increase from transfers but mostly by an increase in revenue from land and asset sales. In contrast, in Sichuan the increase in transfers from above made up only 10 percent of the decline due to the elimination of tiliu. The absence of other sources of income to offset the elimination of tiliu explains the decline in per capita revenue in Sichuan. As the Sichuan experience illustrates, in many villages the tax-for-fee reform was not revenue neutral. In fact, 40 percent of the 101 villages in our study experienced a drop in fiscal revenue of 25 percent or more.

An important feature of the reform (although not set out in the tables) is that there was clearly significant redistribution in favor of the poorest villages. Villages in the poorest quintile experienced an increase of 85 percent in revenues (from 75.2 yuan to 133.9 yuan) compared to an increase of only 1 percent in the richest quintile. As a result, the gap between rich and poor villages fell sharply, from 1.90 in 2000 to only 1.08 in 2004. The reason for this progressive effect lies in the behavior of the transfers. Although all villages increased their revenue from land sales, for the poorest villages the decline in fee revenue was much more than offset by the increase in transfers.[5]

However, the redistribution in favor of the poorest 20 percent of villages may have been mainly at the expense of the middle 60 percent of villages. Nearly 40 percent of all villages reported a decline in revenue between 2000 and 2004 of 25 percent or more, consistent with an increase in the Gini coefficient for per capita fiscal revenue from 0.54 to 0.59 between 2000 and 2004 (see table 12.3). In addition, although the redistribution of resources (through transfers and by increasing investment financed from above) made poor villages less dependent on their own current and future revenues, it had the opposite effect on richer villages. The latter have relied more on debt to increase capital expenditure, thus again raising important questions of sustainability.

Village Expenditure

Table 12.4 summarizes village expenditures. In 2000, almost two-thirds of per capita expenditure was for current expenditures, of which more than half was for salaries and administrative expenses. Slightly less than a quarter went to maintenance expenditures, and expenditure on social welfare accounted for most of the balance. About one-third of the villages reported capital expenditures financed from current

TABLE 12.3
Inequality Measures for Fiscal Revenues and Expenditures

Gini Coefficient	2000	2004
Revenues	0.54	0.59
Total expenditures[a]	0.50	0.57
Current expenditures	0.43	0.44
Capital expenditures[a]	0.68	0.73
Total public goods investment	0.60	0.64

NOTE: [a]These expenditure concepts are those defined as (2) in table 12.1.

---

[5] Even these numbers need to be interpreted carefully. Rich villages typically have populations that are three to four times larger than those of poor villages. Thus, on a per capita basis more went to individuals living in poor villages, but in absolute terms more went to rich villages.

TABLE 12.4
Per Capita Total Fiscal Expenditure: Composition of Expenditures (yuan)

Expenditures	2000 Mean	SD	Percent >0	Percent of Total Expenditures[a]	2004 Mean	SD	Percent >0	Percent of Total Expenditures[a]
Current expenditure	44.8	37.9	100.0	56.8	40.1	41.9	100.0	42.0
Salaries	15.0	11.8	96.0	19.1	14.4	11.7	98.0	15.1
Administrative expenditures	9.0	8.6	99.0	11.4	6.7	7.3	99.0	7.0
Maintenance expenditures	10.6	14.2	80.2	13.4	8.0	10.5	80.2	8.4
Social welfare expenditures	3.8	6.2	71.3	4.8	6.1	17.6	74.3	6.3
Other expenditures	6.4	12.2	76.2	8.1	5.0	8.5	80.2	5.2
Total capital expenditures financed by the village leadership:	23.0	66.8	40.6	29.2	42.5	105.7	66.3	44.5
financed by current revenues or savings	14.6	44.8	35.6	18.5	17.3	47.4	51.5	18.1
financed by debt	8.4	47.3	12.9	10.7	25.2	85.6	32.7	26.4
Repayment of principle	11.0	27.6	32.7	13.9	12.9	33.4	50.5	13.5
Total expenditures (2)	78.8	85.4	100.0	100.0	95.5	138.9	100.0	100.0

NOTE: Row 1 is the sum of salaries, administrative expenditures, maintenance expenditures, social welfare expenditures, and other expenditures. Total capital expenditures financed by the village leadership are the sum of expenditures financed by current revenues or savings and financed by debt. Total expenditures are the sum of current expenditure, total capital expenditures financed by the village leadership, and repayment of principle. SD = standard deviation.

[a] These expenditure concepts are those defined as (2) in table 12.1.

revenues or savings in 2000, and a third also reported debt repayment. Prior to the tax-for-fee reform, villages were investing significant amounts of their own resources into public goods.

Differences in expenditure across provinces in 2000 were smaller than differences in revenue, with consistently one-third or so of current expenditure going to salaries in each province. Although current expenditures differed significantly between the richest and poorest villages, both groups had nearly the same levels of capital expenditures. The main difference was that poorer villages financed nearly 85 percent of their capital expenditures by borrowing, while richer villages were able to finance their capital expenditures from current revenue and savings.

Our village data reveal two significant changes in village expenditures between 2000 and 2004 (table 12.4). First, total village expenditures shifted from current to capital expenditures. Second, much of the increase in capital expenditures was financed by debt, which increased between 2000 and 2004 from 8.4 to 25.2 yuan per capita. There is significant heterogeneity across provinces in these trends, however (not shown in tables). Expenditures declined most in Shaanxi, owing to a sharp decline in debt-financed capital expenditures, and in Hebei, where both current and capital expenditures declined. On the other hand, in Jiangsu and Sichuan capital expenditures nearly quadrupled. The most notable change between rich and poor villages was a reduction in debt-financed expenditures by poor villages; however, such expenditures actually increased in rich villages. However, by 2004 debt repayment became more important in poor villages, with 20 percent of their fiscal expenditure being earmarked for the repayment of debt.

Table 12.5 depicts per capita total public investment and the sources of financing. In 2000, average total public investment financed from all sources was 48.4 yuan. Roads, irrigation, drinking water, and schools (in order of importance) were the most important investment projects. Survey data (not reported here) shows that nearly 30 percent of all villages had investment projects in roads and irrigation. About 15 percent of villages reported investment in drinking water. On the other hand, only 11.9 percent reported investment in schools. Reflecting the highly decentralized nature of public investment in rural China, table 12.5 shows that the most important source of finance in 2000 was the village itself: 46.9 percent from the village committee (through the use of current revenue and savings or financing by debt) and an additional 17.9 percent directly from village households (through special assessments on farmers, or *jizi*). Since only about a fifth of the investment was financed by transfers—slightly skewed toward roads and irrigation projects—much of the heterogeneity observed in levels of total public goods investment presumably reflects structures, including governance structures, at the village level that influence local ability and willingness to undertake investment projects.

Differences across provinces in total public investment in 2000 (not shown in the tables) were relatively small, except that Jilin's total public investment was only a sixth of that reported in the other four provinces. There were also important provincial differences in the composition of public goods investment. For example, roads and irrigation were especially important in Jiangsu; in Sichuan, roads and drinking water consumed more than 80 percent of total public goods investment;

TABLE 12.5
Funding of Public Investment by Project Type (yuan and percent)

Public Goods Investment	2000 Mean	2000 Percent from Higher Levels of Government	2000 Percent from Village Committee	2000 Percent from Households	2000 Percent from Other Sources[a]	2004 Mean	2004 Percent from Higher Level of Government	2004 Percent from Village Committee	2004 Percent from Households	2004 Percent from Other Sources
Roads & bridges	15.1	23.4	46.5	28.6	1.5	123.6	64.8	22.9	11.0	1.3
Schools	8.9	23.8	57.2	14.9	4.1	7.3	30.9	13.5	3.6	52.1
Irrigation	10.2	42.3	31.4	21.2	5.1	20.4	50.5	28.1	10.1	11.2
Drinking water	4.3	4.6	1.5	3.8	90.1	17.6	42.7	24.3	19.3	13.6
Clinic	0.0	0.0	100.0	0.0	0.0	0.9	0.0	3.8	0.0	96.2
Other[b]	9.8	1.2	74.1	6.9	17.8	21.6	61.3	13.5	8.2	17.0
Total public goods investment	48.4	21.3	46.9	17.9	14.0	191.3	59.2	22.1	11.0	7.7

NOTES: [a] Other sources include funds from overseas, donations from local enterprises, investment by small groups (*xiaoxu*) in the village, private investment, and investment by public utilities.
[b] Other includes electricity, village office building construction, green for grain projects, and investment in communications, etc.

and in Shaanxi, more than two-thirds went to investment in schools. Comparing the poorest and richest of villages, in per capita terms the differences in 2000 were marginal. However, poorer villages weighted their own investment heavily toward schools, while in richer villages resources were primarily directed toward roads and other investments. These differences may reflect differences in the existing endowments of public goods between rich and poor villages.

Between 2000 and 2004, when village-level public investment increased substantially, there was clearly a marked bias toward roads and bridges, followed by irrigation and drinking water. In 2000, one-third of villages had a road project; in 2004, two-thirds did. Similar increases occurred in the level of investment in irrigation and drinking water projects. On the other hand, although the number of villages reporting investment in schools also increased, such investment per capita actually declined.[6] As usual, we observe significant heterogeneity across provinces: For example, in Jiangsu, 95 percent of the increase in public investment went to roads. In Sichuan, about half went to roads. In the other provinces, the rise in investment that went to roads was closer to a third. Even in Hebei, where there was no overall increase in public investment, there was a change in its composition, with an increase in roads and drinking water offsetting the decline in "others." These differences between provinces most likely reflect both differences in initial conditions and the source of the funding.

By 2004, the share of total capital expenditures financed by transfers had almost tripled. The effects of the financing shift are also visible when one compares richer and poorer villages. In 2000, per capita investments were very similar between poor and rich villages (65.8 yuan versus 63.4 yuan). In contrast, by 2004 investment in rich villages was 317.2 yuan per capita compared to only 170.5 yuan in poor villages. Although investment in both rich and poor increased substantially, in poor villages increased transfers *substituted for* financing by the village (from current revenues or saving and by debt). On the other hand, in the richest villages, increased transfers were *complemented by* increases in the absolute contribution of the village (from both current revenues or savings and from debt). Associated with this different financial mix is a difference in the composition of investment. In the richer villages, nearly 95 percent of the increase in investment went to roads. In poorer villages, investments in drinking water and the "other" category were especially important in 2004. On the other hand, investments in schools, a major priority in 2000, declined.

Fiscal Reform at the Township Level

The reforms occurring at the village level were directly related to a simultaneous set of reforms at the township level.[7] The tax-for-fee reform not only eliminated

---

[6] The relatively low rise in school investment is likely correlated with the fact that educational reform was just beginning to shift responsibility for school buildings and other infrastructure from the village to the county government. No significant investment in clinics was observed, which largely reflects the fact that these have been subcontracted to individuals to run and manage.

[7] For a detailed analysis of recent township-level fiscal reforms, see Zhang et al. (2006).

tiliu; it also eliminated *tongzhou*, fees from farmers collected at the village level and remitted to the township. In addition, the fiscal reform package included policies that reassigned expenditures, realigned responsibilities, reduced the importance of extrabudgetary and self-raised funds, and, as already discussed, increased investment in infrastructure in rural areas.

On the whole, our data from the fifty townships from the five sample provinces suggest that the broad impact of the fiscal reforms on township fiscal health has not been beneficial. On average, expenditures were almost double local fiscal revenues throughout the 2000 to 2004 period, a period during which township revenues fell by 6 percent and expenditures by 11 percent. Although county-to-town transfers rose, the increase did not come close to covering the reduction of fiscal resources to townships. Moreover, many transfers were earmarked, leaving little latitude for decision making by township leaders. Finally, it was clear during our fieldwork that county financial offices have been given increased control over township expenditure even from own fiscal resources.

One motivation for downgrading the fiscal independence of townships was concern that township governments were not paying enough attention to the provision of rural public services. For this reason, although townships continue to be required to support rural education, they now do so by transferring resources up to the county, which then directly pays teacher salaries. Similarly, a motivation for increased county control over local public investment was to ensure that more was directed to rural areas, particularly to poor rural areas. A positive outcome of the fiscal reform was indeed a substantial increase in rural infrastructure, not least in poorer areas. However, almost all the new investment came from above, and there was little direct involvement at the village level in project selection, design, or implementation. As elaborated on below, this increased top-down control appears to be associated with reduced village-level satisfaction.

We also noted earlier that one result of the fiscal reform was a reduction in the amount of own fiscal resources available to villages. A consequence of this trend has been that revenue-short village leaders often seek funds from townships for a variety of reasons—for example, to repair village irrigation works or bridges. These pressures from below have had the effect of further exacerbating the fiscal pressures on townships resulting from reform. Increasingly pressed from below and directed from above, township fiscal managers have been finding life very difficult in recent years. The undermining of the operating budget at both the village and township levels that appears to have been a major outcome of the fiscal reforms stands in sharp contrast to the obvious intention and effort of the national government to increase investment in rural China as part of its overall strategy of strengthening the rural economy.

Table 12.6 shows the two stories of the effect of the fiscal reforms on township fiscal health. On the one hand, the fiscal reforms have undermined—or at least not improved—the current budgetary condition of townships.[8] Total fiscal revenues are

---

[8] It is important to emphasize, however, that in many ways the fiscal reforms were relatively more beneficial for poorer townships. For further discussion of this point as well as the differences between provinces, see Zhang et al. (2006).

TABLE 12.6
Summary of Township Fiscal Health, Including Summary of Operating Budget, Capital Budget, and Debts, 2000 and 2004 (yuan per capita)

Item	2000	2004
Total township fiscal revenues[a]	211	182
Local taxation revenue	95	129
Town taxation revenue	70	66
Township-to-county transfers	34	93
Mandated township-to-county transfers for expenditure sharing	2	21
County-to-township transfers	58	84
Township disposable fiscal resources[b]	119	119
Supplementary funds shifted from extrabudgetary funds	22	6
Total extrabudgetary revenue	55	53
Total self-raised funds	37	10
Total current expenditure[c]	204	186
Total budgetary expenditure	142	126
Total extrabudgetary expenditure	62	59
Total public investment expenditure	77	217
Total township debts	236	290

NOTES: [a] Total township fiscal revenues is equal to township disposable financial resources plus extrabudgetary revenue plus revenue from self-raised funds.

[b] Township disposable fiscal resources is equal to total township fiscal revenues minus township-to-county transfers plus county-to-township transfers.

[c] Total current expenditure is equal to total budgetary expenditure plus total extrabudgetary expenditure.

down. Although county-to-township transfers have increased, so have township-to-county upward remittances. Even with the additional subsidies associated directly with the fiscal reforms, disposable financial resources at the township level in 2004 were no larger than in 2000. This stagnation in disposable fiscal resources has occurred despite additional fiscal pressures for townships arising from the need to aid villages that have lost fiscal resources.[9]

On the other hand, total investment in rural infrastructure by the township has increased sharply (see also Luo et al. 2007). Assuming road construction is helpful to villagers, the major effort made to increase investment into rural areas during the period of fiscal reform has succeeded. However, the rise in investment has had other, perhaps unexpected, consequences. Given the tight fiscal conditions, when increases in investment by the upper level have been accompanied by demands for matching funds (as has often been the case), the result in many townships has been increased borrowing. On average, per capita debt in townships rose 23 percent between 2000 and 2004.

---

[9] Additional pressure resulted from a mandated national increase in wages: Between 2000 and 2004, the (nationally dictated) average wage for civil servants rose by over 35 percent.

Village Fiscal Health and Farmer Satisfaction

It is still too soon to assess the impact on rural China of the major fiscal reforms of recent years. For example, the linkages (and time lags) between fiscal changes and changes in rural incomes and productivity are complex and may take a long time to work out. All we have attempted here is the much more modest task of reporting in summary form the impacts on village and township finances of the package of fiscal reform introduced in the early years of this century. It is clear from our analysis that these reforms have had substantial, but often mixed, impacts on the fiscal health of both villages and townships.

To examine further the effect of the fiscal reforms on village fiscal health, we consider the impact of six measures of fiscal reform (or its effect on township fiscal health) on three indicators of village fiscal health. The reform measures include two measures of changing township fiscal health, two measures of county fiscal support, and two measures of the support upper-level policy makers give to townships in the form of investment transfers for infrastructure investment. The three measures of village fiscal health are changes in revenue per capita, changes in expenditure per capita, and changes in infrastructure investment per capita.

We ranked townships on the basis of each fiscal reform measure and then divided the sample into quartiles so that we could separate the townships in which expenditure fell the most from those in which expenditure rose the most. We then compared village outcomes in the two extreme quartiles. Table 12.7 summarizes the results.

Panels A and B of the table provide evidence that when township fiscal health is improving (when expenditure per capita is rising or the balance of fiscal resource to expenditure is improving), village revenue per capita tends to rise and village expenditure per capita does not deteriorate as much. In these and other ways, there appears to be some correlation between township fiscal health (in terms of the operating budget) and village fiscal health (in the same terms). However, there is no correlation between township fiscal health in terms of the operating budget and public investment at the village level.

Similarly, as panels C and D of the table show, there is almost no discernible fiscal relationship between the county and township, and the village. Whether the county provides (or demands) more or fewer transfers to (or from) townships, there is no clear pattern in the change in any of the village measures. If this is correct, it would seem that increased county control over townships appears to have had little if any effect on the fiscal condition of villages. The same is true with respect to the relation between county-controlled investment transfers and the health of village operating budgets (panels E and F). Capital accounts in China, it seems, are managed quite independently of operating budgets. This explanation is also supported by the clear relationship between investment from above and village investment. There is more investment in villages in which upper-level governments invest more. Where higher levels invest less, there is less investment.

TABLE 12.7
Correlations Between Measures of Township Fiscal Reform and Village Fiscal Health, 2000 and 2004 (yuan per capita)

Measures	Quartile	Village Fiscal Indicators	2000	2004
Panel A: Impact of Percentage Change in Expenditure				
Measure 1	Lowest quartile	Village revenue per capita	120	112
	(range of variable	Village expenditure per capita	63	51
	−76 to −42)	Village investment per capita	36	131
	Highest quartile	Village revenue per capita	40	72
	(range of variable	Village expenditure per capita	34	34
	32 to 190)	Village investment per capita	52	325
Panel B: Impact of Percentage Change in the Gap Between Disposable Financial Resources and Budgetary Expenditures				
Measure 2	Lowest quartile	Village revenue per capita	115	110
	(range of variable	Village expenditure per capita	56	45
	−177 to −3)	Village investment per capita	33	334
	Highest quartile	Village revenue per capita	87	126
	(range of variable	Village expenditure per capita	58	56
	33 to 233)	Village investment per capita	25	268
Panel C: Impact of Percentage Change in County-to-Town Transfers as a Share of Disposable Fiscal Resources				
Measure 3	Lowest quartile	Village revenue per capita	97	121
	(range of variable	Village expenditure per capita	45	39
	−70 to −8)	Village investment per capita	40	136
	Highest quartile	Village revenue per capita	85	53
	(range of variable	Village expenditure per capita	45	35
	77 to 165)	Village investment per capita	92	153
Panel D: Impact of Percentage Change in Town-to-County Transfers as a Share of Total Tax Revenue Collections				
Measure 4	Lowest quartile	Village revenue per capita	75	74
	(range of variable	Village expenditure per capita	39	26
	−87 to −6)	Village investment per capita	42	176
	Highest quartile	Village revenue per capita	87	63
	(range of variable	Village expenditure per capita	51	43
	82 to 338)	Village investment per capita	71	216
Panel E: Impact of Percentage Change in the Share of Total Investment from Upper-Level Government Transfers				
Measure 5	Lowest quartile	Village revenue per capita	43	75
	(range of variable	Village expenditure per capita	30	24
	−57 to 0)	Village investment per capita	71	70
	Highest quartile	Village revenue per capita	109	90
	(range of variable	Village expenditure per capita	37	28
	74 to 100)	Village investment per capita	15	115
Panel F: Impact of Percentage Change in Absolute Amount of Upper-Level Government Transfer for Public Investment				
Measure 6	Lowest quartile	Village revenue per capita	34	29
	(range of variable	Village expenditure per capita	24	21
	−34 to 9)	Village investment per capita	61	103
	Highest quartile	Village revenue per capita	75	75
	(range of variable	Village expenditure per capita	53	46
	101 to 757)	Village investment per capita	53	336

TABLE 12.7
(continued)

NOTES: Measure 1: Change (in percentage terms) in township expenditure per capita between 2000 and 2004.
Measure 2: Change in the gap between disposable financial resources per capita and per capita budgetary expenditures between 2000 and 2004.
Measure 3: Change in the share of county to town transfers as a share of disposable fiscal resources between 2000 and 2004.
Measure 4: Change in the share of town to county transfers of total tax revenue collections between 2000 and 2004.
Measure 5: Change in the share of total investment from upper level government transfers between 2000 and 2004.
Measure 6: Change in absolute amount of upper level government transfers for public investment between 2000 and 2004. The impact of percentage change in all panels is ranked from lowest to highest and grouped into quartiles.

TABLE 12.8
Regression Results Explaining Villager Satisfaction, 2004

Explanatory Variables	Dependent Variable: Villager Satisfaction with Public Services (satisfied = 1; not satisfied = 0)			
	Model 1	Model 2	Model 3	Model 4
Total investment level	0	0	0	0
	(3.25)***	(2.70)***	(3.58)***	(3.84)***
Share from above	−0.102	−0.124	−0.118	−0.169
	(2.07)**	(2.46)**	(1.94)*	(2.18)**
District dummy	—	province	county	town
Gender dummy (male = 1)	—	yes	yes	yes
Project dummy	yes	yes	yes	yes

NOTE: * significant at 1 percent; ** significant at 5 percent; *** significant at 10 percent.

In other words, if upper-level governments want to get more investment in villages, under the present system they can best manage that by making investments themselves. Unfortunately, as table 12.8 suggests, they may be making less than optimal investments, since the evidence confirms the hypothesis (Liu, Zhang, and Rozelle, 2007) that, holding the level of investment fixed, the more investment is financed by transfers from above—so that the villages' stakeholding in the project is less—the lower farmer satisfaction with rural investment seems to be. This result is robust regardless of the type of project (road, school, etc.), the gender of respondents, or the location (county). Farmers, it seems, appreciate rural investment; but they might appreciate it more if they had some say in selecting and designing the projects.

Conclusions

Unsurprisingly, the set of fiscal reforms generally referred to under the label of the tax-and-fee reduction was popular in rural China: Everyone likes lower taxes. However, although it is too soon to say what the long-term effects of this policy might be, the analysis reported here shows clearly that by most measures and for most areas the effects on the fiscal health of townships and villages are mixed. The increased investment in rural areas by higher-level governments that accompanied the reform clearly has the potential to make many rural people better off. Indeed, one beneficial result of the increased centralization reflected in this package of reforms has been that relatively more resources have been directed to poor rural areas. However, even in those cases the evidence presented here suggests that such investment would, in welfare terms, have had a bigger payoff if there were larger direct village input into the selection, design, and implementation of infrastructure projects. Moreover, in the province of Jiangsu and richer townships, the need for additional matching funds has resulted in increased local debt.

As Wong and Bird (2008) and others have argued, the intergovernmental dimensions of China's public finances remain a work in progress in the sense that there is much that needs to be done before the intergovernmental system is sound. In at least two ways, the recent package of reforms affecting rural public finance appears to have moved in the wrong direction. First, by eroding the fiscal resources and control of both China's lowest official level of government (the township) and its lowest effective "governing" body (the village), these reforms have moved the system even further away from one that can likely accommodate the heterogeneity of China's rural reality and sustain an adequate level of rural public services. Second, by strengthening upper-level control of local public finance, the reforms have made it even more difficult for China to develop an effective and responsible local public finance system.

The marked fiscal recentralization emerging from the recent package of fiscal reforms makes it clear that upper-level leaders are afraid lower-level leaders will not manage fiscal resources responsibly. It is equally clear, however, that when fiscal management is too far removed from local reality, the outcome is not likely to be ideal. Many of the problems manifest at the local level in China result from the inadequacy of local governance institutions and the lack of effective checks on the behavior of local leaders. Changes that "solve" some of the resulting local problems by essentially kicking them upstairs are in the end almost certainly doomed to failure. The development of more responsive and sustainable local fiscal management in China will inevitably require both the devolution of more decision-making power over public finance to local governments and the development of local governments that are more openly and directly responsible to the local people whom they are supposed to serve.

REFERENCES

Fock, Achim, and Christine Wong. 2005. Extending public finance to rural China. Background for presentation at the MOF–World Bank International Seminar on Public Finance for Rural Areas.

Li, Linda Chelan. 2006. Embedded institutionalization: Sustaining rural tax reform in China. *Pacific Review* 19(1):63–84.

Liu, Chengfang, Linxiu Zhang, and Scott Rozelle. 2007. A study on the factors impacting the quality of public goods investments in rural China. *Journal of Agro-Technological Economics* [in Chinese] 2:11–18.

Luo, Renfu, Linxiu Zhang, Jikun Huang, and Scott Rozelle. 2007. Elections, fiscal reform and public goods provision in rural China. *Journal of Comparative Economics* 235:583–611.

National Bureau of Statistics. 2006. *China statistical yearbook*. Beijing: China Statistics Press.

Tao, Ran, and Mingxing Liu. 2005. Urban and rural household taxation in China: Measurement, comparison and policy implications. *Journal of the Asia and Pacific Economy* 10(4): 486–505.

Wong, Christine P. W., and Richard Bird. 2008. China's fiscal system: A work in progress. In *China's great economic transformation,* eds. Loren Brandt and Thomas G. Rawski, 429–467. Cambridge, UK: Cambridge University Press.

World Bank. 2005. Tax for fee reform and public investment in China's rural communities. Report of the World Bank. Beijing.

Zhang, Linxiu, Haomiao Liu, Loren Brandt, and Scott Rozelle. 2006. China's rural public finance: The township perspective. Annex 8: Report to the World Bank–*Fiscal reform and the role of the township*. Washington, DC: World Bank.

Zhang, Linxiu, Yuanyuan Yan, Loren Brandt, and Scott Rozelle. 2005. China's rural public finance: The village perspective. Annex 7: Report to the World Bank–*Village finance: Tax-for-fee reform, village operating budgets and public goods investment*. Washington, DC: World Bank.

Future Reform

Intergovernmental Fiscal Relations and Local Public Finance: What Is Next on the Reform Agenda?

ROY W. BAHL

Is China one of the world's most decentralized countries, or one of the most centralized? In fact, it is both. On one hand, 70 percent of all government expenditures pass through the subnational government budgets. On the other hand, subnational governments have no independent (formal) taxing powers. The question that might be raised is whether the longer-term intention is to develop a system of local public finance that would give subprovincial governments more fiscal discretion, or whether some other structure is envisaged. Either way, the issue to consider is what specific reform packages would move China toward its goal.

On average, subnational governments account for about one-third of all government spending in OECD (Organisation for Economic Co-operation and Development) countries. The economic model that explains the efficiency gains from this fiscal decentralization, however, does not travel so well to transitional and developing countries, where subnational government expenditure autonomy is less prominent in the budgetary makeup. Nor does it fit as well where elected and autonomous local governments are not the norm. The purpose of this chapter is to review structural practices in fiscal decentralization and to ask whether the international practice holds any lessons for China.

The analysis of local public finance in China must be put in a different context than in other countries. This is because taxation powers in China are almost completely centralized and because decisions about tax policy, tax administration, and intergovernmental fiscal relations are inextricably linked (Bahl 1999).[1] Note also that China's formal intergovernmental fiscal system is limited to central-provincial fiscal relations. The "local public finance" system is mostly about provincial-local fiscal relations, and this structure varies from province to province. Since local governments

---

[1] Tax policy decisions and tax administration efficiency affect the total pool of funds available for revenue sharing. The revenue-sharing arrangements can provide incentives for subnational governments to divert funds to extrabudgetary accounts, thereby reducing central government revenues.

have no formal taxing power, and since provincial governments are totally dependent on the center for their revenues, central-provincial fiscal arrangements define the budget constraint for local governments. Central-provincial relations, therefore, cannot be separated from the discussion of local government spending and financing. Finally, when we talk in this chapter about "local government" in China, we will mean the three tiers of government that operate at the subprovincial level.[2]

This said, we begin this discussion by noting the very great importance of subprovincial governments in the fiscal system. This importance might be measured both in terms of the amounts spent by subprovincial governments and in terms of the important functions for which they have responsibility. On average, the 2004 *China Statistical Yearbook* reports that in 2004 subprovincial governments spent 571 yuan per person, an amount that can be compared to the 679 yuan spent by the central government (excluding transfers). Provincial and subprovincial governments have heavy responsibility for the provision of social security, health care, basic education, public safety, and economic development services. The budget emphasis on social services is even greater for subprovincial governments than for provincial governments.

The Decentralization Model: Theory and Practice

China has never formally adopted a fiscal decentralization program in the sense of issuing a white paper that outlines a strategy for empowering its local governments. Nor has it called for significant autonomy and more self-governance at the bottom tier of government, as was done, for example, in the constitutional amendments in India in the 1990s. In fact, China has sent mixed policy signals about whether it will or will not move toward a more decentralized structure of government. On one hand, subnational governments now account for about 70 percent of all government expenditures, and there have been recent policy measures designed to strengthen subprovincial finances (Lou 2008). On the other hand, the major 1994 reform recentralized intergovernmental finances on the revenue side, and policy actions since have continued in this direction. All of this may be due to growing pains, and a country as large as China may eventually find fiscal decentralization irresistible. Or possibly the Chinese style of decentralization, and the way it goes about developing its local public finance system, will be different from that seen in other parts of the world. So the question we might start with is whether the western decentralization model is a good or bad fit for China.

Theory

The fiscal decentralization model is by now well known. At its core, it is about capturing the welfare gains that come from moving government decision making closer to the people. This economic efficiency argument drives the thinking of most economists who work on this subject (Oates 1972). The argument is straightforward. Let us assume that people's preferences for government services vary—for example, because of religion, language, ethnic mix, climate, or economic base. Let us assume further that people have sorted themselves so that those with like preferences live in

---

[2] These include prefectures (prefecture-level cities), counties (county-level cities), and townships.

the same province (city, township).[3] If subnational governments respond to these preferences in structuring their budgets, decentralization will result in variations in the package of services delivered in different places. People will get what they want, and the welfare of the population will be enhanced. Under the same circumstances, but with a centralized system, service provision would be more uniform, and people in different regions would be less likely to get the service mix they want.

Advocates will point out that successful fiscal decentralization can at once attack several of the problems that face developing economies: revenue mobilization, innovation in economic decision making, accountability of elected officials, capacity development at the local level, and grassroot participation in governance.

This story on the benefits of decentralization is a good one, and it is easy to believe that these welfare gains exist, even if they cannot be precisely measured. An important question is whether these gains are large enough to warrant the (possible) disruption of the national public financing system that would be brought about by the required structural changes. There also is the question of whether these gains are attainable in China—that is, whether the necessary conditions are in place to capture the benefits of moving to a decentralized system.

For fiscal decentralization to be fully successful, a number of conditions must be met. First, regional and local government legislatures must be accountable to the regional and local population. If local political leadership is elected, the question becomes whether the electorate has the information and inclination to exercise the vote to assure accountability. If these political leaders are appointed rather than elected, the question becomes whether they see their self-interest as being joined with the satisfaction of the local population.

Second, the chief officers of the regional or local government must be accountable to their legislature. If they are appointed by the center or state, their allegiance will be to a higher level of government, and local programs may not be delivered according to local preferences. One can imagine the problems that could arise. The mayor's directive about enforcement of property tax penalties for failure to pay might have a hollow ring if the chief local tax collector is appointed by a higher-level government. The same might be said for the implementation of local health and education policies.

Third, subnational governments should have some independent taxing powers—that is, provincial and local governments should have the ability to determine at least the tax rate for some important sources of local government finance. This is important if the local population is to hold the political leadership accountable for the quality of public services delivered. The test to which politicians will be put by local voters will be a much harder one if voters pay directly for services than if services are financed by a transfer from the center.

Fourth, subnational governments should be responsible for some important government services. The issue here is that the local voters should care about the quality of services delivered. In most cases, states and provinces are assigned services that affect the quality of people's lives and so this criterion is satisfied. However, in the

---

[3] Note that the economic base and location characteristics of the local government also will shape people's preferences.

case of local (third-tier) governments, this is not always the case. Where these local governments are given responsibility for little more than housekeeping functions, the local population is not likely to revolt over the quality of services delivered.

Fifth, subnational governments should have adequate discretion over the level and composition of expenditures. If a higher-level government mandates the expenditures, the subnational government has little ability to respond to citizen preferences. Excessive mandates can be an important impediment to fiscal decentralization.

What we conclude from this discussion is that the efficiency gains that might be captured with fiscal decentralization are far from automatic. There must be a structure in place to allow the subnational government to capture these gains. In some ways, China would seem a likely candidate to capture the efficiency gains from fiscal decentralization. Certainly, the fourth and fifth (expenditure) tests discussed above are passed because provincial and lower-level governments have control over a significant share of the expenditure budget and can set expenditure priorities. Subprovincial governments in particular are called on to deliver important social services (education, health) that matter to the local populations. Direct central control over chief local officers has been relaxed since the 1980s. Directors of fiscal agencies and tax bureaus are now appointed by provincial governments, though the provincial government leadership itself is appointed by the center.

In other ways, local governments in China are constrained in their fiscal choices. They are saddled with mandates and expenditure controls, and they have little or no independent taxing powers.

Finally, there is the issue of the vote. While half of all government spending does pass through local government budgets, there is little popular political representation (Bahl and Martinez-Vazquez 2006). Without political representation, the local population has no direct way of revealing its preferences for more or fewer public services. The provincial governors are still appointed; thus their accountability is upward, to the level of government and the political body that appointed them and will reward them. This absence of political representation at the local level is the major difference between decentralization in China and that in OECD countries.

Evidence supports the argument that an absence of political representation and the appointment of political leadership have not been impediments to local economic growth. In this respect, the Chinese version of federalism that empowered centrally appointed local officials, rewarded their successes with economic development, and encouraged them to compete with one another appears to have been a successful alternative to political decentralization (Qian and Weingast 1997).

Practice

One might test the hypothesis that the benefits of decentralization outweigh the costs by looking for evidence of the growing fiscal importance of subnational governments. In fact, countries around the world have moved only slowly toward the adoption of more decentralized intergovernmental fiscal systems. Bahl and Wallace (2005) use International Monetary Fund (IMF) *Government Finance Statistics Yearbook* data to estimate that the subnational government share of public expenditures has remained at about 13 to 14 percent in developing countries over the last

TABLE 13.1
Distribution of Government Expenditure and Taxes by Level of Government, 2003 (percent)

	China Exp.	China Taxes	United States Exp.	United States Taxes	Canada Exp.	Canada Taxes	Brazil Exp.	Brazil Taxes
Central	30	100	48	56	41	54	60	70
Provincial	18	0	21	24	45	37	28	26
Subprovincial	52	0	31	20	14	9	12	4

SOURCE: International Monetary Fund, various issues.
NOTE: Exp. = expenditures.

three decades.[4] The subnational government expenditure share is more than two times higher in the OECD countries and also has been stable over this period.

China is an outlier in this comparative empirical picture. First, its subnational government expenditure share is about 70 percent, arguably the highest in the world. Second, it is an outlier in terms of vertical balance—that is, in the extent to which subnational government taxes are adequate in amount to cover subnational government expenditures. To illustrate, we show comparable statistics in table 13.1 for China, the United States, Canada, and Brazil. In the United States and Canada, the local government (subprovincial) share is a smaller, 31 and 14 percent of total government spending, respectively, but local taxes cover two-thirds or more of total local spending. In Brazil, the local government share of spending is 12 percent, and about one-third of this is financed by local taxes.[5]

These average levels of fiscal decentralization hide a great deal of intercountry variation, which several analysts have tried to explain using cross-section regression analysis. Bahl and Wallace (2005) found that the subnational government expenditure share is significantly higher in countries with a higher per capita GDP, a larger population size, and a lower degree of corruption. This more or less matches the findings in other studies.[6] China is not easily "fitted" to the conclusions from this regression analysis. Its low per capita GDP would suggest an expected lower level of expenditure decentralization, but its larger size would suggest an offsetting effect.[7]

The Financial Instruments of Fiscal Decentralization

Subnational government budgets in most countries are driven by expenditure assignments, and financing is provided through subnational government taxation,

---

[4] Decentralization is measured here as the subnational government share of total government expenditure—that is, subnational government expenditures as the numerator and total central plus subnational government expenditures as the denominator. This is a flawed (though commonly used) measure of fiscal decentralization because it does not indicate whether the subnational government has any significant influence over how the money will be spent.

[5] In India, by contrast, state governments finance about half of current expenditures from their own revenue sources (Rao 2009).

[6] For a good literature review, see Letelier (2005).

[7] In the Bahl and Wallace study, the elasticity of expenditure decentralization with respect to per capita GDP, and the elasticities with respect to either population size or land area, are not significantly different.

by intergovernmental transfers, and in some cases by borrowing. The practice of using these instruments, however, is different in China from the international practice, particularly with respect to expenditure and revenue assignment. On this subject, we can say more about provincial government finance than we can about local government finance, since data at the subprovincial level are difficult to come by—in most developing countries and in China.

Expenditure Assignment: International Practice

The division of government expenditure responsibility among central, provincial, and local governments can fall back to four sets of "rules" or "guidelines." The first is that the central government should have primary responsibility for stabilization policy and income distribution policies (Musgrave 1959). Provincial-level stabilization policies—for example, borrowing to stimulate job creation—would fail because factor mobility would result in the benefits from provincially financed programs spilling over to other jurisdictions. In the case of income distribution responsibility, provincial and local governments are not likely to have the resources to address the needs for income security, and, in any case, the mobility of labor and capital could weaken the revenue base and increase the size of the client population in the province. According to the conventional thinking, this leaves subnational governments to concentrate on the allocation function—that is, to decide how resources will be divided among various expenditure heads and how the funds will be raised.

The second set of guidelines address the issue of how to decide which expenditure responsibilities will be allocated to which level of government. In the context of local government finance, one might begin with the decentralization theorem "Services should be delivered at the lowest possible level of government consistent with allocative efficiency." The two qualifications are the following:

1. The presence of economies of scale will push the assignment of responsibility for a function to a higher level of government or to an autonomous body. Examples include public utilities and regional hospitals.
2. The presence of external benefits or costs in the delivery of a function will force its assignment toward a higher level of government. Examples include interprovince trunk roads, research universities, and medical schools.

For the most part, these basic rules are reflected in expenditure assignments. Central governments are usually responsible for at least the financing of transfer payments to individuals, interprovince roads, defense, and the justice system, while provincial or state governments may have responsibility for interlocal roads, regional hospitals, large-scale irrigation projects, and the like. Depending on their size, local governments and autonomous local agencies may have responsibility for general urban maintenance, including local streets, water, sewerage and solid waste disposal, public transportation, basic health services, and primary and secondary education. There are departures from this assignment pattern, of course, but in most countries the expenditure assignments more or less "follow the rules."[8] Problems with expenditure assignment more often arise when there are concurrent assignments, that is, when two levels of government share in the provision of a function. In that case, the responsibility for service delivery can become murky as a result of duplication of effort or failure to deliver the service.

The third guideline for expenditure assignment is the time-tested advice of public finance students: "Finance follows function." The rule here is that the right order for sequencing is to first assign expenditure responsibilities among levels of government and then assign revenue-raising powers. This suggests that the right progression is to determine the revenue needs for a subnational government by first costing out the minimum level of services to be provided. If the process begins instead with allocating a share of the national budget to subnational government, this funding formula becomes the first step in the process of defining the level of services that will be delivered. The whole question of minimum service levels becomes obscured by the issue of affordability.

Despite these good arguments, many (most) countries focus on defining a revenue entitlement for subnational governments and then find a way to make expenditure needs fit this constraint. For example, Indonesia decided on the allocation of 25 percent of central taxes to its local governments, and the Philippines decided on 40 percent, without calculating these percentages according to a detailed assessment of expenditure needs. Another part of this sequencing argument is that efficiency in subnational government financing (particularly for local governments) depends on the specific services that are delivered. For example, efficiency considerations might dictate that education be financed by a combination of local taxes and transfers, parks by general local taxes, and refuse collection by user charges. Absent a knowledge of the expenditure responsibilities of subnational governments, how could the most efficient assignment of revenues be decided?

A fourth guideline is that there should be a (vertical) balance between expenditure assignment and revenue assignment. The counterfactual here is a one-to-one ratio of own revenues to expenditures. Deviations from this norm should occur because transfers are needed to bring public service levels in poorer jurisdictions up to some acceptable level and to correct for underprovision of services where there are large spillover effects. Where a low revenue assignment is made to subnational governments, the intergovernmental transfer system must be set at a high enough level to fill in the gap between local revenues and the minimum level of services. A mistake often made is to over-assign expenditure responsibility to subnational governments, relative to the central government's ability to finance the necessary vertical share with transfers. The result of this is sometimes a soft budget constraint for subnational governments that might be filled by bailout-type grants from the center or by imprudent borrowing by the subnational governments.

---

[8] For a good discussion of the criteria for expenditure assignment and the complexities of making assignments, see Ebel and Vaillancourt (2008).

Expenditure Assignment: China

The assignment of expenditure responsibility is spread across tiers of government in China. Approximately 70 percent of expenditures are made below the central government level and 52 percent below the provincial government level. By comparison with other large countries, China makes heavy use of subnational governments in delivering public services (table 13.1). There are, however, some features of the practice of expenditure assignment in China that are at odds with best international practice. The fact that nearly all subnational government expenditures are financed by central transfers is a significant difference in approach.

One might question whether it makes sense to apply international norms to China. In some ways the international experience of expenditure assignment is not relevant to China. The absence of political representation means that accountability, in the western sense of the concept, is not so relevant an issue. Moreover, many of China's provinces are larger than most countries, so some of the problematic spillover issues encountered in other countries might be less relevant.

On the other hand, some of the international norms are relevant. China's assignment of expenditure responsibilities is still emerging. There remain some anomalies that go back to pre-market times and that are not sustainable under the present economic system. Some rethinking of expenditure assignments might rank high on China's intergovernmental reform agenda (Lou 2008). In this regard, reform thinking might center on the important issues of responsibility for income maintenance functions, clarity in expenditure assignment, and sequencing (whether function should follow finance). Changes in all of these areas are necessary if there is to be a sustainable vertical balance in the Chinese intergovernmental fiscal system.

Income Maintenance. A striking difference between China and most other countries is the degree to which subprovincial governments are responsible for income-maintenance functions. Social welfare and unemployment expenditures are a responsibility of the subprovincial governments in China. This responsibility includes the compensation payments and pensions of former workers in state-owned enterprises. Subnational governments account for a large share of expenditures for "pensions and social relief" and for subsidies to social security. Within the subnational sector, responsibility for the bulk of these expenditures falls to prefectures and counties.

As a result of these expenditure assignments and the reforms of state-owned enterprises (SOEs), the fiscal systems of prefectural and county-level cities have come under pressure. There were defaults on the payment of pensions and unemployment benefits and a wave of popular protests that were most pervasive in the "rust belt" cities of the Northeast (World Bank, forthcoming). In response, the central government intervened with subsidies to bail out subprovincial governments. In many cases, the grants and subsidies from the central government have not been adequate to offset mandated increases in expenditures. The central government has also introduced such measures as social security reforms, the merging of unemployment benefits with the SOE living stipend schemes, *dibao* (minimum living stipend) schemes, and the urban medical insurance scheme, aimed at restoring budgetary stability to local governments.

Unclear Assignments. The assignment of functions is not clear. Expenditure may be assigned to levels of government as exclusive responsibilities or as concurrent responsibilities. While most analysts favor the exclusive route in order to maximize clarity in who is responsible for what, most countries have a significant list of concurrent functions. China is no exception here. Arguably, China's budget laws are less precise in defining expenditure responsibility than is the case in many other countries. In the case of provincial-local governments, the issue is particularly murky (Dollar and Hofman 2008).

The result of this murkiness is underprovision of services for some functions and duplication of services in other cases. This situation could lead to higher-level governments imposing mandates to force spending in "uncovered" areas, and it compromises accountability because it is not clear exactly what functions local governments are responsible for. Moreover, without a clear assignment of expenditure responsibility, it is not possible to define "minimum expenditures" that ought to be the foundation of the intergovernmental transfer system.[9]

1. *Sequencing.* Another departure of China practice from the basic principles of public finance (a departure shared by most developing countries) is that the public finance system is structured with function following finance. That is, the resource distribution appears to be decided independent from the division of expenditure responsibilities. An important international lesson, often hard-learned, is that if these two sides of the public finance equation are separated, significant fiscal disparities can result. Large fiscal disparities now characterize the Chinese intergovernmental fiscal system (Dollar and Hofman 2008; Lou 2008). Interprovince disparities in spending in China are larger than among subnational governments in OECD countries.

2. *Macroeconomic management.* Contrary to the budgeting principles that recommend reserving macroeconomic policy and management for central governments, China assigns significant responsibility in this area to subnational governments. Provincial and local governments have formal responsibility for economic development and industrial policy. They carry this out through various tax incentives, tax preferences, subsidies, and regulatory activities. A mixing of public service responsibility and economic development responsibility has led some local governments to accumulate significant debt. As the market economy continues to develop, some responsibility for macroeconomic management almost certainly will be removed from subnational governments.

3. *Local discretion.* While subnational governments do account for a large share of expenditures, and they do have considerable freedom in rearranging expenditure priorities, their autonomy is limited by mandates placed on them by higher-level governments.

---

[9] For a discussion of the problems that come with concurrent responsibilities for service provision, see Martinez-Vazquez et al. (2008).

4. *Reform direction.* To date, intergovernmental reforms in China have left the question of expenditure assignment mostly untouched. In fact, the comprehensive 1994 reform dramatically recentralized revenues but was mostly silent on expenditure responsibility (Bahl 1999). More recently, the rural fee reform and elimination of the agricultural income tax, without revenue-neutral compensating grants, had the same effect. These policy changes significantly exacerbated the vertical imbalance and put great pressure on the intergovernmental finance system to both fill the financing gap and equalize the fiscal disparities.

Revenue Assignment: International Practice

The revenue assignments made in a country answer the question about what levels of government will be allowed to levy what taxes. There is no complete agreement among scholars and practitioners about which taxes are best assigned to subnational governments. There are, however, a number of general guidelines in the public finance literature:

1. In a system of fiscal decentralization, subnational government officials should be accountable to their voting constituency if the welfare gains are to be fully captured. Local voters will put their elected officials to a harder test on efficient service delivery if services are substantially financed by locally imposed taxes.
2. Local taxation promotes efficiency in local government spending. Without provincial or local government taxation, the tax price for public services will be set too low, and the subnational government will tend to overspend. Or the demand for local government services will outrun the allocation of intergovernmental transfers, and without taxing powers local governments will underspend. By "subnational government taxing powers" we mean the autonomy to determine the level of tax revenue, at least by setting the tax rate.
3. The choice of tax instruments to be used by subnational governments should be influenced by administrative costs, and by "correspondence"—that is, the burden of the tax should be borne within the jurisdiction where the benefits of the resulting expenditures are enjoyed.
4. Provincial-level governments can levy broad-based income and sales taxes where administration permits. In the case of income taxes, this might take the form of a piggyback on the central tax.
5. Lower-level governments should tax immobile factors. This is usually taken to include taxes on property, licenses on local businesses, and certain taxes on motor vehicles.
6. The smallest of local governments should focus on user charges or benefit taxes. Because of administrative problems, their tax structures should stress simplification.

The practice of subnational government taxation in most industrial countries is in step with these principles, but the practice in developing countries is not. The practice in OECD countries includes using income and sales taxes at the state (provincial) level and allowing the subnational governments to set the tax rate. At the local level, cities and municipalities rely heavily on the property tax and on taxes on motor vehicles, but they also may use piggyback sales or income taxes (as in the United States and Denmark) or profits tax (as in Switzerland).

The story is very different in developing countries, where local government taxes, on average, account for only about 10 percent of total taxes. There often is intense resistance on the part of central governments to delegating taxing powers to the third tier. In fact, there are relatively few instances in developing countries where local governments, or even provinces, have been given significant taxing powers.[10] The assignment of taxes to subnational governments in many countries appears to have been more ad hoc than based on first principles. Subnational governments in low-income countries often have inherited taxes that are too politically hot for the center to handle (taxes on agriculture) or very difficult to administer (property taxes or sales taxes on services). Often, the "local taxes" are not local taxes at all because the rate and base are defined by higher-level governments.

Revenue Assignment: China

The most important characteristic of the Chinese practice is that subnational governments have no control over setting the rate or base of the major taxes in the system. In effect, all taxes are central. Subnational governments can influence revenue outcomes by their use of industrial policy to grow the tax base, and in some cases by their collection efforts, but the international practice of setting the tax rate at the provincial or local government level is not followed.

Chinese terminology treats the subnational government share of central taxes as "own-source revenues."[11] In part, this is because the tax-sharing arrangement is viewed as an entitlement of the recipient government. Another justification is that subnational governments feel that they have some discretion in influencing the revenues from these taxes. First, they may influence the growth in the tax base by providing a better climate for investment and for growth in productivity. Second, they may be more efficient collectors of taxes, have some formal responsibility for tax administration, and have better knowledge about local taxable activities. This reasoning leads some Chinese analysts to think of increases in own-source revenues as increased revenue mobilization by subnational governments.

By this categorization, subprovincial governments in China received nearly 40 percent of their revenues from "own sources" in 2003 (World Bank 2006), but this percentage fell over the 1995–2003 period. In part, this is because the central government has reduced its revenue sharing with the provinces—for example, the subnational shares of the personal income tax and the enterprise income tax have been reduced. The World Bank (2002) argues that provinces have passed on some of this decline in revenue sharing to lower-level governments. There is another important implication, however. Since the financing of subprovincial governments has been shifting from shared taxes (an entitlement approach) to transfers (a more

---

[10] There are, of course, exceptions—for example, Argentina, Brazil, and India.

[11] In most countries, own-source revenues of a local government are those over which the local government has some discretion to set the tax rate. A shared tax whose rate and base is determined by a higher-level government is more properly thought of as an intergovernmental transfer (Bahl and Linn 1992).

discretionary approach), decisions about the sectors and regions where public resources will be invested are increasingly determined by provincial governments.

Little detail can be given about revenue assignments at the subprovincial level, because these assignments vary from province to province. In general, the pattern seems to follow the central-provincial pattern: No independent taxing powers, and now a shift from revenue-sharing entitlements to grants-in-aid.

Local governments can make use of extrabudgetary funds—that is, nontax revenues that can be used for financing public services. Martinez-Vazquez et al. (2008) estimate that extrabudgetary expenditures were equivalent to 23 percent of budgetary expenditures in 2002. While down from levels in the early 1990s (Bahl 1999), this share is still significant.

Revenue Assignment: Reform Directions for China

China's development of a harmonious society could benefit from a reform of its revenue assignment model. Depending on national development strategy, and on the issues that the government would like to address, a number of reform directions might be considered. First, the present system will not establish an accountability of political leaders to local taxpayers to the same degree as would provincial and local government taxation. If the longer-term goal is to bring some political accountability to the system, the option of giving rate-setting powers to subnational governments might be considered. This could also address the problem of soft budget constraints.

A second issue that might be addressed with revenue assignment is equalization. Under the present system, subnational governments have no possibility for substituting locally raised revenues for intergovernmental transfers in order to meet expenditure demands. Such a substitution could free up intergovernmental transfers for the equalization fund at either the central or the provincial level.

A third issue has to do with the present approach of rewarding local officials for promoting economic development and growing the tax base. This practice may not be sustainable in the long run because of the perverse incentives that it embodies—for example, zoning out migrant workers because of their high public-sector costs, undervaluing congestion and other environmental costs, and failing to take full account of the additional infrastructure and social costs of continued industrial expansion. Another reform direction might be to reward provincial and local officials on the basis of quality of services delivered.

Intergovernmental Transfers: International Practice

There are no hard and fast rules about the best way to structure a system of intergovernmental transfers. Moreover, the practice varies widely, from country to country. There are, however, some generally accepted rights and wrongs that can guide the practice. The following are some principles that are often discussed:

1. The desired impacts of the transfer system should guide its design. For example, if a conditional grant is meant to stimulate the production of a particular public

service, the design of the grant should provide an adequate incentive for the subnational government to stimulate that production. Or if the idea is to allow local governments to tailor their spending programs to local preferences, unconditional grants should be used. This guideline may seem evident, but it is not always followed.
2. The structure of intergovernmental transfers should be transparent—that is, every recipient government should understand how the size of its transfer will be determined. Formula-based distributions or derivation-based shared taxes are examples of transparent distributions of transfers. The impact of changes in these formulae also can be understood by recipients.
3. Intergovernmental transfers should not be distributed according to the level of the deficit incurred by a subnational government. Deficit grants are the enemy of fiscal discipline at either the provincial or the subprovincial level.
4. Higher-level governments should regularly evaluate their transfer programs to determine whether the objectives are being achieved. For example, if a particular transfer program is meant to be equalizing, it should be subjected to a regular evaluation to determine whether it is achieving this objective.

Even if these general rules are followed, there is ample room to design grant instruments in different ways. A taxonomy of intergovernmental transfers, developed by Bahl and Linn (1992), defines two distinct components: a vertical sharing mechanism and a horizontal sharing mechanism. There are three more or less common approaches to determining the size of the total grant pool (i.e., the vertical dimension). *Shared taxes* are most consistent with decentralization in that they guarantee subnational governments a vertical share, usually a share of a broad-based tax. Moreover, these transfers often are distributed on an unconditional basis, and so give subnational governments discretion over how the money will be spent. *Ad hoc transfers* determine the vertical share on a political basis, usually on a year-by-year basis, and reduce the amount of budgetary certainty given to subnational governments. The *cost reimbursement determination* of the vertical share is used mostly for the conditional grants that are in the portfolio of most governments. This is a centralizing approach in that it makes transfers from this pool conditional upon spending the money for a designed purpose. The "right" approach to vertical sharing depends on what the central government is trying to accomplish with its transfer system.

The horizontal sharing mechanism, the allocation of revenues among eligible recipients, might take the form of *derivation*—that is, subnational governments may retain a share of what is collected within their boundaries. Alternatively, they may receive grants distributed by *formula*, by *cost reimbursement*, or according to *ad hoc* methods. Until one decides on both the horizontal and the vertical dimensions, the transfer system is not defined and its impacts cannot be evaluated.

Intergovernmental Transfers: Chinese Practice

We can follow this same taxonomy to describe the Chinese central-provincial transfer system (table 13.2). This schematic allows us to focus on a number of potential strengths

TABLE 13.2
China's System of Intergovernmental Transfers

Method of Allocating the Divisible Pool Among Eligible Units	Method of Determining the Total Divisible Pool		
	Specified Share of National or State Government tax	Ad Hoc Decision	Reimbursement of Approved Expenditures
Derivation	tax sharing and rebates (62.5 percent)	—	—
Formula	grants to minority regions (0.1 percent)	equalization grants (4.9 percent)	wage grants (6.1 percent)
Total or partial reimbursement of costs		grants for rural fee reform (3.5 percent)	—
Ad hoc		original system (quota) subsidies	earmarked grants (21.2 percent)

SOURCE: Adapted from Bahl and Linn, 1992.

and weaknesses of the transfer system. The system of transfers to provinces is summarized in table 13.3.

First, we might observe that the system is mostly transparent. Over 60 percent of transfers are distributed by revenue sharing on a derivation basis. The earmarked grants (about 20 percent of the total) are the exception to this transparency.

Second, the Chinese system has little equalization built into it, despite the existence of very great fiscal and economic disparities across provinces. Several researchers have pointed out the absence of equalization in the Chinese system of transfers (Bahl 1999; Dabla-Norris, 2005; Dollar and Hoffman 2008; Lin, 2011; Shah and Shen 2008). This result might be expected. About two-thirds of transfers are allocated according to the derivation of collections of VAT and income tax (see table 13.3). The equalization grant per se accounts for less than 5 percent of total transfers and is weakly equalizing at best. The remaining transfers in the system are equalizing but account for a small share of the total.[12]

Lou (2008, 159) takes another view. He acknowledges large interregional disparities but argues that these have been reduced by the transfer system: "In 2005 the ratio of fiscal revenues in the eastern, central and western parts of China stood at 60:23:17, while the ratio of their expenditures stood at 46:29:25."

While we can describe the arrangements for vertical and horizontal sharing as between the central and provincial governments, we cannot provide a parallel description for provincial-local government allocations. The latter vary by province, and provinces are not required to report on their arrangements. Nor does the central government regularly monitor their policies.

The central government now raises about 70 percent of all revenues but directly accounts for only about 30 percent of expenditures. It is left to the transfer system to fill

---

[12] For a review, see Shah and Shen (2008).

TABLE 13.3
Central-Provincial Intergovernmental Transfers: Vertical and Horizontal Shares

Transfer Type	Date Introduced	Vertical Share	Horizontal Share
VAT and excise tax rebate	1994	The base for the rebate to each province was fixed in 1994, to allow maintenance of its previous level of expenditure. Thereafter, the rebate grows by 30 percent of the growth of revenues from these taxes collected in the province.	Derivation basis.
Income tax rebate	2002	The amount was fixed in 2002 for each province, to allow it to maintain its previous level of expenditures.	Derivation basis.
General transfer (formerly transitional transfer)	1995	No fixed share until 2002. Since 2002 the vertical share has included the incremental revenues accruing to the central government from EIT and PIT over the 2001 level.	According to a needs-based formula that includes a component for the ethnic minority population.
Original system (quota) subsidy	1980s	No fixed share.	Distributed only to poor and ethnic minority provinces. Amounts were fixed in nominal terms in 1987, with only minor changes for compensatory adjustments.
Wage increase subsidy	1999	No fixed share.	Initially, this subsidy was given only to the poorer inland provinces in the central and western regions, to offset the costs of civil service wage increases mandated by the central government. Since 2001 Liaoning, Shandong, and Fujian have also been eligible, albeit only for partial compensation.
Minority region subsidy	2000	No fixed share.	For the 14 provinces and regions with large concentrations of ethnic minority populations. Funding comes from (1) central budget appropriation, and (2) 80 percent of the incremental VAT collected in the 14 provinces. Half of the second component is returned to the collecting provinces and regions by derivation. The other half is pooled with central appropriations (1) and distributed according to a needs-based formula.
Rural fee reform subsidy, subsidies for agricultural tax reduction and adjusting responsibilities	2001, 2003	No fixed share.	All provinces are divided into four groups, to receive compensation for revenue losses under the rural tax-for-fee reform and the abolition of agricultural taxes, at rates of 100% (central and western grain-producing provinces), 80% (non-grain-producing provinces in central and western provinces), 50% (major grain-producing provinces in the coastal region), and 0% (other coastal provinces).
Subsidy from the issuance of additional state debts	1999	A share of additional state bonds issued under the fiscal stimulus program.	Tilted toward the western and central provinces.

this vertical gap. Much the same might be said of provincial-local transfers. Subprovincial governments account for an estimated 52 percent of subnational government expenditures, with virtually no taxing power. Few if any other intergovernmental transfer systems in the world are asked to carry this much of the financing load.

The Property Tax

The property tax is almost everyone's choice for a principal local government tax revenue source in both developing and industrialized countries.[13] Despite all of the good work that has been done in designing more efficient property tax structures and administrations, however, the revenue yield of the property tax in developing countries is very low. The best comparable data available (International Monetary Fund, various years) suggest an average yield equivalent to only about 0.6 percent of GDP (table 13.4). De Cesare (2004) finds a similar result in her more detailed analysis for Latin American countries. Note also from this table that the property tax share of GDP is more than three times higher in the OECD countries than in developing countries. Lotz (2006), however, observes a limit on property taxes in OECD countries, perhaps at no more than 3 percent of GDP.

A number of hypotheses have been offered about why property tax revenues are so low in developing countries. Arguably, the most important reason is that the property tax works best as a local government tax, and fiscal decentralization has not been as embraced in developing as in industrialized countries. Bahl and Martinez-Vazquez (2008) use data from a panel of 70 countries for 1990, 1995, and 2000 to show a significant positive effect of both expenditure decentralization and the level of per capita GDP on the level of the effective property tax rate.[14] Higher-income countries and countries that are more decentralized use the property tax more intensively. Again, China can be seen as a mixed bag, with its relatively low per capita GDP a dampening factor and its high level of expenditure decentralization a stimulative factor.

Man (2011, chapters 1 and 6) argues that the burden of the property tax falls on capital and as such may lead to slower economic growth. Her econometric analysis of data for over 2,000 counties in China is consistent with this hypothesis. This suggests that land and property taxes would not be favored by local officials who are graded on a basis of the economic performance of their jurisdiction.

Another argument for the low level of revenues raised by the property tax is that efficient administration is very costly, both in terms of the setup (fixed cost) and the operating costs. In particular, proper valuation and revaluation are thought to be beyond the reach of most subnational government tax administrations, unless very significant expenditures are made to put the capacity in place. The barriers to efficient administration include the absence of a full and up-to-date survey of all land (urban and rural) and records of title that would allow tax liability to be determined. Putting the human resource infrastructure and the information base in place to effi-

---

[13] Three books of essays that review property tax practice in developing and transitional countries are Bahl (1979); Bird and Slack (2004); and Bahl, Martinez-Vazquez, and Youngman (2008).

[14] The effective rate of property tax is measured as the ratio of property tax collections to GDP.

TABLE 13.4
Property Tax as Share of GDP (percent)

	1970s	1980s	1990s	2000s
OECD countries (number of countries)	1.24 (16)	1.31 (18)	1.44 (16)	2.12 (18)
Developing countries (number of countries)	0.42 (20)	0.36 (27)	0.42 (23)	0.60 (29)
Transition countries (number of countries)	0.34 (1)	0.59 (4)	0.54 (20)	0.68 (18)
All countries (number of countries)	0.77 (37)	0.73 (49)	0.75 (59)	1.04 (65)

SOURCE: Bahl and Martinez-Vazquez, 2008.
NOTE: The average for the 2000s is for the years 2000 and 2001.

ciently administer the property tax would also be an expensive proposition. At current yields of the property tax, it would be difficult to justify such outlays, by either the central or the subnational levels of government. The result is that most developing countries improve their administrations with marginal changes rather than with comprehensive reforms.

Neither is the property tax a major source of revenue in China. Its yield is well less than the average level of revenues (relative to GDP) raised in developing countries.[15] Though the present yield is low relative to other taxes in the system, the growth in revenues has been significant in recent years (Man, 2011, chapters 1 and 6). Will the property tax become a major source of revenue for China in the future? If this is to happen, are there lessons in the international experience?

Chinese authorities are reported to be considering developing a local property tax. This policy initiative has been discussed for several years (Bahl, 1999; Ter-Minassian and Fedelino 2008). Various rationales have been offered for imposing a property tax in China.[16] In fact, taxes on land and buildings in China already exist.[17] The one that is most like the standard property tax is a notional charge per unit of area used, which varies by location within the urban area (Bahl and Zhang 1989).

Clearly, China could build on this structure to develop a property tax that would finance a significant share of subprovincial government revenue. An ambitious target for property tax revenues—after a suitable transition period—is 1 percent of GDP. This is about the same share of GDP as that raised from property taxes in Sweden and Poland. In 2003, it would have yielded 121 billion yuan in revenue.

Defining the Tax Base

The base of the Chinese property tax would likely be real property and land. It could initially be an urban tax, perhaps levied only by municipalities. Agricultural

---
[15] This includes revenues from all recurrent and transfer taxes.
[16] These rationales include the need for subprovincial governments to switch their emphasis away from economic growth and toward the provision of social services and the belief that a better tax system would lead to more rational subprovincial government behavior, especially regarding land conversion and off-budget financing.
[17] For a description of the existing eight taxes on land and buildings, see Hong (2009).

land would be excluded because of the recently rolled-out rural fee reform and the elimination of the agricultural tax (a land-based tax).

It does not seem feasible for China to adopt a U.S.-style capital value property tax on land and improvements. Apart from the administrative constraints, the absence of a property market where land is bought and sold means that there is no good basis for establishing the values of individual parcels. Some land is leased through a bidding process, but this remains a small percentage of total land. In most cases, user rights are assigned. An area-based tax with notional rates, as presently exists, might be workable if two issues could be resolved. First, rates of tax would have to be increased dramatically before the property tax could become a meaningful source of revenue. Second, some method would need to be developed to periodically upgrade the notional location values.

Determining Tax Rates

In many countries, subprovincial governments have discretion in setting property tax rates. This discretion is justified on the basis of equating the benefits received from local public services with their (tax) price. Since the quality and cost of public services differ from city to city, one would expect the property tax payment also to differ. Allowing discretion in determining tax rates could strengthen the accountability of Chinese local officials in financing and delivering local services. For example, they could raise the property tax rate in line with expanding the local budget to improve service delivery.[18] In the past, local officials have been willing to raise extrabudgetary fees and charges, so it seems reasonable to suggest that they might be willing to impose higher levels of property tax if they could retain the revenues.

Administering a Property Tax

Administrative considerations will strongly influence the structure of the Chinese property tax. Given the lack of private ownership of land and the absence of an open market in property transfers, the task is daunting. While there clearly is a market for real estate, it is not clear what process could be used to assign a value to every parcel. Moreover, there is no existing cadre of skilled valuers to develop the tax base. Finally, there is the issue of educating taxpayers and local officials to accept this new levy. All of this suggests that implementing a significant property tax will be a gradual process in China.

Leasing

A major issue to be resolved in China is reconciling the concept of a property tax with the Chinese land tenure arrangements. Hong (2009) poses the question simply: "How is the government going to get lessees to pay property tax when they do not own the property?" At present, enterprises and individuals have user rights that are gained from a competitive bid, negotiation, or a transfer from government. Should a

---

[18] There is some limited rate-setting power for urban subprovincial governments under the present land use tax.

property tax, or charge, be placed on these users? More to the point, should those who have purchased leases be charged again with the property tax?

One view is that when a new property tax is enacted, the existing users of leased land should be taxed, just like anyone else. In other words, leaseholds should *not* be given a property tax exemption, nor "grandfathered" (i.e., held harmless in their treatment). Leasing and property taxes coexist in many other countries (e.g., the U.K.), and there are many systems (e.g., in The Netherlands) that tax ownership and use separately.

A tax on land that has been leased may be thought of as a charge for public service benefits, whereas the lease amount is a payment for the use of the property. However, the original lease amount may well have been higher because expected subprovincial government public service benefits were capitalized into the value of the lease. But if these public expenditures were not financed by a property tax, there would not have been a corresponding land value reduction due to tax capitalization. If the property tax is new, and the services it finances are new, the case for levying property tax on top of the lease is stronger.

There is another view. Advocates of grandfathering argue that current leaseholders have already paid many fees on their leasehold that can be considered as taxes. Research has found that up to 40 percent of the total costs of a lease can consist of fees, many of which are quasi-taxes. If the property tax were to replace some of the levies and fees already charged, there could be an argument for grandfathering: Existing leaseholders would have paid "extra" taxes in the past. This case is strongest if the new tax does not finance the provision of new or enhanced services. Still, a property tax does not differ from any new tax imposed to provide better services. This case for grandfathering is not a strong one.

If the government feels bound to consider compensation for existing leaseholders, a better way would be to relax the restriction on transferability of a lease (which is currently not possible) or on the use of the land that is leased. Transferability would increase the value of the land for the leaseholder, it would promote better utilization of land, and it would soften the blow on current leaseholders who feel they have been double taxed.

Property Taxation: The Way Forward

Successful implementation of a local property tax requires much planning. The higher the revenue targets, the greater the amount of planning required. The following areas require detailed planning before introducing a property tax:

- *Develop a policy framework for property taxation in China.* This framework would include establishing the tax base and exemption policy and addressing the question of discretion for subprovincial governments to set tax rates. This framework must be completed and debated before further reforms are undertaken. When approved, this framework would become the basis for drafting the property tax law.
- *Make provision for the tax administration and for the division of tasks among the levels of government.* This includes establishing acceptable valuation procedures

and collection procedures. Some processes for training and certifying valuers must be considered. This step also includes establishing a venue for appeals—a property tax court. After the administrative planning is complete, implementing regulations can be drafted.
- *Establish an appropriate data base to support the levying of the property tax.* Every taxing jurisdiction will need an up-to-date cadastre with particulars for each property, including information on assigned user rights.

Other Local Tax Options

There are at least two other options for subnational government taxes that are worth consideration in China. Access to the individual income tax has been mentioned in previous studies (Ahmad 2008; Bahl 1999). The international experience also would suggest taxes on motor vehicles as an option.

Individual Income Tax

If subnational governments in China are to be given an independent source of revenue, in which rate setting can be at least partially delegated to provincial or subprovincial governments, the individual income tax could be a good candidate. This option has some desirable features as a local revenue source:

- It could give subnational governments some discretion in determining the size of their budgets, and hence could create accountability for their decisions and the quality of services they provide.
- The burden of such a tax, if levied on payrolls, would likely remain within the local area. There would be little exporting to other provinces or other subprovincial governments. Even in cases where nonresident workers are taxed, part of the levy could be seen as a charge for using locally provided services.
- This could be a productive revenue source, at least for the more urbanized local areas. Note from the discussion above that at present it constitutes only a small percentage of provincial and subprovincial government revenue.
- Provincial governments could use this reform to improve equalization. By reducing transfers to higher-income subprovincial governments (e.g., prefectures), which could make up the loss by increasing individual income tax rates, funds could be freed up for transfers to lower-income subprovincial governments. Or if provincial governments levied the income tax surcharge, they could allocate the increased vertical share to an equalization fund.
- Higher-income tax rates in wealthier provinces would reflect the access to a better quality of services in those provinces.
- Administration for this tax is already in place.

There also are many reasons a subnational individual income tax might not be a good fit with China's fiscal strategy. The most obvious is that the central government has chosen to control tax policy at the central level and has not given discretionary taxing powers to subnational governments. The Chinese government may not soon be ready to shift away from this long-standing component of its economic strategy. Another weakness of local income taxation in China is that its revenue benefits might be captured by relatively few subprovincial governments. Zhang and Martinez-Vazquez (2003) point out that the nine coastal provinces collect 70 percent of income taxes. This concentration of revenues in higher-income places strengthens the argument that a locally levied income tax could be a good replacement for transfers to higher-income subprovincial governments.

Competition between the central and subprovincial government sectors for the revenue base also argues against decentralizing the individual income tax. Recently, the central government has increased its share of income taxes. Even if it did decentralize this base, again, there would be some concern that it would be reclaimed. Stability would be an issue.

Another argument against reassigning the individual income tax to subnational governments is that there are income-redistribution objectives for individual income taxation that are more properly the responsibility of the central government. In its present form, the Chinese individual income tax structure is built around a progressive marginal rate schedule. How could China reconcile the income-distribution objective, which suggests centralization, with the proposal for provincial and local income taxes as a quasi-user charge for local services provided?

The answer is that these goals for the individual income tax will not conflict if the tax structure is designed properly. There would seem to be two choices for the design. One route is retaining the present system, whereby the central government determines the rate and base of the income tax and can introduce whatever degree of progressivity is desired. But this approach fails in two ways. It is counter-equalizing across regions, and it offers no provincial-local choice as to the level of the tax rate. A resident would pay the same income tax rate in Shanghai as in Yantai, even though the marginal cost of delivering local public services in the two urban areas might be quite different.

The second route is for subprovincial governments to be given some discretion to determine the income tax rate. Such an arrangement could work as follows: The tax base would be nationally uniform and defined by the central government. The central government would also prescribe a minimum and maximum rate of tax, and local (provincial) governments would be given discretion to set their rate within this range. This is essentially the system used in the Nordic countries (Lotz 2006). One version of the local discretion approach, and arguably a good transition, would be to allow urban subprovincial governments (prefectures) to impose a tax as a surcharge on central income tax liability, with permission from the higher-level government. The prefecture would retain both its normal share and 100 percent of the surcharge amount. The center could prescribe a minimum and maximum value for the surcharge.[19] If the local tax rate were simply added to the present progressive rate structure, the government's income distribution intent would be preserved.

---

[19] This approach is also favored by Bird (2006) in his review of the world practice of subprovincial government revenue mobilization.

Motor Vehicle Taxes

A good revenue source for subprovincial government, particularly for the more urbanized local areas, is the taxation of motor vehicle use. This could take the form of tolls, parking taxes, licenses, and even the taxation of motor fuel consumption (Bahl and Linn 1992). Taxes on motor vehicle purchases are better left to higher-level governments, but there are good arguments for considering motor vehicle use as an object of subprovincial government taxation:

- It could be a very productive revenue source. Certainly the number of motor vehicles is growing rapidly.
- It might serve a social purpose in that it taxes those who impose pollution and congestion costs on the public.
- Charging higher taxes for operating motor vehicles in larger cities (assuming that larger cities choose to impose higher motor vehicle taxes) would reflect the higher cost of providing services in those cities. This would move the Chinese fiscal strategy a step closer to asking residents and workers in different cities to pay the different marginal costs of the local public services they demand.
- It should be administratively feasible. Tolls, licenses, and parking fees are all relatively easy to assess and collect. Taxes on motor fuels are more problematic; moreover, if there are differential tax rates across local jurisdictions, some fuel carrying could result. Nevertheless, fuel taxes levied in urban areas may be feasible.

Arguments against allowing motor vehicle use to become a subject of local tax are, first, that it could be seen as an encroachment on central government revenues. This is particularly true for taxes on motor fuels. Second, some would see this as discouraging economic growth in larger cities, if larger cities were forced to adopt higher rates of tax. Third, there would be a political cost of imposing a higher tax on motor vehicle operation. Finally, the door would be open for tax avoidance measures that could lead to unfairness—for example, special tax treatment for the use of motor vehicles assigned to government officials.

Conclusions and Reform Options

China's intergovernmental reforms must be part of a larger reform package that will define how provincial and local governments fit into the national economic development strategy. In this connection, a number of questions might be raised:

- Will the equalization of public service levels, across and within provinces, become a higher priority goal?
- Will the practice of rewarding the local leadership based on economic growth be discontinued in favor of rewards based on more traditional measures of governmental performance, such as the quality of services delivered?
- Will internal migration policies be relaxed to allow rural "floating" workers full access to local services?

With these and a number of other questions answered, the government might consider intergovernmental reforms that would lay the groundwork for a system of local public finance.

China's system of local government finance is an important component of its development strategy. About 70 percent of all government expenditures in China pass through subprovincial government budgets, including expenditures for crucial education and health services and some income maintenance functions. While China has used subprovincial governments in important ways, it has not embraced a local government finance system like those that exist in many industrialized countries. Whether such a system should be an objective in China is a matter of government economic policy and governance strategy. That larger question is not addressed here. Rather, this chapter is focused on the lessons that could be learned from the international experience if China were to adopt an approach of developing a local government finance system.

If China were to be guided by international practice, the following primary issues might be addressed with intergovernmental fiscal policy:

- There is a significant vertical imbalance in China. Subnational governments account for about 70 percent of government expenditures but have virtually no taxing powers. Subprovincial governments account for about 50 percent of government expenditures and also have virtually no taxing powers. By comparison with OECD countries, this is a very large vertical fiscal imbalance. The traditional approach to resolving such a large vertical imbalance is to assign taxing powers to subnational governments.
- The intergovernmental system suffers from a horizontal fiscal imbalance, as well. This shows up in the form of significant fiscal disparities among provincial and subprovincial governments and in the degree of mismatch between expenditure needs and revenues available. Other countries address this type of imbalance with an equalization program. China's revenue-sharing system tends to be counter-equalizing, and some past research suggests that it exacerbates these disparities. This issue could be addressed by increasing the size of the equalization fund. The increase might be financed by reducing transfers to higher-income provinces in return for new taxing powers.
- Neither provincial nor subprovincial governments have independent taxing powers. In many industrialized countries, subnational governments have been given such taxing powers (at least rate-setting powers), and this has allowed them to meet demands for public services. Among the opportunities for subnational and subprovincial taxation in China are property taxes, individual income taxes, and motor vehicle taxes.
- As a prerequisite to developing an OECD-style local finance system, China would need to rethink its present expenditure assignment model. First, there is a need for more precise delineation of the responsibilities at various levels of government. Second, the present practice of assigning significant responsibility for social welfare and pensions to subprovincial governments might be rethought.

REFERENCES

Ahmad, Etisham. 2008. Taxation reforms and the sequencing of intergovernmental reforms in China: Preconditions for a xiaokang society. In *Public finance in China: Reform and growth for harmonious society*, eds. Jiwei Lou and Shuilin Wang, 95–128. Washington, DC: World Bank.

Bahl, Roy, ed. 1979. *The taxation of urban property in less developed countries.* Madison: University of Wisconsin Press.

———. 1999. *Fiscal policy in China: Taxation and intergovernmental fiscal relations.* San Francisco: 1990 Institute.

Bahl, Roy, and Johannes Linn. 1992. *Urban public finance in developing countries,* chapter 13. New York: Oxford University Press.

Bahl, Roy, and Jorge Martinez-Vazquez. 2006. Fiscal federalism and economic reform in China. In *Federalism and economic reform: International perspectives,* eds. Jessica Wallack and T. N. Srinivasan, 249–300. New York: Cambridge University Press.

———. 2008. The property tax in developing countries: Current practice and prospects. In *Making the property tax work: Experiences in developing and transitional countries,* eds. Roy Bahl, Jorge Martinez-Vazquez, and Joan Youngman. Cambridge, MA: Lincoln Institute of Land Policy.

Bahl, Roy, Jorge Martinez-Vazquez, and Joan Youngman. 2008. The property tax in developing countries: Current practice and prospects. In *Making the property tax work: Experiences in developing and transitional countries,* eds. Roy Bahl, Jorge Martinez-Vazquez, and Joan Youngman. Cambridge, MA: Lincoln Institute of Land Policy.

Bahl, Roy, and Sally Wallace. 2005. Public financing in developing and transition countries. *Public Budgeting and Finance,* Silver Anniversary Issue: 83–98.

Bahl, Roy, and Jun Zhang. 1989. *Taxing urban land in China.* Washington, DC: World Bank, Infrastructure and Urban Development Department (March).

Bird, Richard M. 2006. Local and regional revenues: Realities and prospects. In *Perspectives on fiscal federalism,* eds. Richard M. Bird and Francois Vaillancourt, 177–196. WBI Learning Resources Series. Washington, DC: World Bank.

Bird, Richard, and Enid Slack, eds. 2004. *International handbook of land and property taxation.* Cheltenham, U.K.: Edward Elgar.

Dabla-Norris, Era. 2005. Issues in intergovernmental fiscal relations in China. IMF Working Paper No. 05/30. Washington, DC: International Monetary Fund.

De Cesare, Claudia M. 2004. General characteristics of property tax systems in Latin America. Paper presented at 7th International Conference on Optimizing Property Tax Systems in Latin America, Guadalajara, Jalisco, Mexico.

Dollar, David, and Bert Hofman. 2008. Intergovernmental fiscal reforms, expenditure assignments and governance. In *Public finance in China: Reform and growth for a harmonious society,* eds. Jiwei Lou and Shuilin Wang, 39–52. Washington, DC: World Bank.

Ebel, Robert, and Francois Vaillancourt. 2008. Intergovernmental assignment of expenditure responsibility. In *The Kosovo briefing book,* eds. Robert Ebel and Gabor Peteri, 75–88. Budapest: Open Society Institute.

Hong, Yu-Hung. 2009. Taxing public leasehold land in transitional economies. Paper presented at the UN-Habitat Conference on Financing Affordable Housing and Infrastructure in Cities: Towards Innovative Land and Property Taxation, Warsaw, Poland (October 15–16).

International Monetary Fund. Various years. *Government finance statistics yearbook.* Washington, DC.

Letelier, Leonardo. 2005. Explaining fiscal decentralization. *Public Finance Review* 33(2):155–183.

Lin, Shuanglin. 2011. China's central government transfers: For equity or growth? In *China's local public finance in transition,* eds. Joyce Yanyun Man and Yu-Hung Hong. Cambridge, MA: Lincoln Institute of Land Policy.

Lotz, Jorgen. 2006. Local government organization and finance: Nordic countries. In *Local governance in industrialized countries,* 223–264. Washington, DC: World Bank.

Lou, Jiwei. 2008. The reform of intergovernmental fiscal relations in China: Lessons learned. In *Public finance in China: Reform and growth for harmonious society,* eds. Jiwei Lou and Shuilin Wang, 155–170. Washington, DC: World Bank.

Man, Joyce Yanyun. 2011. Local public finance and property taxation in China. In *China's local public finance in transition,* eds. Joyce Yanyun Man and Yu-Hung Hong. Cambridge, MA: Lincoln Institute of Land Policy.

Man, Joyce Yanyun, and Xinye Zheng. 2011. Tax structure and economic growth. In *China's local public finance in transition,* eds. Joyce Yanyun Man and Yu-Hung Hong. Cambridge, MA: Lincoln Institute of Land Policy.

Martinez-Vazquez, Jorge, Baoyun Qiao, Shuilin Wang, and Heng-Fu Zou. 2008. Expenditure assignments in China: Challenges and policy options. In *Public finance in China: Reform and growth for a harmonious society,* eds. Jiwei Lou and Shuilin Wang, 77–94. Washington, DC: World Bank.

Musgrave, Richard A. 1959. *The theory of public finance.* New York: McGraw-Hill.

National Bureau of Statistics. 2004. *China statistical yearbook.* Beijing: China Statistics Press.

Oates, Wallace. 1972. *Fiscal federalism.* New York: Harcourt Brace Jovanovich.

Qian, Yingyi, and Barry Weingast. 1997. Federalism as a commitment to preserving market incentives. *Journal of Economic Perspectives* 11(4):83–92.

Rao, Govinda. 2009. Fiscal federalism in India: Trends and reform issues. In *Decentralization policies in Asian development,* eds. Roy Bahl and Shinichi Ichimura. Singapore: World Economic Press.

Shah, Anwar, and Chunli Shen. 2008. Fine-tuning the intergovernmental transfer system to create a harmonious society and a level playing field for regional develoment. In *Public finance in China: Reform and growth for a harmonious society,* eds. Jiwei Lou and Shuilin Wang, 129–154. Washington, DC: World Bank.

Ter-Minassian, Teresa, and Annalisa Fedelino. 2008. Fiscal policy and reforms: Toward realizing a harmonious society. In *Public finance in China: Reform and growth for a harmonious society,* eds. Jiwei Lou and Shuilin Wang, 53–75. Washington, DC: World Bank.

World Bank. 2002. *China—National development and subnational finance: A review of provincial expenditures.* Report 22953-CHA. Washington, DC.

———. 2006. Governance, investment climate and harmonious society. Report CHA 37759-CN. Washington, DC.

———. Forthcoming. Reforming subnational finance: Lessons from northeast China. Washington, DC.

Zhang, Zhihua, and Jorge Martinez-Vazquez. 2003. The system of equalization transfers in China. Working Paper No. 03-12, p. 37. Atlanta: Georgia State University, International Studies Program (July).

Contributors

Editors

YU-HUNG HONG
Lincoln Institute of Land Policy
and
Massachusetts Institute of Technology

JOYCE YANYUN MAN
Lincoln Institute of Land Policy
and
Peking University–Lincoln Institute Center for Urban Development and Land Policy

Authors

JOHN E. ANDERSON
University of Nebraska–Lincoln

ROY W. BAHL
Georgia State University

BAOYUN QIAO
Central University of Finance and Economics

RICHARD BIRD
University of Toronto

LOREN BRANDT
University of Toronto

DONALD J. S. BREAN
University of Toronto

DIANA BRUBAKER
Lincoln Institute of Land Policy
(2007–2009)

ALFRED TAT-KEI HO
University of Kansas

SHUANGLIN LIN
University of Nebraska at Omaha

LINXIU ZHANG
Chinese Academy of Sciences

JUN MA
Sun Yat-Sen University

JORGE MARTINEZ-VAZQUEZ
Georgia State University

JOHN L. MIKESELL
Indiana University

MEILI NIU
Sun Yat-Sen University

SCOTT ROZELLE
Stanford University

SUSAN H. WHITING
University of Washington

WEIPING WU
Virginia Commonwealth University

XINYE ZHENG
Renmin University of China

LI ZHANG
Central University of Finance and Economics

Index

accountability: fiscal, 135; infrastructure financing and, 78; intraparty, 135; of local governments, 34, 37
ad hoc transfers, 259
ad valorem property tax, 165–166
ad valorem real estate tax, 157, 162
Agell, J., 114
agricultural land, ownership of, 64
agricultural tax, 129–130, 137–138, 149, 227, 230, 264
Anderson, John E., 154, 160
Anhui: education expenditures in, 211; expenditures in, 209, 211; health care expenditures in, 211; land revenues in, 13; tax-for-fee program in, 149
Areddy, James T., 147
Argentina, 11
Asian Development Bank, 66
asset management system, 85

Bahl, Roy, 165n1, 250, 251, 259, 262
bank loans, 64–65
Bank of China, 65
Bao, Helen X. H., 148
Barro, R. J., 115
basic education, 28–29
basic public services: expenditure assignments for, 27–30; underprovision of, 33–34, 37
Becsi, Zsolt, 114
Beijing: education expenditures in, 211; expenditures in, 44, 208; health care expenditures in, 211; housing prices in, 146, 178; land revenues in, 13; property tax per capita in, 11; tax revenue in, 8; urban infrastructure investment in, 52, 54; urban maintenance and construction revenues in, 49
Bird, Richard, 242
blueprints, 59–60
Bohai area, 52

Bolivia, 22
borrowing: for infrastructure financing, 41, 44–46, 63–66, 78–79, 82; local system for, 82; restrictions on subnational, 46, 63, 64, 78
Brazil, 251
Break, George F., 203
brownfield land sites, 146
Brueckner, Jan, 160
budget: budgets required by law, 84; capital, for infrastructure development proposals, 59–60, 84–85; general governmental, for infrastructure financing, 62
budget expenditures. *See* expenditures
buildings, as private property, 167
building tax, 165, 183
business tax, 95, 117, 119–120, 123, 136–137

Canada, 251
capital budgets, for infrastructure development, 59–60, 84–85
capital construction investment, in Guangdong, 66–72, 68t, 69t
capital improvement plans, 79–80
Cashin, P., 114
central government: education services provided by, 28–29; expenditure management processes in, 32–33; expenditure responsibilities of, xi, xii; and fiscal relations with local governments, 91–96, 96n; health care services provided by, 29–30; power and authority of, 128; revenues of, xi, xii, 7t; tax revenues of, 91–92, 93t, 94–95. *See also* intergovernmental transfers
centralization, 4, 126–135, 247. *See also* decentralization; recentralization
central-local fiscal relations, 42–44, 91–94, 126–135; disparities in, 205–211; expenditure responsibilities, 130–131; fiscal gap, 131; guiding principle in, 96n; political

central-local fiscal relations (*continued*)
    factors in, 135; revenue assignments and control, 127–130, 129t. *See also* intergovernmental relationships
China Agriculture Bank, 65
China Commercial Bank, 65
China Compendium of Statistics 1949–2004, 216
China Construction Bank, 65
China Development Bank (CDB), 65
China Internet Information Center, 96
China Land and Resources Yearbook, 71
China Regional Economy, 216
China Statistical Yearbook, 178–179, 216, 219
China Taxation Abstracts, 116
China Transportation Bank, 65
China Yearbook on Land and Resources, 67
Chinese Communist Party, 135
Chinese Statistical Abstracts, 116
Chongqing, urban infrastructure financing in, 52
city construction tax, 101
civil service, 134
Colombia, 22
commercial property prices, tax capitalization effect on, 179–184
company tax, 101
contract tax, 95, 101, 126
corporate income taxes, 5, 136
cost reimbursement, intergovernmental transfers and, 259
counties: fiscal matters of, 130; intergovernmental transfers to, 191, 195–201; and villages' fiscal health, 239

decentralization: benefits of, 248–249; conditions for successful, 249–250; degree of, 247; financial instruments of, 251–262; fiscal effects of, on local governments, 42–44, 148; overview of, 126–135; in practice, 250–251; role of expenditure assignments in, 22, 24; theory of, 248–250
De Cesare, Claudia M., 262
deed tax, 11
Deng, F. Frederic, 146
Deng Xiaoping, 92
Denmark, 257
Department of Construction (DOC), 71–72, 72t
Department of Land and Resources, 60–61
derivation, 259
developing countries: decentralization in, 247, 249, 250; expenditure assignments in, 255; expenditure responsibilities in, 130; fiscal imbalances in, 5; foreign direct investment in, 53–54; property taxes in, 11, 41, 262; revenue assignments in, 256–257
Development and Reform Commission (DRC), 58–59
Development and Reform Department (DRD), 60
disparities. *See* regional disparities
domestic investment, 53–54, 64–65
Dongguan: foreign direct investment in, 53; self-raised funds in, 47

earmarked transfers, 133–134
Easterly, W., 114
Economic Census (2000), 116
economic growth: endogenous theory of, 113–114, 122; exogenous (neoclassical) theory of, 113; tax structure/tax rates and, 113–123; urban infrastructure and, 52–54
economy: infrastructure financing's effect on, 52–55, 53t; intergovernmental transfers and, 195–201; 1978 reforms and, 92; public and private sector roles in, 21–22; stabilization of, 23; twentieth-century development in, 48. *See also* economic growth
Ecuador, 22
education: economic growth in relation to, 120; government provision of, 28–29, 33, 209, 211
efficiency, criterion of, 22–23
Engen, Eric M., 114
equalization purpose transfers, 193, 195–200, 260
equity, in provision of public services, 23
European Charter of Local Self-Government, 22n
excise taxes, 5, 95
expenditure assignments, 21–39; accountability regarding, 34; for central vs. subnational governments, 27f; challenges of, 25–36; common problems with, 24–25; concurrent responsibilities in, 25, 27–28, 38; current, 26–33, 254–56; "delegated" vs. "own" responsibilities in, 38; for education, 28–29; efficiency in, 22–25, 35–36; enforcement of, 39; equity and redistribution in, 23; exclusive, 38; expenditure structures and, 30–31; formal (explicit and clear), 24, 34–36, 255; guidelines for, 252–253; for health care, 29–30; hierarchical management structure underlying, 31; information required for, 39; intergovern-

mental administration of, 39; international practices of, 252–254; legal specification of, 38; levels of, 38; for levels of government, 28t; main issues with, 33–36; mismatch between revenues and (*see* revenues insufficient for); origins of system of, 25–26; primacy of, 22; principles of, 21–25; reform proposals for, 36–39; revenues insufficient for, 5, 25, 33, 42, 125, 193, 203–204, 237, 253; for social security, 30

expenditure responsibilities: amalgamation of, 39; asymmetric, 39; central share of, by country, 208t; central vs. local, 193f, 206–207t; closed list, 38; concurrent, 25, 27–28, 38; decentralization and, 130–131; "delegated" vs. "own," 38; exclusive, 27–28; general competence, 38. *See also* expenditure assignments; local governments: expenditure responsibilities of

expenditures: composition of budget, by government level, 30t; disparities in, 34t; extrabudgetary, 32, 32t; hierarchical model for managing, 31; international comparison of, 251t; local autonomy for, 31–32; subnational, 31t, 35t, 250–251; of villages, 232, 233t, 234, 236

extrabudgetary funds: amount of, 12; for central vs. subnational governments, 32; defined, 46, 132, 132n (*see also* off-budget funds); expenditures of, 32, 32t; for infrastructure financing, 46–47, 63; reliance on, xi, 3, 12, 132–133; sources of, 12, 132, 132n; uses of, 47. *See also* fees

extra-extrabudgetary funds, 47. *See also* off-budget funds

extra-system revenues, 47. *See also* off-budget funds

farmer satisfaction, 241
farmland occupation tax, 11
feasibility reports, 59
fees: for assessments on farmers (*tiliu*), 228, 230; farmers' village-to-township payment of (*tongzhou*), 237; for infrastructure financing, 45; for land development, 157–159; local reliance on, 3, 5, 63, 125, 149; for public services, 23, 44–47, 67; real estate, 145–150. *See also* land transfer fees
feigaishui. *See* tax-for-fee reforms
finance departments, and infrastructure development, 77–80, 85
Finance Yearbook of China, 219

fiscal centralization, 4
fiscal contract system, 5
fiscal gap, 4, 44, 131, 237
fiscal system, evolution of, 4–5, 126. *See also* central-local fiscal relations
Fisher, Ronald C., 203
fixed capital investment, 120
Fock, Achim, 141
foreign investment in China: economic performance in relation to, 53–54; for infrastructure financing, 46, 66; in real estate, 147
Franz, M. G., 114
Fujian, urban maintenance and construction revenues in, 49, 52

Gansu: education services provided by, 130; expenditures in, 44; tax revenue in, 8
Gaoxin, 139
GDP. *See* gross domestic product
General Office of the Governor (GOG), 59
general purpose transfers, 134, 193, 212
Gini Index of Inequality, 108, 108n, 110, 111t, 112, 232, 232t
Glasock, John L., 148
Gong, Tina, 175
Government Finance Statistics (IMF), 250
Government Finance Yearbook of China, 216
government structure, 127, 128t
government transfers. *See* intergovernmental transfers
greenfield land sites, 146
Grenadier, Steven R., 152
gross domestic product (GDP): intergovernmental transfers and, 218–222; property tax as share of, 263t; provincial rankings by per capita, 96, 97t, 98; regional disparities in, 108, 109t; revenues as share of, 126, 127t; tax revenues in relation to, 91–92, 93t, 94–95
Gu, Yizhen, 178
Guangdong, 81–85; budgetary spending on infrastructure in, 70t; capital construction investment in, 66–72, 68t, 69t; Department of Construction revenue sources in, 72t; expenditures in, 209; growth rates of GDP, population, and infrastructure investment in, 76t; infrastructure accomplishments in, 72–77, 73t; infrastructure development process in, 57–62, 61f; infrastructure financing in, 62–86; obstacles to analyzing infrastructure in, 66–67; off-budget funds in, 132; recommendations for, 81–85; remaining infrastructure issues in, 77–81;

Guangdong (*continued*)
  among top-performing counties, 136;
  urban maintenance and construction
  revenues in, 49, 52
Guangdong Finance Yearbook, 66, 67
Guangdong International Investment
  Company, 78
Guangdong Land and Resources Yearbook,
  66
Guangdong Statistical Yearbook, 66
*Guangdong Yearbook on Land and
  Resources*, 67
Guangxi: expenditures in, 209; urban
  infrastructure investment in, 67–72
Guangzhou City, expanding infrastructure
  in, 75t
Guizhou: expenditures per capita in, 133; tax
  revenue in, 8
Guo, Xiao-Yu, 178

Hainan: land revenues in, 13; urban
  maintenance and construction
  revenues in, 52
Han, Sun Sheng, 147
Hangzhou, housing prices in, 178
health care services, 29–30, 33–34, 211
Hebei: expenditures in, 234; public
  investment of, 236; revenues in, 231
Heilongjiang, expenditures in, 209
Henan: education expenditures in, 211;
  expenditures per capita in, 133, 208–209;
  welfare expenditures in, 211
higher education, 29
Ho, Samuel P. S., 175
Hong Kong, foreign direct investment
  from, 66
housing prices, 146–148, 160, 178
Hubei: land transfer fees in, 132; local income
  taxes in, 129–130
Hui nationality, 209
Hu Jintao, 147
Hunan: education services provided by, 130;
  expenditures in, 44; health care
  expenditures in, 211; off-budget
  funds in, 132

IMF. *See* International Monetary Fund
improvements tax, 154–160
income maintenance, 254–255
income support schemes, 35
indirect borrowing, 65, 78–79, 84
individual income tax, 101, 212, 266–267. *See
  also* personal income tax
Indonesia, 11, 253

infrastructure. *See* public services; rural
  areas: infrastructure in; urban
  infrastructure
infrastructure financing: accomplishments
  of, 72–77; borrowing for, 41, 44–46, 63–66,
  78–79, 82; central control of, 43; and
  current fixed assets information, 80, 85;
  economic performance in relation to,
  52–55, 53t; extrabudgetary funds for,
  46–47, 63; fiscal fragmentation in, 77–78;
  foreign investment in, 66; general budget
  financing for, 62; and governance
  problems, 80–81; government funds for,
  63–64; in Guangdong, 62–86; international
  funding for, 66; mechanisms for, 44–47;
  and multiyear capital improvement
  plans, 79–80; municipal responsibility
  for, 41–43; in other countries, 41; politics
  and, 60, 80–81; private donations
  for, 66; proprietary funds for, 63–64;
  recommendations concerning,
  81–85; regional disparities in, 48–52,
  54; remaining issues in, 77–81;
  self-fundraising for, 47, 63–66; sources of,
  44, 62–72, 74; transparency in, 77–79;
  uniqueness of Chinese, 41–42, 54–55
initial project proposals, 58–59
Inman, Robert P., 203
Inner Mongolia, expenditures in, 209
intergovernmental relationships:
  recommendations concerning, 83–84;
  taxes and, 91–94. *See also* central-local
  fiscal relations
intergovernmental transfers: Chinese
  practices concerning, 259–262, 260t, 261t;
  to counties, 195–201; dependence on,
  133–134; determinants of, 191–201;
  empirical analyses of, 216–224; growth
  stimulation as result of, 204; guidelines
  for, 258–259; international practices
  concerning, 258–259; local fiscal needs
  covered by, 131; local-to-central, 92n;
  methods of allocation in, 259; politics and,
  191; problems with, 242; by province, 217t;
  regional disparities addressed by, 33, 42,
  133–134, 192–224; reliance on, 192–193,
  203; revenue in relation to, 205, 208; rich
  vs. poor governments as recipients of, 192,
  195–201, 204–205, 214–215, 219–222, 236;
  transparency in, 260; types of, 133–134,
  193, 194f, 203–204, 212; U.S., 203; vertical
  and horizontal shares in, 261t. *See also* tax
  rebates
International Monetary Fund (IMF), 66, 250

international organizations, funding from, 66
international practices: decentralization, 247, 250–251; expenditure assignments, 252–254; fiscal policy, 269; intergovernmental transfers, 258–259; revenue assignments, 256–257

Janssen, Christian T. L., 151–152
Jia, Sheng-Hua, 178
Jiangsu: expenditures in, 209, 234; land revenues in, 13; off-budget funds in, 132; public investment of, 234, 236; revenues in, 230–231; among top-performing counties, 136; urban infrastructure investment in, 52, 54, 67–72
Jiangxi, property tax revenues in, 11
Jilin: public investment of, 234; revenues in, 230–231
Jilin, expenditures in, 209

Kahn, Matthew, 178
Katz, C. J., 114
Koester, Reinhard B., 114
Kormendi, Roger, C., 114

land: in communist China, 145; government reclamation of, 64–65; ownership of, 167, 167n; reforms and attitudes about, 146. *See also* real estate tax
land and property taxes, 8–12, 118–119, 123, 262–266; administering, 264; challenges for reform of, 165n1; deed tax, 11; determining tax base for, 263–264; determining tax rates for, 264; economic growth and, 117; exemptions from, 150; farmland occupation tax, 11; land value-added tax, 10–11; leases and, 169, 264–265; local, 83; local government's incentive to collect, 175–176; model of, 154–157; proposals for, xi–xii; and public leaseholds, 165–185; rate for, 150; rationale for, 148; real estate tax, 9–10; revenues from, 11, 12f; as share of GDP, 263t; and tax incidence, 170–175; transition to, 145–150, 159–162, 263–266; in 2008, 10t; urban land use tax, 8; utilization of revenues from, 176, 177t, 178
land appreciation tax, 176
land appreciation value (LAV), 11
land banks, 141
land conversion, xi
land development: basic model of, 152–154; fees for, 157–159; policy options for, 158–162; structural density of, 152–162; with taxes on land and structures, 154–157; timing of, 152–162
land leases: basic, 150–152; conditions of, 167; consolidation of, into budget, 84; duration of, 151–152; explanation of, 8, 64; and leasehold acquisition, 146; methods involved in, 140, 146, 167; problems with, 79; property tax and, 169, 264–265; reliance on, 47, 64; value of, 151–153. *See also* public leaseholds
land public finance, 145–162; attracting industry with land, 139; basic model of, 152–154; defined, 123; generating taxes with land, 139–140; land as collateral, 141; models of, 150–162; model with development fee, 157–159; model with taxes on land and structures, 154–157; policy options for, 158–162; in Zouping, 138–141. *See also* land transfer fees
land requisitions, 138
land revenue, 13t
land transfer fees: as extrabudgetary vs. self-raised funds, 47; fiscal expenditure in relation to, 13t; generating, 140–141; growth of, 132; official government control over, 140; problem of, 139; regional disparities in, 12–13; reliance on, 12; in Zouping, 140–141
land use rights transfer, 145–146, 167
land use tax, 183
land value, components of, 167–169, 167f
land value-added tax, 10–11, 176
land value allocation, under public leaseholds, 167–169
land values, xi
Latin America, 22
leasing. *See* land leases
Li, Ling Hin, 147
Liaoning, expenditures in, 209
Lin, George C. S., 175
Lin, Justin Yifu, 149
Lincoln Institute of Land Policy, 13
Lindh, T., 114
Linn, Johannes, 259
Liu, Mingxing, 136n7, 148, 149
local cadres, 135, 141
local governments: accountability of, 34, 37; aggregate expenditure composition of, 31t; counties, 130, 191, 195–201; decentralization's fiscal effects on, 42–44; education services provided by, 28–29, 33, 209, 211; expenditure management by, 30–31, 30t, 37; expenditure responsibilities of, xi, 3, 5, 6f, 25–36; under fiscal

local governments: (*continued*)
    centralization, 4; fiscal disparities between, xi, xii, 4, 8, 14, 33, 34t, 37, 42, 44, 133–134, 192, 255; fiscal gaps in, 4, 5, 25, 33, 42, 44, 125, 131, 193, 203–204; fiscal needs of, 131; fiscal performance of, 96–112; health care services provided by, 29–30, 33–34, 211; income maintenance provided by, 254–255; income support provided by, 35; land revenues of, 13t; macroeconomic management by, 255; minority, 209, 215, 220; pensions provided by, 35–36, 254; practical influences on fiscal practices in, 135; property tax collection by, 175–176; revenues of, xi, xii, 5, 6f, 7t; revenue sources for, xi, 3, 33; social security provided by, 30, 33–37; tax revenues of, 9t; townships, 130–131, 236–238; unemployment compensation provided by, 35, 254; villages, 227–242; welfare provided by, 211, 254. *See also* intergovernmental transfers; provinces
local public finance, 247–269; expenditure assignments, 252–256; financial instruments of, 251–262; importance of, 247–248, 269; individual (personal) income tax, 266–267; intergovernmental transfers, 258–262; issues for, 268–269; motor vehicle taxes, 268; overview of reform of, xi, 3–17; property tax, 262–266; revenue assignments, 256–258; subnational expenditures, 251; uniqueness of Chinese, 247–248
local public goods, expenditures on, 176, 177t, 178
Local Tax Service (LTS), 5, 129
Lotz, Jorgen, 262
Lou, Jiwei, 260
Luo, Renfu, 149

Ma, Jun, 59
macroeconomic management, 255
Mahler, V. A., 114
Man, Joyce Yanyun, 262
Man nationality, 209
Mao Zedong, 92
Martinez-Vazquez, Jorge, 262, 267
matching funds, 133, 137, 212
Meng nationality, 209
metropolitan areas. *See* prefecture-level cities
Miceli, Thomas J., 151
minimum living standard, 30
Ministry of Construction, 71
Ministry of Finance, 27, 39, 116, 132, 134

minority regions, 209, 215, 220
motor vehicle taxes, 268
Mullen, J. K., 114
multiyear capital improvement plans, 79–80
municipal governments: borrowing by, 82; infrastructure development process in, 60–62, 61f. *See also* local governments
Munnell, Alicia H., 52

National Economic Research Institute, China Reform Foundation, 148
nationally designated poverty counties (NDPCs), 191, 196–198
National People's Congress (NPC), 128, 146, 167
National Statistical Bureau of China, 96, 116
National Tax Service (NTS), 5, 129
NDPCs. *See* nationally designated poverty counties
Newell, Graeme, 147
Nicaragua, 11, 22
1994 tax reforms, 94–96, 126, 130, 193, 195, 203, 205
Ningbo, urban maintenance and construction revenues in, 52–53
Ningxia, expenditures in, 209

off-budget funds, 47, 132
Ohlsson, H., 114
Oi, Jean, 176
operations tax, 101
own-source revenues, 176, 178, 183, 257, 257n11

Palmon, Oded, 174
Peking University–Lincoln Institute Center for Urban Development and Land Policy, 13
pensions, 35–36, 254
People's Congress: elections for, 135; land use policy of, 61; oversight function of, 62, 84, 86; role of, 135. *See also* National People's Congress
personal income tax, 120, 123. *See also* individual income tax
Philippines, 253
Ping, Xinqiao, 132, 136
planning departments, and infrastructure development, 79–80, 85
Poland, 11
politics: infrastructure financing and, 60, 80–81; and intergovernmental transfers, 191; popular representation in, 250

population growth, intergovernmental transfers in relation to, 215, 219–220, 222
prefecture-level cities, economic data on, 52–54, 52t
premium water networks, 47
pricing mechanisms, 23
private donations, 66
private property, buildings as, 167
private sector: economic role of, 21–22; expenditure assignments and, 26–27
Promulgation of the Plan for Sharing the Individual Income Tax, 212
property taxes. *See* land and property taxation
provinces, 91–112; annual percentage change of per capita revenue in, 101, 104–105t; fiscal performance of, 96–112; GDP per capita disparities in, 108, 109t; GDP per capita rankings of, 96, 97t, 98; GDP-to-tax revenue ratio in, 92, 93t, 94; and 1994 tax reforms, 94–96; revenue elasticity by tax category in, 101, 106–107t; tax per capita disparities in, 108, 110t; tax revenue-GDP ratios in, 98, 100t, 101; tax revenue per capita by tax category in, 101, 102–103t; tax revenue per capita in, 98, 99t. *See also* local governments
provincial tax Gini coefficients, 108, 110, 111t, 112
public finance system, 4–6. *See also* local public finance
public good, expenditures on local, 176, 177t, 178
public land, reclamation of, 64–65
public leaseholds, and property taxes, 165–185. *See also* land leases
public sector: economic role of, 21–22; expenditure assignments and, 26–27
public services: local governments' responsibility for, 205; underprovision of, 42; villages' provision of, 227, 234, 235t, 236. *See also* basic public services
public spending, and capitalization of tax liabilities, 178–185
public utility surcharge, 44

Qin, Ping, 131
Qinghai: expenditures in, 209; land revenues in, 13; property tax revenues in, 11

real estate, market allocation of, 146–148. *See also* land
real estate tax, 9–10, 44, 149–150
Rebelo, S., 114, 120

recentralization, 33, 44, 94, 128, 148
reclamation of public land, 64–65
redistribution, in public service provision, 23
reform agenda, 247–269; decentralization, 248–251; expenditure assignments, 252–256; individual income tax, 266–267; intergovernmental transfers, 258–262; issues for, 268–269; motor vehicle taxes, 268; property tax, 262–266; revenue assignments, 256–258. *See also* 1994 tax reforms; tax-for-fee reforms
regional disparities, 205–211; in education expenditures, 209, 211; expenditure responsibilities and, xi, xii, 4, 8, 14, 33, 34t, 37, 42, 44, 255; expenditures per capita, 209f, 210t, 211f; in GDP per capita, 108, 109t; geographic distribution of, 48–49, 54, 98; in health care expenditures, 211; in infrastructure provision and financing, 48–52, 49t, 54; intergovernmental transfers as means of addressing, 33, 42, 133–134, 192–224; intraprovincial disparities, 136; and rich-to-poor ratio, 133; tax sharing system and, 44, 48; in village finances, 232; in welfare expenditures, 211
resource tax, 101
revenue assignments, 256–258
revenue distribution, 131t
revenues: central-local division of, 194f, 206–207t; central share of, 126, 127t; central share of, by country, 205, 208t; Chinese practices concerning, 257–258; intergovernmental transfers in relation to, 205, 208; international practices concerning, 256–257; as share of GDP, 126, 127t; village, 230–232
revenues assignments and control, 127–130
revenue-sharing systems, 4–5
rural areas: education services in, 28–29; fiscal reforms in, 148–149; health care services in, 29–30; infrastructure in, 149, 237–238; intergovernmental transfers to, 195, 198–201, 198t, 200t, 201t; population of, 227; taxes in, 148. *See also* villages
rural collectives, 64
rural public finance, 227–242; outcomes of, 241–242; township finances, 236–238; village expenditures, 232–236; village finances, 228–230; village fiscal health, 239–241; village revenues, 230–232
rural tax-for-fee-reforms. *See* tax-for-fee reforms
Russia, 11

Sala-i-Martin, X., 115
self-raised funds, 47, 63–66
Shaanxi: expenditures in, 234; public investment of, 236; revenues in, 230–231
Shandong: intraprovincial disparities in, 136; off-budget funds in, 132; property tax revenues in, 11; among top-performing counties, 136; urban infrastructure investment in, 67–72
Shanghai: and borrowing for infrastructure, 46; education expenditures in, 211; expenditures in, 44, 208–209, 211; expenditures per capita in, 133; health care expenditures in, 211; land revenues in, 13; property tax per capita in, 11; tax revenue in, 8; urban infrastructure investment in, 52, 54; urban maintenance and construction revenues in, 49, 52; welfare expenditures in, 211
Shanghai Jiushi Company, 46
shared taxes, 259
Sichuan: expenditures in, 234; land revenues in, 13; public investment of, 234, 236; revenues in, 230–231; urban infrastructure financing in, 52
Sirmans, C. F., 151
Skinner, Jonathan, 114
Smith, Barton A., 174
social security, 30, 33–37, 134
SOEs. *See* state-owned enterprises
Solow, Robert M., 113
South Africa, 11
State Administration of Taxation, 116, 149, 166
State Council, 128, 130, 212, 220
state-owned enterprises (SOEs), 26, 32, 132n, 211
Stokey, N. L., 120
submissions, 212
subnational governments. *See* local governments
subprovincial governments. *See* local governments
subsidiarity principle, 22–23
subsidies, 212–213
surplus land value, 168
Swan, T. W., 113
Switzerland, 257

Taiwan, foreign direct investment from, 66
Tao, Ran, 131, 136n7, 148, 149
tax burdens, 148. *See also* tax incidence, property tax and

taxes: ad valorem property tax, 165–166; ad valorem real estate tax, 157, 162; agricultural tax, 137, 149, 227, 230, 264; building tax, 165, 183; business tax, 95, 117, 119–120, 123, 136–137; central government and, 91–92, 93t, 94–95, 247; central taxes, 94–95; city construction tax, 101; company tax, 101; contract tax, 95, 101, 126; corporate income taxes, 5, 136; distortionary, 113–114, 118, 123; excise taxes, 5, 95; improvements tax, 154–160; individual (personal) income tax, 101, 120, 123, 212, 266–267; international practices concerning, 256–257; land appreciation tax, 176; land use tax, 183; land value-added tax, 10–11, 176; local structure for, 6–8, 44; local taxes, 94–95; motor vehicle taxes, 268; 1994 reforms concerning, 94–96, 126, 130, 193, 195, 203, 205; operations tax, 101; provincial, 91–112; real estate tax, 9–10, 44, 149–150; resource tax, 101; rural vs. urban, 148; shared taxes, 94–95, 259; tax sharing system, 5, 43–44, 48, 94–95, 128, 133, 193n; urban land use tax, 8, 44, 162; urban maintenance and construction tax, 44, 45t, 49, 50f, 51t; urban real estate tax, 165, 183; value-added tax (VAT), 5, 95, 101, 117, 123, 128, 137, 139, 204, 213–215. *See also* land and property taxes
tax-for-fee reforms, 134, 148–149, 199–200, 200t, 227–242, 264
tax incidence, property tax and, 170–175. *See also* tax burdens
tax liabilities, capitalization of, 178–185
tax rates, and economic growth, 113–123
tax rebates, 133, 192, 193, 195–201, 204, 212–213, 221–222
tax sharing system (TSS), 5, 43–44, 48, 94–95, 128, 133, 193n
tax structure, and economic growth, 113–123
Tianjin: expenditures in, 208; health care expenditures in, 211; land revenues in, 13; tax revenue in, 8; urban infrastructure investment in, 52, 54
Tibet: expenditures in, 209; property tax revenues in, 11; tax revenue in, 8
tiliu (fees for assessments on farmers), 228, 230
tongzhou (farmers' village-to-township fees), 237
townships, finances of, 130–131, 236–239, 238t, 240t

Transfer Mechanism during the Transition Period, 212
transition period transfers, 212
Turnbull, Geoffrey K., 151
turnover taxes, 5, 95, 128
Turnovsky, S. J., 120
two-item funds, 44

unemployment compensation, 35, 134, 254
United States: expenditures in, 251; intergovernmental transfers in, 203; taxation in, 257
urban areas: economic growth in relation to infrastructure in, 52–54; intergovernmental transfers to, 198–201, 198t, 200t, 201t; population in, 57, 117; taxes in, 148
urban infrastructure: blueprints and capital budgets for, 59–60; under central government, 43; defined, 42; demand for, 41; development process for, 57–62, 61f, 74, 77, 79–81; economic performance in relation to existing, 54; feasibility reports for, 59; initial project proposal for, 58–59; property taxes invested in, 171–174; regional disparities in, 48–52, 49t, 54. *See also* infrastructure financing
urbanization. *See* urban areas: population in
urban land use tax, 8, 44, 165
urban maintenance and construction tax, 44, 45t, 49, 50f, 51t, 137
urban real estate tax, 165, 183
urban real property tax, 10
user charges, 45

value-added tax (VAT), 5, 95, 101, 117, 120, 123, 128, 137, 139, 204, 213–215
VAT. *See* value added tax (VAT)
villages, 227–242; expenditures of, 232, 233t, 234, 236; finances of, 228, 229t, 230; fiscal disparities between, 232; fiscal health of, 239, 240t, 241; population of, 227; public services in, 227, 234, 235t, 236; resident satisfaction in, 241; revenues of, 230–232; sources of revenue in, 231t; tax-for-fee reforms and, 228, 230
vocational education, 28

wage adjustment subsidies, 134
Walker, Anthony, 147
Wallace, Sally, 250, 251
Weiqiao Group, 138
welfare expenditures, 211, 254
Wen, Hai-Zhen, 178
Wen Jiabao, 148
western region, intergovernmental transfers to, 220, 222
Western Regional Development Initiative, 133
Widmalm, F., 118, 120
Williams, M., 114
Wong, Christine P. W., 134, 141, 242
work units, 147
World Bank, 52, 66

Xinjian, expenditures in, 209
Xu, B., 120
Xu, Dashan, 146

Yangtze Delta area, 52
Yulin, urban maintenance and construction revenues in, 53

Zang nationality, 209
Zhang, Yanlong, 132, 141
Zhang, Zhihua, 267
Zhang, Zing Quan, 147
Zhejiang: expenditures in, 209; land revenues in, 13; off-budget funds in, 132; among top-performing counties, 136; urban infrastructure investment in, 52, 54, 67–72; urban maintenance and construction revenues in, 49
Zheng, Siqi, 178
Zhou, Sherry Z., 148
Zhou, Yan, 59
Zhu, Jieming, 146
Zhuang nationality, 209
Zouping County, fiscal practices in, 135–141

About the Lincoln Institute of Land Policy

The Lincoln Institute of Land Policy is a private operating foundation whose mission is to improve the quality of public debate and decisions in the areas of land policy and land-related taxation in the United States and around the world. The Institute's goals are to integrate theory and practice to better shape land policy and to provide a nonpartisan forum for discussion of the multidisciplinary forces that influence public policy. This focus on land derives from the Institute's founding objective—to address the links between land policy and social and economic progress—that was identified and analyzed by political economist and author Henry George.

The work of the Institute is organized in three departments: Valuation and Taxation, Planning and Urban Form, and International Studies, which includes programs on Latin America and China. We seek to inform decision making through education, research, demonstration projects, and the dissemination of information through publications, our Web site, and other media. Our programs bring together scholars, practitioners, public officials, policy advisers, and involved citizens in a collegial learning environment. The Institute does not take a particular point of view, but rather serves as a catalyst to facilitate analysis and discussion of land use and taxation issues—to make a difference today and to help policy makers plan for tomorrow. The Lincoln Institute of Land Policy is an equal opportunity institution.

LINCOLN INSTITUTE OF LAND POLICY

113 Brattle Street
Cambridge, MA 02138-3400 USA

Phone: 1-617-661-3016 x127 or 1-800-526-3873
Fax: 1-617-661-7235 or 1-800-526-3944
E-mail: help@lincolninst.edu
Web: www.lincolninst.edu